Understanding MS-DOS®

Second Edition

The Waite Group

Kate O'Day

John Angermeyer

Harry Henderson

A Division of Macmillan, Inc.

11711 North College, Carmel, Indiana 46032 USA

SECOND EDITION
FIRST PRINTING—1989

International Standard Book Number: 0-672-27298-9

From The Waite Group:
Development Editors: Mitchell Waite and James Stockford
Content Editor: James Stockford
Managing Editor: Scott Calamar

From Howard W. Sams & Company:
Acquisitions Editor: James S. Hill
Development Editor: James Rounds
Manuscript Editor: Don MacLaren, BooksCraft, Inc.
Illustrator: Donald B. Clemons
Cover Art: DGS&D Advertising, Inc.
Cover Photo: Cassell Productions, Inc.
Indexer: Sherry Massey
Compositor: Shepard-Poorman Communications Corp.

Printed in the United States of America

Contents

Preface to the Second Edition

MS-DOS is the powerful disk operating system developed by Microsoft for use in today's microcomputers. It provides the instructions that enable microcomputers to manipulate files, handle interactions between the computer and the user, and manage peripherals.

This book is different from many books on MS-DOS and other operating systems in several ways. First, you don't need a computer background to read it. Second, it is written with the belief that computer concepts don't have to be complicated or boring. Third, when you have finished this book, you'll find that in addition to having had fun reading it and working the examples, you will have learned how to utilize the power of MS-DOS.

Understanding MS-DOS, Second Edition begins with a description of what a computer is and why it needs an operating system. You then learn how to start your system, how to handle disks, and how to get information into and out of your system. You are shown how to shape up your files before you move into high gear and learn about the power of the keyboard—function keys and keystroke combinations that can make everyday tasks easier. You're shown, in a clear and entertaining style, ways to develop routines so that repetitive tasks are automated. The real power of MS-DOS is revealed in the tree-structured directories, pathnames, and in advanced features of redirection, piping, and filtering. For the hard-disk user, the BACKUP and RESTORE commands are explained clearly and concisely. This revised edition includes a tutorial on the DOS Shell utility that simplifies MS-DOS operation and also includes expanded information on file management. There is also a new chapter on configuring your system. An appendix shows how to maximize the editing capabilities of MS-DOS's line editor, EDLIN, and another explains the most common error messages in MS-DOS and possible solutions.

Like other books in this series, this book builds understanding through the subject in a step-by-step manner. You gain knowledge and confidence as you complete each subject. A quiz is included at the end of each chapter for self-evaluation of what has been learned. Answers to the questions are found in the back of the book.

The Waite Group would like to thank Harry Henderson for doing a splendid job revising this book. Thanks to John Angermeyer and Kate O'Day for their contributions to the first edition. Thanks, too, to James Stockford for his diligent editing of this project. Thanks to Don MacLaren for his editiorial work. Finally, thanks to the talented staff of Howard W. Sams & Company for their production work.

Introducing MS-DOS

ABOUT THIS CHAPTER

In this chapter, you will see how this book will help you discover the power of MS-DOS. You will also take a look at the parts of your computer system and get started on the road to building a vocabulary of important computer terms.

WHAT'S IT ALL ABOUT?

MS-DOS is the most popular operating systems available for microcomputers.

This book is about using your computer system. It is especially for new computer owners. To read, use, and enjoy *Understanding MS-DOS* you don't have to know a thing about MS-DOS, operating systems, or computer terminology. The only thing you need to know right now is that MS-DOS is the operating system that comes with your computer.

MS-DOS is one of the most popular operating systems used in microcomputers today. It is available for a wide variety of computers, from self-contained portables and laptops to the many IBM PC compatibles. The IBM PC itself uses a special version of MS-DOS.

Understanding MS-DOS employs a well-known educational technique—"learning by doing." Computer folks call this the "hands-on" approach. Whichever term you prefer, this book is not merely descriptive, it also presents examples and exercises for each part of MS-DOS. You will "get your hands wet" typing information into the computer and seeing the results of your labor. These projects are designed to help you understand the topic being discussed.

WHAT'S AHEAD?

By moving through the chapters, you will gradually build on your growing knowledge of MS-DOS. The chapters are best read in order. When you have finished this book, you will find it a valuable reference tool.

If you've just bought your PC and haven't installed MS-DOS yet, see the appendix on Installing MS-DOS before reading Chapter 3. Alternatively, you can have the dealer or a knowledgeable user install it for you.

There are several implementations of MS-DOS. One of them, PC-DOS, is used on all models of the IBM PC/XT/AT and PS/2. Some completely PC-compatible computers run PC-DOS. Other computers such as Compaq and Zenith run versions of MS-DOS tailored to their hardware. As a user, however, you will notice few differences among the various MS-DOS versions. If your computer has its own MS-DOS manual, see it for details.

If this is your first experience with computers, just start with this chapter and don't look back. This chapter introduces computer systems. In Chapter 2, "Your Operating System," you will learn about operating systems in general, and MS-DOS in particular. You will begin using your operating system in Chapter 3, "Getting Started with MS-DOS." If you are already familiar with the components of a computer system and understand what an operating system is and does, you might want to go directly to Chapter 3.

Chapter 4, "Using the Command Line," starts by showing you how to use special features of your PC's keyboard to speed the entry of MS-DOS commands. It also shows you to use "wildcard" characters to create more powerful commands. Chapter 5, "Floppy Disks," shows you how to prepare floppy disks for use and how to copy files to and from them. In Chapter 6 you will learn more about files and how to create, view, and print them. Chapter 7 shows you how to create directories and subdirectories to organize your applications and data files—this is especially important when you are using a hard disk. Chapter 8 continues this theme, and you will learn how to manage your hard disk and perform the "housekeeping chores" needed to keep your work going smoothly. This includes making regular backups, an important "insurance policy" for every PC user. Chapter 9, "Advanced File Manipulation," shows you how to control the input, processing, and output of data using the keyboard, screen, disk drive, or printer, and how to combine MS-DOS commands to find, sort, and display data. Chapter 10, "Using Batch Files," explains how you can create lists of often-used commands that will run automatically without your having to remember the details. If you have MS-DOS 4.0, you'll want to read Chapter 11, "Using DOS Shell," to explore an alternative way to look at your programs and files. The new DOS Shell enables you to use graphic windows and the keyboard or a mouse to perform most of the common file-management tasks. You can also create menus for yourself or other users, simplifying access to regularly used programs. Finally, Chapter 12 shows you how to customize your system using MS-DOS configuration commands, the CONFIG.SYS file, and the AUTOEXEC.BAT file. Topics covered include speeding up disk access, specifying information to be used to control MS-DOS or your application program, and using expanded memory to help your applications run faster.

The appendices include a brief introduction to EDLIN, a simple text editor provided with MS-DOS; a guide to installing MS-DOS on a hard disk or floppy disk; a list of common error messages and what to do about them; a glossary of MS-DOS and general computer terms; and a list of other Waite Group books that you may find to be of interest after completing this one.

What You Need to Use This Book

To learn about MS-DOS you'll need a personal computer equipped with one of several versions of MS-DOS.

To use this book you need a personal computer equipped with a keyboard, monitor, and the MS-DOS operating system. You also need at least one disk drive (two are preferable). Since most computer users today have hard disks, most of the book's examples refer to the hard disk. If you have only floppy disk drives, you can still do the examples, however—any differences will be noted. Most of the material in this book is applicable to MS-DOS versions 2.0 or later. Important features added with MS-DOS versions 3.0 and 4.0 are also fully covered.

Other than the hardware and software mentioned, all you need is a willing mind and a little time to try out the examples as you read along.

WHAT IS A COMPUTER SYSTEM?

Microcomputer systems range from single, self-contained units, such as laptops and portables, to desktop machines with several external components attached.

A microcomputer system can range from a small portable or laptop machine that you can store under an airplane seat to a desktop machine featuring fancy graphics capabilities and several printers. Most likely, your system falls somewhere between the extremes. MS-DOS is available for almost all of these machines and many more that fall inside the broad definition of "computer system." Even Apple Macintosh users can buy plug-in cards that allow them to run MS-DOS software; some systems that run UNIX (an operating system that is MS-DOS's "big brother") can run MS-DOS as well.

Check your computer or components manuals for specific information on names, displays, keys, or messages.

This book should help make your learning experience more enjoyable, but you may sometimes be confused when our discussion or illustrations do not match your specific computer layout. Because MS-DOS is available for many types of computers, our discussion will deal with generalized definitions and components of computer systems, shown in *Figure 1-1,* and generic elements of MS-DOS. If at times you are confused about specific names, displays, keys, or messages, check the manual that the manufacturer packages with your system.

The hardware includes the main system unit, keyboard, disk drives, monitor, and optional equipment called peripherals.

Your computer system is made up of many different components. The machine parts are called *hardware.* This includes your keyboard, disk drives, and monitor. You can connect *peripherals* (additional hardware) to your machine through specialized ports, or connectors (the places where they plug into your machine). One typical peripheral is a printer.

The part of your computer system that makes this hardware perform is called *software*—the programs that control the operation of your machine. You are getting acquainted with one type of software, your MS-DOS *operating system*. The operating system controls how the computer performs its work. Other types of software include application programs (e.g., word processors, games, accounting packages) and utility programs (e.g., file managers and "pop-up" calculators and notepads). Software also includes

Figure 1-1. Hardware and Software

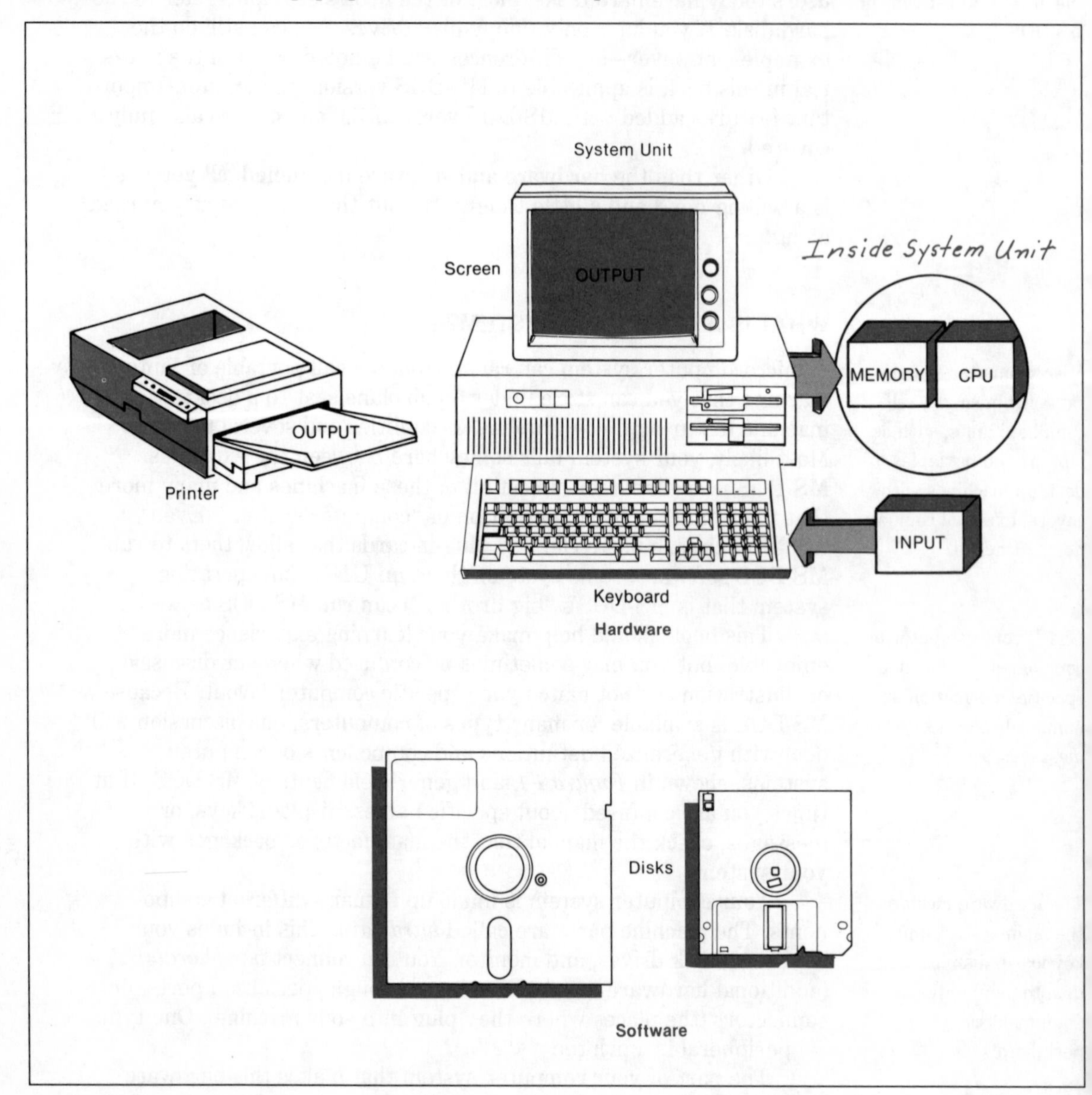

programming languages, such as BASIC, C, or assembly language, which are essentially programs that let you create new programs.

HARDWARE

MS-DOS is used to control how the computer does its work.

One of the advantages of MS-DOS is that many different machines can operate with it. This versatility allows you to choose the specific computer system you want and still use the most popular operating system on the market.

Whether your computer system is a laptop or a specialized workstation that is part of a large office network, it has several features in common with all other systems:

- Information that is fed into the computer is called *input.* Most often this input comes from you. You will use a keyboard to type in your entries. (Some application programs also allow you to use a "mouse" pointing device to select among options shown on the screen or to manipulate text. The mouse is discussed further in Chapter 11.)
- The information that comes from the computer to you is called *output.* Messages and results are displayed on a monitor, or screen.
- When the computer is not actually using some information, the information is put into storage. Computers use floppy disks or hard disks to store data.
- Inside every microcomputer is a microprocessor chip. This chip is what makes your computer compute—that is, manipulate data. Also inside the machine is some memory.

Let's explore the inside of the machine first.

Central Processing Unit (Microprocessor)

Computers containing a microprocessor chip are called microcomputers.

The "brain" of your computer is contained in the central processing unit (CPU). CPUs vary in size, speed, and the amount of work they are capable of performing in a given amount of time. MS-DOS works fine with older CPUs such as Intel's 8086 and 8088, but newer CPUs such as the Intel 80286 and 80386 can do many jobs faster. A new operating system, OS/2, can run MS-DOS programs as well as including features that take advantage of the newer CPUs. (Learning MS-DOS is a good introduction to learning OS/2.)

Memory

Computers have two types of memory: random-access memory and read-only memory.

The computer has two types of memory (depicted in *Figure 1-2*), each with very specific characteristics.

Figure 1-2. ROM and RAM

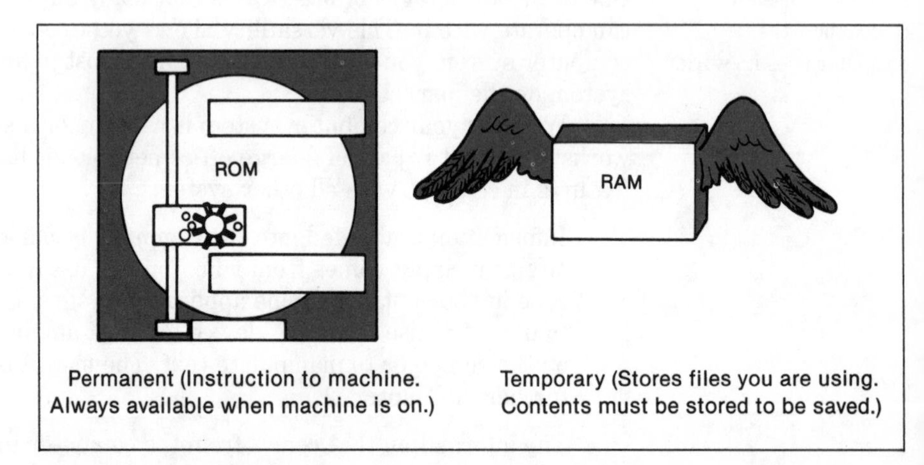
ROM
RAM
Permanent (Instruction to machine. Always available when machine is on.)
Temporary (Stores files you are using. Contents must be stored to be saved.)

Random-Access Memory

Random-Access Memory (RAM) is used by the computer to hold the information it is currently working on. Information in RAM changes as you edit and enter data. It is very important to remember that RAM is transient: things stored in RAM are only temporary; when you turn off the machine, RAM is wiped clean.

You must transfer any data in RAM to storage (on a floppy disk or hard disk) before you turn off your machine. Application programs, which come on their own disks, or information that you do not alter and already have on a disk do not need to be returned to storage at the end of a working session. Some applications programs save new or changed data to disk automatically. Nearly all applications will warn you if you try to leave the program without saving your data. This is a good reason why you should always give your program's "exit" command rather than just shutting off your computer.

Read-Only Memory

Read-Only Memory (ROM) is permanent. It is actually contained in hardware on your CPU. ROM contents are determined by your computer manufacturer.

Measurement

The amount of memory in your computer is measured in *bytes*. Each byte contains 8 bits. A byte can be thought of as one character such as the letter "A." It takes 6 bytes to store "MS-DOS" (actually 8, if you count the quotation marks).

Computer memory is usually measured in bytes (8 bits) or kilobytes (1024 bytes). For example, 640K of memory actually means 655,360 bytes (640 × 1024) or 5,242,880 bits (640 × 1024 × 8).

Computer memory is often described in terms of *K*, as in "I know where I can get some additional K real cheap!" K is shorthand for *kilobytes*, which means 1024 bytes. You may have seen the claim "expandable to 640K." This means the total computer memory of that system could be 640 × 1024, or 655,360 bytes.

Newer computers can hold even more memory—1024K or more. 1024K is usually called "1MB," or "1 megabyte." A *megabyte* means a million bytes.

The relationship between bits, bytes, K, and MB is shown in *Figure 1-3*.

Storage Devices

The devices most often used to store information permanently are floppy-disk drives and hard-disk drives.

Many computer systems use disk drives to read information from and write information to storage. There are two kinds of drives, floppy-disk drives and hard-disk drives.

Floppy disks are small magnetic disks that are coated to contain information. You insert these disks into disk drives. Your system may have one, two, or several disk drives. Although many types of computers use the same size disks, generally you cannot interchange disks between computers that use different operating

Figure 1-3. Bits, Bytes, K, and MB

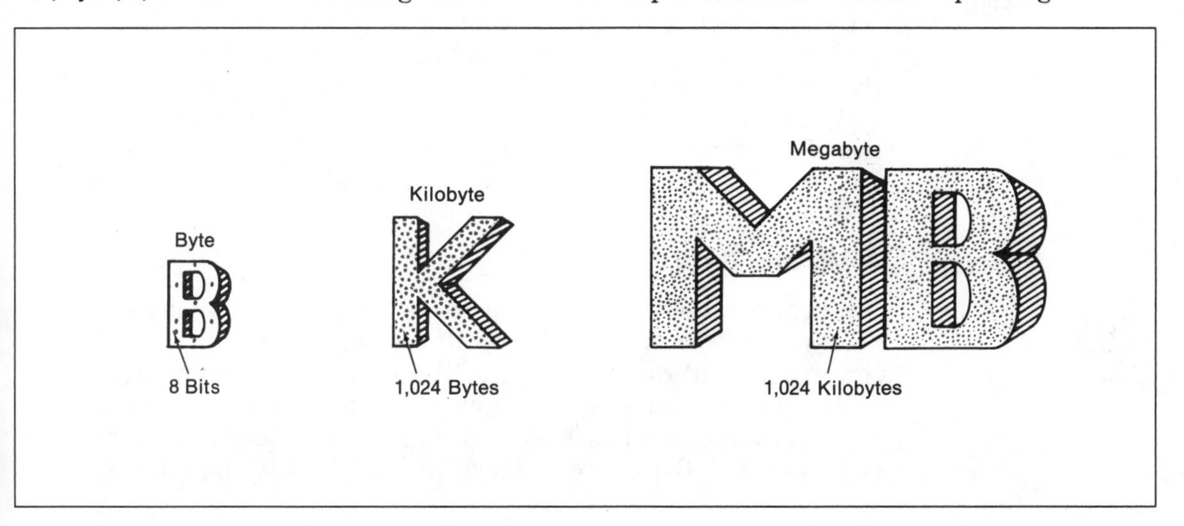

Floppy disks for MS-DOS systems today come in two sizes, 5¼″ and 3½″. Older desktop systems use the 5¼″ disks, while the IBM PS/2 series and most laptops use 3½″ disks. It is useful to have access to at least one drive of each size.

Storage disks are used together with your system's RAM. As the computer requires information, it reads it from the disk, stores it in the RAM, and manipulates it as necessary. When instructed to, the computer copies information from RAM and stores it on the disk.

A computer's hardware is not very useful without software that's applicable to your needs.

systems. Thus you could use the same 3½″ disk in an MS-DOS laptop computer and an IBM PS/2 desktop computer (which also uses a version of MS-DOS).

Most desktop computers now include a hard-disk drive. (IBM calls this a "fixed-disk drive.") Hard-disk drives can be built into your machine, or they can be peripheral. The hard disk inside one of these drives is usually not removable although drives with removable hard disks are now available. The advantages of hard disks are that they can store much more information than floppy disks and they are faster than floppies. They are also more expensive, however. The various kinds of disk drives and disks are shown in *Figure 1-4*.

As mentioned earlier, disks store programs and data that you are not actively using. Information is read from the disk into the computer's RAM (temporary memory). As you need more information, the drive retrieves it from your disk. When you are finished working, the information is sent to the disk for storage.

Your understanding of these few terms that apply to software may clear away any confusion you experience inside your friendly computer store. Knowing these terms should boost your computer confidence considerably.

SOFTWARE

Software is another name for "computer programs." According to buying experts, when you choose a computer system, you should first find the software you want and then buy the computer to fit the software's specifications. That's how important the software is in a computer system. Although you want convenience and ease of use in the system hardware, if the software does not do what you want, you really have nothing but an easy-to-use white elephant. The interaction of software with your computer hardware is depicted in *Figure 1-5*.

Application Programs

A program that does something for you is an application program. Some of the common types of application programs are word processors (e.g., WordPerfect or Microsoft Word), database programs (e.g., dBASE IV or Paradox), spreadsheets (e.g., Lotus 1-2-3 or Microsoft Excel), and integrated (multiple-use) packages (e.g., Microsoft Works or Framework). Games are also considered application programs.

Programming Languages

Another type of software lets you write instructions, in the form of programs, for your computer. This software is known as a programming language. You can use languages to design your own application programs. Your computer probably includes the BASIC programming language. BASIC may be contained inside ROM, or you may have it on your operating-system disk. Other programming languages include Pascal, C, and assembly language. (If you want to learn how to program, see the appendix on Related Waite Group books.)

Figure 1-4. Storage Devices

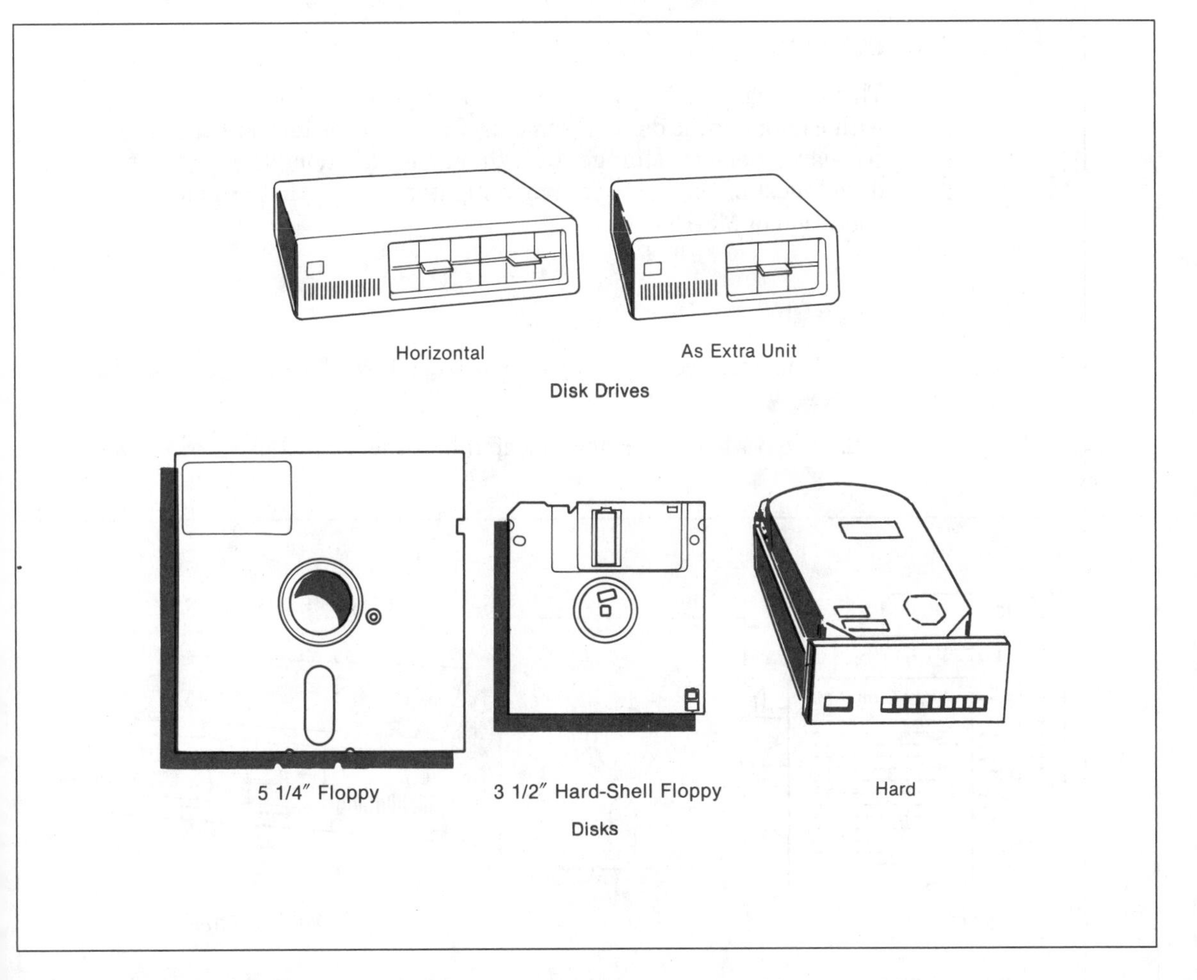

Operating Systems

Your operating system is a type of specialized software. The operating system manages all the disk input and output operations of your computer. You are an important part of the input and output system because you originate and receive this input and output. How well you, the information, and the machine work together is the secret of an effective operating system. You will learn about your operating system in Chapter 2.

SUMMARY

This first chapter has served several purposes. If you are unfamiliar with computers, it defined some useful computer terms: hardware, software, memory, storage, input, and output. Along the way it introduced most of the parts of your computer system that are used in the operation of MS-DOS.

REVIEW

1. Your microcomputer system is composed of hardware and software.
2. The brain of your microcomputer is the central processing unit (CPU).

Figure 1-5. Software

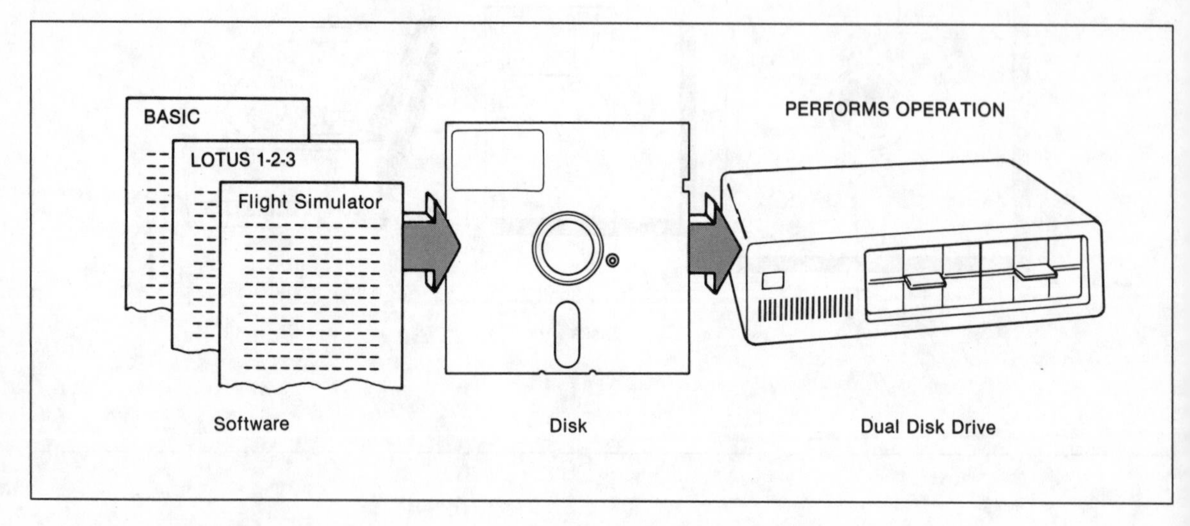

3. Random-Access Memory (RAM) is a temporary storage place to hold data that the CPU is working on currently. Be sure to transfer data from RAM to a storage device, such as a floppy disk or hard disk, before you turn off the system.
4. Read-Only Memory (ROM) is permanently contained in the hardware; its contents are determined by the manufacturer.
5. Floppy-disk drives are built to read from and write on removable disks coated with magnetic material. Each operating system writes data on floppy disks in its own characteristic way.
6. Hard-disk drives contain built-in disks; they are faster, hold more information, and are more expensive than floppy drives.
7. Application programs are those that let you do a useful, specific kind of work.
8. Programming languages let you write programs of instructions for your computer.
9. Operating systems help your computer system manage the input and output of the data.

Quiz for Chapter 1

1. MS-DOS is:
   a. a microcomputer operating system.
   b. a minicomputer operating system.
   c. a mainframe operating system.
   d. an operating system for any computer.
2. MS-DOS's popularity is due to:
   a. its capabilities.
   b. its availability for a wide variety of computer systems.
   c. the large number of application software programs compatible with it.
   d. all of the above.
3. The physical components of a computer system are:
   a. software.
   b. hardware.
   c. programming languages.
   d. the operating system.
4. Almost all microcomputers consist of:
   a. a system unit.
   b. a keyboard.
   c. a screen, or monitor.
   d. a floppy-disk drive.
   e. all of the above.
5. Input to your computer is accomplished by using the:
   a. screen.
   b. keyboard.
   c. memory.
   d. carrying handle.
6. Output from your computer can go to:
   a. the screen, or monitor.
   b. the printer.
   c. either of the above.
   d. none of the above.
7. The central processing unit (CPU), or microprocessor, is:
   a. the part that "computes."
   b. a type of memory.
   c. a type of disk drive.
   d. none of the above.

8. The type of memory almost all microcomputers contain are:
   - a. random-access memory (RAM).
   - b. read-only memory (ROM).
   - c. both of the above.
   - d. none of the above.

9. Your computer's random-access memory (RAM) is used for:
   - a. temporarily holding information that is currently being worked on by the computer.
   - b. permanently storing information.
   - c. discarding unwanted information.
   - d. storing only random numbers.

10. When your computer's power is turned off, information stored in RAM will:
    - a. always remain intact.
    - b. remain intact for a predetermined period of time.
    - c. immediately be erased.

11. Your computer's ROM is used to contain:
    - a. permanent information.
    - b. manufacturer-specific software.
    - c. software that can only be read.
    - d. all of the above.

12. Computer memory is usually measured in:
    - a. bits.
    - b. bytes.
    - c. kilobytes (1024 bytes).
    - d. megabytes (1024K).
    - e. all of the above.

13. A byte equals:
    - a. 8 bits.
    - b. 16 bits.
    - c. 1 character (sometimes).
    - d. b and c.
    - e. a and c.

14. A kilobyte, also referred to as K, always equals:
    - a. 1000 bytes.
    - b. 1024 bytes.
    - c. 1500 bytes.
    - d. none of the above.

15. Storage devices usually used in microcomputers are:
    - a. floppy-disk drives.

b. hard-disk drives.
c. compact cassette tape recorders.
d. card punches.
e. a and b.
f. all of the above.

16. Disk-storage devices can be:
a. part of the system unit.
b. a peripheral to the system unit.
c. removable or fixed.
d. any of the above.

17. Floppy disks cannot always be interchanged between different computers because:
a. different operating systems put information on disks in different ways.
b. not all computers use the same size disks.
c. they are not easily removed.
d. they are too fragile.
e. a and b.

18. Examples of application software are:
a. word-processing programs.
b. data management, or integrated, programs.
c. game programs.
d. all of the above.

Your Operating System

ABOUT THIS CHAPTER

This chapter explains what an operating system is, what it does for the computer, and what it can do for you. It also takes a brief look at the evolution of operating systems, the history of MS-DOS, and the unique position of MS-DOS in the operating system world of today.

WHAT IS AN OPERATING SYSTEM?

When you first encountered the term "operating system," it was probably in the small print of an advertisement or part of an eager salesperson's technobabble. Among all those other incomprehensible terms, such as RAM, ROM, modem, expandability, peripherals, RS232, and CPU, its significance may have escaped you. But operating system is not really a complex or confusing concept. Let's start with definitions from the *Random House Dictionary of the English Language*:

> Operate (1) to work or perform a function, like a machine does; (2) to work or use a machine.

That's clear. Operate has to do with performing machine-like actions.

> System (1) A complex or unitary whole; (2) a coordinated body of methods or a complex scheme or plan of procedure.

MS-DOS, like other operating systems, runs the computer by organizing information going into and coming out of the computer.

So, an operating system is a coordinated body of methods or a plan of procedure for controlling machines. MS-DOS, the operating system in your computer, organizes the information that goes into and comes out of the machine, and it controls how the parts of your computer system interact. The operating system runs the computer.

WHAT DOES AN OPERATING SYSTEM DO?

As you read in Chapter 1, a computer system is a collection of hardware (the machine parts) and software (the instructions that tell the computer how to perform the actual computing operations).

You use the hardware, such as the keyboard, disk drives, monitor, and printer, to coordinate data. Hardware provides the physical tools to type in data, feed data to or from a disk, receive data from other machines, or copy data to the printer.

The computer's software, particularly the operating system, gives instructions to the computer about what to do, when to do it, and with what data.

Software, usually in the form of programs, gives instructions to the computer. Software tells the computer what to do, at what time, and with what data. Without software, the hardware is useless. The operating system is software that carries out the basic procedures for controlling the hardware. As you will soon see, you can give commands directly to the operating system: for example, you can tell it to run WordStar. Your application program (such as a word processor) can also ask the operating system to carry out tasks such as saving data from memory to disk.

The main function of the operating system is to manage the information you enter into, store in, and retrieve from your computer. The scope of this management chore is shown in *Figure 2-1*.

In the course of its work, the operating system is an interface between you, who understands what you want to happen to the data you type in, and the mechanics of the computer, which demands that instructions be in a form that *it* can understand. Let's see how MS-DOS responds to this challenge.

Information Management

MS-DOS's major responsibility is to act as the master program for keeping all incoming and outgoing information in order. This task is accomplished by storing information in files.

The major responsibility of the operating system is to keep all the incoming and outgoing information in order. MS-DOS accomplishes this task by storing information in files. Computer files are no different from paper files; both hold a collection of related data. You give each file a name, and the operating system does the rest: storing the file where it can find it quickly, updating the file when you enter new information, and eliminating the file when you don't want it anymore. Computers may not be terribly interesting to converse with, but they are very good file clerks.

Let's compare this idea of a master program to something equally complex in everyday life. Suppose that instead of speaking of a DOS (an acronym for disk operating system), we were speaking of an ATC (air traffic controller). This ATC is in charge of all operations at a major international airport.

The controller is responsible for coordinating the overall traffic flow and is constantly aware of which planes are coming in, on which runways they'll land, their speed, and their arrival gates. An ATC must be sure those runways and gates have been cleared for landing, must know the relative position of each plane waiting to take off and which flight paths they will follow as they ascend, and must often make quick decisions so that all planes arrive and depart on schedule safely.

Listening to the conversation in a control tower can be confusing. You know that the instructions being passed back and forth are in English, but it's hard to believe these people are conversing sensibly. It might sound something like this:

Figure 2-1. Managing Files: DOS's Main Job

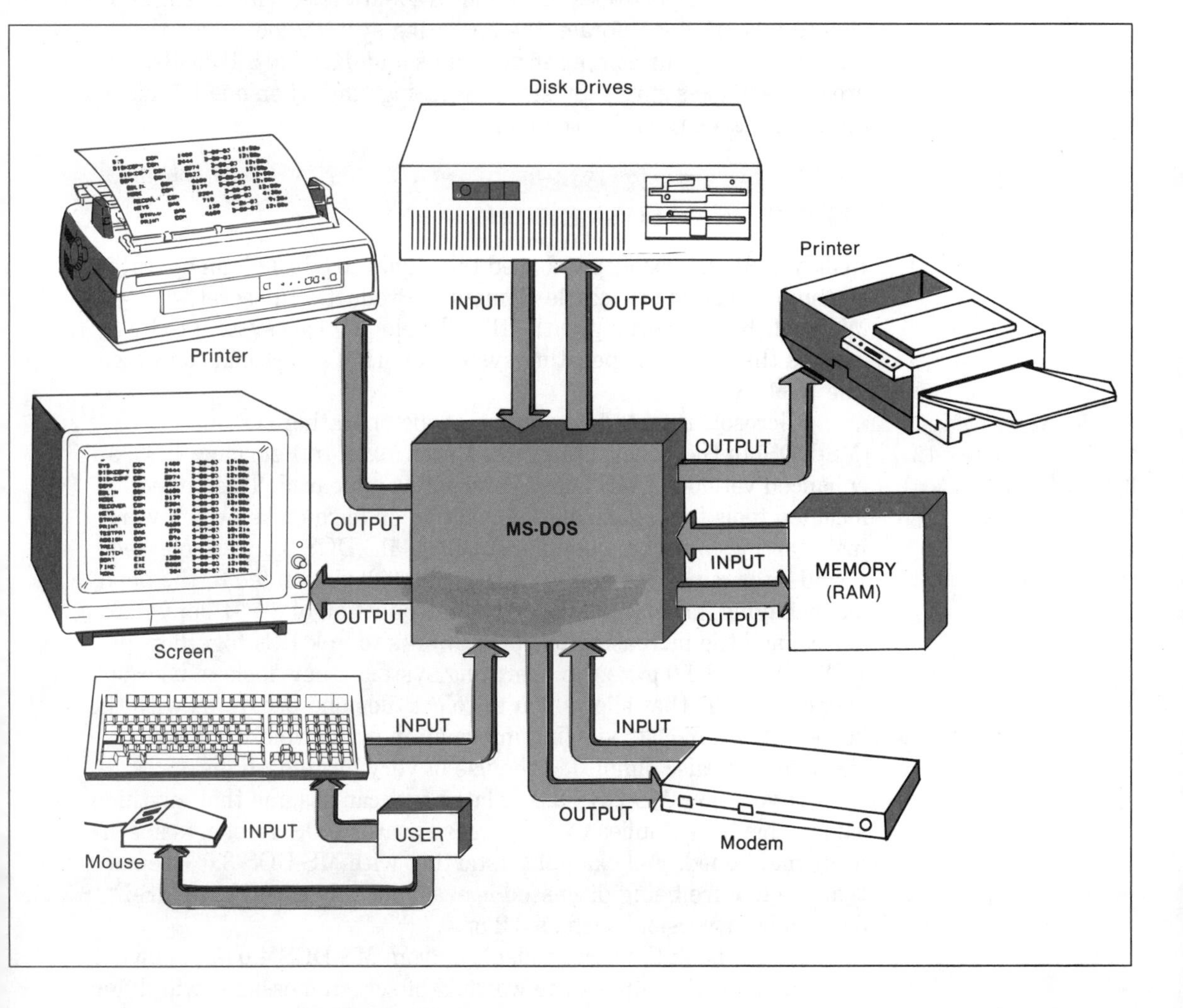

"United 9er9er 7 heavy, clear for takeoff on 2-1-left. You're number 3 behind the company."

You can't really understand it, but obviously it's working.

The operating system is like an air traffic controller in the way it controls the system: it organizes, schedules, and updates information.

The operating system is like that controller. It monitors all the incoming and outgoing activity of your computer system. Just as the controller knows constantly the position of every plane in the air or on the ground, the operating system knows the location and size of all the files currently in its memory or stored on its current disk. And like the controller, the operating system constantly updates all of its information according to changing conditions.

The controller's job is to make sure that each plane scheduled to come into the airport does indeed arrive and that each plane scheduled to take off does. Again, the operating system does much the same thing for your computer programs and data files. It loads programs, makes sure they start executing, and when one is finished, the DOS makes room for the next.

HISTORY OF MS-DOS VERSIONS

In July 1981, Microsoft purchased the rights to 86-DOS, an operating system developed by Seattle Computer Products. In secret, Microsoft began working with IBM, developing this system to be used as the PC-DOS operating system for IBM's personal computer (the IBM PC).

The first version of MS-DOS was released in 1982 for the IBM PC. Several versions of MS-DOS have been released since then.

Microsoft released its version of the operating system (MS-DOS) to the general public in March 1982. In February 1983, an enhanced version of MS-DOS, Version 2.0, appeared. This version included tools for organizing information on hard disks, which were just starting to become popular. In 1984, MS-DOS 3.0 was released. It and later minor revisions (3.1, 3.2, and 3.3) responded to the need for managing larger hard disks, the introduction of 3½″ floppy disk drives, and the increasing use of networks to link PCs together. In 1988, MS-DOS 4.0 gave the operating system a new look—a user-friendly "shell" that allows you to select files and programs with the keyboard or a mouse, viewing information in multiple windows on the screen. It also simplified the use of very large hard disks.

If you have MS-DOS 2.0 or later, you can assume that anything said in this book applies to you, unless a later DOS version is specifically mentioned. For example, "starting with MS-DOS 3.0" means that the feature being discussed is available only if you have MS-DOS 3.0 or a later version, such as 3.2 or 4.

In this book the screen displays from MS-DOS 4.0 are shown in the examples. Sometimes the wording of screen messages will differ slightly in earlier DOS versions, but the substance will be the same. The few significant differences will be noted.

It is important to realize that MS-DOS versions are highly "upwardly compatible"; most programs (and nearly all data files) created under one version of DOS will also work with later versions. This means that in most cases you can upgrade your DOS version without having to replace your expensive software. (The exceptions include some special utility programs and a few games.) The appendix on Installing MS-DOS also explains how to upgrade your DOS version.

WHAT MS-DOS MEANS TO YOU

Every computer needs an operating system. But the fact that your computer uses the MS-DOS operating system brings you some extra advantages.

MS-DOS provides some clear advantages to microcomputer users today: a wide variety of commands, its availability for many different computers, and the availability of a great amount of compatible application software.

Because the operating system is the interface between you and your computer's operation, you want it to be easy to use. With MS-DOS, most of the operations you want to accomplish can be performed with a few, easy-to-understand commands. Yet MS-DOS also incorporates some sophisticated and complex functions in its structure. As your computer knowledge grows, so will your appreciation of MS-DOS's capabilities. If you have MS-DOS 4.0, you will find an extra measure of "friendliness" is available, as you'll see in Chapter 11.

One of the biggest advantages of MS-DOS is its popularity. Because MS-DOS is the chosen operating system of so many personal computer manufacturers, software programmers have responded with a deluge of application programs. This means you can usually find the programs you want, and they will work with no modifications on your machine.

SUMMARY

This chapter discussed the concept of an operating system. It told you that MS-DOS manages files to keep track of the information put into the computer. Finally, it showed how new features were added as MS-DOS evolved, helping the operating system keep up with the development of new peripheral devices.

REVIEW

1. The MS-DOS operating system manages the way in which you enter, retrieve, and store information as files within the computer system.
2. DOS is an acronym for Disk Operating System.
3. MS-DOS 3.0 and 4.0 have expanded the capabilities of DOS to keep up with today's more powerful PCs.

Quiz for Chapter 2

1. An operating system can be compared to the function of:
   a. an application program.
   b. a peripheral device.
   c. a shopping mall.
   d. a programming language.
   e. an air-traffic controller.

2. Software is:
   a. a collection of instructions that tell a computer how to perform certain computing operations.
   b. soft and pliable if manipulated by a computer.
   c. built into every computer.
   d. data that is typed into a computer.

3. The main function of an operating system is to:
   a. manage all information that is input, stored, and output.
   b. take absolute control over the system on its own.
   c. show you how to operate the system.
   d. determine what information should be input and output.

4. MS-DOS maintains the order of incoming and outgoing information by using:
   a. special scale software.
   b. files.
   c. manual control.
   d. folders.

5. In the world of computers, DOS is used as an acronym for:
   a. disk optimizing software.
   b. density optically sensed.
   c. disk operating system.
   d. none of the above.

6. Most of the material covered in this book applies to:
   a. MS-DOS 4.0 only.
   b. any operating system.
   c. MS-DOS 2.0 and later.
   d. MS-DOS 3.0 and later.

7. The main reason later versions of MS-DOS were developed was:
   a. to run on non-IBM computers.
   b. to accommodate foreign languages.
   c. to allow you to run more than one program at a time.
   d. to accommodate new peripheral devices.

8. If you upgrade to a new version of DOS:
   a. you must buy new software.
   b. your existing hardware and software should work fine.
   c. you must retype all of your data into the computer.
   d. you must buy new peripheral devices.
   e. both a and d.

Getting Started with MS-DOS

ABOUT THIS CHAPTER

Using MS-DOS is very simple. In this chapter you'll learn how to start, or *boot,* your system and how to get the computer to respond to MS-DOS commands. Two commands are introduced in this chapter, the DIR (directory) command and the CLS (clear the screen) command.

BEFORE YOU BEGIN

Now that you are familiar with the basic facts about computer systems and you know that MS-DOS helps operate your system, it's time for you to begin computing. Just as a pilot approaches takeoff in a logical step-by-step fashion, you too are going to follow a simple "pre-flight" routine.

First, make sure that your machine is properly set up and ready to go (your user's manual will give you all the necessary instructions). Second, sit down at the controls, and try not to be intimidated by the intricacies of being in command of your computer. After all, you will do everything one manageable step at a time.

MS-DOS should be installed on your computer. This means that if you have a hard disk, the various files that make up MS-DOS have been copied to the hard disk, and the hard disk has been set up so that MS-DOS will be loaded when you turn on the computer. If your machine has only floppy disk drives, there should be a "system disk" that has the MS-DOS files on it. Insert that disk in the disk drive before turning on the computer. If you have just bought your computer, MS-DOS may not be properly set up yet. If MS-DOS doesn't load when you follow the instructions given below, turn for help to the appendix on Installing MS-DOS.

BOOTING THE SYSTEM

The first step in getting MS-DOS off the ground is booting, or loading, the system.

To begin using your computer, you must boot the system. This doesn't mean you deliver a sharp kick to the backside of the machine! The term is derived from "pulling oneself up by the bootstraps." In computereze, booting means getting the machine ready to accept your instructions.This sounds very simple, but logically it creates a Catch-22 situation. How can the machine start, if the instructions it needs to begin are located inside the machine (which you can't get to until the machine starts)?

After the computer is powered up, or reset, it receives instructions from the bootstrap loader program stored in ROM on how to boot MS-DOS and reads the hard disk or the disk in drive A for further instructions.

This problem is solved by a handy little program called the *bootstrap loader.* This small program located in ROM (remember, that's the part of memory that is permanent) is the first thing the computer reads when the power is turned on. The bootstrap contains one simple directive—"start reading the instructions on the disk in drive A." If you have no hard disk drive, you start the computer after putting your MS-DOS system disk or another boot disk in drive A. (When the floppy drives are housed side by side, drive A is the one on the left. If they are housed one on top of the other, drive A is usually the top drive.)

If your system has a hard disk, however, don't put any disk in drive A. When the bootstrap loader discovers there is no disk there, it will look on the hard disk instead. (On most systems, the hard disk drive is called drive C.) MS-DOS will be loaded from the hard disk, which is much faster than using floppies. (Again, if you have trouble, turn to the appendix on Installing MS-DOS.) That's all MS-DOS needs to be up and running.

Be sure you have handy the user's guide supplied by the manufacturer. Because not everyone has the same system, there may be slight differences in the wording or order of the messages that appear on the screen and the wording used in this book. If things seem inconsistent to you, just consult your user's guide. If you have started MS-DOS from your hard disk, you can skip over the next section, which deals with starting from a floppy disk.

The Operating-System Disk

To begin the booting-up process, locate your operating-system disk. This will be labeled MS-DOS or some variant of a DOS name. Because this disk contains your operating system, it is the key to your computer's operation.

Next insert the disk into disk drive A. If you have a question about how to insert the disk or which drive is A, consult your user's guide. Every computer sage can recount a favorite story of trying for hours to get something to work, using all kinds of procedures, only to discover that the disk was put in wrong or was hiding in the wrong drive. Be sure to close the drive door after inserting the disk; you can't get any information from a disk unless the door is closed. (Disk drives for 3½″ disks don't have a door. Instead, the disk drops into place with a "click." You remove the disk by pushing on the square "Eject" button on the bottom right of the drive housing.) Inserting the two kinds of floppies is shown in *Figure 3-1.*

Figure 3-1. Disk Insertion

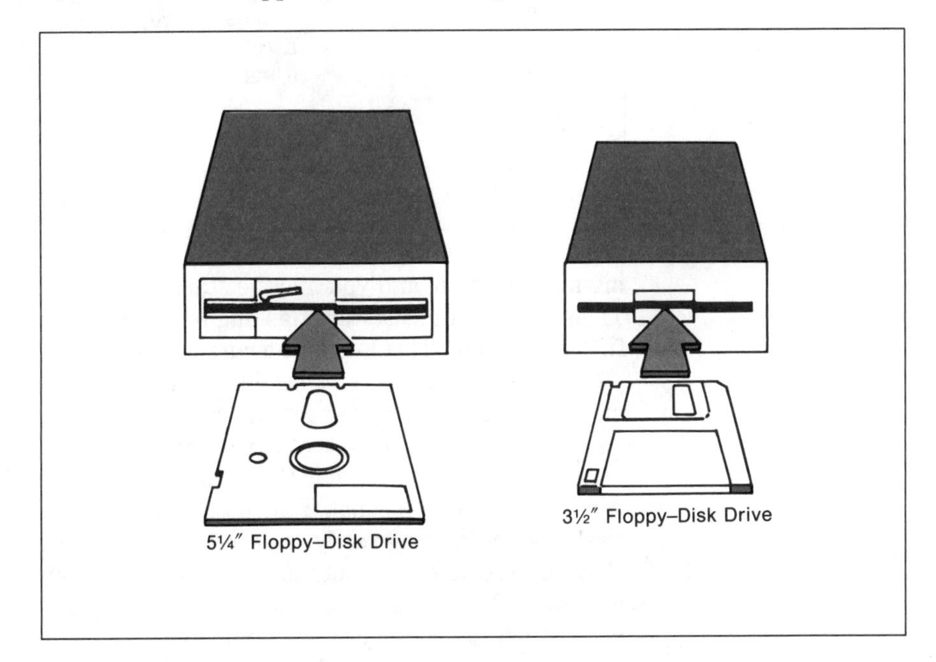

The Power Switch

Now you're ready to fire up. But where's the on switch? This is another question for your user's guide, but the switch is probably on the side or back of your machine. (The power switch on the IBM PS/2 machines is on the right side of the front panel.) If your monitor has a separate power switch (it does on most systems), be sure to turn it on as well. Turn on the power and wait patiently.

To help you through the booting-up process, a checklist is provided in *Figure 3-2.*

MS-DOS Comes to Life

It takes a few seconds for the machine to wake up. Then several things happen at once. You'll hear some whirring sounds as the cool-

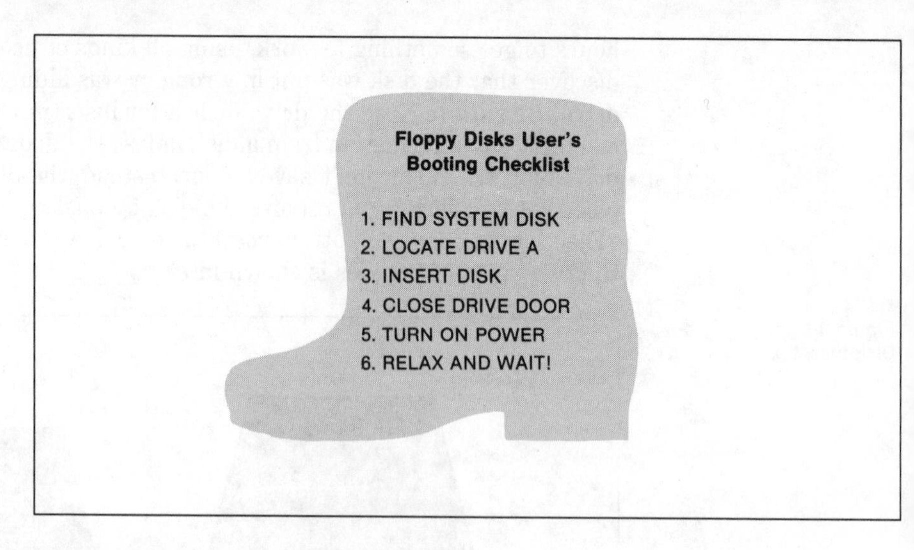

Floppy Disks User's
Booting Checklist
1. FIND SYSTEM DISK
2. LOCATE DRIVE A
3. INSERT DISK
4. CLOSE DRIVE DOOR
5. TURN ON POWER
6. RELAX AND WAIT!

Figure 3-2. Booting Checklist for Floppy-Disk Systems

ing fan comes on, and you may be startled by a short electronic beep. Then a small line will start flashing on the screen. Good, this is the first sign of life. This line is the cursor, a small marker that indicates your place on the screen. Your cursor may or may not flash, and it may not be a line. More about the cursor in a moment.

You will also notice the drive's indicator light (usually red) flashing on and off. You can hear the drive moving when the light is on. All of this is quite normal. Your machine is just doing some self-checking and getting ready to receive instructions. (If none of the above occurs after a minute or two, check to be sure the machine is plugged in.)

When the activity stops, a number of messages may appear on the screen, if someone such as your dealer has already installed some programs that are run at startup. Don't worry about any of these now—in Chapter 12 you'll learn how to do your own system customization. Eventually, you should see a short message, or "prompt," that will look something like this:

```
C>
```

or

```
C:\>
```

(If you used a floppy disk to boot the system, the prompt will show the letter A instead of C.)

SETTING THE CALENDAR AND CLOCK

Most MS-DOS systems today keep track of the date and time using a battery-powered clock. The appendix on Installing MS-DOS shows you how to tell MS-DOS to refer to this clock automatically on startup. If the calendar and clock haven't been set up for MS-DOS, you will see a message like this:

```
Current date is Tues 1-01-1980
Enter new date (mm-dd-yy):
```

The date you see on the screen will not be today's date. Let's say that today is August 1, 1991. This is the new date you want to enter. You can enter the date in a variety of ways:

8-1-91   08-1-91   8/1/91   08/01/91

Almost all prompts displayed by MS-DOS requiring that you type in something on the keyboard also require that you press the <ENTER> key after you've finished typing your input.

Whichever method you use to enter the date, separate the parts of the date with hyphens or slashes. Notice that you don't enter the day of the week, just the numeric equivalents of the month, day, and year. Enter the date now.

```
Current date is Tues 1-01-1980
Enter new date: 8-1-91 <ENTER>
```

Immediately after you enter the date, MS-DOS returns the current time and asks you if you want to enter a new time.

```
Current time is 0:00:46.08
Enter new time:
```

At this point, the computer has no hours and no minutes, so enter the current time now. Our current hypothetical time is 9:30 in the morning. Here are the various ways you could enter the time:

9:30:00.0   9:30:0   09:30:0   9:30

Your computer follows the international standard of the 24-hour clock. This means that the hours from 1 A.M. to noon are indicated by 0 to 12. After noon the hours go from 13 to 24 (midnight). (If you are using MS-DOS 4.0, you can use the regular 12-hour clock instead. Just type *a* or *p* after the time to indicate whether it is A.M. or P.M. For example, 9:30 in the morning can be entered as 9:30a.) You can enter the time according to the precise hours, minutes, seconds, and tenths of seconds, but for most applications the hour and minutes suffice. When entering the time, separate the hour, minutes, and seconds with a colon. If you do add the tenths of seconds, they are preceded by a period. Now enter the time.

```
Current time is 0:00:46.08
Enter new time: 9:30 <ENTER>
```

Your clock and calendar are now right on the mark; you did very well with your first computer encounter.

What we have been describing is the ideal sequence of events when setting the time and date. But what happens if you follow the instructions (you think perfectly), and this message appears on the screen?

```
INVALID DATE or INVALID TIME
```

There is nothing to worry about, just try the entry again. You may have put a period where you need a slash.

ENTERING DATA INTO THE MACHINE

The C> or A> prompt indicates that MS-DOS is waiting for some information. You will use the keyboard to enter data into the computer. Sometimes your entry is in response to a request such as the "Enter new date" statement. Sometimes *you* initiate the interaction with a request of your own.

Understanding Instructions

At first, what information to enter and how and when to enter it may seem mysterious. To help you, this book uses different type faces and special symbols to distinguish between what you type at the computer and what MS-DOS displays on the screen. *Table 3-1* shows the usages involved.

Some Common Misconceptions

To the computer, each key means a different character. You must not type the 1 (number one) if you really mean the l (lowercase ell). The same is true of the 0 (number zero) and the O (uppercase oh).

The spacebar on your computer does not simply move the cursor across the screen. It also sends a message to the computer: "make this a blank space." There are a number of keys that you can use to move the cursor around the screen, such as the arrow (cursor-control) keys. How these keys work depends mainly on what program

Table 3-1.
The Symbols Used in This Book

How Text Is Shown	Meaning
`A>Format another? (Y/N)`	Information shown in regular type is supplied by the computer.
`A>format b:`	Information shown in color is supplied by you. When you type your entries be sure to include all punctuation and leave blank spaces where indicated.
< >	These brackets indicate a key on the keyboard (other than the letter or number keys).
`<ENTER>`	The <ENTER> key is your signal that you have finished typing in an entry. You must press the <ENTER> key before the computer can respond to most commands or instructions. The <ENTER> key may appear on your keyboard as <RETURN> or <↵>.

you are running. Chapter 4 will show you how these keys can be used to help you enter MS-DOS commands.

Correcting Mistakes

Because you are just beginning your exploration of the computer, it's natural that you will make mistakes (especially if you're also new at typing). So double-check your entries before you press the <ENTER> key. If you find a mistake, just use the <BACK-SPACE> key (it may look like this <←>) to erase characters until you back up to the error. Then retype the entry.

If you can't get the keyboard to accept your data, or if you've lost track of what is going on, just press the <Esc> (Escape) key. If all else fails, remove your floppies and turn off the machine and start over, following the instructions given earlier.

These keys are shown in *Figure 3-3*. Take a moment to find the keys on your keyboard. There is a wider 101-key keyboard that comes with many newer systems such as the IBM PS/2. The <Esc>, <BACKSPACE>, and <ENTER> keys are in the same place on both this and the older keyboards, however.

Figure 3-3. Position of <Esc>, <BACKSPACE>, and <ENTER> Keys on Keyboard

Regular keyboard

Enhanced keyboard

BOOT TEMPERATURE (COLD VS. WARM)

Using the power-off/power-on method of booting the system is called cold booting. The system can also be warm booted while power remains on by pressing the <Ctrl> key, and while holding <Ctrl> down, pressing the <Alt> and <Del> keys.

When you turn on the PC's power, you are performing a cold boot, or starting the machine from a power-off position. There is another kind of boot that occurs when you are already working on the machine (the power is on), but you want to start over again from the beginning. This is called a warm boot. To warm boot the system, press down the <Ctrl> (control) key, and while holding down <Ctrl>, press the <Alt> and <Del> keys. Be careful, though. Warm booting your system is just like turning off the power, as far as any data you may have had in RAM is concerned. If possible, save your work to disk first. Of course, one reason why you might be warm booting in the first place is that the machine won't respond to any of your commands, and you need to reset it. In that case you've lost any data created or changed since the last time you saved. Fortunately, the system gets "hung up" like this rarely—it indicates a problem with your software or hardware. The main advantage of warm booting is that it saves wear on your power switch and on the electrical circuits in your computer—every time you turn on your computer, it gets a surge of power that can eventually weaken internal components. For this reason, it is a good idea to leave your computer running throughout the workday.

Control Key

You will find that the <Ctrl> key is always used in conjunction with other keys. When used with another key, it changes the message that key sends to the computer. When you use <Ctrl>, you must hold it down while pressing another key or keys. Release all the keys together.

PROMPTS

Now that these preliminaries are out of the way, it is time to learn how to enter MS-DOS commands. The capital letter (C or A) followed by the greater-than symbol (>) is the MS-DOS prompt. Some systems use a prompt that has the letter C or A followed by a colon and a backslash, like this: C:\>. From now on, this prompt will be shown in most listings; if you have started MS-DOS from a floppy disk, remember that your prompt will be A> or A:\>. (In Chapter 7 you will learn how you can " customize" your MS-DOS prompt.) A prompt tells you that the machine is waiting for you to enter some information. Notice that the cursor follows the prompt, indicating the location of the next entry.

Prompts vary with the program in use. For example, C> is the DOS prompt, "ok" is the prompt for the BASIC programming language, and "*" is the prompt for the EDLIN program: a program that can be used to create text files (see the appendix on EDLIN).

In response to the C:\> prompt, you are going to give MS-DOS your first command. Commands are nothing more than instructions to the operating system. They consist of short words or abbreviations that tell MS-DOS to perform specific actions. Right now, you want to find out what's on a disk.

COMMANDS

The DIR Command

Files, or collections of related data, are the way MS-DOS keeps track of which information is stored where. You will learn how to create your own files in Chapter 6. You use the DIR (short for DIRectory) command to see the names of all the files that are on a disk or to find out if a specific file is located on a particular disk.

Listing All the Files

The first command you should enter after having booted MS-DOS for the first time is the DIR command, which causes a list of files to be displayed on the screen.

You can now use the DIR command to see what's on your hard disk. When you enter a command, you can use either upper- or lowercase letters (don't forget to include all punctuation and blank spaces). Enter this command now.

```
C:\>dir <ENTER>
```

If no files are listed, or only a few, try typing the command this way instead:

```
C:\>dir c:\dos<ENTER>
```

(This will be explained further in Chapter 7.) If you started with a floppy disk, you'll be looking at the contents of the floppy disk in drive A instead. In both cases you will be looking at the files that come with MS-DOS.

MS-DOS responds with a listing of the files. Did the entire screen fill up and then move on quickly to another screen? No one can read anything that fast! What do you do now?

Scrolling

There is a simple explanation for this phenomenon. If the disk contains only a few files, after they are listed the display stops. But when a disk contains many files, they cannot fit on the screen at one time, and the display will scroll. Scrolling means that as the screen is filled with information, new data is added to the bottom of the display as old data rolls off the top. There is a simple way to freeze the screen and stop this scrolling action.

Because lists of files generated by the DIR command can be lengthy, the list may scroll off the screen before you can read it. To stop the display at any time, press and hold down the <Ctrl> key, then press the S key. Press any key on the keyboard to resume scrolling.

To stop scrolling, you press and hold down the <Ctrl> key and then press the S key. Release both keys together. In some systems you stop scrolling by holding down <Ctrl> and pressing the <Num Lock> key. On the enhanced keyboard found on the PS/2 and many AT-compatible systems, you can also use the <Pause> key to stop the scrolling. This key is located at the right end of the row of function keys across the top of the keyboard. (Don't use the <Ctrl> key with the <Pause> key.) After pressing <Pause>, press any key to resume scrolling.

Try using the DIR command to list the disk contents again. If your display is more than one screen long, freeze the scrolling action by using the <Ctrl> S combination.

```
C:\>dir <ENTER>
<Ctrl> S
```

Press any key (<ENTER> is a good one to use) to begin the scrolling again until the display is finished.

The Directory Listing

The exact file names and the numbers on your screen will vary according to the version of MS-DOS you are using (the examples here use MS-DOS 4.0). *Figure 3-4* shows the pattern in which the files are listed.

Figure 3-4. Directory Output Sample

```
 Volume in drive C is MSDOSDISK
 Volume Serial Number is 1454-3E20
 Directory of C:\
.            <DIR>       01-31-91  11:15a
..           <DIR>       01-31-91  11:15a
COMMAND  COM      37637 01-31-91  12:00p
FORMAT   COM      22923 01-31-91  12:00p
MORE     COM       2166 01-31-91  12:00p
GRAPHICS COM      16733 01-31-91  12:00p
XCOPY    EXE      17087 01-31-91  12:00p
CHKDSK   COM      17771 01-31-91  12:00p
BACKUP   COM      33754 01-31-91  12:00p
DISKCOPY COM      10428 01-31-91  12:00p
LABEL    COM       4490 01-31-91  12:00p
MODE     COM      23056 01-31-91  12:00p
SYS      COM      11472 01-31-91  12:00p
DOSSHELL BAT        311 01-31-91   3:25p
FASTOPEN EXE      16302 01-31-91  12:00p
FDISK    COM      70151 01-31-91  12:00p
IFSFUNC  EXE      21653 01-31-91  12:00p
KEYB     COM      14759 01-31-91  12:00p
SHARE    EXE      10301 01-31-91  12:00p
APPEND   EXE      11186 01-31-91  12:00p
ASSIGN   COM       5785 01-31-91  12:00p
ATTRIB   EXE      18247 01-31-91  12:00p
BASIC    COM       1065 01-31-91  12:00p
BASICA   COM      36285 01-31-91  12:00p
COMP     COM       9491 01-31-91  12:00p
DEBUG    COM      21606 01-31-91  12:00p
DISKCOMP COM       9889 01-31-91  12:00p
```

Continued

Figure 3-4
(continued)

```
DOSUTIL  MEU       6660 01-31-91  12:00p
EDLIN    COM      14249 01-31-91  12:00p
FILESYS  EXE      11125 01-31-91  12:00p
FIND     EXE       5983 01-31-91  12:00p
GRAFTABL COM      10271 01-31-91  12:00p
GRAPHICS PRO       9413 01-31-91  12:00p
JOIN     EXE      17457 01-31-91  12:00p
MEM      EXE      20133 01-31-91  12:00p
NLSFUNC  EXE       6910 01-31-91  12:00p
PCIBMDRV MOS        295 01-31-91  12:00p
PCMSDRV  MOS        961 01-31-91  12:00p
PCMSPDRV MOS        801 01-31-91  12:00p
PRINT    COM      14024 01-31-91  12:00p
RECOVER  COM      10732 01-31-91  12:00p
REPLACE  EXE      17199 01-31-91  12:00p
RESTORE  COM      40030 01-31-91  12:00p
SHELL    CLR       4438 01-31-91  12:00p
SHELL    HLP      65667 01-31-91  12:00p
SHELL    MEU       4588 01-31-91  12:00p
SHELLB   COM       3937 01-31-91  12:00p
SHELLC   EXE     154377 01-31-91  12:00p
SORT     EXE       5914 01-31-91  12:00p
SUBST    EXE      18143 01-31-91  12:00p
TREE     COM       6334 01-31-91  12:00p
DOSSHELL GRA        213 01-31-91   3:56p
SHELL    ASC       1680 01-31-91  10:44a
        52 File(s)   18409120 bytes free
```

The first items, the *volume* and *volume number*, are optional, and you don't need to worry about them now. They will be discussed in Chapter 7. Following them is the name of disk whose directory you are viewing (this will be A:\ rather than C:\ if you are using a floppy disk).

The body of the listing is divided into five columns. Column 1 gives the name of the file: for example, SORT, FIND, MORE, BASIC. This name identifies the contents of the file. Column 2 is an extension of the file's name. EXE and COM tell what type of files these are. Pay no attention to these particulars right now. File naming is discussed in detail in Chapter 6.

Column 3 tells how big the file is. File size is measured in bytes; so the SORT file takes up 5914 bytes on the disk. Columns 4 and 5 tell the date and time that the file was last updated as obtained from the system disk.

Finally, MS-DOS performs a little housekeeping chore. It reports the total number of files on the disk and the space available on the disk for new files. This information will be very useful to you later, when you are deciding if a file will fit on a certain disk.

That's a lot of information from one small three-letter command.

Notice that when MS-DOS is finished performing the DIR command, it returns you to the operating system. You know this has happened when you see the DOS prompt C:\>.

Listing a Specific File

When the DIR command is entered without qualification, it causes the entire list of files on the disk to be displayed. You can also use DIR to see if a specific file exists on the disk by typing in the file's name.

In addition to listing all the files on a disk, DIR can also tell you if a specific file is on a particular disk. To get this information, enter the command followed by a file name. Although you already know the contents of your system disk, assume that you are trying to find a file named COMMAND.COM. Enter the DIR command, leave a blank space, and enter the name of the file.

```
C:\>dir command.com <ENTER>
 Volume in drive C is MSDOSDISK
 Volume Serial Number is 1454-3E20
 Directory of C:\
COMMAND  COM     37637 01-31-91   12:00p
        1 File(s)   18288640 bytes free
```

And there it is—all of the same information listed in columns 1 through 5, as they describe this particular file.

If the file you request is not on the disk, MS-DOS returns this message:

```
File not found
```

Sorry, try again. Either you never put the file on this disk or you are looking at a different disk than you thought. (You may also be looking at the wrong *directory* on your hard disk. Directories are used to divide the hard disk into more manageable parts. They are discussed in Chapters 7 and 8. For now, just be aware that you may be looking at only part of your hard disk.)

Now you are reaping the fruits of your labors (either a DIR of the entire disk or a DIR of the COMMAND.COM file). But how do you remove this information from the screen? The next command provides the answer.

CLEARING THE SCREEN

The CLS Command

To clear the screen, you can enter the CLS command at any time in response to the MS-DOS prompt. Using CLS does not alter any information stored in memory or on disk.

As you use your computer, you will realize that you don't need to keep looking at all the information after you have seen it. With mistakes and changes of mind, you can fill up a screen pretty quickly. For instance, in one use of the DIR command, you displayed all the files on your system disk. You don't really need this information once you have looked at it. The CLS (CLear Screen) command is a handy way of getting rid of all the stuff on the screen. Try using CLS now to empty the screen.

```
C:\>cls <ENTER>
```

Like magic, the screen is cleared. After you execute the CLS command, the cursor waits in the upper left corner of the screen for the next entry. This is sometimes called the cursor's home position.

CLS affects only the information currently on the screen. It does nothing to data in memory or to information stored on disks. The corollary is that it also saves nothing. Use CLS only when you don't need the information on the screen.

SUMMARY

In this chapter you've learned how to perform a cold and a warm boot. You've learned some simple rules for entering data into the machine and entered your first MS-DOS commands. The DIR command enabled you to display the listing for a disk, and <Ctrl> S showed you how to freeze that display. The CLS command cleaned up your screen when you were finished looking at the displayed information.

In the next chapter you'll take a closer look at one piece of computer technology that helped spawn the personal computer revolution: the floppy disk.

REVIEW

1. To boot from your hard disk, simply turn on the power for the computer and monitor.

2. To boot your floppy-disk system, you first place a copy of your MS-DOS disk into disk drive A.

3. To enter a new date, you must type absolutely correctly; use the backspace key to erase errors. You can enter the current date and time in several ways, but remember that the computer follows the international twenty-four-hour clock (DOS 4.0 lets you use A.M. and P.M. instead).
4. Cold boot refers to starting the machine from a power-off condition.
5. Warm boot refers to restarting the machine without having turned off power; to warm boot your machine, press the <Ctrl> key, the <Alt> key, and the <Del> key, all at the same time.
6. The C:\> prompt indicates that MS-DOS is loaded and that the computer system is ready for your command.
7. The DIR command presents information on one or all of the files on a disk in a given disk drive.
8. The CLS command removes all information displayed on the screen and places the cursor in the upper left corner of the screen.

Quiz for Chapter 3

1. Booting the system is the process of:
   a. kicking the system.
   b. loading the MS-DOS operating system.
   c. applying polish to the system.
   d. dismissing the system.
2. The first program that is executed when the system is powered up is the:
   a. shoehorn loader.
   b. bootstrap loader.
   c. MS-DOS operating system.
   d. a predefined application program.
3. In addition to this book, it is also recommended that you keep handy your:
   a. computer's serial number.
   b. BASIC language manual.
   c. computer manufacturer's documentation.
   d. screwdriver.
4. If you don't have a hard disk, your booting checklist should include:
   a. finding the system disk.
   b. locating drive A.
   c. inserting the disk.
   d. closing the drive door.
   e. turning on the power.
   f. all of the above in the order shown.
5. If your system hasn't been set up to read the clock automatically, the first thing MS-DOS displays after it has been booted is the:
   a. blank screen.
   b. prompt requesting that you enter the current date.
   c. prompt requesting that you enter the current time.
   d. list of files stored on the disk.
6. Some keys can be easily confused with each other. They are:
   a. 0 (zero) and O (letter) keys.
   b. 1 (one) and l (lower case ell) keys.
   c. both of the above.
   d. none of the above.

7. You can correct typing errors at an MS-DOS prompt by using the <BACKSPACE> key and retyping the text:
   a. after pressing the <ENTER> key.
   b. after pressing the <Esc> key.
   c. before pressing the <ENTER> key.
   d. before pressing the <ScrollLock> key.

8. You can enter the date July 4, 1991, as:
   a. 7-4-91.
   b. 07-4-91.
   c. 7/4/91.
   d. 07/04/91.
   e. any of the above.

9. A cold boot means the system is booted:
   a. immediately after power has been turned on.
   b. without having to turn the power off.
   c. only in cold temperatures.
   d. using a cold floppy disk.

10. A warm boot means the system is rebooted while power remains turned on and is accomplished by pressing the:
   a. <Del> key.
   b. <Ctrl> key.
   c. <Ctrl> key, and, while holding it down, pressing the <Alt> and <Del> keys.
   d. <Ctrl> key, and, while holding it down, pressing the <Alt> and <SPACEBAR> keys.

11. In response to the standard MS-DOS prompt C:\> that is displayed after the system has been booted you can:
   a. enter any text you want.
   b. enter only the DIR command.
   c. enter only MS-DOS commands.
   d. enter any MS-DOS or BASIC command.

12. The DIR command is used to:
   a. look at the contents of files.
   b. display a list of files stored on the disk.
   c. erase files.
   d. copy files.

13. Pausing the scrolling of text on the screen is accomplished by:
   a. pressing and holding down the <Ctrl> key and then pressing the S key.
   b. pressing and holding down the <Ctrl> key and then pressing the <NumLock> key (on some computers).

   c. pressing the <Ctrl>, <Alt>, and <Del> keys.
   d. turning the power off and then on again.
   e. any of the above.
   f. a or b.

14. The CLS command is used to:
   a. clear out memory.
   b. clear the screen.
   c. clear out the contents of a disk.
   d. clear the CPU.

15. After pausing the scrolling of text on the screen, you can resume scrolling by:
   a. pressing any key.
   b. pressing and holding down the <Ctrl> key and then pressing the S key.
   c. pressing the <Esc> key twice.
   d. pressing the <SPACEBAR> key.

Using the Command Line

ABOUT THIS CHAPTER

This chapter is going to refine your computing skills. You have already learned how to enter simple MS-DOS commands (DIR and CLS). In doing so, you may have become acquainted already with some of the special keys on your computer keyboard. You are probably becoming familiar with the location of the standard alphabet, number, and punctuation keys. will be learning are longer and more complicated. Before you learn them, though, it will be useful to learn how special keys on your PC can help you correct errors or start over if necessary. You will also expand your knowledge of commands by learning how to use switches with the DIR command. By the time you finish this chapter, you'll know how MS-DOS processes your commands, and this will help you deal with errors or problems.

A QUICK REVIEW

The two most commonly used keys on an MS-DOS system are the <ENTER> and <BACKSPACE> keys.

The first two special keys are already in your repertoire. They are illustrated in *Figure 4-1* and included here for review.

Figure 4-1. The <ENTER> and <BACKSPACE> Keys

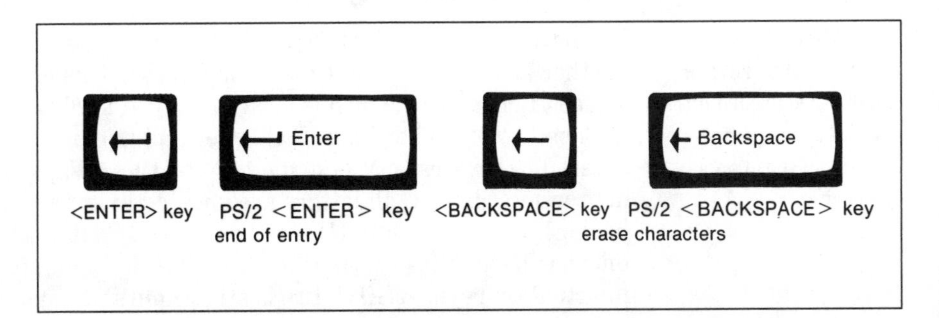

The <ENTER> Key

You wouldn't be this far along unless you had already mastered the <ENTER> key. This important key indicates the end of an entry and must be pressed to give the go-ahead signal to MS-DOS. This key may look like this <↵> on your keyboard.

The <BACKSPACE> Key

And unless you are perfect, you've probably had a lot of experience with the <BACKSPACE> key as well. Using this key is an easy way to erase characters to correct mistakes. It moves the cursor on the current line to the left and erases characters as it moves. You will learn some additional procedures for correcting mistakes later in this chapter. This key may be represented as a left arrow <←> on your keyboard.

SPECIAL KEYS

Now we are going to introduce some other keys that make using MS-DOS more convenient. One word of caution: your keyboard may not contain all of these keys. But by reading through the entire section on editing characters, you will find out how to use your keyboard to the best advantage.

Most of these keys are operational only when you are using MS-DOS or EDLIN, although there are exceptions. Usually they are inoperative or perform different functions in other programs. With a little experience in a variety of computing applications, you'll learn the quirks of each key and its uses.

The <Caps Lock> Key

The <SHIFT> and <Caps Lock> keys on a computer keyboard often operate a little differently from those on a typewriter.

You have used the <SHIFT> key to enter uppercase letters, but another key also lets you type in uppercase. This is the <Caps Lock> key, which is located for you in *Figure 4-2*. When <Caps Lock> is not in use, all letter and number keys are normally entered in lowercase. When you turn on the <Caps Lock> mode by depressing this key, all letters are entered in uppercase without your having to press the <SHIFT> key. The <Caps Lock> key affects only the letter keys on your key board; it does not affect number or punctuation keys. <SHIFT> is still required to enter the punctuation symbols found above the number keys and on the upper section of other keys. <Caps Lock> mode stays in effect until you depress the key again.

Figure 4-2.
<Caps Lock> Key

Here is one unique result of using the <Caps Lock> key that may surprise you: when you are in the <Caps Lock> mode, pressing the <SHIFT> key causes all letters to be entered in lowercase. Try using <Caps Lock> to enter some information just to get the general idea.

In normal mode (<Caps Lock> off), pressing *M* results in *m*; pressing <SHIFT> *M* results in *M*; and pressing <SHIFT> *2* results in @.

In Caps Lock mode (<Caps Lock> on), pressing *M* results in *M*; pressing <SHIFT> *M* results in *m*; and pressing <SHIFT> *2* results in @.

The <Esc> Key

Suppose you discover that you have made a mistake on an entry just as you finish typing in the entire line. Of course, the mistake is way back at the beginning of the line. You just don't feel like sitting there using <BACKSPACE> to erase the whole thing. There is a way to cancel an entire line.

The <Esc> key is used for many programs to "escape" from a particular operation. If you press <Esc> while typing a command at the MS-DOS prompt, a backslash (\) is displayed, indicating that the command is canceled.

To eliminate the current line you use the <Esc> (Escape) key. <Esc> puts a backslash (\) on your command line to indicate that the command is canceled. It then moves the cursor down one line so you can enter a new command. When you cancel a line with <Esc>, it is not received by the computer. Remember that you must press <Esc> *before* you press the <ENTER> key. Once you've pressed <ENTER >, your command is sent to MS-DOS and executed, and you can't change it. The <Esc> key is located for you in *Figure 4-3*. Try this now: imagine that you are looking for a file on the directory called "fishing.123." As you enter the extension you realize that you have made a mistake.

```
C:\>dir wishing.123 <Esc>
```

The <Esc> key cancels your command and moves you down to the next line. The cursor appears, waiting for a new command.

```
C:\>dir wishing.123\
    ■
```

Now you could enter the correct information and continue with your work. Additional editing commands will be explained later in this chapter.

Figure 4-3. The <Esc> and <PrtSc> Keys

Regular keyboard

Enhanced keyboard

The <PrtSc> Key

The <PrtSc> (or Print Screen) key (only available on IBM-compatible keyboards) is used in combination with other keys to cause text displayed on the screen to be output to a printer. <SHIFT><PrtSc> prints the entire contents of the screen to the printer, whereas <Ctrl><PrtSc> causes each line on the screen to be printed as it is displayed.

Often, when you are entering or editing commands or text, you may want to have a printed copy of what is being displayed on the screen. To do this, you use the <PrtSc> (Print Screen) key. This key, found only on IBM-compatible keyboards, is located for you in *Figure 4-3*. If you don't have this key, there is still a way for you to print out your display. See the <Ctrl> P description in Table 4-2.

To print out everything that is currently displayed on your screen, be sure your printer is turned on and ready. Printing the contents of a display is known as "dumping the screen." To perform a screen dump, hold down one of the <SHIFT> keys and press <PrtSc>.

You can also make a printed copy of each line you enter on the screen, as you enter it. This is called "echoing the screen" to the printer. To echo each line as it is entered, hold down the <Ctrl> key and press the <PrtSc> key. All typed-in entries are echoed to the printer until you press <Ctrl><PrtSc> again. (Anything displayed by MS-DOS, such as a directory listing, is also printed.)

You can also print graphics (pictures) on the screen if you have a printer that can print graphics (most dot matrix and laser printers can print graphics). To use this feature, you must enter the MS-DOS GRAPHICS command, which is explained in Chapter 12.

The <Num Lock> Key

The <Num Lock> key is used on IBM-compatible keyboards to switch the modes of the keypad between numeric input and cursor control.

The keys on the numeric keypad on your machine have a dual purpose, as shown in *Figure 4-4*. You can use them to enter numbers as input or to control the movement of the cursor. These keys have a set of arrows and are named <Home>, <End>, <PgUp> (page up), and <PgDn> (page down). The <Num Lock> key controls which function these keys perform.

Normally <Num Lock> is in the cursor-control mode. This means that pressing the keys moves the cursor up, down, left, right, or to a certain location on the screen or in a file. These cursor control keys are not normally used in MS-DOS operation but they are used in many application programs.

Pressing <Num Lock> while it is in this cursor-control mode shifts the keyboard to the numeric mode. Now when you press these keys, the numbers are entered as input. When using MS-DOS, however, you will probably use the number keys across the top of the keyboard for numeric input. The numeric keypad comes into its own when you are using an application that involves many numeric entries—a spreadsheet program, for example.

Figure 4-4. The Numeric Keypad (Regular Keyboard)

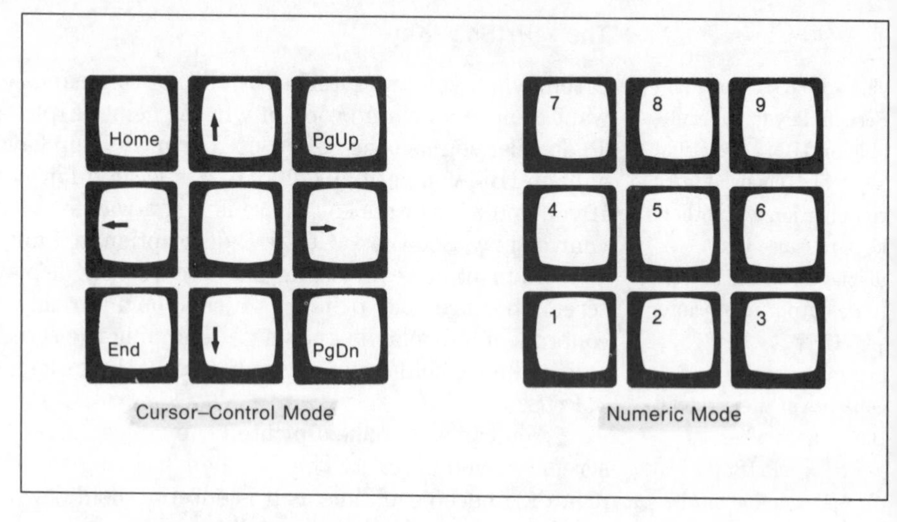

You may also remember from Chapter 3 that you can stop a listing from scrolling off the screen on some PCs by using the <Ctrl> and <Num Lock> keys together. To "unfreeze" the screen, press the <SPACEBAR> key or <Ctrl> <Break>. If you do not have <Num Lock> on your keyboard, you can still stop the screen from scrolling. See the <Ctrl>S description on page 32.

If you have the new enhanced keyboard, you will see that this keyboard has the numeric keypad discussed above, but it also has a separate cursor-control keypad between the main keyboard and the numeric keypad (see *Figure 4-5*). This means that you don't have to use the <Num Lock> key to switch between numeric and cursor-control modes, though you can if you want to. This keyboard (and many newer keyboards) also has indicator lights that come on when the <Num Lock>, <Caps Lock>, or <Scroll Lock> keys have been pressed.

CORRECTING YOUR MISTAKES

Whether you are writing the great American novel, figuring how you can make the most of your new tax shelter, or creating your first BASIC program, most of your interactions with the computer take place via the keyboard. And unless you are a typing champion, you will frequently make mistakes while entering your information.

Most computer programs provide some help for you in correcting these mistakes. A word processor, for example, allows for certain keys that help you move forward and backward in a line or around in a file to change information. Most even provide spelling checkers. BASIC, a programming language provided with MS-DOS,

Figure 4-5.
Enhanced Keyboard with Separate Cursor-Control and Numeric Keypads

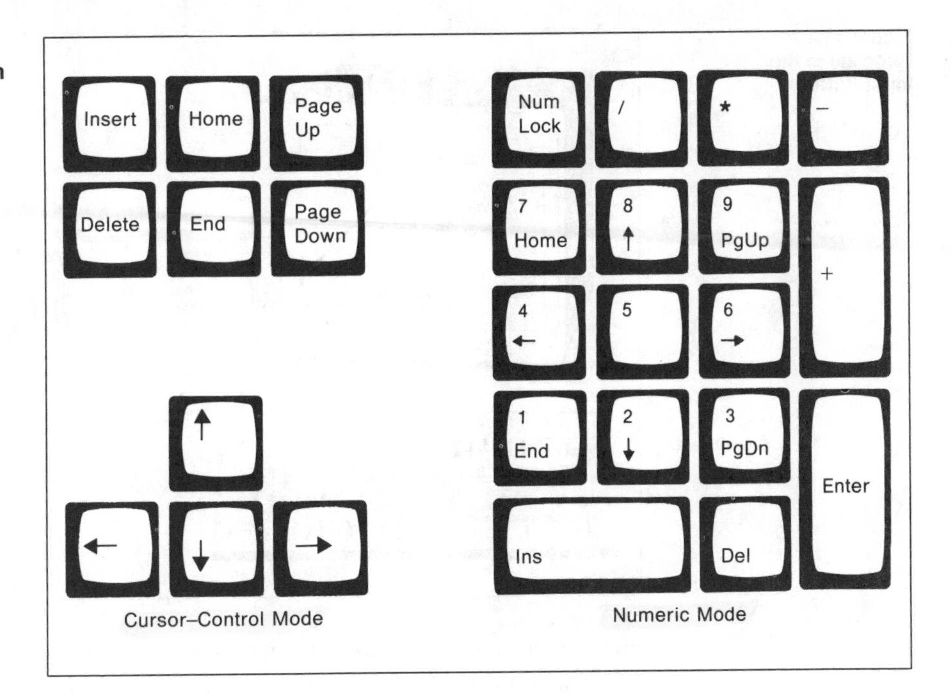

has a built-in editor to help make correcting errors easier. MS-DOS provides some special keys to speed up the editing process when you are entering commands or using the EDLIN program. (See the appendix on EDLIN for details.)

Any line that you type into the computer is stored in a special place in the computer's memory called the *input buffer.* After you press <ENTER>, the line you typed is retained in the input buffer. The line currently stored in the input buffer is called a *template.* By recalling this template, you can use it as a pattern to make minor changes within a line with just a few keystrokes. This storage sequence is shown in *Figure 4-6.*

How can this template help you? Well, most of the commands and other information you enter into MS-DOS consist of very short lines. Commands, after all, are rarely more than four letters, and file names cannot exceed twelve characters. MS-DOS editing keys are designed to make correcting mistakes in these short lines easier and faster.

THE FUNCTION KEYS

Some of the editing keys are already familiar to you. You know about using <Esc> to cancel the line you are typing, and you have used <BACKSPACE> to erase characters on a line. The other editing

Figure 4-6.
Template in the Input Buffer

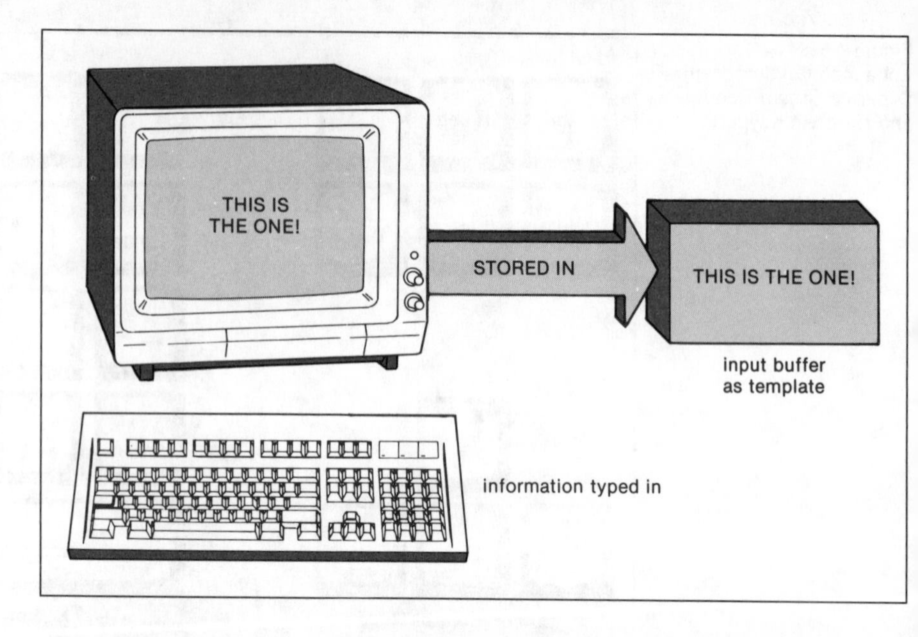

operations require the use of function keys, those strange keys with F1, F2, and so forth enscribed on them, or a combination of two keys. The function keys on two different keyboards are located for you in *Figure 4-7*.

Figure 4-7.
Location of Function Keys

The function key pad (the <F1> through <F10> keys) are assigned special functions according to whether you're at the MS-DOS prompt or are running a program. On enhanced keyboards, the function key pad goes through <F12>.

One problem with explaining the editing keys is that they are one of the least standardized parts of personal computer systems. That means, unfortunately, that this discussion can tell you how the editing keys work, but it can't identify exactly which keys perform these functions on your computer. Here is another situation where you must check your user's guide to find out the specifics for your machine.

If you have numerous function keys on your keyboard, you are probably in luck. Most often these function keys provide the editing operations with one keystroke. When positioned at the MS-DOS prompt, the system always retains the last command entered in the input buffer. By using the function keys <F1> through <F5>, you can retrieve all or part of the command and reissue it or edit it and turn it into a new command.

Table 4-1 lists the most frequently used key for each function. If the keys your computer uses are different from those listed, write down the keys you use in the blank box before the description of each operation.

How do you actually use the editing keys? First type the DIR command again:

```
C:\>dir
```

By now, you know that you'll see the directory of your disk. The command you typed is now the stored line in the input buffer. Put a floppy disk (such as your MS-DOS system disk) in drive A. How can you see its directory? The DIR command will show you the directory of the disk in any drive, so long as you include the drive letter. You could type the DIR command over again, but it's easier to use the <F3> key to copy the template line (*dir*) back to the screen.

The <F3> (Copy All) Function

This function copies the entire template. Once you have pressed the <ENTER> key, the last line on the screen becomes the template in your input buffer. If you decide to add more information at the end of the line, first you need to recall the line from the template. To retrieve the entire line you use the copy all function.

```
dir
```

You press <F3> (copy all) and MS-DOS returns the template. To add more information, type in the new text. In this case, type a

Table 4-1. Editing Functions and Keys

Your Key	Key	Function	Explanation
	<Esc>	Cancel	Cancel the last line.
	<BACKSPACE> <←>	Back up	Erase the last character.
	<F3>	Copy all	Copy the entire template.
	<F1>	Copy one	Copy one character.
	<F2>	Copy up to	Copy up to a specified character (character is not included in the copied template).
	<Del>	Skip one	Skip one character in template.
	<F4>	Skip up to	Skip up to the specified character (specified character not included in the template).
	<Ins>	Enter new characters	Insert new information in the middle of the template.
	<F5>	New template	Make this line the new template (if a command, not executed until <ENTER> is pressed).

space, the letter of the drive whose directory you want to see, a colon, and then the <ENTER> key:

```
C:\>dir a:
```

You get a directory of the disk in drive A. Now *dir a:* is your template.

The <F1> (Copy One Character) Function

You can use the editing keys to copy part of a line. There are several ways to do this. The simplest is to copy one character at a time.

```
dir a:
```

Press <F1>.

```
d
```

If you press <F1> four times.

```
dir
```

Now that you're seeing *dir* you can add whatever you want. Why might this be useful? Well, if you have two floppy-disk drives and you want to see the directory of a disk in drive B, you can change the command to specify drive B. With *dir* showing, just add *b*: and press <Enter>:

```
C:\>dir b:
```

You will now get the directory for the disk in drive B.

When the Disk Drive Is Empty . . .

If you accidentally try to look at the directory in an empty floppy-disk drive you'll see a message like this:

```
Not ready reading drive A
Abort, Retry, Fail?
```

(Some earlier versions of DOS will say *Abort, Retry, Ignore?* instead.) There are two things you can do. You can put a disk in the drive and press the *r* key, for "retry," and the DIR command should then run correctly. If you decide that you don't want a directory after all, you can press the *a* (for "abort") key, and the DIR command will quit without trying to show a directory, and you will see the *C:\>* prompt again. (Don't worry about the *Fail* option: it is of little use.)

The <F2> (Copy Up To) Function

There is a quicker way to copy part of the template, however. You can use the copy up to function, <F2>. "Copy up to" means retrieve all of the template up to the first occurrence of the specified character. The specified character is not included in the new template.

```
dir a:
```

Press <F2> and then *a*.

```
dir
```

"Copy up to" copies up to the first occurrence of the indicated letter.

This again gets you *dir*, and you can add *b:* (or another drive letter) as before. If you want to copy up to a later occurrence of a letter, just repeat the use of <F2> until you get there. For example, if the template read *the quick brown fox* and you wanted to change it to *the quick brown fax*, you would press <F2> and *o* to get to the *o* in *brown*, and press <F2> and *o* again to get up to the *f* in *fox*. (Remember that this operation copies up to, but not including, the letter specified.)

The <Del> (Skip Over One Character) Function

You can also use the editing keys to skip over part of the template. You use the <Del> key to skip over one character.

```
dir a:
```

You press <Del> and then <F3> to copy the remaining characters.

```
ir a:
```

While you are practicing these functions, by the way, it is a good idea to use the <BACKSPACE> key to erase any lines that don't make sense to DOS (for example, *ir a:*). You may remember that the <Esc> key cancels the entire current line. If you use <Esc>, however, the whole template is also erased, and you will have to type the entire command in again.

Press <Del> and <F3> again.

```
r a:
```

The <F4> (Skip Up To) Function

Just as you can copy up to, you can also "skip up to." To do this you use the <F4> key and indicate the character you want to skip up to. The specified character is not included in the template.

```
This is the final line of this program.
```

You press, <F4> and then *n*. Press <F3> to copy the remaining characters.

```
nal line of this program.
```

Just as "copy up to" copies up to the first occurrence of the character, "skip up to" skips all characters up to the first occurrence of the letter given.

```
This is the final line of this program.
```

You press <F4> and then *l*. Press <F3> to copy the remaining characters.

```
l line of this program.
```

You may have been intending to skip up to the word "line" but DOS encounters the *l* in *final* first. Pressing <F4> and *l* again brings you up to the desired location in the template.

When You Type an Invalid Command

It's quite possible that by now you've accidentally typed in an invalid command, especially while practicing use of the function keys for editing. An "invalid command" is something that MS-DOS doesn't recognize as something it knows how to do. For example, try typing:

```
C:\>list
```

You'll see:

```
Bad command or file name
```

This means that MS-DOS couldn't find any command or program called "list" and therefore couldn't carry out your wishes. Sometimes there really *is* such a program on your disk, but MS-DOS can't find it anyway! Later you'll learn how to help DOS out in that situation.

The <Ins> (Insert a New Character) Function

By combining the use of function keys <F1> through <F5> to manipulate the input buffer with other keys such as <BACKSPACE>, <Del>, <Ins>, and <Esc>, you can significantly cut down on the amount of typing required to issue similar commands over and over again.

You can also insert new information into the middle of the existing template. To do this you use the <Ins> key, as shown in this example:

```
This is the final line of this program.
```

You press <F2> and then o.

```
This is the final line
```

Press <Ins>, type *and end* and then press <F3>.

```
This is the final line and end of this program.
```

First you copied the template up to the first occurrence of the letter o (in the word *of*). Then you pressed the <Ins> key to indicate that you wanted to add new characters: *and end*. The <F3> then copies all the remaining character s in the template, resulting in the new line. Once you get used to them, these function keys will cut your editing time.

The <F5> (Create a New Template) Function

The <F5> editing key makes the most recently entered line the new template. In the previous example, pressing <F5> after you had finished editing the line, but before you had pressed <ENTER>, would make *This is the final line and end of this program* the template. Note that although this line is now the template, it has not been sent to the computer. If the new line were a command, it would not be executed by the computer.

```
COPY a: b:
```

You do not press <ENTER> at the end of the line, but instead press <F5>, then <F3>.

```
COPY a: b:
```

This is the new template but the command has not been sent to the computer.

The <Esc> (Escape) Function

You already know how to use this function. This is just a reminder that <Esc> is a function as well as a key. When you use <Esc> to cancel a line, the template is not changed (that is, it is not canceled and left blank). The last line entered is still the current template. The backslash on the line indicates that it has been canceled.

```
This is the final line
```

You press <Esc>.

```
This is the final line \
```

The line entered just before this one would still be the template.

Using editing keys takes a bit of practice, and you may be confused until you get the hang of it. But these keys can be useful when you are entering duplicate or repetitive commands or when you want to correct mistakes without typing in the entire line again. Experiment with these keys and see if they are helpful to you.

Table 4-1 summarizes the editing functions and the probable keys used to perform each function.

<CTRL> KEY COMBINATIONS

Throughout this book you've been gradually introduced to the <Ctrl> key in its various guises. You used <Ctrl> <Alt><Del> to perform a warm boot, and you used <Ctrl>S to stop the screen from scrolling.

An alternative to using the <Ctrl><PrtSc> key function to cause lines of text to be printed as they are entered on non-IBM-compatible keyboards is the <Ctrl>P function.

Some computer keyboards use specific keys to perform specific actions such as <PrtSc> and <Scroll Lock> described previously. But if your machine does not have these special keys, you can use <Ctrl> in conjunction with another key to perform these actions. Even if you do have these special keys, you can use the <Ctrl> combinations too, because these keys are standard on all computers using MS-DOS. These control functions operate not only in MS-DOS but also in a wide variety of application programs. They are presented in *Table 4-2* for a quick reference.

Table 4-2. Control Functions and Keys

Keys	Explanation
<Ctrl><Alt><Del>	Reboots the MS-DOS system.
<Ctrl>C	Cancels the current line (like the <Esc> key) or cancels the currently running program.
<Ctrl>H	Moves the cursor to the left and erases the last character, just like the <BACKSPACE> or <←> key.
<Ctrl>P	Echoes the display to the printer, line by line.
<Ctrl>N	Turns off the echoing function.
<Ctrl>S	Stops the scrolling on the screen; to resume scrolling, press any key.
<Ctrl>Z	End-of-file marker.

MS-DOS COMMANDS

Not all of the MS-DOS's commands are stored on the disk in the same manner. Some, called internal commands, are built into MS-DOS itself; others, called external commands, are stored in their own individual files.

Just as "file" was familiar to you from earlier chapters, so is the term "commands." You've been issuing commands since your first DIR experience. But now you're going to expand on that experience.

"Command" is another word that is not restricted to computer use. Any of you who have been in the Army or have suffered through dog-obedience courses with lovable Rover know about commands. Commands are simply clear and comprehensible instructions.

Commands in MS-DOS are instructions to the computer. As mentioned earlier, MS-DOS, while true and loyal, is rather stupid. It can understand instructions only when they follow a preordained pattern. The commands that you give MS-DOS must be very specific. Fortunately for users, MS-DOS commands make sense in English too. It's pretty simple to remember that DIR stands for DIRectory, and CLS stands for CLear the Screen. FORMAT and DISKCOPY are self-explanatory. You'll find the commands in this chapter just as clear and concise.

Internal Commands

The advantage of internal commands is that they can be accessed at any time, regardless of the disk inserted in a drive, because they are accessed directly from memory.

Some commands are resident in your computer's RAM when you are operating under MS-DOS control, that is, when you are responding to the MS-DOS prompt (C:\, A>, or B>). These commands are called "internal" because they are inside the machine's memory, ready for use whenever you are operating in MS-DOS. *Table 4-3* shows the "typical" MS-DOS internal commands.

Table 4-3. Internal Commands

Command	Action
COPY	Makes copies of files
DATE	Sets or displays the date
DIR	Displays a list of files
ERASE (DEL)	Eliminates a disk file
RENAME (REN)	Changes a file's name
TIME	Sets or displays the time
TYPE	Displays the contents of a file

The internal commands in your version of MS-DOS may include other commands. Check your user's guide for the internal commands associated with your system.

You can use an internal command without having to worry about which disk drive you are using or whether the files used to run MS-DOS commands are on the disk in the current drive. (The current drive and how to change it is discussed in more detail in Chapter 5.) For example, since the internal COPY command is kept in memory, no program needs to be loaded from disk before you can copy files from one disk to another.

External Commands

Many MS-DOS commands aren't kept in memory, however, because doing so would use up too much memory, making it hard to run your word processing or other application programs. Commands that are not kept in memory are called "external." To run an external command, MS-DOS must be able to find the program file for that command on disk. For example, to run the external command DISKCOPY, the program file DISKCOPY.COM must be loaded and run from one of your disk drives. If you get the error message

```
Bad command or file name
```

first check to make sure that you spelled the command correctly. If you have, the message indicates that MS-DOS can't find the command file.

If you have a floppy-only system, you may have to replace the disk in drive A with the system disk before you can run the command. (You can also use the COPY command to copy DISKCOPY.COM to your word processor disk, and then you can run the DISKCOPY command without having to swap disks.)

If you are running MS-DOS from a hard disk, your system is probably set up so that you can run external MS-DOS commands from the hard disk without worrying about which disks are in your floppy drives. If MS-DOS can't find your external commands, however, you may have to use the PATH command (discussed in Chapter 7) to tell MS-DOS where to find the system files.

If you enter an external command, you can instruct MS-DOS to retrieve the command from a disk drive other than the default drive by preceding the command with a disk-drive identifier. For example, if the file DISKCOPY.COM is on a disk in drive B, you can type B:DISKCOPY.

Before you begin studying specific commands in detail, here are some helpful hints for entering all MS-DOS commands:

- Wait until you see the MS-DOS prompt (C:\> for a hard disk) before entering a command. The prompt means DOS is ready.
- When a command requires a filename to operate, be sure you include all the necessary parts of the file specification (drive indicator, filename, and extension). (The parts of a filename are discussed in Chapter 6.)
- Use a blank space to separate the different parts of a command. Leave spaces between command and filename. Don't leave a space between the optional drive indicator and the filename.
- You can enter commands in either upper- or lowercase.
- When commands don't work, check your typing. Is the command correct, did you leave the appropriate spaces, did you

spell the filename correctly? Are you trying to use an external command without inserting the system disk?

- End each command with the <ENTER> key.

WILDCARD SYMBOLS

Special keys, function keys, and control-key combinations help you use MS-DOS and EDLIN with little wasted motion. Not surprisingly, filenames also have shortcuts that can increase your efficiency.

You probably haven't thought of your experience in computing as resembling a card game, although you have probably taken a few chances. But now you are going to learn to use wildcards.

MS-DOS provides a simple method of specifying a group of files within a filename when used with a command. Like the jokers in a deck of cards, the * and ? keyboard characters can represent wildcards (also called global characters). A wildcard means "any character." Use the * wildcard to represent a group of characters and the ? wildcard to represent a specific character position. Using wildcards can greatly enhance the capabilities of file-related commands.

Like their playing card antecedents, wildcards can stand for something else or a lot of something elses. When used in filenames, wildcards replace one or more specific characters in the filename or extension.

As you know, each file's name must be unique, but many of your filenames probably have a lot in common. Wildcards allow you to use one command to perform an action on a group of similarly named files. The wildcard replaces one or more characters in the filename. Wildcards are especially useful when you are using the DIR, COPY, DEL, and RENAME commands, because in these situations you often refer to groups of files.

The wildcard symbols (sometimes called "global characters") are the question mark (?) and the asterisk (*).

The question mark is used to match a character in a specific position in a filename or extension. For example, assume you had all your monthly salary records on one disk.

```
JA-MAR.SUM
JANSAL.
FEBSAL.
MARSAL.
MARTOT.
JA-JUN.SUM
```

If you want a directory of all the files that concern monthly salaries, you could look at the whole directory or use DIR to check on the presence of each individual salary file. But you can get this information much quicker by entering a wildcard command.

```
C:\ACCT>dir ???sal <ENTER>
```

A directory would appear.

```
 Volume in drive C is MSDOSDISK
 Volume Serial Number is 1454-3E20
 Directory of  C:\ACCT
JANSAL            128 01-31-91  10:21a
FEBSAL            128 01-31-91  10:21a
MARSAL            128 01-31-91  10:21a
        3 File(s)   2015232 bytes free
```

This command tells MS-DOS to look through the directory of the disk in drive C and list all files that end in "sal." Any characters may be used in the first three positions. This is the key to the question mark wildcard; any character can occupy the position indicated by the ?, but the rest of the name must be exactly as you specified. If you had entered

```
C:\ACCT>dir mar????? <ENTER>
```

then only files beginning "mar" would have been listed.

```
 Volume in drive C is MSDOSDISK
 Volume Serial Number is 1454-3E20
 Directory of  C:\ACCT
MARSAL            128 01-31-91  10:21a
MARTOT            128 01-31-91  10:21a
       2 File(s)   18015232 bytes free
```

In response to this command, MS-DOS looks for files that have "mar" in the first three positions and any characters in the last five positions.

The * and ? wildcards can often be combined in a filename specification to provide specific instructions to a file-related command.

When you include the ? wildcard as the last character in a filename or extension, you must account for all eight characters in the filename proper or all three characters in the extension.

Using the asterisk wildcard is just like using a lot of question marks. When you include an * in a filename specification, any character can occupy that position or any of the remaining positions in the filename or extension. An asterisk pretends that there are as many question marks in the filename as there are positions.

Asterisks do not include the extension of a filename unless you specify this with another asterisk after the period. Then it will accept any extension.

```
C:\>dir ja*.* <ENTER>
```

If you entered this command for the files above, MS-DOS would list the following files that begin "ja."

```
 Volume in drive C is MSDOSDISK
 Volume Serial Number is 1454-3E20
 Directory of  C:\ACCT
JA-MAR   SUM        128 01-31-91  10:21a
JANSAL              128 01-31-91  10:21a
JA-JUN   SUM        128 01-31-91  10:21a
        3 File(s)    18015232 bytes free
```

Here MS-DOS is looking for any files that contain "ja" in the first two positions. Any characters can occupy the remaining positions in the filename. Since you also included an asterisk in the extension, the filename can contain any extension.

You can also use a completely wild filename.

```
*.*
```

As you have probably guessed, this means all files.

Wildcards can be useful because of their power, but they can also be dangerous. When you want to copy all the files on a disk (*COPY* *.*) to list an entire directory (*DIR* *.*), they can make your task easier.

Beware of the use of wildcards with the DEL command. As you probably have guessed, DEL*.* would mean goodbye to all the files in the current directory. When you do use *.* with the DEL command, however, MS-DOS gives you a chance to back out.

```
C:\>DEL*.* <ENTER>
```

When you enter this command, MS-DOS asks a question.

```
Are you sure (Y/N)?
```

Enter *y* if you are really sure or *n* if you have any doubts about what you're doing.

The keys' functions and tools described in this chapter increase your knowledge of MS-DOS. Now you're going to learn some new uses of familiar commands.

SWITCHES

As you become better acquainted with MS-DOS, you not only are able to use it more easily, but you come to appreciate some of its finer points. Up until now, you have been using commands in their simplest form. These are valid uses of commands, but many commands have command options that make them even more useful.

Many of MS-DOS's commands can be entered with optional switches. A switch usually consists of a single character and is preceded by a slash (/).

Commands can contain switches. As the name implies, switches can turn on and off certain operations within a command. When you add a switch to a command you indicate it with a slash (/) and a letter. Switches always follow the command and any drive indicators.

Switches and the DIR Command

You are familiar with the DIR command. You know this command lists the files on a directory, displaying their names, extensions, sizes, and the time and date they were last accessed. If the directory contains more files than will fit on one screen, the display scrolls until it reaches the end of the listing.

The DIR command has two optional switches: /w is used to display the directory in several columns across the screen, and /p is used to instruct DIR to pause at every screenfull of text. Both switches can be used together if desired.

There are two optional switches you can include in the DIR command that alter how the directory is displayed: /w and /p. The /w switch lists the files in several columns across the screen. Only the filenames are displayed. The /p pauses the listing after each screenful is displayed.

The /w Switch

Assume you want a listing of the disk in drive A. Enter the *DIR/w* command.

```
C:\>dir a: /w <ENTER>
```

If this disk is a typical system disk, the command will produce a multicolumn list of filenames.

```
 Volume in drive A has no label
 Volume Serial Number is 2533-07FF
 Directory of  A:\
APPEND   EXE ASSIGN   COM ATTRIB   EXE BACKUP   COM BASIC    COM
BASICA   COM CHKDSK   COM COMP     COM DEBUG    COM DISKCOMP COM
DOSUTIL  MEU EDLIN    COM FILESYS  EXE FIND     EXE FIND     EXE FORMAT   COM
GRAFTABL COM GRAPHICS COM GRAPHICS PRO JOIN     EXE LABEL    COM
MEM      EXE MORE     COM MORTGAGE BAS NLSFUNC  EXE PCIBMDRV MOS
PCMSDRV  MOS PCMSPDRV MOS PRINT    COM RECOVER  COM REPLACE  EXE
RESTORE  COM SHELL    CLR SHELL    HLP SHELL    MEU SHELLB   COM
SHELLC   EXE SORT     EXE SUBST    EXE TREE     COM
       39 File(s)     51200 bytes free
```

This horizontal layout of the directory is useful when the disk holds a lot of files and you only want to see their names. Note that this directory gives you no information about file size or the date or time the file was last accessed.

The /p Switch

The other switch you can use with the DIR command is /p. The /p switch operates like an automatic scroll control. It stops the display of a directory when the screen is filled. This switch is useful when you want to look at the listing of a large directory. You can study the display and then press any key when you are ready to proceed. Again, the switch follows the command. (*Figure 4-8* illustrates the effects of the /w and /p switches.)

Figure 4-8. The DIR Command

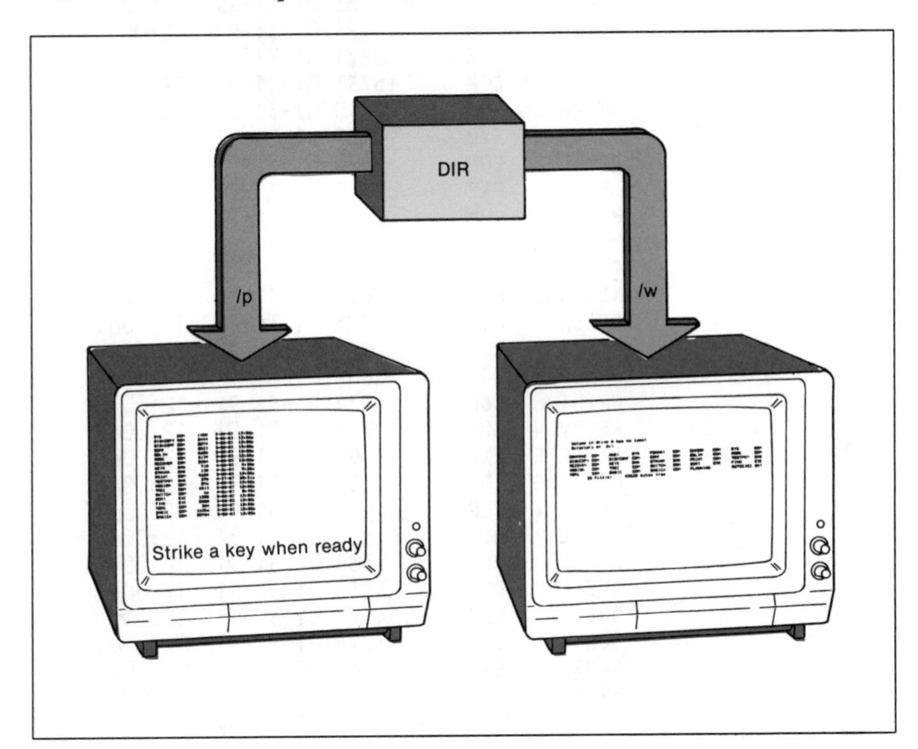


```
C:\> dir a: /p <ENTER>
```

This command results in a list of filenames and attributes.

```
 Volume in drive A has no label
 Volume Serial Number is 2533-07FF
 Directory of  A:\
APPEND   EXE     11186 01-31-91   12:00p
ASSIGN   COM     15875 01-31-91   12:00p
ATTRIB   EXE     18247 01-31-91   12:00p
BACKUP   COM     33754 01-31-91   12:00p
BASIC    COM      1065 01-31-91   12:00p
BASICA   COM     36285 01-31-91   12:00p
CHKDSK   COM     17771 01-31-91   12:00p
COMP     COM      9491 01-31-91   12:00p
DEBUG    COM     21606 01-31-91   12:00p
DISKCOMP COM      9889 01-31-91   12:00p
DOSUTIL  MEU      6660 01-31-91   12:00p
EDLIN    COM     14249 01-31-91   12:00p
FILESYS  EXE     11125 01-31-91   12:00p
FIND     EXE      5983 01-31-91   12:00p
FORMAT   COM     22923 01-31-91   12:00p
GRAFTABL COM     10271 01-31-91   12:00p
GRAPHICS COM     16733 01-31-91   12:00p
GRAPHICS PRO      9413 01-31-91   12:00p
JOIN     EXE     17457 01-31-91   12:00p
LABEL    COM      4490 01-31-91   12:00p
MEM      EXE     20133 01-31-91   12:00p
MORE     COM      2166 01-31-91   12:00p
MORTGAGE BAS      6207 01-31-91   12:00p
Press any key to continue . . .          ← press any key
NLSFUNC  EXE      6910 01-31-91   12:00p
PCIBMDRV MOS       295 01-31-91   12:00p
PCMSDRV  MOS       961 01-31-91   12:00p
PCMSPDRV MOS       801 01-31-91   12:00p
PRINT    COM     14024 01-31-91   12:00p
RECOVER  COM     10732 01-31-91   12:00p
REPLACE  EXE     17199 01-31-91   12:00p
RESTORE  COM     40030 01-31-91   12:00p
SHELL    CLR      4438 01-31-91   12:00p
SHELL    HLP     65667 01-31-91   12:00p
SHELL    MEU      4588 01-31-91   12:00p
SHELLB   COM      3937 01-31-91   12:00p
SHELLC   EXE    154377 01-31-91   12:00p
SORT     EXE      5914 01-31-91   12:00p
SUBST    EXE     18143 01-31-91   12:00p
TREE     COM      6334 01-31-91   12:00p
       39 File(s)      51200 bytes free
```

SUMMARY

You have now acquired the basic knowledge of your keyboard and of MS-DOS that you need to "take command" of your computer system. You have learned how to use special features of the keyboard, including keys for editing your commands. You have learned how to enter MS-DOS commands and how to use optional switches to specify command features.

REVIEW

1. The <Esc>, <Num Lock>, <Home>, <End>, <PgUp>, <PgDn> keys and the ten function keys are used to reduce time and effort at the keyboard.
2. MS-DOS gives you an error message when it doesn't understand your command or when a particular device such as a disk drive isn't ready.
3. Using the ? and * wildcards enhances the capabilities of file-related commands.
4. The special switches for DOS commands allow you to specify optional features.
5. You can use the DIR command to view a list of files on a disk.
6. The /w switch makes DIR display filenames only, using several columns.
7. The /p switch makes DIR pause after listing each screenful of information.

Quiz for Chapter 4

1. In addition to <ENTER> and <BACKSPACE>, other special keys are commonly used, such as:
   - **a.** <Caps Lock>.
   - **b.** the left and right <SHIFT> keys.
   - **c.** <Esc>.
   - **d.** <PrtSc>.
   - **e.** <Del>.
   - **f.** all of the above.
2. The <PrtSc> key is used in the following ways:
   - **a.** <SHIFT><PrtSc> prints everything currently displayed on the screen.
   - **b.** <Ctrl><PrtSc> causes each line displayed on the screen to be printed as it is entered.
   - **c.** When pressed by itself, it causes the * to be displayed.
   - **d.** all of the above.
   - **e.** a and b.
3. <Num Lock> is a toggle key that is used to:
   - **a.** switch between numeric and cursor-control modes.
   - **b.** switch between special and normal characters.
   - **c.** switch between insert and command modes.
   - **d.** lock and unlock all numbers.
4. The area in memory where MS-DOS stores the last command entered is called the:
   - **a.** transient buffer.
   - **b.** input buffer.
   - **c.** output buffer.
   - **d.** input/output buffer.
5. The function keys used to manipulate the input buffer are:
   - **a.** <F1> through <F5>.
   - **b.** <F6> through <F10>.
   - **c.** <F1> through <F10>.
   - **d.** The even-numbered ones.
6. Which of the following is *not* correct?
   - **a.** <F1> is used to retrieve the previously entered command one character at a time.
   - **b.** <F2> is used to retrieve all of the previously entered command up to the character subsequently specified.

c. <F3> is used to execute the entire previously entered command.
d. <F4> is used to skip over characters of the previously entered command up to the first occurrence of the character subsequently specified.
e. <F5> puts a newly edited command back into the input buffer.
f. All of the above are correct.

7. While at the MS-DOS prompt, the <Esc> key is used to:
   a. execute the typed command.
   b. cancel the typed command.
   c. either a or b.
   d. none of the above.

8. For some nonstandard keyboards, an alternative command to the <Ctrl><PrtSc> function is:
   a. <Ctrl> S.
   b. <Ctrl> C.
   c. <Ctrl> P.
   d. <Ctrl> Z.

9. The * and ? characters, used as special characters in file names specified with file-related commands, are called:
   a. wildcards.
   b. special characters.
   c. aces.
   d. jokers.

10. The * wildcard is used to specify:
    a. a single character position.
    b. a group of characters.
    c. numbers only.
    d. alphabetic characters only.

11. The ? wildcard is used to specify:
    a. a single character position.
    b. a group of characters.
    c. numbers only.
    d. alphabetic characters only.

12. The optional switches that can be used with the DIR command include:
    a. /w to cause the directory to be displayed in several columns across the screen.

b. /p to cause DIR to pause each time the directory fills up the screen.
c. both a and b.
d. none of the above.

5

Floppy Disks

ABOUT THIS CHAPTER

Only a few years ago, hard disks were uncommon and expensive, and many PC users had to use floppy disks to store their programs and data. Today, however, most serious PC users have a hard disk, and much of the discussion in later chapters of this book will be devoted to the hard disk. Remember that this book assumes that you have installed MS-DOS on your hard disk (if you haven't, see Appendix B). This means that the command prompt will be shown in the listings as *C:\>*. If you don't have a hard disk, your prompt will be A>or A:\>, but you will type the commands as shown, except as otherwise noted.

The importance of protecting yourself by making a backup copy of your MS-DOS operating system disk cannot be overstated. It should be one of the first things you do when first using your system. Losing data that has not been backed up can be disastrous.

Even if you have a hard disk, however, you must learn how to use and care for floppy disks. MS-DOS and your application programs come to you on one or more floppy disks, and you need to make backup copies of the MS-DOS system disks and your other program disks. Having a backup copy ensures that you can reinstall MS-DOS and your programs after a hard disk failure, without having to depend on your original copies remaining flawless. (In Chapter 8 you will learn how to copy everything on your hard disk to a set of floppy disks.)

Becoming familiar with floppy disks is an important part of becoming comfortable with your computer system. Floppy disks are also a common medium of exchange between PC users. By learning how to copy them, you can share files with other users.

DISKS AND DISK DRIVES

Although floppy disks got their name because they are flexible, their flexibility should not be tested. Floppy disks should always be handled with care.

It is staggering to think of how much information is stored on one magnetically coated piece of plastic. Detailed instructions about how the computer is to receive input, manage files, deliver output, and operate its equipment are all there on your operating-system disk. Before you actually insure this precious commodity, let's take a closer look at what makes up a disk.

Just as the size, speed, and capabilities of computer hardware have undergone a remarkable technological evolution in the last three decades, so have the methods for storing the programs and data the computer needs to operate.

Floppies

There is a variety of floppy disk types. The disks differ in physical size, number of recordable sides, storage density, and data format. The most common disk size used with MS-DOS computers is 5¼ inches. According to the data format used, storage capacity can range from 360K to 1.2MB.

The most common kind of removable disk used in PCs today is 5¼ inches in diameter. The amount of data the disk can hold depends on how densely it can pack the magnetic "marks" together. The most common format holds 360K per disk, and this is often referred to on the disk box as "double-sided, double density." Many systems (especially the IBM PC/AT or compatibles) can also use disks that hold 1.2MB (more than a million bytes) of information. This is referred to as "double-sided, quad density." A drive that can use 1.2MB disks can also use 360K ones, but a drive designed only for 360K disks cannot use 1.2MB ones.

Microfloppies

A more recent innovation is the microfloppy. These disks are approximately 3½ inches in diameter. They are held in a rigid, rather than flexible, sleeve. There are two common formats for microfloppies: 720K and 1.44MB. The 3½″ disk drives are found in nearly all laptop computers, and they are standard in the IBM PS/2 models.

The relative proportions of the two kinds of disks are shown in *Figure 5-1*.

Figure 5-1. Disk Evolution

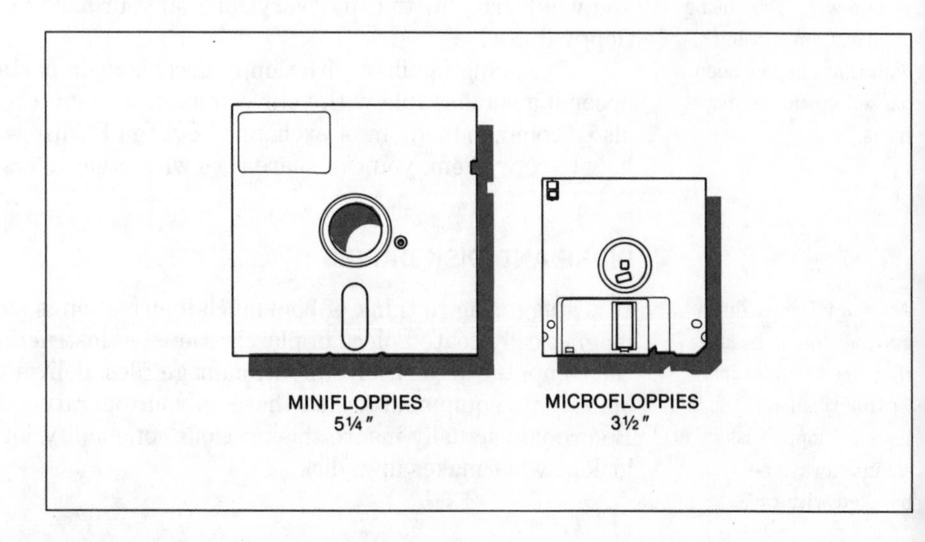

How data gets put on disks is covered later in this chapter. For now, the only thing you need to know about your disks is what type your computer uses. Check your owner's manual for the specific types of disks you should buy. For convenience in exchanging data, many users are now buying add-on drives so their systems can use both 5¼″ and 3½″ disks.

PROTECTING YOUR DISKS

Whatever their size or density, all disks have several features in common. This discussion describes the most common features found on 5¼″ floppy disks. These features are illustrated in *Figure 5-2.*

Figure 5-2. Features of Disks

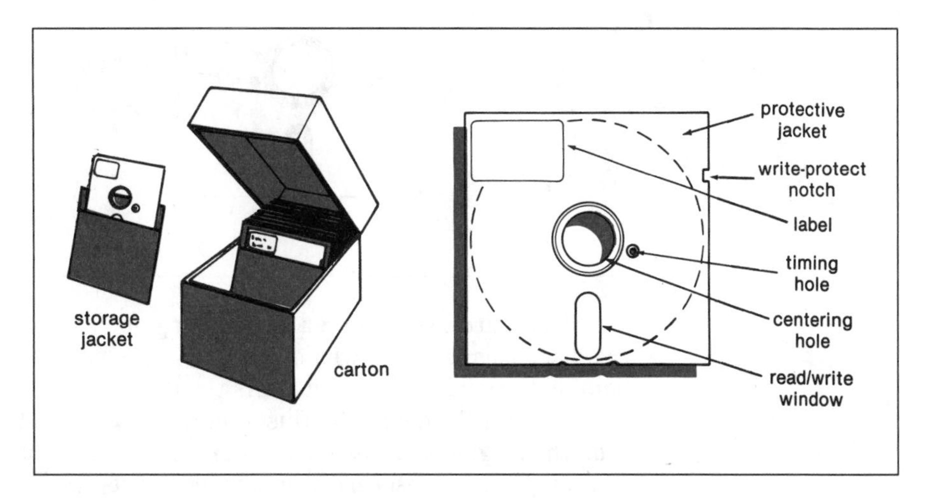

Storage

While a disk is not in use, it should always be placed in its protective jacket. Never touch the exposed surfaces of the disk.

Disks are usually sold in convenient boxes (save these for storing your disks). Inside the box, each disk is nestled inside a paper envelope. This is the disk's storage jacket. It's a good idea to put this paper jacket on the disk whenever you're not using it.

The actual disk is round and completely enclosed in the square plastic protective jacket. This plastic jacket is permanent and should never be removed. In fact, you won't be able to remove it without using a sharp instrument. If the disk is not square, something dreadful has happened to the protective jacket (and undoubtedly to any information that was on the disk).

Handling

Figure 5-3 indicates the three areas where the recording surface is exposed on the disk. Take care not to put your fingers (or anything else) on these sections. One exposed area is around the centering hole of the disk. The disk drive uses this area to be sure the disk is in the right place before it begins operation. The timing, or indexing, hole is just off to the side of the centering hole. This too is used to align the disk correctly.

Figure 5-3.
Exposed Surfaces

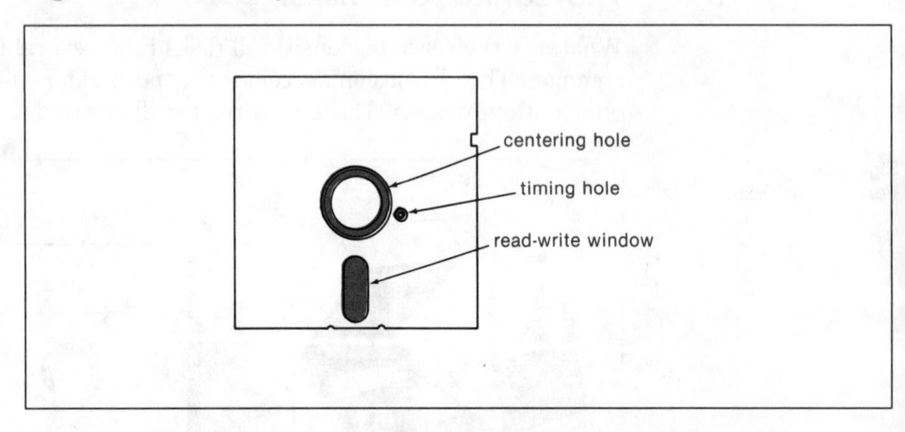

The third exposed area is an oblong opening along one edge of the disk. This area is a window used by the drive to read and write data on the surface of the disk. As the disk revolves, the special heads within the disk drive (just like the heads on a tape recorder) code the magnetic surface with information that contains the pattern of your data. It is especially important to keep this window free of dirt or dust. Imperfections in this window can be transferred to the drive heads and can damage your drives as well as your disks.

Write-Protection

When the write-protect notch on a 5¼″ disk is open, the computer may store data on the disk as well as retrieve data from it. When the write-protect notch is covered with special write-protect tabs, data may only be retrieved from the disk.

Along one edge of the disk, you will see a distinct square cutout indentation. This is the write-protect notch. A clever design feature, this small space can prevent you from erasing vital information by inadvertently writing over it.

New information can overwrite, or erase, previous information. But before the computer writes to a disk, it checks this notch. If the notch is covered, the disk is write-protected; that is, it cannot receive new data. If the notch is open, the disk is fair game for both reading and writing. *Figure 5-4* shows covered and open notches.

When you want to make sure that the contents of a disk will not be altered, cover the notch with one of the write-protect tabs included in your box of purchased disks (there will be several oblong tabs stuck on one sheet; they are usually silver or black). These pieces of adhesive foil or paper seal off the notch and prevent any new information from being written to the disk. (You can peel off the seal if you change your mind.)

By the way, 3½″ disks don't use a write-protect notch. Instead, as shown back in *Figure 5-1*, there is a little sliding box near the corner of the disk. To write-protect the disk, slide the box so that the tiny square hole is open.

You may notice that some disks, especially those containing application programs, have no write-protect notch. If you can't write to the disk, you don't run the risk of altering or destroying the program.

Figure 5-4.
Write-Protect Notch

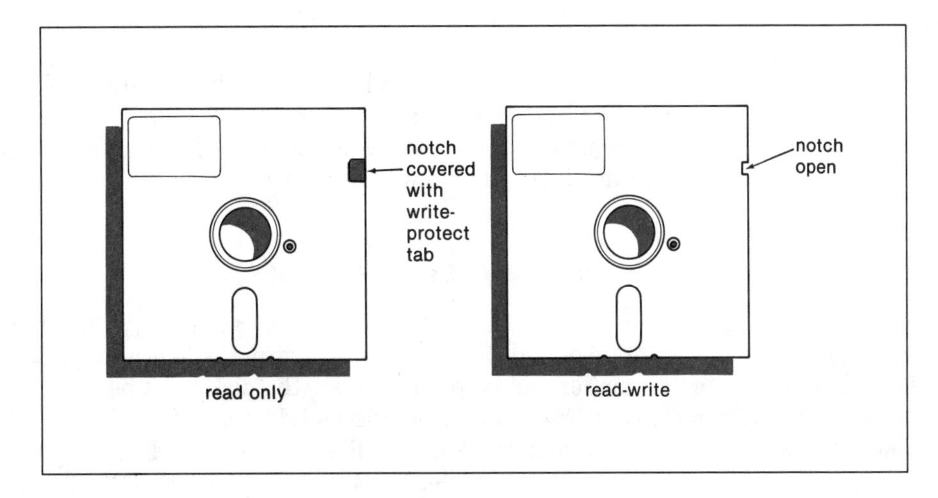

Labeling

Using adhesive labels with clearly written information can help you organize your disk library.

Also in your carton of purchased disks, you will find a packet of adhesive labels (they come in many colors and usually have lines on them). These are content labels, a means of identifying each disk. Without labeling, most disks look alike. How much information you put on these labels is up to you, but your labeling should be clear enough so that you'll know what's on your disk when you pick it up next month—or next year. Your label should be positioned as illustrated in *Figure 5-5*. (If you write on a label that's attached to a disk, write gently—a felt-tip pen is best.)

Figure 5-5. Labeling

All these do's and don'ts may have you wondering if you will ever have the courage to pick up a disk, let alone use it in your computer. But by following the rules listed in *Figure 5-6*, you should have little trouble with your disks.

STORING DATA ON THE DISK

New disks are made compatible with MS-DOS by formatting them with the FORMAT command. The disk formatting process establishes the data storage characteristics of the disk, such as the number of tracks, the number of sectors per track, and the number of bytes per sector.

MS-DOS is a careful and efficient manager, so when it stores information on a disk it does so in an orderly, logical way. Before any information can be put on a disk, the disk must be prepared using the FORMAT command (discussed later in this chapter). Fresh from the box, your blank disk is like a newly paved running track—one large, unmarked surface. The first thing that FORMAT does is divide this area into specific tracks. As shown in *Figure 5-7*, the tracks run in concentric circles around the disk, much like the painted lanes that mark boundaries for runners on a running track.

The tracks are divided into small sections called sectors (also shown in *Figure 5-7*). This makes storage and retrieval of your data faster and more efficient because MS-DOS knows just which track and sector holds each file. The amount of data stored in a sector is dependent upon your computer system. On a 360K disk, for instance, there are 9 sectors per track. Each sector can hold either 512 or 1024 bytes.

Figure 5-6.
Rules for Disk Handling and Usage

1. Do not rest heavy objects on disk surfaces. Such objects include reference books, instruction manuals, and the omnipresent elbow.
2. Do not eat, drink, smoke, or comb your hair near your disks. These seemingly innocent activities can cause deposits on the surface of a disk.
3. Do not bend, staple, paper clip, or mutilate your disks by rough handling or improper storage.
4. Protect disks from the common forces of nature. This encompasses the peril of destruction by sunlight or exposure to high temperatures or excessive humidity.
5. Do not allow your disks to be near X-ray machines (including those at the airport inquisition), telephones, speakers, or any other source of magnetic energy (beware the magnetic paper-clip dispenser!). These "fields of force" can wreak havoc on your disks.
6. Handle your disks gently—by the edges only.
7. Label your disks properly. When writing labels, use only a felt-tip pen, for pencils and ballpoints damage disks. Unlabeled disks carrying precious information have been known to succumb to the destructive prowess of the FORMAT command.
8. Store your disks carefully. Specifically, refrain from resting them on their sides or crowding them too closely in their box. If you are going to send a disk to someone, use one of the padded disk mailers available at office supply stores. It is a good idea to write "Magnetic Media—do not bend or x-ray" on the outside of the package (disk mailers already have this notice printed on them).
9. When not in use, your disks should be kept in their storage jackets.
10. Remember that the quality of the performance of your disks is directly related to the quality of the care you give them.

Figure 5-7.
Tracks and Sectors

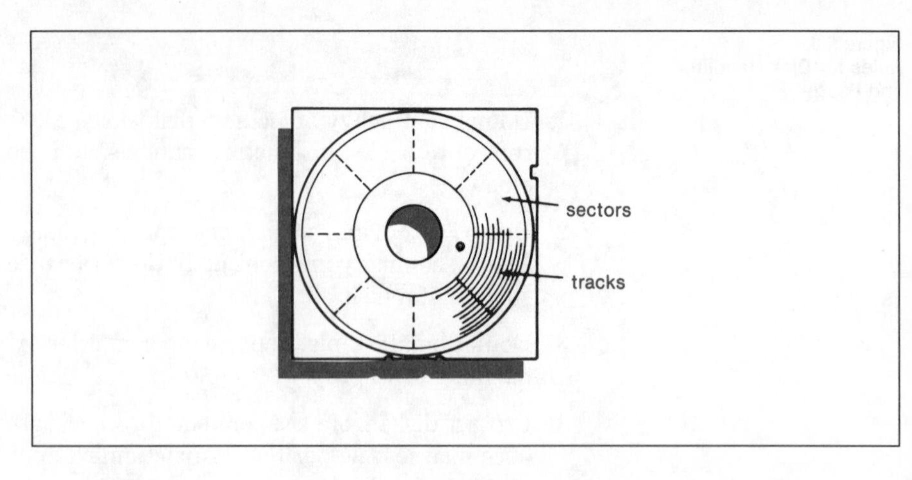

The first section of the first track on every disk is reserved for storage of the operating system. Thereafter, as data are written to the disk, they are stored on a first-come, first-served basis. You do not need to remember the order in which you store data on the disk, MS-DOS keeps track of that for you.

Differences for 3½″ Disks

Most of the preceding discussion applies also to 3½″ disks, although the number of tracks and sectors is different. A special advantage of 3½″ disks is that their rigid construction protects them from being bent, while the spring-loaded access window keeps dust and dirt out. While sturdier and more compact than their larger cousins, 3½″ disks aren't invulnerable. In particular, data on them can be obliterated by a magnetic field just as easily as on their flimsier 5¼″ friends.

GETTING THE DISK READY TO BE USED

It's easy to prepare your disks for use. Don't let this new challenge make you nervous. After all, you already know how to handle disks and how they go into your disk drive (remember how well you executed the DIR command). But a little planning can make things easier for you as you perform this procedure.

1. Have the computer up and running.

2. Have your computer instruction manual nearby.

3. Have ready the system disk and several new, blank disks.

The instructions for the following MS-DOS commands are given in terms of the typical MS-DOS system. The typical system has two disk drives.

Disk Drives

Although your computer may be equipped with only one floppy disk drive, most MS-DOS commands assume that two drives (A and B) are installed.

When asking questions and giving responses to commands, MS-DOS assumes that you have two disk drives, A and B. (It usually considers your hard drive, if any, to be drive C.) Operating with at least two drives is the most efficient method for MS-DOS because it simplifies transferring information from one disk to the other and makes giving instructions easier. With two drives, MS-DOS can easily differentiate where the information is coming from and where the information is going.

The operating system is quite set in its ways on this point. So much so that even if you have a single drive, MS-DOS behaves as though you have two. It always issues instructions in terms of drive A and drive B. How can single-drive owners use this system? *Figure 5-8* shows you how.

One easy way to do this is to think of your disks as drives. That is, one disk represents drive A, and the second represents drive B. Then when the display tells you to do something with the disk in drive A, you use the first disk. When you need to do something with the disk in drive B, you remove the first disk and insert the second disk before performing the action. Both the operating system and you are happy and no one is any the wiser.

With these preliminaries out of the way, you're ready to prepare some new disks. To accomplish this, you will call upon the FORMAT command.

The FORMAT Command

The FORMAT command readies a disk to receive data by dividing up the disk specifically for MS-DOS, marking the sectors and providing a directory area to store special information that MS-DOS later will use to find particular files.

Figure 5-8.
Two Drives Versus One Drive

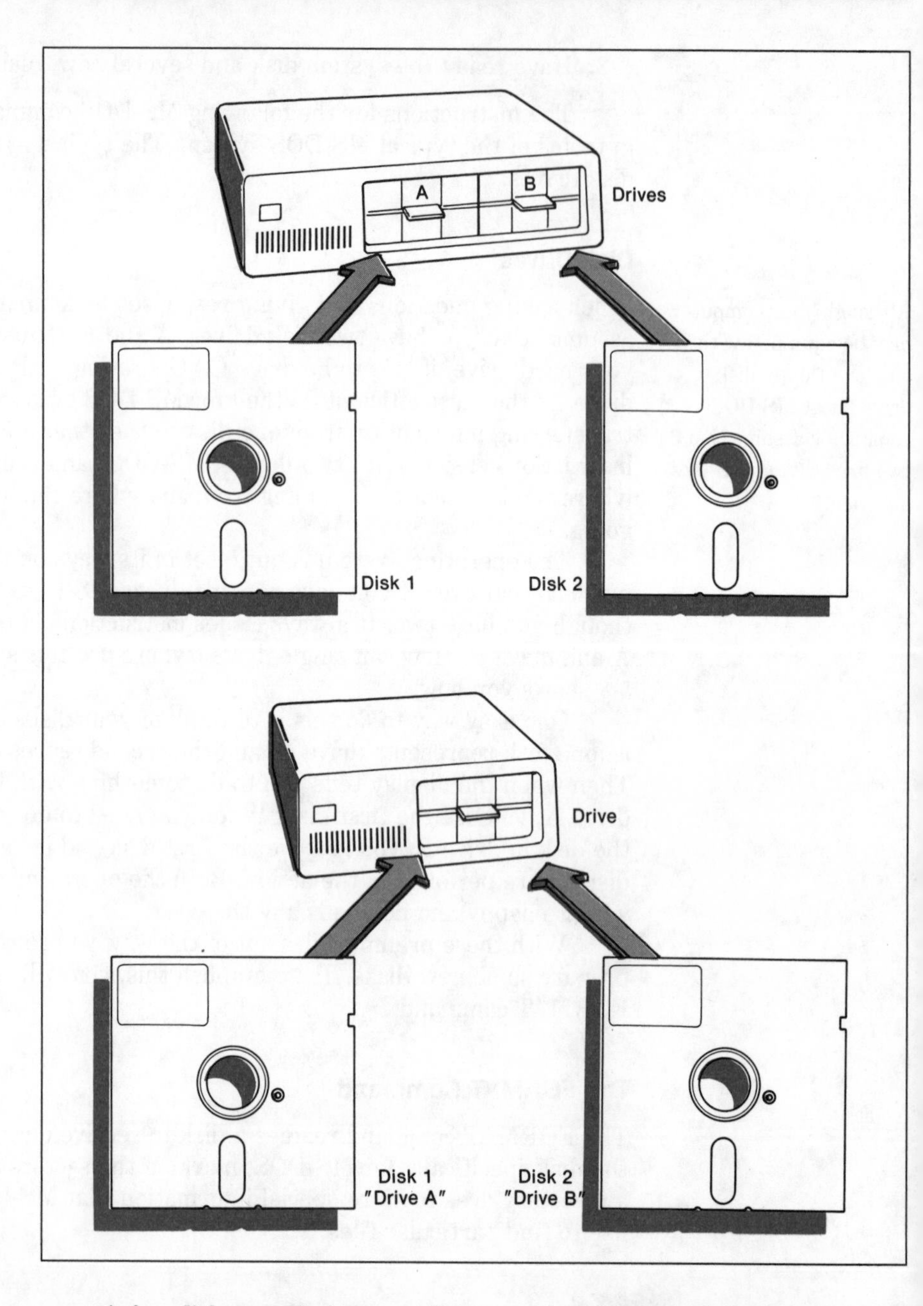

A few disk manufacturers sell boxes of preformatted disks (at a higher price). Unless your new disks are preformatted, you must use the FORMAT command on each disk before you can store any data on it. How do you format a disk? The method described here assumes that you are running MS-DOS from a hard disk. Put your new blank disk in drive A. If you have only floppy drives, boot the system by putting your MS-DOS system disk in drive A. You will use drive B to hold the blank disk to be formatted; where we say "drive A" use "drive B." (Refer to *Figure 5-9* for a graphic representation of the formatting sequence.)

Figure 5-9. The Format Sequence: Step 1

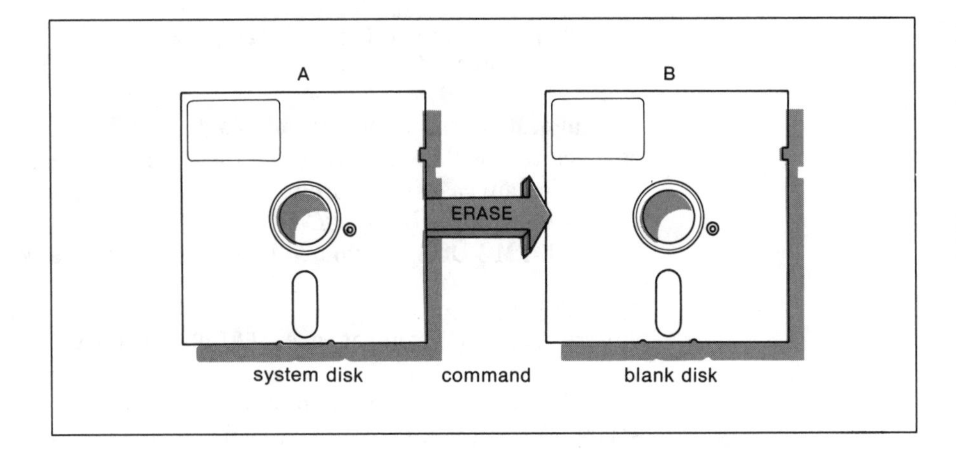

Now you are going to tell the operating system to FORMAT the disk in drive A. You must include the letter A in your command or else you might destroy your system disk. Enter the command.

```
C:\>format A: <ENTER>
```

Be sure to include the space between the command and the drive specifier, and the colon after the letter A. Now watch the screen. It will answer your command.

```
Insert new diskette for drive A:
and strike any key when ready
```

Because you have already put a new, blank disk in drive A, you can press any key.

The drive will click and whirr, and the indicator light will go on and off. Do not interrupt this process, just let the machine do its work. The operating system lets you know what is going on by displaying a message showing how much of the disk has been formatted thus far:

```
XX percent of disk formatted
```

where "XX" represent a running total percentage. (In versions of MS-DOS prior to 4.0, only the message "Formatting . . . " is displayed.)

Once the formatting is complete, it tells you this also.

```
362496 bytes total disk space
362496 bytes available on disk
   512 bytes in each allocation unit
   708 allocation units available on disk
Format another (Y/N)?
```

(An "allocation unit," usually called a "cluster" is the smallest amount of space that will be allocated to a file. You can change the cluster size in certain cases to improve storage efficiency, as explained in *The Waite Group's Using PC DOS.*)

With MS-DOS 4.0, you will also be asked for a *volume label*:

```
Format complete
Volume label (11 characters, ENTER for none)?
```

You can use a name with up to 11 characters, or press <ENTER> if you do not want to use a label. (Volume labels are discussed a bit later in this chapter.)

MS-DOS 4.0 also automatically generates a volume serial number for each newly formatted disk. This has no particular use to you as a user, so it won't be discussed further.

Let's take a moment to look at the messages MS-DOS is giving you. First you are told that the formatting of the disk has been completed. Then the total number of bytes on the disk is given. Because formatting has not put any information on the disk, but has only divided up the space, the amount of total disk space and the amount available on the disk are the same.

You must now make a decision. Do you want to format any additional disks? If you answer *y*, you will be instructed to insert another disk in drive B. It's a good idea to format several disks at a time. Then, when you're working on a project and need another disk, you won't have to stop, insert your system disk, and prepare the disk. Go ahead and format several disks now.

Good. You've got everything moving along smoothly, and you now have several disks awaiting use. When you're finished formatting, just answer *n* to the "Format another" question, and you will be returned to the MS-DOS prompt.

Formatting Other Sizes of Disks

The preceding listing assumes that you are formatting a 360K 5¼″ disk. If you are using a 1.2MB disk or a 720K or 1.44MB 3½″ disk, the totals shown will be different, but their meaning is the same. When you type FORMAT, MS-DOS uses the *default* capacity of the disk drive in question, so you should use the appropriate physical disk type. For example, if your drive uses 1.2MB 5¼″ disks, use a double-sided quad-density disk. Otherwise, MS-DOS will attempt to format a 360K disk as a 1.2MB disk, and this will not work properly.

If you want MS-DOS to format a disk of smaller capacity than the default for the type of drive in use, you can do so by using option switches with the FORMAT command. To format a 720K 3½″ disk in a 1.44MB 3½″ drive, type *format a: /n:9*. To format a 360K 5¼″ disk in a 1.2MB 5¼″ drive, type *format a: /4*. (If you are formatting the disk in a drive other than A, of course, use the appropriate drive letter.) With MS-DOS 4.0 you can use the alternative switch of /f:xxx, where "xxx" is the formatted capacity of the disk. Thus, you can format a 720K disk with *format a: /f:720*.

In general, it is not a good idea to format 360K disks in a 1.2MB drive, because drives designed only for 360K disks are often unable to accurately read disks formatted in this fashion.

Labeling Formatted Disks

Be sure to label those disks. This label can be short or long, just so its meaning is clear to you. One simple label consists of the letter F, or the word "formatted," followed by the date. This leaves lots of room for you to fill in the contents of the disk as you store information on it. (Use a felt-tip pen or marker when labeling 5¼″ disks. Pressure from a pen or pencil can damage the disk surface.)

Electronic Disk Labels: the LABEL Command

Don't confuse the physical label on the disk jacket with the volume label used with the FORMAT command. The volume label is stored in the disk's file directory and displayed when you type the DIR command. It provides a convenient way of identifying the disk in a particular drive without physically removing and inspecting it.

In MS-DOS 4.0, FORMAT automatically requests a volume label. For earlier MS-DOS versions, use the /v option switch with the FORMAT command if you want to establish a volume label.

In versions of MS-DOS before 3.0 you cannot change the volume label without reformatting the disk. Starting with MS-DOS 3.0, however, you can use the LABEL command to change a volume label (or add one to a disk that lacks one). For example, to label the disk in drive B, type

```
C:\>label b: <ENTER>
Volume in drive B has no label
Volume label (11 characters, ENTER for none)?ACCOUNTING
```

Here you have given the disk in drive B the label ACCOUNTING.

You can also specify a label in your LABEL command, in which case you won't be prompted for one:

```
C:\>label b:accounting <ENTER>
```

Notice there is no space between the drive letter and the label.

The FORMAT command is an effective command, but it can be destructive. If you format a disk that contains data, the data will be destroyed after the formatting process is complete. Always make sure you are formatting a disk that is blank or one that contains data you no longer need!

One note of caution in using the FORMAT command. When you tell MS-DOS to format, you are indicating that this is a new, blank disk. FORMAT ignores any information already on a disk and lays down new track and sector divisions. This can be useful if you want to erase an entire disk. Just use FORMAT. But this operation can also backfire. Once you format a disk that contains something you really want, the data are erased. (You can buy special utility programs that may be able to recover the data, but MS-DOS by itself can't do so.) This only emphasizes the importance of labeling all disks. Keep this fact in mind whenever you use the FORMAT command: FORMAT treats each disk as blank; it will erase any information on the disk.

Occasionally, when you format a disk, you will receive an unexpected message.

```
Bad sector on track xxx
```

or

```
xxxxx bytes in bad sectors
```

If this message appears, do not continue to use the disk. There is probably a manufacturing fault in the disk (and possibly with the entire carton of disks). Return these disks to your dealer and request a refund or replacement.

Making Bootable MS-DOS Disks with the /s Switch

The optional FORMAT switch /s is used to instruct FORMAT to automatically copy the MS-DOS operating system to the disk after it has been formatted.

A disk formatted with the plain FORMAT command is ready to store data, but it doesn't have the MS-DOS system files on it. You cannot start the system with such a disk. To make a "bootable" disk that has the required system files, you can use the /s option switch with your FORMAT command.

The /s switch on the FORMAT command allows you to put a copy of the operating system on a disk during the formatting procedure. This can be a timesaver because it allows you to boot the system from any disk that has been formatted this way. To put the system on a disk, you *must* include the /s switch at the time you format the disk.

For example, you may write a program that you know you will use quite often. This program requires you to input information from a data disk. If you have the system on your program disk, you can just insert it in drive A, insert the data disk in drive B, turn on the machine, and proceed. No more inserting the system disk in drive A, then removing this disk to put in your program disk, and then beginning to run the program.

When you include the /s switch in the FORMAT command to set up a system disk, it transfers three files to the new disk. Two of these files are hidden, which doesn't mean DOS can't find them. It means you won't see them listed among the files on the disk when you use the DIR command. To tell if a disk contains any hidden files, use the CHKDSK command. You cannot access hidden files, so you can't change them or do anything to make the system fail to operate properly. The third file transferred by the /s switch is COMMAND.COM. This file does appear as part of a disk's contents when you use DIR to look at the disk. All three of these files make up the system.

Putting the system on the disk does take up some space. Not every disk needs to have the system on it. However, if you think you are likely to be booting from a disk or you know you will need the internal commands handy when you are using the disk, put the system on it. (If you have a hard disk you won't need system disks, though you should have a copy of your original system disk to use if your hard disk should fail.)

To format the disk in drive B and make this disk a system disk, enter the command and the switch.

```
C:\>format b:/s <ENTER>
```

MS-DOS follows the usual steps in the formatting sequence.

```
Insert new diskette for drive B:
and strike any key when ready
Formatting...Format complete
```

The new twist is an added message.

```
System transferred
```

The space occupied by the system is included in the message at the completion of the formatting operation.

```
362496 bytes total disk space
40960 bytes used by system
321536 bytes available on disk

Format another (Y/N?)n
```

And that's all there is to it. You now have a self-booting disk ready for your data or programs.

You can put a volume label and the system on the same disk. Simply enter both switches at the time you FORMAT the disk.

```
C:\>format b:/v/s <ENTER>
```

On some computers the order of the switches does not matter. Others require the /s to come last. You can't go wrong by putting the /v first and the /s second.

You will see the "system transferred" message and be asked for a "volume label" during the formatting procedure. The difference between the two FORMAT switches is illustrated in *Figure 5-10.*

Remember, the /s switch is only for transferring the system to a new, blank disk. Because you will quickly find how convenient it is to have the system on a disk, you may want to know how to put the system on disks that already contain information.

Figure 5-10.
The FORMAT Command

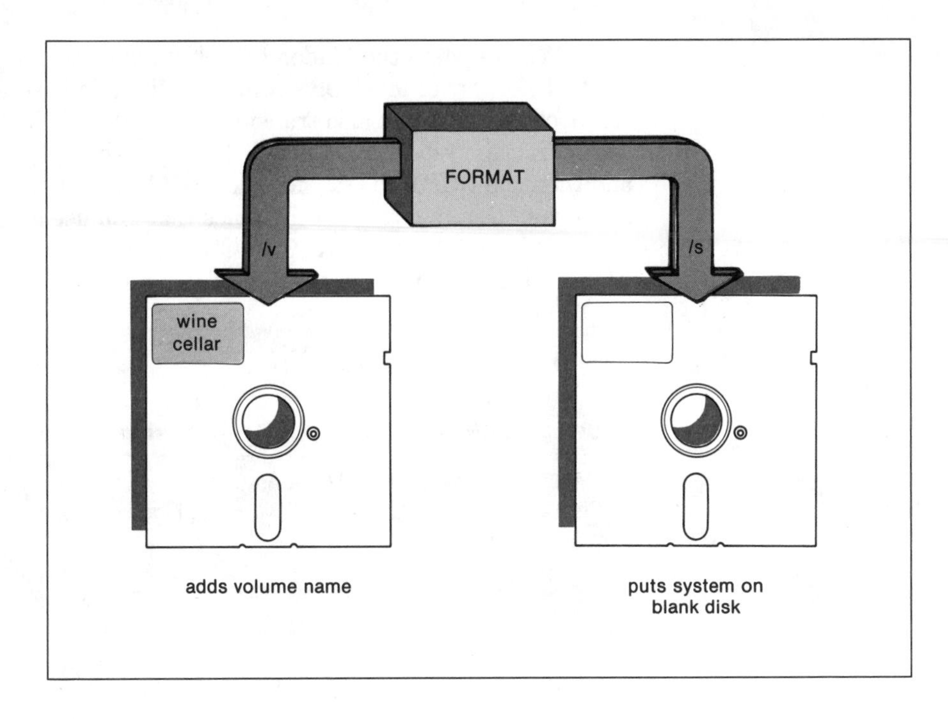

The SYS Command

An alternative to using FORMAT with the /s switch is the SYS command, which can be used after a disk has been formatted to transfer the MS-DOS operating system. One drawback, however, is that, unlike FORMAT, SYS does not copy the file COMMAND.COM to the new disk, thus requiring that it be copied separately with the COPY command.

The SYS command performs the same function as the /s switch in the FORMAT command; that is, it transfers the operating system onto a designated disk but does not transfer the command files of MS-DOS. Because the use of FORMAT erases all previous information on a disk, you cannot use FORMAT/s to put the system on preprogrammed or application disks. A few of these disks (mainly games) cannot be copied to customized disks because they are "copy protected." But, by using SYS, you can put the system on most of these disks.

Just like the /s switch in FORMAT, SYS transfers two hidden files to the specified disk. You can't see these files, but don't worry, MS-DOS knows if they are there. In most versions of MS-DOS, system files occupy a unique position on the disk; they are always located in the first track, at the very beginning of the disk. Even if the files are not on the disk, MS-DOS allocates this space to them when you format the disk. When you use the SYS command, you put the system in this already available location. Most preprogrammed or application disks are produced with this predefined location for the system files. If you save data to a formatted disk, this reserved area will be written over, and you won't be able to transfer the system files successfully.

SYS transfers the hidden files, but unlike the /s switch, it does not transfer any of MS-DOS's command files. To have a disk that is self-booting, you must also transfer the COMMAND.COM portion of the operating system. First use SYS to put the system on the disk, and then use COPY to transfer the COMMAND.COM file. You may also use COPY to transfer other files that you use a great deal, such as FORMAT.COM or DISKCOPY.COM. (The difference between FORMAT/s and SYS is outlined in *Table 5-1.*)

Table 5-1. Putting the System on a Disk

Using FORMAT/s	Using SYS
On a blank disk, FORMAT/s transfers the COMMAND.COM file and two hidden files.	On a blank disk, SYS transfers two hidden files.
	Use the COPY command to transfer the COMMAND.COM file.

Because SYS is an external command, you must have your system disk in drive A before issuing the command (if you're running with floppies only). Don't forget to put your target disk in drive B. If you have a hard disk, you can make a system disk in any floppy drive.

```
C:\>sys b: <ENTER>
```

MS-DOS tells you when the transfer has been completed.

```
System transferred
C:\>
```

When you look at the directory of this disk, you will see that COMMAND.COM is now one of its files. But how can you be sure that the hidden files were also transferred? The next command gives you that information.

Sometimes you can use the SYS command to transfer the system files to a disk that already has data on it, making it a bootable disk. This nearly always works with MS-DOS 4.0, provided there is enough room on the disk to hold the system files. With earlier MS-DOS versions, you can often use SYS to upgrade a bootable disk containing system files. This won't work with disks that contain only data, however.

INSURING THE SYSTEM DISK

The DISKCOPY command provides a quick and effective method of making an exact copy of an entire disk. As with the FORMAT command, DISKCOPY will destroy any data previously stored on the target disk.

Before you do anything else, you are going to make an insurance copy of each of your MS-DOS system disks. Each copy will be an exact duplicate of the original disk. You do not want to add or delete any information. When you want to copy an entire disk, use the DISKCOPY command. (Early versions of MS-DOS come on a single disk, but later versions, especially MS-DOS 4.0, come on several disks depending on the disk capacity used. After completing each copy, DISKCOPY will ask if you want to copy another disk. Continue replying *y* until all of your system disks have been copied.)

The DISKCOPY Command

This command makes a duplicate of an entire disk. Normally, before transferring any information to a disk, you must prepare it with FORMAT. The DISKCOPY command is the exception that proves the rule. DISKCOPY automatically formats the disk as it makes the duplicate copy. As it does, it erases any previous information on the disk. Because this is true, you should observe the same precautions you follow when formatting.

If you wish to copy only certain files to another disk, use the COPY command instead of DISKCOPY.

It's important to distinguish between DISKCOPY and COPY (an MS-DOS command introduced in Chapter 6). DISKCOPY automatically formats the disk and it copies the entire disk. COPY needs a formatted disk and it copies only designated files. When you only want to copy some of the files on a disk, use the COPY command.

Now let's make DISKCOPY jump through its hoops. Insert an unformatted, blank disk in drive B. Again, a hard disk is assumed in this discussion. If you are using floppy drives, run DISKCOPY from your MS-DOS system disk in drive A. You will be looking at the *A>* command prompt.

Before you enter this command, take a close look at the exact wording of the example.

```
C:\>diskcopy a: b:
```

This command tells MS-DOS to copy the entire contents from the disk in drive A to the disk in drive B. Be sure you enter the command in this exact order; otherwise, you may erase your entire system disk.

How could this happen? As the DISKCOPY transfers the information, it wipes out anything previously on the disk. So when you are using this command you must be sure to clearly indicate where the information is coming from and where it is going.

Source and Target Disks

The DISKCOPY command can be used with only one drive or with several drives to copy disks.

The disk that holds the original information is your source disk: it contains the information you want to copy. In this case, the source disk is your system disk, currently in drive A. The disk that receives the copy is your target disk: it is the destination of the information you are copying. Your target disk (as yet empty) is currently in drive B.

It's wise to become familiar with these terms because they are used in the instructions MS-DOS uses to perform copying commands. You'll see an example of this now as you execute DISKCOPY.

```
C:\>diskcopy a: b: <ENTER>
```

Include the blank spaces and colons. MS-DOS will remind you of what to do next.

```
Insert SOURCE diskette in drive A:
Insert TARGET diskette in drive B:
Press any key when ready...
```

You already have the source and target disks in place, so press any key.

The operating system now performs the same sequence of events that accompanied the FORMAT command, and copies the contents of the disk at the same time. Again the drives will whirr and the indicator lights will flash on and off. When the light under drive A is lit, information is being read from the system disk. When the light under drive B comes on, information is being written to this disk. Do not attempt to open the drive doors or remove any disks while this command is in operation.

During this process, a message will be on the screen.

```
Copying 40 tracks
9 Sectors/Track, 2 Side(s)
```

Depending on the type of disk your system uses, your message may read a bit differently (it may have more than 9 sectors). In any case, MS-DOS tells you when the disk is copied.

```
Copy complete
Copy another (Y/N)?
```

At this point, you are offered a choice. As you can use FORMAT repeatedly without retyping the command, similarly you can use DISKCOPY to make more than one duplicate of the source disk. If you answer *y* to MS-DOS's query, you are instructed to insert a new target disk in drive B and to start the copying process with a keystroke. If you answer *n*, you are returned to the system prompt. If you want to be doubly protected, make an extra copy of your "insurance" disk.

If you have only one floppy-disk drive, type the command above, substituting *a: a:* for the command *a: b:* above. DOS will tell you when to insert and remove source and target disks.

Now you are all set. You have taken out an insurance policy on your system disk (properly labeled, of course). You can take your original system disk and store it in a dry, safe place. Keep your backup system disk and your newly formatted disks handy; you will need them in Chapter 6.

Drive Indicators

DISKCOPY is the first MS-DOS command you have encountered that requires the use of two disks, one in each drive. Many MS-DOS commands rely on this kind of transfer of information from one disk to another. It is important that you understand how MS-DOS identifies which drive is the source and which drive is the target. You inform MS-DOS as to which is the source and which is the target through the use of drive indicators.

After you complete a command, MS-DOS returns you to the system prompt:

```
C:\>
```

MS-DOS is ready for your next command. Besides being the system prompt, the C symbol gives you another important piece of information. It informs you that the system is working off the C drive. It expects that any information you request or store will be on this drive. So this C is also a drive indicator. *Figure 5-11* shows the positions of drives in a typical PC.

Figure 5-11.
Drive Positions in an AT-Type System

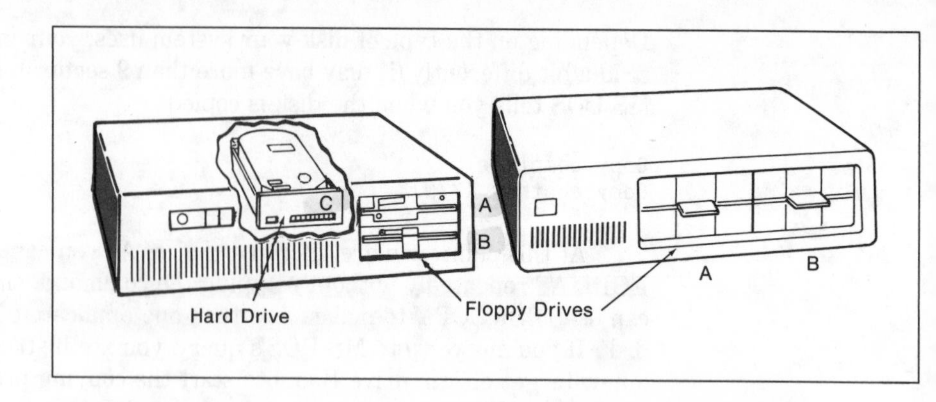

MS-DOS keeps track of the current, or default, drive by displaying the drive's indicator (name) in the MS-DOS prompt, such as A> for drive A and B> for drive B. The current drive is always accessed by MS-DOS if you enter a command without indicating which drive is to be accessed.

To keep track of itself, MS-DOS uses the concept of current drive. The current drive is the one represented by the drive indicator. This is also called the default drive because, unless you tell it otherwise, MS-DOS will always look for information or store information on the current drive.

Take, for example, the DIR command. You want a listing of the disk in drive A. You ask for this information by entering the command, followed by a drive indicator. Drive indicators in commands are separated from the command by a space and must be followed by a colon.

```
C:\>dir a: <ENTER>
```

This command produces a listing of all the files on the disk in drive A. But suppose you leave out the drive letter.

```
C:\>dir<ENTER>
```

This will give you a listing of the current directory on drive C, your hard drive. Notice that the prompt always shows the current drive (drive C, in this case). When you don't specify a drive in your command, the current drive is assumed to be the one you want to use.

This default feature is very handy when you are working extensively with one disk. But it does have its drawbacks. You can cause some pretty weird and unwanted file changes if you neglect to include a drive indicator in a command. Because it does no harm to include a drive indicator, when in doubt write it into the command. Even if the operation involves only the current drive, it doesn't do any harm to include the default indicator in your command. Specifying drive indicators is always a good idea when you are transferring information from one disk to another, just as an extra measure of protection.

You can issue commands to be performed on the disk in other drives without changing the current drive. Suppose you want to see a directory of the data files on the disk in drive B. To do so, include the drive indicator in the command. The command is followed by a blank space, the drive indicator, and a colon.

```
C:\>dir b: <ENTER>
```

The screen displays the listing of the files on the disk in drive B. After the listing you will be returned to the system prompt.

```
C:\>
```

The current drive is still C because you have only taken a peek at the files on the disk in drive B. When you issue your next command, MS-DOS will look for the information or write the information to drive C, as the C:\>prompt indicates that A is still the current drive.

The current, or default, drive can be changed at any time by entering the drive indicator followed by a colon. For example, to change the default drive from A to B, enter *B:* in response to the C:\> prompt, whereupon the prompt will change to B:\>.

When you are working extensively with the disk in drive B, it can be inconvenient to keep including the drive indicator in every command. There is a simple solution, however—change the current drive. To make drive B the current drive, just type in the drive indicator in response to the system prompt.

```
C:\>b: <ENTER>
```

The new current drive now appears as the system prompt.

```
B:\>
```

Now that you have changed the current drive, what would be the result of the following command?

```
B:\>dir <ENTER>
```

This command produces a listing of the files on the disk in drive B. Because B is now the current drive, and you did not include a drive indicator in the command, MS-DOS automatically performs the command on the disk in drive B.

If you are still confused about when to include a drive indicator, think of it this way: the computer can do only what you tell it to. Including drive indicators is like making a will: you can only be sure the goodies go to the right recipients if you make your wishes known (preferably by writing them down). If you tell MS-DOS that drive B is the current drive, it will return to that drive after every command until you tell it differently. It will also perform the entered command on the data in the current drive unless you tell it to go to another drive.

To return to C as the current drive, enter the drive indicator in response to the B prompt.

```
B:\>c: <ENTER>
```

The current drive is again C.

```
C:\>
```

As you become familiar with other MS-DOS commands, the significance and use of drive indicators will become clearer. This will be especially true as you move into more advanced MS-DOS commands in Chapter 6.

SUMMARY

This chapter has been about protecting yourself. This includes using and handling your disks wisely and making sure you back up your original system disk. In addition, you have actually done something with a disk. You've used FORMAT to prepare your disks and DISKCOPY to make your insurance copy. Finally, you have begun to see more of the inner operations of MS-DOS by learning the basics of source and target disks and the current drive indicator.

REVIEW

1. Floppy disks reside inside a permanent square plastic protective jacket. Parts of the floppy disk are exposed through holes in the protective jacket; never touch those areas of the disk.

2. You can prevent the disk drive from writing information on the floppy disk by covering the write-protect notch that is cut out on one edge of the disk or by sliding open the square window on a 3½″ disk.

3. A disk must be formatted to define its tracks and sectors before it can store information.

4. If you format a disk that already has files on it, you will erase all the information on the disk, so be very careful not to reformat a disk that you still need to use.
5. Specify the drive name—FORMAT A:, for example—in order to use the FORMAT command.
6. The DISKCOPY command will copy all information on one disk (the source disk) to a second disk (the target disk), and it will automatically format that second disk as part of the process.
7. To specify which disk drive you want to control with an MS-DOS command, include the name of the drive on the same line following the MS-DOS command.

Quiz for Chapter 5

1. Making regular backups of your disk data is:
   a. always important.
   b. only occasionally necessary.
   c. to be done only if you have extra floppy disks.
2. The sizes of floppy disks in common use today are:
   a. 5¼ inch and 8 inch.
   b. single-sided and double-sided.
   c. 5¼ inch and 3½ inch.
   d. all of the above.
3. Although floppy disks are flexible, testing their flexibility by bending them:
   a. never causes damage.
   b. may cause damage and is therefore not recommended.
   c. will always cause damage.
4. Touching the exposed surfaces of a floppy disk:
   a. will most likely damage the disk and therefore must never be attempted.
   b. will probably not cause damage but shouldn't be attempted anyway.
   c. cannot hurt the disk.
5. A covered write-protect notch on a floppy disk will:
   a. not allow new data to be stored.
   b. not allow data to be erased.
   c. allow data to be retrieved.
   d. all of the above.
6. Clear labeling of your disks will:
   a. help keep track of what is stored on each disk.
   b. be of marginal use.
   c. keep them nicely decorated.
7. The FORMAT command is used to establish:
   a. the data storage characteristics of a disk.
   b. the number of tracks.
   c. the number of sectors per track.
   d. the number of bytes per sector.
   e. all of the above.
8. Although most MS-DOS commands assume that you have two disk drives installed, the minimum number of drives an MS-DOS computer can have is:

a. none.
b. one. (Hard Drive)
c. two.
d. three.

9. Formatting a disk with the FORMAT command will:
   a. copy any data stored on it.
   b. destroy any data stored on it.
   c. restore any data stored on it.
   d. leave any data stored on it intact.

10. The DISKCOPY command will:
    a. make an exact copy of a disk.
    b. destroy any data originally stored on the target disk.
    c. copy all files stored on a disk.
    d. automatically format the target disk if it wasn't previously formatted.
    e. all of the above.

11. Changing the current, or default, drive is accomplished by:
    a. typing the drive indicator.
    b. typing the drive indicator, followed by a colon. B:, C:, etc.
    c. pressing the <Ctrl> and D keys.
    d. typing the drive indicator, followed by the greater-than character (>), and then pressing the <ENTER> key.

Managing Your Files

ABOUT THIS CHAPTER

The term "file" is not unknown to you. You've been working with files for a while now. You listed files with DIR, copied files with DISKCOPY, and you may have created files with a word processor or EDLIN. In this chapter you'll learn about the intricacies of naming files and how to use MS-DOS to manage your files. First we'll look at a quick summary.

WHAT IS A FILE?

A file stored on a magnetic disk is much like a paper file folder placed in a file cabinet, in that it stores a group of related data and is stored in one location. When the DIR command is used to display a list of files stored on disk, the effect is similar to opening a file drawer and visually scanning its contents.

A file is a group of related data stored together in one location. Files are not restricted to the high-tech world of computers; as illustrated in *Figure 6-1,* you use files every day in different ways. When you stack all your phone bills in one pile, you're creating a file. When you add a memo to a project report at work, you're expanding a file. When you delete from your address book the names of people who moved away ten years ago, you're updating a file.

Computer data files perform this same organization and storage function, but they happen to reside on disks. When DIR displays the contents of a disk, it details the information about each file: its filename, its size in bytes (remember, each byte represents one character in a file), and the time and date the file was created or last modified. To MS-DOS, all data are part of one file or another.

FILENAMES

To keep MS-DOS from getting confused, each file stored on a particular disk must have a unique name.

To create, store, and retrieve files, they must be named. Otherwise, how would MS-DOS differentiate among the thousands of files it has to keep track of? And how would you know what was in each of those files? To alleviate confusion, there is a very simple rule: *each file on a disk must have a unique name.*

If you attempt to use an existing name for a new file, you will either get an error or warning message, or you will lose the old file.

(What happens depends on the command or program that you are using.) Files on different disks can have the same name—and they normally will if you make backup copies of your important files, which is strongly recommended.

It is important that you take your time in working with your files. Before copying over an old file (or deleting it), make sure you know what is in it, and make sure you don't need the data any more. As you will see, choosing good filenames will help you remember what is where.

Many MS-DOS commands require that you supply the names of one or more files to be worked with.

Figure 6-1. Types of Files

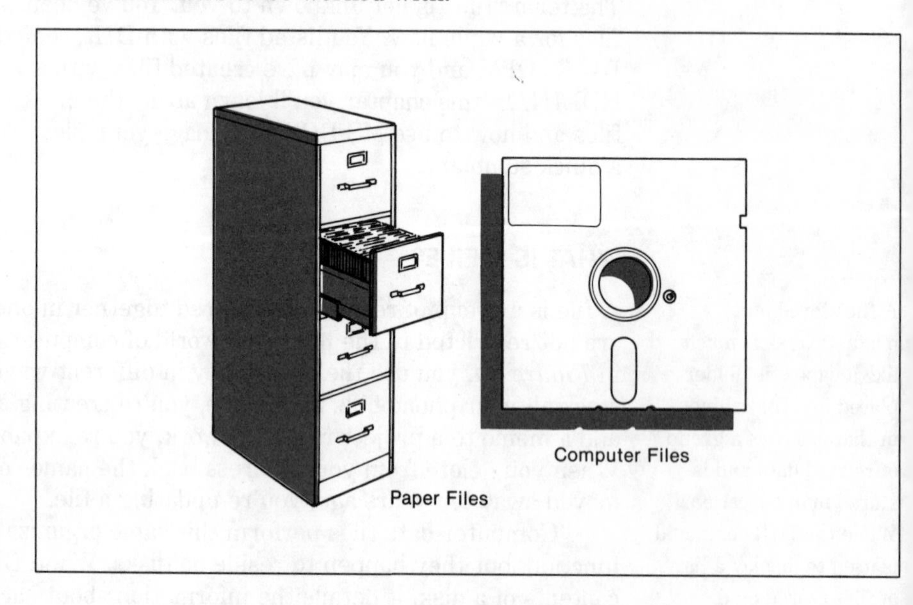

Many of MS-DOS's commands must be followed by a filename or a group of filenames. Otherwise, MS-DOS doesn't understand what you are trying to accomplish.

One of the commands you will learn about in this chapter is COPY.

```
C:\>copy
```

If you type in the command like this, MS-DOS cannot respond. Copy what, from where, to where? You'll see how you should enter this command with all the necessary information in just a second.

Rules and Regulations

All file naming follows a set pattern: filename.extension. The filename must consist of at least one character but may not exceed eight characters. The extension is optional; it may be omitted, or it may contain one, two, or three characters. When a file contains an extension, a period must be used to separate it from the filename. Not all characters may be used in a filename or extension. Some symbol characters have special meaning for certain MS-DOS command functions.

When you assign each file a unique filename, both you and MS-DOS know exactly which file is to be created, modified, operated on, or stored away. A filename must follow a specific pattern.

filename.extension

The filename can be from one to eight characters. An optional extension, not exceeding three characters, may be added to the name. When you give a filename an extension, use a period to separate the extension from the filename itself.

Filenames must be made up of valid characters. *Table 6-1* is a list of these characters. The exact list of special characters may vary, depending on your computer type and the version of MS-DOS on your machine.

In general, the symbols listed in *Table 6-2* may not be used in filenames. These symbols have special meanings in MS-DOS and are misinterpreted if included within a filename.

Table 6-1. Valid Characters for Filenames

All letters of the alphabet, numbers 1 through 9 and 0, and the following special characters:	
@ (at sign)	´ (single quote)
# (number sign)	` (grave accent)
$ (dollar sign)	~ (tilde)
% (percent sign)	((opening parenthesis)
^ (caret)	) (closing parenthesis)
& (ampersand)	{ (opening brace)
- (hyphen)	} (closing brace)
_ (underscore)	

Table 6-2. Invalid Characters for Filenames

. (period, except to delineate an extension)	/ (slash)
, (comma)	\ (backslash)
: (colon)	¦ (vertical bar)
; (semicolon)	" (double quote)
* (asterisk)	+ (plus sign)
? (question mark)	= (equal sign)
< (less than)	[(opening bracket)
> (greater than)	] (closing bracket)

Some filenames are reserved by MS-DOS as command names or device names. Attempting to name new files the same as these reserved names will either cause immediate errors or future problems.

There are also some special groups of characters, listed in *Table 6-3*, that MS-DOS reserves for its own use. One group comprises the names of the MS-DOS commands and program files. You shouldn't use such existing filenames. (If you copied another file to one of these names, you would lose access to part of MS-DOS—the DISKCOPY command, for example.) Another group consists of device names. These are abbreviations that MS-DOS uses to refer to pieces of computer equipment. By the time you finish reading this book, you'll know most of these terms.

Table 6-3. Reserved Filenames and Device Names

Files			
ASSIGN	COPY	FDISK	MORE
ATTRIB	CITY	FIND	PATH
BASIC	DATE	FORMAT	PRINT
BASICA	DEBUG	GRAPHICS	PROMPT
BREAK	DEL	GRAFTABL	RECOVER
CD	DIR	KEYB	RENAME
CHDIR	DISKCOMP	LABEL	REN
CHKDISK	DISKCOPY	LINK	REPLACE
CLS	EDLIN	MEM	RESTORE
COMMAND	ERASE	MKDIR	RD
COMP	EXE2BIN	MODE	RMDIR

Table 6-3.
(continued)

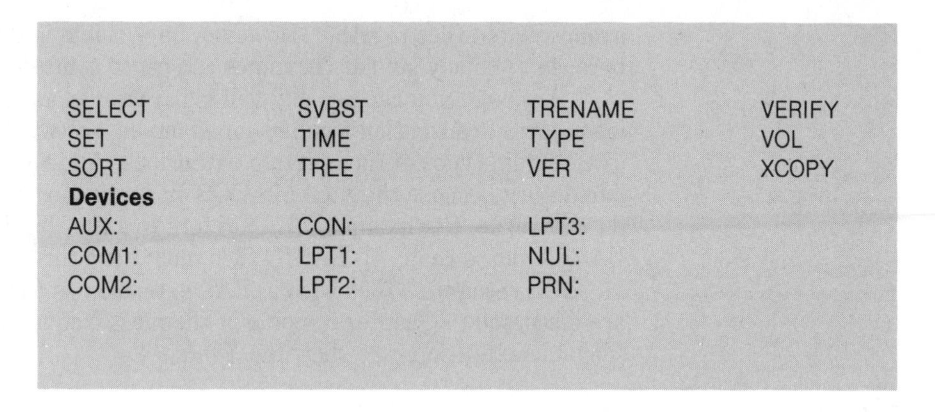

SELECT	SVBST	TRENAME	VERIFY
SET	TIME	TYPE	VOL
SORT	TREE	VER	XCOPY
Devices			
AUX:	CON:	LPT3:	
COM1:	LPT1:	NUL:	
COM2:	LPT2:	PRN:	

If you use these combinations of characters in filenames, MS-DOS gets confused. Again, this list may vary from system to system. To be sure about filename limitations, check your computer's user's guide.

Except for these special cases, you can name your files almost anything: for example, "bills," "scores," "games," "letters."

For convenience and to make typing them easier, this book always shows filenames in lowercase letters. When you are using filenames in commands, you can enter them in either upper- or lowercase. When filenames are included in the text, they are enclosed in quotation marks (" ").

Extensions

A file's extension is normally used to identify the type of file. Some file extensions always mean certain things to MS-DOS or your application program; others can be determined by you according to your preferences.

A three-character extension in any filename is optional. Extensions are useful for clarifying or categorizing the contents of a file. For example, you have a file named "letters." Now, if you put all your letters into this one file, not only would it be very large, it would also be extremely difficult to use. Each time you wanted to look at a specific letter, you would have to search through the entire file. By subdividing this file into three smaller files with identifying extensions, you can save yourself a lot of time and trouble.

letters.bus	These are your business letters.
letters.sue	These letters are of a more personal nature.
letters.tax	This is legal correspondence concerning tax shelters.

At first glance it would seem that these three files violate the uniqueness rule for filenames. All the files are named "letters." But the extension, as a part of the filename, can be the differentiating factor. Sometimes it is even desirable to use similar filenames to group related files together. However, be sensible in doing so, because too many similar filenames can cause confusion.

Although you can use any valid character in an extension, a loose sort of convention has developed among software designers to give certain types of files certain extensions. A few extensions are mandatory because they tell MS-DOS or application program what to do with a file. For example, .BAS refers to a file that is written in BASIC source code. All BASIC files must have this extension. MS-DOS recognizes files with a .BAT extension as *batch files,* which are discussed in Chapter 8. Some of the most frequently used filename extensions are shown in *Table 6-4.*

Table 6-4. Most Frequently Used Filename Extensions

Extension	Meaning
.BAK	A backup copy of a text file
.BAS	A BASIC source code file
.BAT	A batch processing file
.COM	An executable program in memory-image format
.DAT	A general data file
.DBF	A dBASE data file
.EXE	An executable program in relocation format
.TXT	A text file from a word processor
.WKS	A Lotus spreadsheet

Don't worry if you don't understand these explanations. The only reason these extensions are mentioned at all is so you won't be alarmed if some strange extension shows up on one of your directory listings.

Probably the most important rule of naming files is to assign a name that makes sense to you. Although you can use many special symbols in filenames, what good is a file when you can't remember what's inside it?

File Specification

Filenames are often preceded by disk-drive identifiers.

The name of a file is made up of the filename (up to eight characters) and the optional extension (up to three characters). But when you use a filename in a command, MS-DOS must have one more piece of information: which drive contains the disk that holds the file? You

Table 6-5. What's Wrong with These Filenames?

ZZZ#9HUH.YUK	This is a legal filename, but what's in it?
MYOWN/.TEXT	Two things are wrong here: / is an illegal character, and there are too many characters in the extension.
FASTNOTES	A filename can have only eight characters.
COPY.BAT	Although COPY can be used in a filename, the file should not be an executable file (with the .BAT, .COM, or .EXE extensions), because COPY is a reserved command name. The wrong copy is likely to be executed.
DING.BAT	This is a perfectly valid filename, and you're sure to remember what you put in it.

direct MS-DOS to the correct drive by including the letter of the drive (the drive indicator a:, b:, or c:) in the filename. You were introduced to this concept in Chapter 5 when you learned about the current drive and source and target disks. A quick review of drive indicators is presented in *Table 6-6.*

Table 6-6. Drive Indicators

Drive Indicator	Meaning
`C:\>c:games`	The drive indicator is optional because C is the current drive (as shown by the C prompt).
`C:\>games`	Produces the same results as the above command.
`C:\>b:games`	The drive indicator is mandatory because the file is not on the disk in the current drive.
`B:\>c:games`	The same situation in reverse.
`C:\>format b:`	Drive indicator is mandatory for MS-DOS to perform the operation on the correct disk.
`C:\>diskcopy a: b:`	When you are transferring data from one disk to another, you should include both drive indicators.

Because you are going to use the COPY command later in this chapter, learning to use drive indicators takes on added significance. These three elements of a filename—the filename itself, the optional extension, and the drive indicator—make up a file specification. And that's all you really need to know about naming files. This is one area where you can let your imagination run free; just remember a few special rules:

1. Give each file a unique name.
2. Make the filename easy to remember.
3. Include a drive indicator if necessary.
4. Use no more than eight letters in a filename.
5. Use no more than three characters in an extension.
6. Don't use invalid characters or reserved names.
7. Separate the filename from the extension with a period.

Now that you know about filenames and how to specify drives and files, it's time to learn some more MS-DOS commands that are useful for working with files. You will learn how to create, view, delete (erase), and rename files.

CREATING A NEW FILE

Unless you have been using an application program such as a word processor, the only files you probably have so far are the files provided with MS-DOS. You don't want to experiment with these essential files, so it's time to create some files of your own—*text files*, which contain characters you can read. (The other kind of files, *binary files*, are executable programs. Their contents make sense only to programmers.)

If you have a word processing or "text editing" program, you can use it to create text files. The easiest thing to do in that case is to use your word processor or editor to create a sample file with a few lines of text in it as you'll see in a minute. You will use this sample file later to try out these MS-DOS commands: COPY, TYPE, MORE, DEL, and REN.

Another alternative is to use EDLIN, a simple text editor provided with MS-DOS. This program is not as easy to use (nor as versatile) as a word processor, but it works fine for creating short text files, and you've already paid for it. If you wish to use EDLIN, please read Appendix A.

Finally, there is a way to create a text file using just the MS-DOS COPY command. Here is how you could start the Great American Novel with a little assistance from MS-DOS:

```
C:\>copy con: novel
There was a 50/50 chance the world would end today.
            ← press <ENTER> after each line
EVEN MONEY
It was down to just the three of us now.
The "Stranger" kept watching the darkening sky.
Finally he saw the signal.
Tossing the quarter in the air, he laughed "Call it"...
            ← press the F6, or Ctrl-Z, key
            ← press <ENTER>
     1 file(s) copied
C:\>        ← prompt: now waiting for your next command
```

ASCII Text Files Make Sense to MS-DOS

ASCII stands for American Standards Committee for Information Interchange. It is a set of characters used by all PCs, with a particular version found in the IBM PC and compatible computers running MS-DOS. This set includes some characters that won't show up on your screen, or that will do special things involving files or the printer. (The <Ctrl>Z shown in the last listing is an example. It doesn't show up on the screen, but it tells MS-DOS that it has reached the end of the text file.) For learning to use MS-DOS commands with text files you just want to use regular "printable" characters such as the letters of the alphabet, numerals, and punctuation marks. Many word processors use special formatting characters that are useful for making fancy printouts. For these examples, however, if you are using a word processor, instruct it to save the text to disk in ASCII format. (You may have to check your manual to find out how to do this. It is sometimes called "DOS text" format.)

CON is one of the special device names mentioned earlier: it refers to your CONsole, or keyboard and screen display. This command is telling MS-DOS "copy whatever I type at the keyboard into a disk file called 'novel.'" After you press Enter, each line is sent to the disk file. Finally, when you press the <F6> key (or <Ctrl>Z), you send a special character that tells MS-DOS that it has reached the end of the file. When you press <ENTER>, MS-DOS then wraps up everything and closes your new disk file, leaving a copy on the disk for future perusal.

At this point, you should have used one of the methods mentioned above to save the file novel to disk.

If you want to, you can use DIR to verify that the file is on the disk.

```
C:\>dir novel <ENTER>
 Volume in drive C has no label
 Directory of C:\
NOVEL                241 02-10-91  10:11a
        1 File(s)    18430720 bytes free
```

If you are eager to see your work in print, you can use a new MS-DOS command to see the contents of this file.

REVIEWING WHAT YOU WROTE

The TYPE Command

With the commands such as EDLIN and TYPE, computers equipped with MS-DOS can be excellent tools for the creation of text files for many applications, such as letters, recipes, reports, documents, and books.

TYPE is a very straightforward command, as you can see in *Figure 6-2.* Used in conjunction with a filename, it displays the contents of the file. The text of the file must be in ASCII format, or you'll have a tough time deciphering it.

```
C:\>type novel <ENTER>
```

The file contents appear (without line numbers).

```
EVEN MONEY
There was a 50/50 chance the world would end today.
It was down to just the three of us now.
The "Stranger" kept watching the darkening sky.
Finally he saw the signal.
Tossing the quarter in the air, he laughed, "Call it"...
```

Figure 6-2.
The TYPE Command

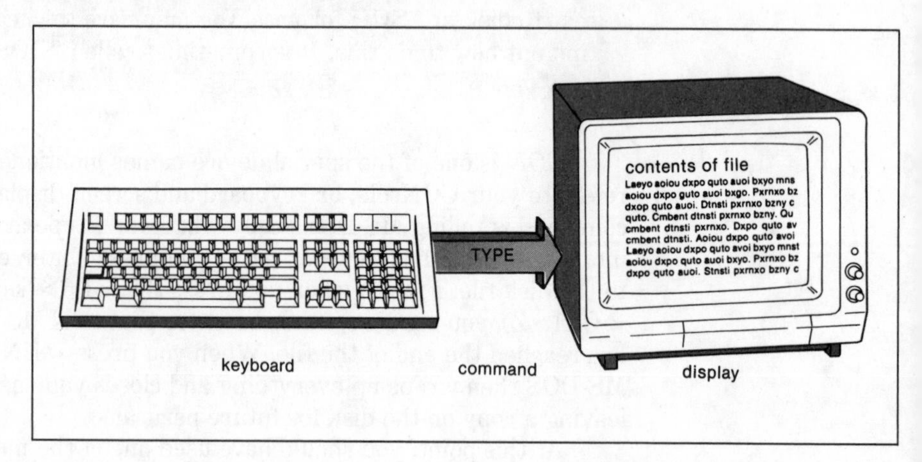

Seeing "MORE" of What You Wrote

An alternative command for viewing your files is the MORE command. The MORE command is convenient because it shows your file one screenful at a time. (This may not matter now, but it will when your novel has gotten a bit longer.) To use the MORE command, type MORE followed by the less-than symbol (<), followed by the filename (with drive specifier if necessary):

```
C:\>more < c:novel
```

← Text will be displayed: if there is more than a screenful, you will see this prompt:

```
--MORE--
```

← press any key to see the next screen, or press Esc to break out of the listing

(You will learn more about the special < symbol in Chapter 9.) MORE is an external command, so if you are using a floppy-only system you will need to have your system disk available to use it.

MAKING COPIES

The importance of making of regular backup copies of all your disks each time they're updated cannot be overstressed. If you are able to retrieve backed-up files if the disk containing the original files is damaged, you will save time and money and reduce considerably the amount of irritation computer mishaps can cause.

In today's world of information proliferation, rarely do you make just an original of anything. From term papers to tax forms, it's always smart to keep a copy. When the documents are on paper, you type multiple copies or, more likely, run down to the copy machine.

Copies are useful for many reasons. They are handy if two or more people are referring to the same document. They allow you to share with someone else information that might not otherwise be available to them. They provide a record of interaction between two companies or communication between two people. But by far the most persuasive argument for copies is that they provide insurance in case something should happen to the original. (This was discussed in some detail in Chapter 5.)

All of these reasons for making copies hold true for your computer files too. It is just as easy to copy a computer file as it is to copy a paper file, but you don't need any extra copying equipment. All you need is another disk. How important are copies? Let's go back to your life as a writer.

Much as you would like to, you can't earn a living as an unpublished author. So your writing times are squeezed between the demands of the office and the need for sleep. Naturally, this time is precious to you. Late one evening, you start to work on some changes that your agent has suggested. After hours of work, you have incorporated the revisions into the text. But the very next day your agent phones and says, "Scratch those changes, there may be a question of libel involved."

Unfortunately, while you were editing the work, you entered and exited the word processing program several times, so even its automatic backup file no longer contains your original version. You do have a printout of the first few chapters, but that means entering lots of text again. To avoid situations such as this, it is important that you make a backup of your original file (on a separate disk) before you make any significant changes.

Now you finally have your book back in order. You have been talking to a friend in Chicago about the possibility of turning this book into a screenplay. Your friend is eager to see the latest revision, so you send your disk to Chicago. Your friend spills a cup of coffee on your disk, and it is ruined. This is one reason you should make a copy of all files before they leave your possession.

Are you beginning to get the picture? The thing that is helpful to remember about disk files, as opposed to paper files, is that unless you make one, there is no copy of anything in the file. You can't hunt through the wastepaper basket for the piece of information you deleted. You should make copies for insurance, in case a disk is accidentally damaged; in case you need a copy of an earlier version of the files; and to reorganize files. There are other reasons to make copies. You might copy files when you want to put them in new groups on a disk or use parts of a file to reorganize its contents. Some of these reasons are shown in *Figure 6-3*.

Earlier in this chapter you saw the advantage of grouping files using extensions.

letters.bus, letters.sue, letters.tax

Suppose the "letters.bus" file has become too large to be efficient. Here's how you would use a copy to solve that problem. Of course, you should already have an updated backup of this file.

First, you make a copy of the entire "letters.bus" file. You want to make a new file that contains only the letters from the Live Now, Die Later company. By deleting all the other correspondence in your newly copied file you are left with only the relevant letters. You then give this file a new name using RENAME (a command discussed later in this chapter). Your results are one file, "letters1.bus," which holds only a part of your original file, "letter.bus."

In most cases, you will be copying from your hard drive to a disk and then often from one disk to another. This means you have to tell MS-DOS where to find the original and where to put the copy.

Figure 6-3. Making a Backup Copy of a File

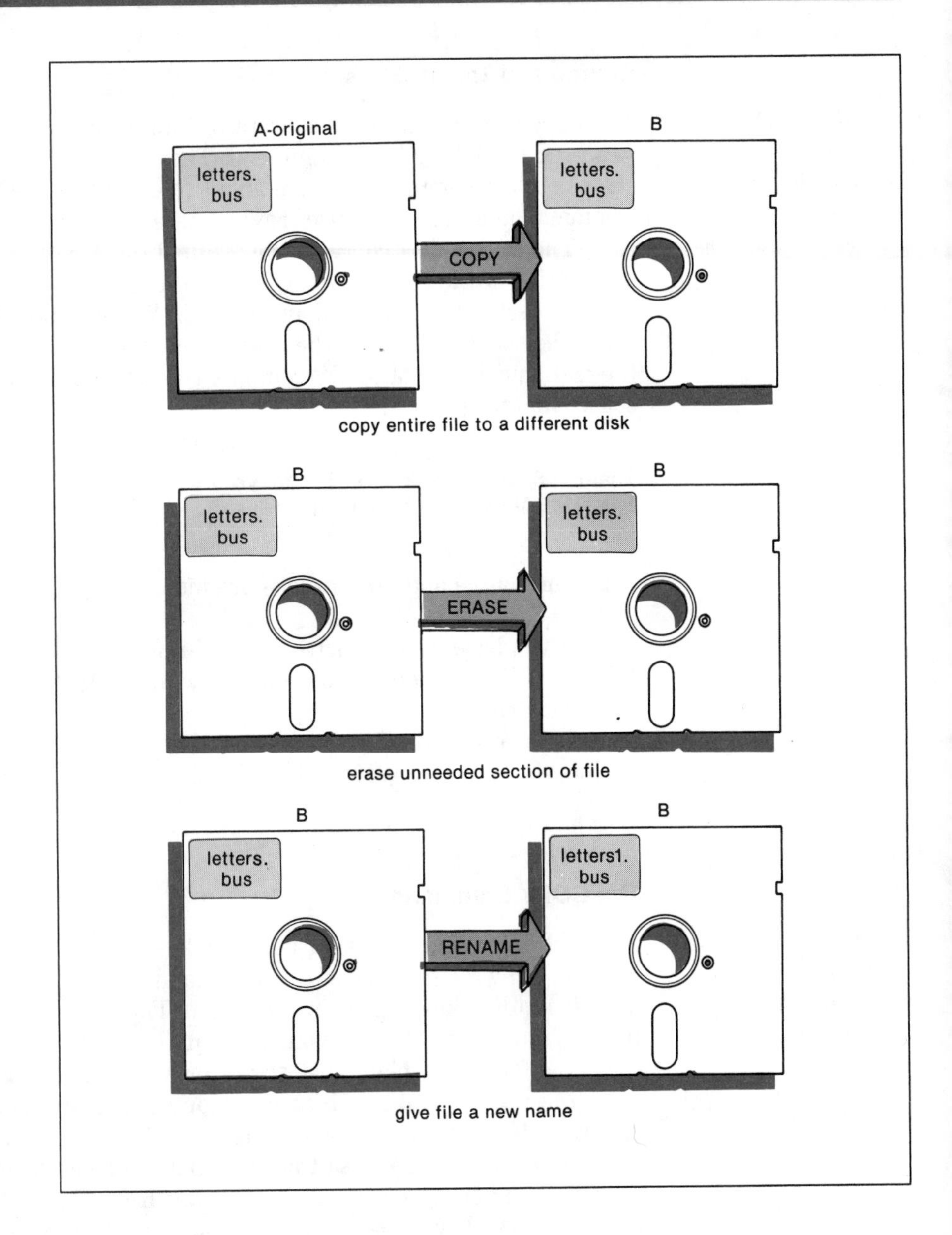

Source and Target Disks

The DISKCOPY command provides a method of backing up entire disks that is quicker than using the COPY command to copy files individually.

You were introduced to the concept of source and target disks when you used the DISKCOPY command. They are equally important in the use of the command you are about to execute, the COPY command, and deserve a brief review here.

The source disk contains the original file. The target disk is the destination of the copied file. (Often the source will be your hard disk and the destination will be drive A or B.) When floppy drives are used, the source is usually the disk in drive A, and the target usually the disk in drive B. MS-DOS reminds you to keep track of your source and target.

```
Insert SOURCE diskette in Drive A:
Insert TARGET diskette in Drive B:
```

The source and target disks are indicated by drive specifiers (a: and b:).

If you have a single-drive system, refer to the discussion of DISKCOPY in Chapter 5 to review how MS-DOS "pretends" you have two drives.

With this theoretical discussion of why and when to make copies behind you, revert to your novelist's role as you learn to use the COPY command.

The COPY Command

Use the COPY command to copy individual files or a group of files between disks.

The COPY command is versatile. It makes copies of a file or a group of files. You will often use of this command to copy a file from one disk to another, keeping the same name. (This is the backup.) Let's try this now. You will need your system disk containing the "novel" file and a formatted blank disk to perform these copying exercises.

You want to make an insurance copy of the first edition of your "EVEN MONEY." Take the disk containing "novel" and put it in drive A. Put the target disk that will contain the copy in drive B.

Remember the earlier discussion about drive specifiers and the current drive? If your hard disk is your current drive (as it usually is if you have one), C is your current drive, and you are looking at the C:\> prompt. If you want to copy from a disk in drive A to one in drive B, you'll have to use the specifiers a: and b: as appropriate.

Okay, now copy "novel" to the target disk.

```
C:\>copy a:novel b: <ENTER>
```

With this command you tell MS-DOS to copy the file "novel" now on the disk in drive C to the disk in drive B. The name of the copied file will also be "novel."

MS-DOS will respond to this command.

```
1 File(s) copied
```

This message is short and simple but to the point. It says, "fine, your request has been honored." This message is a convenient part of MS-DOS, because it lets you know several things at once. It tells you that the specified file was found on the indicated disk, that there is no problem with the target disk, and that the copying procedure is complete. If anything had gone wrong—an incorrect disk inserted in A or an unformatted disk in B, for example—you would have received an error message. The COPY command procedure is depicted in *Figure 6-4*.

Figure 6-4. Copy to a Different Disk

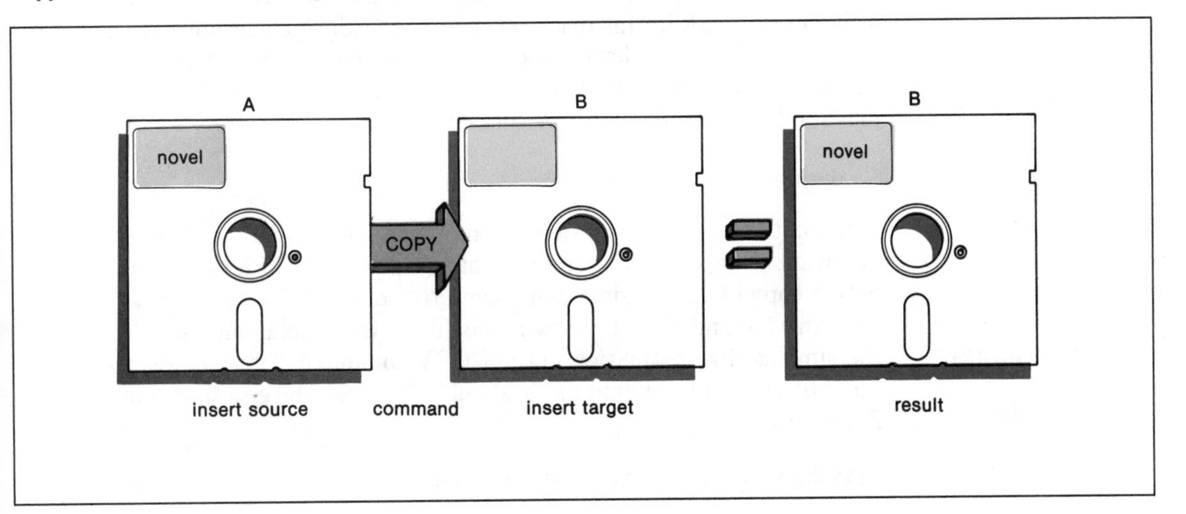

As a nervous writer, you may want to be sure the copy is on the disk in B. To relieve your skepticism, request verification with the DIR command.

```
C:\>dir b: <ENTER>
```

MS-DOS will respond.

```
 Volume in drive B has no label
 Directory of B:\
NOVEL            241 02-10-91   10:11a
        1 File(s)     183614 bytes free
```

If you are going to be working with several files (or use several commands) involving one drive, it is often easier to make that drive the current drive. To perform the preceding copy operation using drive B, type

```
C:\>b:
B:\>
```

which makes B the current drive. You can now type

```
B:\>copy novel a:
```

to perform the copy. Notice that you didn't need to use the B: specifier with the filename "novel," since MS-DOS always assumes you mean the current drive if you don't specify another.

The B:\> prompt shows you that drive B is your current drive. It is not necessary to include the drive indicator B: when referring to a file on this disk in this drive. Just to keep things clear, however, it's easier to include the drive indicator in these copy commands. As you become more at ease with MS-DOS, you will probably exclude the drive indicator when it is unnecessary.

Changing the Filename

The COPY command can be used to copy and rename a file at the same time. Copying and renaming can be accomplished on the same disk or between two disks.

You don't have to use the same name when you copy a file. Suppose you want to copy the file and try changing sections of it. You want both a copy of the original and a copy to fool around with. You can copy the file and give it a new name. To do this, include a new filename as the destination in the COPY command. Try copying your file, but change the name to "bestsell." The procedure is shown in *Figure 6-5*.

```
C:\>copy a:novel b:bestsell <ENTER>
```

Again your instruction will be confirmed.

```
1 File(s) copied
```

If you have done both of the preceding exercises, you now have two files copied on the target disk. One is called "novel" and the other is "bestsell." Both files contain exactly the same information. To make sure both copies are on the disk, use the DIR command.

```
C:\>dir b: <ENTER>
 Volume in drive B has no label
 Directory of B:\
NOVEL               241 02-10-91   10:11a
BESTSELL            241 02-10-91   10:11a
          2 File(s)   182580 bytes free
```

Figure 6-5. Copy to a Different Disk, Changing Name

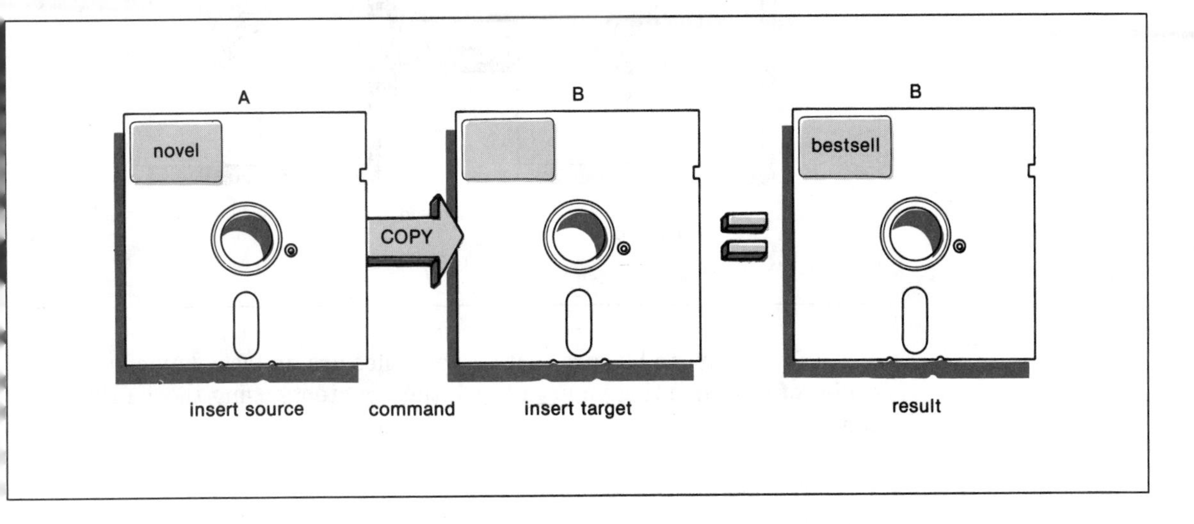

You can also have two copies of a file on the same disk. But to copy a file to the same disk, you have to give the copy a different name because two files on the same disk cannot have the same name. Let's make a duplicate of "novel" on the disk in drive A. In this case, the disk in drive A is both the source and target disk. This time try leaving out the drive indicator (first make sure A: is your current drive).

```
A:\>copy novel bestsell <ENTER>
            1 File(s) copied
```

You now have two copies of the file on the same disk. Only the names are different; the contents are the same. *Figure 6-6* shows how this is done.

If you attempt to copy a file to a disk and that disk already contains a file with an identical filename, MS-DOS will respond with an error message.

```
File cannot be copied onto itself
        0 File(s) copied
```

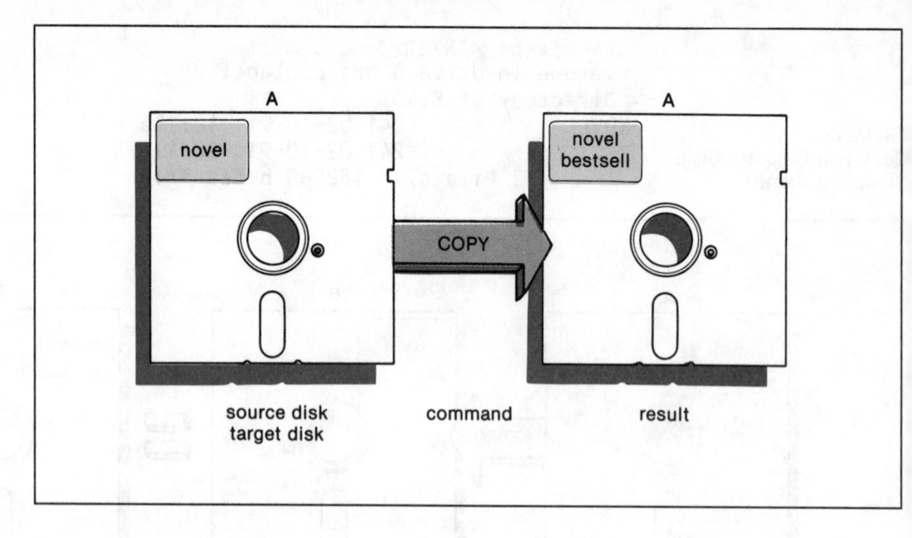

Figure 6-6. Copy to Same Disk, Changing Name

If you want to be sure that all your files are, in fact, duplicate copies of the same file, you can check their contents using the TYPE command.

```
A:\>type novel <ENTER>
A:\>type bestsell <ENTER>
A:\>type b:novel <ENTER>
A:\>type b:bestsell <ENTER>
```

The results of all these commands are the same because you have not altered the contents, just the filenames. The next command also allows you to change the name of a file.

RENAMING FILES

There are several reasons you might want to rename a file. It could be that you have files with similar names and there is a danger of confusing them. Perhaps you have given your file an esoteric name and now can't remember what's in it. Or you may want to group a set of files together under a new name, as when the Handydandy Company becomes At Your Service Company, and you need to change its name in all your files dealing with it.

The RENAME Command

Use the RENAME command when you don't want to copy a file but want only to change its name. When renaming a file, the new filename also must be unique.

This command, abbreviated REN, changes the name of a file. You also use the RENAME command to remove the .BAK extension from files so that you can use backup files for editing purposes.

Copying, Renaming, and Backups

Don't be confused about the differences among copying a file to another name on the same disk, renaming a file, and copying a file to a different disk. If you make a copy of a file on the same disk, you have two separate files that have different names but the same contents. This gives you some protection if one small area of the disk "goes bad," but it won't help you if the disk has coffee spilled on it or is buried by your dog in the backyard.

Renaming a file changes the file's name but not its contents. It does not create a new file—you started with one file and you ended with one file. No backup copy was made.

Copying a file to another disk (or copying the whole disk with the DISKCOPY or BACKUP commands—BACKUP is discussed in Chapter 8) is the only way to make a true backup copy that won't be lost if the original disk is damaged.

As an aspiring writer, you realize that there is another novel you want to write. The filename "novel" is now too limiting. You'll want to know *which* novel. So you decide to give your file the name "opus1." Using the RENAME command, change the filename. You can enter this command with its entire name, "RENAME," or you can use the abbreviation "REN." You must include the old and the new name. To rename the file on the current drive you don't need to include drive indicators.

```
C:\>ren novel opus1 <ENTER>
```

This is a silent job by MS-DOS. It simply returns you to the C:\> prompt after renaming the file. To verify the name change, you must use DIR.

```
C:\>dir <ENTER>
```

This gives you a listing of the entire disk. Notice that the listing no longer contains "novel" but does contain "opus1."

You can also make sure that the change has occurred by using DIR with the new filename.

```
C:\>dir opus1 <ENTER>
```

MS-DOS confirms that the filename has been changed.

```
 Volume in drive C has no label
 Directory of C:\
OPUS1                  241 02-10-91   10:11a
        1 File(s)    18430208 bytes free
```

If you want to be absolutely sure that "novel" no longer exists, you can ask for a directory of that file.

```
C:\>dir novel <ENTER>
```

If no file by that name is on the disk, MS-DOS will tell you.

```
File not found
```

As you can with the other commands, you can rename a file on a drive other than the current drive by including a drive indicator. Now, rename the "novel" file on the disk in the B drive by including the drive indicator in the command.

```
C:\>ren b:novel opus1 <ENTER>
```

"Novel" is no more. Again you will be returned to the system prompt. You still have two copies of the file on each disk, but they are now named "opus1" and "bestsell." A listing of the files on the disk in B confirms this change.

```
C:\>dir b: <ENTER>
 Volume in drive B has no label
 Directory of B:\
OPUS1                  241 02-10-91   10:11a
BESTSELL               241 02-10-91   10:11a
        2 File(s)      182580 bytes free
```

Finally, if you've been carefully trying to help MS-DOS understand what you want, you may have been using drive specifiers with all of your filenames. If you type

```
C:\>ren a:novel a:opus1
```

you get

```
Invalid number of parameters
```

because MS-DOS gets confused. It doesn't want a drive specifier for the destination, though you can use one for the source if needed. The reason why MS-DOS isn't looking for a destination drive specifier is because RENAME doesn't copy the file to another disk; the file stays put but gets a new name.

You may be confused as to how this command is different from using the COPY command with a new filename; both change the name of the file. *Table 6-7* outlines the distinction.

Table 6-7.
COPY Versus RENAME

Command	Action
A:\>copy novel bestsell	Creates a duplicate file with a new name
A:\>ren novel opus1	Changes the name of the existing file

ERASING FILES

The DEL and ERASE commands provide the identical function of erasing a file or a group of files from a disk. Only when you want to erase *all* files with either of these commands, however, will a prompt ask you if this is what you want. These commands should therefore be used with caution.

Files seem to multiply at an alarming rate. Many of the files you use, such as program files, will serve you well for many years. Other files quickly become outdated or irrelevant. Even the worst pack rat shouldn't want to save every file forever. Sooner or later you'll want to do some housekeeping and clean up your files. You eliminate unneeded files with the DELETE command.

The DELETE Command

The DELETE command erases files from a disk (you can use ERASE as a synonym for DELETE).

Before using the command, make sure that the file to be erased is a duplicate or useless file. Also, enter the filename with care; if your files have similar names, a simple typing error can cause you grief because you cannot retrieve files once they have been erased (except with the use of a special utility program).

When using the COPY, RENAME, or ERASE (or DEL) commands, always use the DIR command beforehand to verify what it is that you're trying to accomplish. Use the DIR command again afterward to make sure that the command you entered accomplished what you wanted.

At this point, you have copies of your file on each of two disks. You want to do a little tidying up, so you are going to erase one of the files on each disk. You decide to stick with the name "opus1" because it most clearly defines the file for you. Before you do any erasing, it's a good idea to make sure exactly which files are on a disk. If you have a directory in front of you, you're less likely to enter a filename by error and find out too late that you made a mistake. A directory also confirm s that the file you want to delete actually resides on the disk.

With all of the copying and renaming that you have done on this file, you may be confused as to which names are still valid filenames. Get a directory of each disk.

```
C:\>dir a: <ENTER>
C:\>dir b: <ENTER>
```

First eliminate the "bestsell" file from the disk in drive A. For convenience, type a: to make A the current drive. Then type

```
A:\>del bestsell <ENTER>
```

You don't get any response from MS-DOS when you use the DELETE command. To make sure the file is gone, use the DIR command.

```
A:\>dir bestsell <ENTER>
```

The DELETE procedure is shown in *Figure 6-7.*

Figure 6-7. The DELETE Command Result

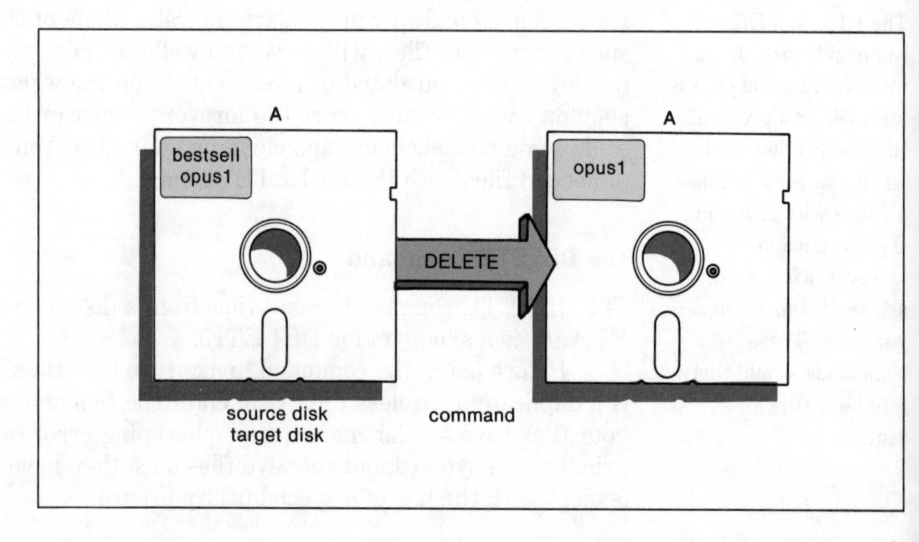

If the DELETE command has been executed properly, you get this message:

```
File not found
```

Are you worried that you have eliminated all traces of your book? Just ask for it by name.

```
A:\>dir opus1 <ENTER>
 Volume in drive A has no label
 Directory of A:\
OPUS1                241 02-10-91  10:11a
        1 File(s)     183614 bytes free
```

Perform the same procedure on the disk in drive B.

```
A:\>del b:bestsell <ENTER>
```

Use the DIR command to make sure the file is gone.

```
A:\>dir b: <ENTER>
 Volume in drive B has no label
 Directory of B:\
OPUS1                241 02-10-91  1:29p
        1 File(s)    183614 bytes free
```

Everything is as it should be. You're right back where you started, with two copies of the file, one on the disk in drive A and the backup on the disk in drive B.

If you are a bit confused by all this, it is worth some time now to practice creating, copying, typing, renaming, and erasing some more files. These commands are the "bread and butter" of your everyday work with MS-DOS. COPY, especially, is essential, because you will be making frequent backups of your files. You may be surprised by how often you use TYPE or MORE to see the contents of a file. RENAME and ERASE are commands that become increasingly useful as you accumulate more and more files and want to clarify and clean your various directories.

SUMMARY

This chapter set a new pace for your conquest of MS-DOS. First you discovered files and learned the ins and outs of file naming. In the guise of a struggling writer, you created a text file. Using this file, you put MS-DOS to work by using the TYPE, MORE, COPY,

RENAME, and DELETE commands. You are well on your way to effective file management using MS-DOS.

REVIEW

1. Every file must have a unique name, which can be up to eight characters in length followed by a period and an extension of up to three characters.
2. DOS does not allow a colon, asterisk, hyphen, or many other punctuation characters in a filename.
3. Certain names are reserved for DOS use and may not be used for any other purpose.
4. In using a command to manipulate a file, you often need to specify the name of the disk drive in which the file is stored.
5. The TYPE command is an internal command that prints the contents of a file to the screen: A:\>type b:fancy.one.
6. The MORE command is an external command that displays the contents of a file one screenful at a time. You use it with the < symbol and a filename.
7. The COPY command is an internal command that lets you copy the contents of a file to another disk or to its own disk under a different name.
8. The RENAME and DELETE commands are internal commands that let you change the names of files and erase files, respectively.

Quiz for Chapter 6

1. Data stored in files by MS-DOS can be compared to:
   - a. files stored in a file cabinet.
   - b. files stored within folders.
   - c. a stack of files in the in-basket.
   - d. a stack of files in the out-basket.
   - e. any of the above.
   - f. none of the above.
2. A filename can have up to:
   - a. no characters.
   - b. eight characters.
   - c. twenty characters.
   - d. any number of characters.
3. A file's extension is an optional part of a file's name and is normally used to indicate the type of file. An extension can be composed of:
   - a. no characters (if not used).
   - b. one character.
   - c. two characters.
   - d. three characters.
   - e. any of the above.
   - f. none of the above.
4. Filenames and extensions can be made up of:
   - a. any characters.
   - b. only numerical characters.
   - c. all alphabetic and numeric characters and some special symbol characters.
   - d. only alphabetic characters.
5. Considering the importance of regularly backing up your data files, MS-DOS provides the following commands to help you in this task:
   - a. BASIC
   - b. COPY and DISKCOPY
   - c. EDLIN
   - d. RENAME
6. An ASCII text file is a file that has:
   - a. readable characters.
   - b. only letters of the alphabet.
   - c. special formatting characters.
   - d. binary numbers.

7. The COPY command can be used to:
   a. copy a file between two disks.
   b. copy and rename a file at the same time between two disks or on the same disk.
   c. copy all files or a group of files between disks.
   d. create a short text file.
   e. all of the above.
   f. none of the above.

8. The TYPE and MORE commands are used to:
   a. make backup copies of files.
   b. display the contents of text files.
   c. list the names of all files on the disk.
   d. create text files.

9. The REN, or RENAME, command provides the function of:
   a. copying a file.
   b. renaming a file.
   c. deleting a file.
   d. listing a file.

10. The DELETE command, which is used to erase a file, a group of files, or all files on a disk, can also be accessed by entering:
    a. DEL or ERASE
    b. ERA
    c. DESTROY
    d. COPY

Tree-Structured Directories

ABOUT THIS CHAPTER

By now you are well acquainted with the use of directories. Directories are a quick reference index to the contents of your hard disk or a floppy disk. When listed with the DIR command, directories give the names and sizes of files and a date-time reference indicating when they were created or last modified.

Directories, of course, are not unique to the computer world. One frequently used directory is the phone book. The phone book is a simple directory. The entries are alphabetized by last name. An entry is listed in one location only, according to surname. When you know exactly the name you are looking for, the correct spelling, the first initial or name and the address, you can find a number quickly.

But a phone directory also illustrates a problem with simple directories. When you have too much of one kind of information, as when there are pages and pages of the same last name and that's all the information you have, phone books lose their effectiveness. Instead of being a shortcut to information, they become a burden.

This same situation can occur in your information-retrieval system. When you accumulate too many files, you may actually dread the output of the DIR command. A hard disk can hold hundreds or even thousands of files, and listing the directory can involve several screens. Examining these screens can take a lot of time. In this chapter you will learn a new method of structuring directories.

FILE STORAGE

The difficulty of accessing and storing many files demands a solution in two different areas. First, a tool is needed that can store many files in a small space. This tool, the hard, or fixed, disk, is borrowed from larger mainframe computer systems, which have always had a great deal of information to process. Hard disks are quite inexpensive, and start at 20MB capacity. Many users have hard disks that hold 40, 60, or more megabytes of data.

A tree-structured directory, introduced in MS-DOS Version 2.0, is a concept borrowed from mainframes and minicomputers. Tree-structured directories, especially on hard disks, provide considerable flexibility in the way you can store files.

The hard disk necessitates a new method of directory structuring. MS-DOS, again borrowing from mainframe computers and minicomputers, has provided the answer with the use of tree-structured directories.

In this type of structure, a main, or root, directory branches into several subdirectories, which in turn can branch into other subdirectories. To move around from root to subdirectory or from subdirectory to subdirectory, you use a path that is included in a command as a *pathname*. (You have already seen the use of a pathname. When you want to work with a file called "letter" on drive A, for example, you refer to it as *a:letter*. The use of tree-structured directories simply means that pathnames get longer because they often include one or more subdirectories.)

PREPARING YOUR DISK

Arranging the storage of files on a floppy or hard disk using tree-structured directories is especially useful when you have a large number of files and you want them organized into groups of files.

Tree-structured directories are designed to help you create order from the confusion of many, many files. But their use is not limited to the larger capacity of fixed-disk systems. You can use this structure on your floppy-disk system as well.

Your hard disk may already have directories and subdirectories on it. Although they aren't as necessary with floppy disks, you can have tree-structured directories on a floppy disk, too. In fact, in this chapter you'll be starting from scratch using a blank floppy and creating directories and subdirectories on it. That way you won't have any danger of inadvertently messing up the organization of your hard disk while you experiment. Toward the end of this chapter, and in particular in Chapter 8, you will apply and extend the ideas of this chapter to your hard disk.

First you will need an example disk. Preparing this disk is going to do two useful things for you. First, it will show you just how much you have learned. Second, it will provide you with the tools necessary for greater directory control.

If you are running MS-DOS from a hard disk, you will be working mainly from the C:\> prompt, specifying other drives as necessary. If you have a floppy-only system, make sure your system disk is in drive A. Whether or not you have a hard disk, you will be creating your new directories on the disk in drive B.

Put a blank, formatted disk in drive B. (If you need to format a disk, or run into problems with your floppy disks, please review Chapter 5.)

Now you're going to create some "dummy" files. You can use EDLIN (see Appendix A) or a word processor (in ASCII text mode) instead of COPY CON if you prefer. To make the job easier, make B your current drive first.

```
B:\>
B:\>copy con: weather <ENTER>
```

The contents of the files do not matter. We are making them short and to the point.

```
File contains weather information. <ENTER>
^Z <ENTER>
  1 File(s) copied
B:\>copy con: b:soil <ENTER>
File contains soil information. <ENTER>
^Z <ENTER>
  1 File(s) copied
B:\>copy con: yields <ENTER>
Record of last year's yields. <ENTER>
^Z <ENTER>
  1 File(s) copied
B:\>copy con: texture <ENTER>
Notes on fruit texture. <ENTER>
^Z <ENTER>
  1 File(s) copied
B:\>copy con: color <ENTER>
Notes on fruit color. <ENTER>
^Z <ENTER>
  1 File(s) copied
```

That's all there is to it. Five files created, just like that. You can take a look at your example disk with DIR.

```
B:\>dir <ENTER>

COMMAND  COM    17664   3-15-91  12:00p
TREE     COM     1513   3-15-91  12:00p
WEATHER            36   3-15-91   1:04p
SOIL               33   3-15-91   1:04p
YIELDS             31   3-15-91   1:05p
TEXTURE            25   3-15-91   1:05p
COLOR              23   3-15-91   1:06p
       7 File(s)      314368 bytes free
```

ROOT DIRECTORY AND SUBDIRECTORIES

When you use the FORMAT command to format a disk, it automatically creates the root directory. The root directory can also contain subdirectories.

Creating a root directory is easy. You have done it many times already; FORMAT automatically creates a root directory every time it formats a disk. The number of entries (names of files or other directories) that can be kept in the root directory depends on the way the sectors are grouped on the disk. It ranges from 112 entries for 360K floppy disks up to 512 or more for hard disks. The directory is the root directory of the tree-structured system. This root directory can also hold subdirectories.

A subdirectory is used to contain files separate from the root directory or other subdirectories. A subdirectory stems from the root directory much like the trunk and branches stem from the roots of a tree. Therefore, a subdirectory that originates in the root directory can also contain other subdirectories, and those subdirectories can contain more subdirectories.

This is a good time to review what you know about the DIR command (and try it out with a disk that has some files on it). If you use the DIR command with the name of a file, you get a directory listing of just that file. If you use it with a directory, however, you get a listing of every file in the directory. When, as you have been doing, you use DIR with just the name of a drive (such as DIR B:), you get a listing of that drive's root directory.

Think about the maps you use when you go into the forest. These maps contain a maze of trails, as illustrated in *Figure 7-1.* Suppose a group of hikers starts from the same point. This starting point, the "straight and narrow" trail, is like the root directory. It is the source of all other paths.

Some hikers follow the "straight and narrow" to "dead end" or "direct." These are their final destinations. Like a root directory, "straight and narrow" contains final destinations (locations where files are stored).

For other hikers, the "straight and narrow" is just the first step on a journey to "boomerang" or "over the hill." In this case, the root is the path to other subdirectories. The subdirectories "boomerang" and "over the hill" may contain final destinations of their own, where files are stored, or they may be links to other subdirectories such as "far away" and "diversion."

A subdirectory is actually viewed by MS-DOS as a special type of file containing information about the files (normal files and other subdirectories) stored within the subdirectory.

The only function of a subdirectory is to group files. Like filenames, the names of subdirectories may contain up to eight characters plus an optional three-character extension. Each subdirectory must have a unique name and it cannot be a name of a file already contained in the root directory. Subdirectory names follow all the other rules for filenames.

It is important to realize that directories and subdirectories contain files. Any of these files (locations) can also be subdirectories—paths to other files.

SPECIAL COMMANDS

There are some special commands MS-DOS reserves for creating and maintaining tree-structured directories: MKDIR, CHDIR, RMDIR, TREE, and PATH. Let's look at each of these commands. Be sure the disk you are using is in drive B.

Figure 7-1. The Map

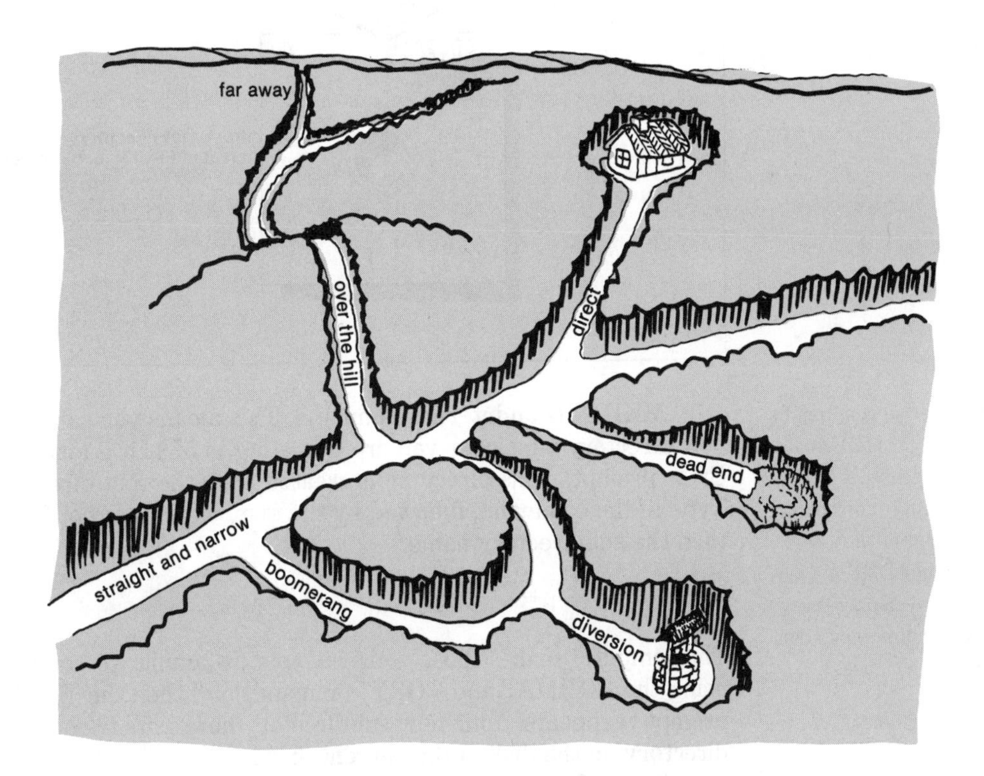

The MKDIR Command

When you format a disk it contains one directory, the original root directory. To create subdirectories on the disk, use the MKDIR (MaKe DIRectory) command. (The process is illustrated in *Figure 7-2.*) Use MKDIR (or its abbreviation, MD) to create the subdirectory FRUITS.

Figure 7-2.
The MKDIR Command

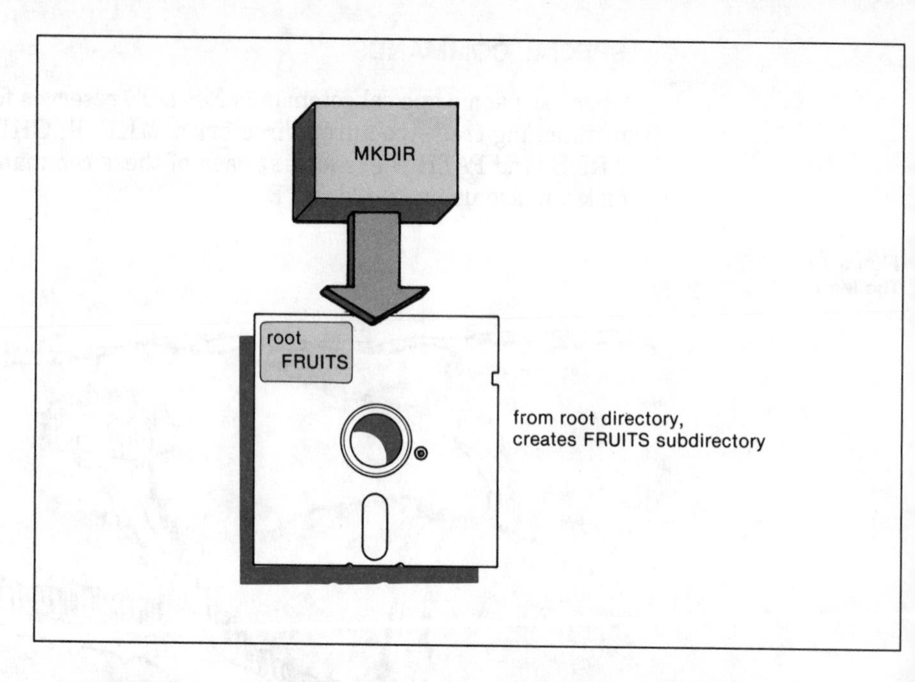

The internal command MKDIR (or MD) creates a subdirectory. After creating a subdirectory, use either of the commands DIR or TREE to display the updated directory structure of your disk.

MKDIR is an internal command. This means you can create a new directory whenever you are operating in MS-DOS (usually the C:\> prompt). This directory is created from the root directory. Type in the command, followed by the symbol for the root (\) and then the subdirectory name.

```
B:\>mkdir \fruits <ENTER>
```

The computer makes those whirring sounds familiar to you from using the FORMAT and COPY commands and then the MS-DOS prompt reappears. Your new subdirectory now exits in the root directory on the disk in the current drive.

To verify the creation of FRUITS, use DIR to list the contents of the root directory. This the same DIR command you have used before.

```
B:\>dir <ENTER>
 Volume in drive B has no label
 Directory of B:\
WEATHER              36  3-15-91   2:19p
SOIL                 33  3-15-91   2:20p
YIELDS               31  3-15-91   2:22p
TEXTURE              25  3-15-91   3:27p
COLOR                23  3-15-91   3:32p
FRUITS        <DIR>      3-15-91   3:45p
         6 File(s)   332521 bytes free
```

A subdirectory is always shown with the symbol <DIR>. Although a subdirectory is in fact a file, it cannot be copied or renamed. Only the files stored within a subdirectory can be treated as normal files.

Right there at the bottom of the list is FRUITS. MS-DOS helpfully reminds you that this is a subdirectory by including the <DIR> extension. You are also given the date and time of its creation. The second line of this listing (Directory of B:\) tells you by means of the backslash, which is the root symbol, that you are looking at the root directory of B.

Because you created this subdirectory from the root directory, you could have eliminated the first backslash. MS-DOS will always begin a directory operation from the directory you are in. In this case, you are in root, so you don't need to include the initial \.

```
B:\>mkdir fruits <ENTER>
```

Suppose you wanted to do a lot of work with the FRUITS subdirectory. You were going to copy many files and perhaps create a few new subdirectories. You can always get to a subdirectory by starting at the root and moving down one level with the pathname \FRUITS. But, just as you often change your current drive when you want to use drive B extensively, you can also change your current directory. This makes it easier to issue commands that refer only to a specified subdirectory.

The CHDIR Command

The internal CHDIR command (or CD) changes the default directory. After you start up the system, the root directory is the default directory. The CHDIR command can be used to make a subdirectory the default directory or to change the default directory back to the root.

Changing directories is as easy as making them: simply give the CHDIR (CHange DIRectory) command. The command is followed by the name of the directory that you want as your base of operations. You may use the abbreviation CD if you wish. Because you are currently in the root directory, you don't need to include the opening \ in this command.

```
B:\>chdir fruits <ENTER>
```

This command instructs MS-DOS to change from the current directory to the subdirectory FRUITS. If you have been using the recommended prompt that shows the current drive and directory, the prompt will change to B:\FRUITS. If you are using the older standard MS-DOS prompt, the prompt will still be B>. (You can now see an advantage of the fuller prompt—you always know where you are in your file system, without having to type DIR to find the current directory. These listings will show the fuller prompt.)

Having Your Prompt Show the Current Directory

If your prompt doesn't show the current directory, simply type the command PROMPT pg <ENTER>. You can put this command in your AUTOEXEC.BAT file (see Chapter 12) so that your prompt will be set up automatically at the start of each session.

You can check which directory you are in by using DIR. No beginning slash is necessary, because you believe you are currently in the FRUITS subdirectory.

```
B:\>dir <ENTER>
```

What you are requesting is a directory listing of the current directory (your numbers may be different).

```
 Volume in drive B has no label
 Directory of B:\FRUITS
.            <DIR>      3-15-91   1:29p
..           <DIR>      3-15-91   1:29p
        2 File(s)   313344 bytes free
```

The second line of the directory message tells you what you want to know. It indicates that this is a directory of the disk in drive B:\FRUITS. Because the directory name is preceded by one slash, indicating the root directory, you know that this directory is a first-level subdirectory. The next two lines of the directory listing are something you have not seen before. The single period and the double period stand for the directory itself and its parent directory. You'll explore these directory symbols a bit later. The final line of the directory listing puts you back on familiar turf. It says there are two files in this directory and gives the number of bytes still available on the disk.

While you are in this directory, you can do all the normal file operations—as long as the files exist in this directory. If you try to do something with files in the root directory or in another subdirectory, MS-DOS will respond with a "File not found" error message. You are currently stuck in this subdirectory. You must issue another CHDIR command to get out of the subdirectory.

A review of the CHDIR command appears in *Figure 7-3*.

Figure 7-3.
The CHDIR Command

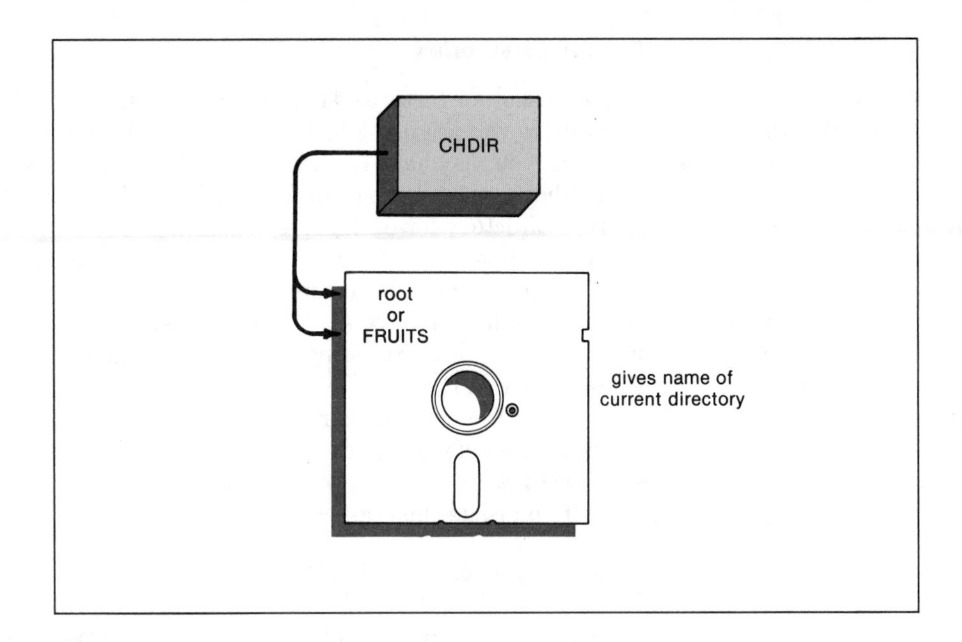

Returning to the Root Directory

When a pathname contains a single backslash it means "reference the root directory," regardless of which directory is the default.

There is a quick and easy way to get back to the root directory no matter where you are within the subdirectory structure. Issue the CHDIR command with the root symbol, the single backslash (\). This changes the default directory to the root.

```
B:\>chdir \ <ENTER>
```

Use DIR to verify that you have returned to the root directory.

```
B:\>dir <ENTER>
 Volume in drive B has no label
 Directory of B:\
WEATHER              36  3-15-91  2:19p
SOIL                 33  3-15-91  2:20p
YIELDS               31  3-15-91  2:22p
TEXTURE              25  3-15-91  3:27p
COLOR                23  3-15-91  3:32p
FRUITS        <DIR>      3-15-91  3:45p
         6 File(s)   332521 bytes free
```

You can tell you are in the root directory by the second line of the display, the directory message with a single backslash. Of course, you probably know that you are in the root because of the files listed. But when you have many files and disks, this second line will be helpful in identifying your current directory.

Current Directories

It is always important to keep track of which directories are current in each disk drive in a system. By quickly using the DIR command, you can check the current directory status of any disk drive in the system before issuing other commands.

There is another factor to keep in mind about current directories. Each drive you are using has its own separate current directory. For instance, you may have the example disk in drive B. In drive A you have other data and program files. MS-DOS keeps track of a separate current directory for each drive. This can cause some confusion when you want to perform operations from one drive to another.

Suppose you want to copy the file "yields" into the root directory on the disk in drive A. When you last worked on drive A you were using a word-processing program contained under its own subdirectory, WP.

MS-DOS views the current directories as follows: in drive B is the root directory of the example disk; in drive A is the WP subdirectory.

If you issue this copy command,

```
B:\>copy yields a: <ENTER>
```

MS-DOS would comply with your wishes. Because the current directory on drive A is WP, however, that is the directory to which it would copy the file. You can see how this might confuse you when you went searching for "yields" in the root on A. (It is simple to get the file to the right directory, but you must be sure to include the correct path.) For safety's sake, it is always a good idea to check on your current directories before you perform any operation.

To find out the current directory, just enter CHDIR by itself.

```
B:\>chdir <ENTER>
```

In this case, the change directory command really becomes the command to check (or identify) the current directory. If you were in the root directory, you would see this listing:

```
B:\
```

If you were in a subdirectory, the current directory would look like this:

```
B:\FRUITS
```

Remember that if your prompt is set up to show the current directory, it will change to show the root directory: in this case, B:\>. With the fuller prompt you don't need to use CD or DIR to check the current directory on the current drive, though you will still need to use one of these commands to check the current directory on another drive. For example, the command CD A: lists the current directory on drive A.

You can see that CHDIR is a versatile command, one that you will use a great deal. It allows you to change directories easily and to return quickly to the root directory, and it provides quick identification of the current directory. The operation of this command is outlined in *Figure 7-4*.

Figure 7-4. Current Directory

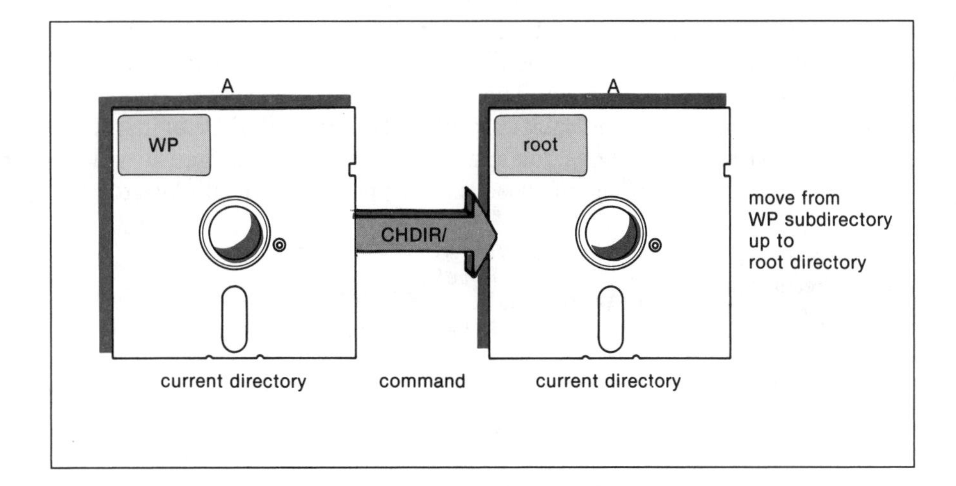

COPYING FILES TO A SUBDIRECTORY

When you listed the contents of the FRUITS subdirectory, you noticed that the directory listed only the . and .. files; the rest of the subdirectory was empty. How do you get files into a subdirectory? The same way you always move files, with the COPY command.

On the disk in drive B you have two files, “weather” and “soil,” along with some other files. Because the “weather” file contains weather data on all fruit crops and the “soil” file contains soil data on all fruit crops, we would like to have these files in the FRUITS subdirectory.

Make sure that root is your current directory. Enter CHDIR to check the current directory status; if necessary, enter CHDIR \ to get to the root directory. “Weather” and “soil” are now part of the root directory. To be sure that everything is according to plan, use DIR to check the directory.

```
B:\>dir <ENTER>
 Volume in drive B has no label
```

```
 Directory of B:\
WEATHER                36  3-15-91  2:19p
SOIL                   33  3-15-91  2:20p
YIELDS                 31  3-15-91  2:22p
TEXTURE                25  3-15-91  3:27p
COLOR                  23  3-15-91  3:32p
FRUITS         <DIR>       3-15-91  3:45p
        6 File(s)   332521 bytes free
```

When you are copying files between directories, only the destination directory name needs to be specified with the command, much like a disk-drive identifier is used. Likewise, when you display the contents of a subdirectory that isn't the default, only the subdirectory's name needs to be specified.

Because this is the same procedure you use to copy files from one disk to another, think of the transfer in terms of source and target. The directory that currently holds the files is the source directory. The subdirectory to which the files will be copied is the target directory. To MS-DOS, FRUITS is just like any other file. As long as you specify a source and a target, it will copy the files, even if one of those files happens to be a subdirectory.

```
B:\>copy weather fruits <ENTER>
        1 File(s) copied
B:\>copy soil fruits <ENTER>
        1 File(s) copied
```

You now have two new files in your FRUITS subdirectory. The files have not been deleted from the root directory; they have simply been duplicated in the FRUITS subdirectory. The procedure is reviewed in *Figure 7-5*. You can check this by using DIR. First make sure the files are still in the root directory. Because this is your current directory, just enter DIR.

```
B:\>dir <ENTER>
 Volume in drive B has no label
 Directory of B:\
WEATHER                36  3-15-91  1:04p
SOIL                   33  3-15-91  1:04p
YIELDS                 31  3-15-91  1:05p
TEXTURE                25  3-15-91  1:05p
COLOR                  23  3-15-91  1:06p
FRUITS         <DIR>       3-15-91  1:29p
        6 File(s)   292119 bytes free
```

You can see that both "weather" and "soil" are still in this directory.

One way to verify that "weather" and "soil" are also part of the FRUITS subdirectory is to change the current directory to FRUITS and then use the DIR command.

```
B:\>chdir fruits <ENTER>
B:\>dir <ENTER>
```

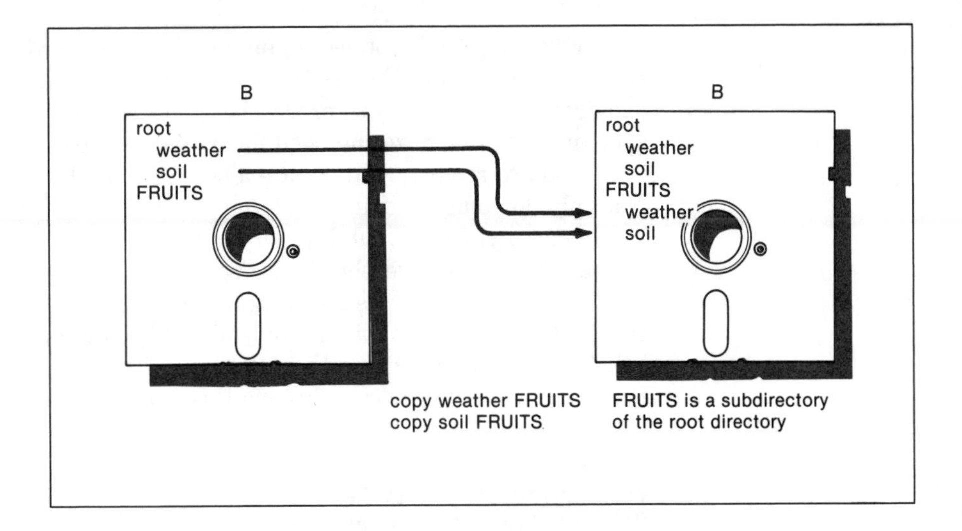

Figure 7-5. Copying Files to a Subdirectory

You can also check on FRUITS without leaving the root directory—that is, without changing the current directory. Just use a pathname to ask for a directory listing.

```
B:\>dir \fruits <ENTER>
 Volume in drive B has no label
 Directory of B:\FRUITS
.            <DIR>      3-15-91   1:29p
..           <DIR>      3-15-91   1:29p
WEATHER              36 3-15-91   1:04p
SOIL                 33 3-15-91   1:04p
        4 File(s)   292119 bytes free
```

You can see that the two files have been added to the listing of the FRUITS directory. A comparison of the amount of bytes still free will show you that the space on the disk has been reduced by the number of bytes in these two files.

Both root and FRUITS exist on the same disk. More important, two copies of "weather" and "soil" now exist on the same disk, and they both have the same name. This violates one of the cardinal rules of file naming: every file *on a disk* must have a unique name.

We have to make a slight modification of the rule. From now on, every file *in a directory* must have a unique name.

This capability of having duplicate files has many advantages. With tree-structured directories, you cannot perform an operation on a file unless it is located in the subdirectory in which you are working. So sometimes, if files are not very long, it is convenient to have duplicates of certain files in different subdirectories.

For instance, if you were going to do some word processing on specific files, it would be useful to have these files in the same subdirectory as your word-processing program. (Later you'll learn some ways to minimize the need for duplicate files.)

You are ready now to create a new subdirectory on this disk. Not only do you grow fruits, but you also have extensive lumber holdings. So your new subdirectory is named LUMBER. It so happens that your "weather" and "soil" files also contain information on conditions related to effective forest management. So you want these files in this new subdirectory also. If you are still in the \FRUITS directory, change back to root with CHDIR\. Starting in the root directory, you can perform this operation with three simple commands.

```
B:\>mkdir lumber <ENTER>
B:\>copy weather lumber <ENTER>
        1 File(s) copied
B:\>copy soil lumber <ENTER>
        1 File(s) copied
```

To check on the creation of this subdirectory, ask for a directory of root, your current directory.

```
B:\>dir <ENTER>
 Volume in drive B has no label
 Directory of B:\
WEATHER             36  3-15-91   1:04p
SOIL                33  3-15-91   1:04p
YIELDS              31  3-15-91   1:05p
TEXTURE             25  3-15-91   1:05p
COLOR               23  3-15-91   1:06p
FRUITS       <DIR>      3-15-91   1:29p
LUMBER       <DIR>      3-15-91   1:42p
         9 File(s)  289047 bytes free
```

The new subdirectory LUMBER is now part of your root directory.

Now make sure that the two files have been copied to the new subdirectory.

```
B:\>dir \lumber <ENTER>
 Volume in drive B has no label
 Directory of B:\LUMBER
.            <DIR>      3-15-91   1:42p
..           <DIR>      3-15-91   1:42p
WEATHER             36  3-15-91   1:04p
SOIL                33  3-15-91   1:04p
         4 File(s)  289047 bytes free
```

You can now create new directories and modify their contents to fit your needs.

PATHNAMES

A file stored anywhere in the directory tree-structure of a disk can be referenced or accessed from any other location by using a pathname.

You find your way around in the directory by specifying a pathname. This is simply a list of names that tells MS-DOS where to start and which subdirectories to use to get to a final destination. Each subdirectory is separated from the next with a backslash (\). In *Figure 7-1,* the path to the "edge of the forest" would be

\boomerang\diversion\edge of the forest

Notice that the root directory, "straight and narrow," is not mentioned in this pathname. That is because the root directory is indicated by the initial backslash in the pathname. You never actually enter the directory name "root," instead you use an initial backslash as a shorthand for this directory.

Assume you are an agriculturist anxious to begin organizing your files. Your files are now on a disk (the one you created earlier), and they are stored in the root directory. Files are always stored in the root directory until you change directory or tell MS-DOS to put them somewhere else. First, you already have a subdirectory called FRUITS. Within FRUITS you are going to create a subdirectory called CHERRIES. The CHERRIES subdirectory will contain a file named "yields." To clear a path to this file, tell MS-DOS where to start and then give clear directions.

ROOT→FRUITS→CHERRIES→YIELDS→
\fruits\cherries\yields

This path translates into: start from the root (indicated by the initial backslash), go to the file FRUITS (which is a subdirectory), go to the file CHERRIES (which is a subdirectory), and then find the file "yields."

Almost all the commands in MS-DOS can be performed on specific files in different subdirectories. All you need to do is to tell MS-DOS which path to take to get to the file.

Pathnames are the organizing tools for sophisticated use of your disks. Subdirectories can save you lots of time and help you keep your files better organized. Pathnames are a quick way to create, copy, delete, and reorganize files. But don't get carried away. The best tree-structured directory is one that is simple. If you make your structure too complicated, you will get lost on the path, and MS-DOS will spend a lot of time getting to the specified destination. One good idea, until you are more familiar with subdirectories and pathnames, is to limit your subdirectories to the root directory.

ACCESSING FILES

Your tree-structured directory currently has two levels. The home base is the parent, or root, directory. This is level zero, or the starting point. Beneath this level there are two first-level subdirectories, FRUIT and LUMBER. But what about the files contained in these directories? How do you get to a specific file within a specific subdirectory?

With the correct use of pathnames, you can easily move around in or reference any part of a directory structure.

To find a file, MS-DOS must have two pieces of information: the name of the file and the name of the directory that contains that file. Because subdirectories can contain other subdirectories, you need to specify the exact path that leads to the file you want.

You can get to a file in two different ways. The first is to start in the root directory and then list all of the subdirectories that intervene between the root and the directory holding the file. The second is to change to the desired subdirectory with CHDIR and then specify the file.

Suppose you want a listing of a file in the FRUITS directory called "weather." You are now in the root directory. Ask for the listing using the correct pathname.

```
B:\>type fruits\weather <ENTER>
```

Or use CHDIR to change the current directory.

```
B:\>chdir fruits <ENTER>
```

Then use the TYPE command.

```
B:\>type weather <ENTER>
```

Your FRUITS subdirectory contains files that pertain to all your fruit crops. But now you want to create within FRUITS another subdirectory, CHERRIES. CHERRIES will be a second-level subdirectory; that is, it will be two levels down from the root directory. Get back to the root directory by using CHDIR\ (you might still be in LUMBER). To create subdirectories within subdirectories you use the MKDIR (or simply MD) command.

```
B:\>md \fruits\cherries <ENTER>
```

In this pathname you specified two directory names: the subdirectory that already exists and the new subdirectory you are creating. All directories must be separated by slashes. The actual message received by MS-DOS from this command translates as, "Starting from the root directory (indicated by the initial backslash), go down to the first-level subdirectory FRUITS and create a new second-level subdirectory named CHERRIES."

As usual, MS-DOS does not inform you that the directory was created; it simply returns to the prompt (though the prompt may change). You can confirm that this subdirectory now exists directly from your current position in the root directory.

```
B:\>dir fruits <ENTER>
```

Here is how the display looks:

```
 Volume in drive B has no label
 Directory of B:\FRUITS
.              <DIR>      3-15-91   1:29p
..             <DIR>      3-15-91   1:29p
WEATHER               36  3-15-91   1:04p
SOIL                  33  3-15-91   1:04p
CHERRIES       <DIR>      3-15-91   1:45p
         5 file(s)   288023 bytes free
```

You can see that the CHERRIES subdirectory is now part of FRUITS.

If you want to check the contents of CHERRIES, you must give the correct path.

```
B:\>dir \fruits\cherries <ENTER>
```

The first backslash tells MS-DOS that FRUITS is a subdirectory of the root; the next slash indicates that CHERRIES is a subdirectory of FRUITS. If you wish, you can eliminate the first slash because root is your current directory, and MS-DOS always begins its search with the current directory. Here is the listing for the previous command:

```
 Volume in drive B has no label
 Directory of B:\FRUITS\CHERRIES
.              <DIR>      3-15-91   1:45p
..             <DIR>      3-15-91   1:45p
         2 File(s)   288023 bytes free
```

The second line in the listing confirms that this is a second-level directory, a subdirectory of a subdirectory. The entire directory structure is shown in *Figure 7-6.* Of course, the subdirectories can contain many other files, but for simplicity we show only the ones we are using in our examples.

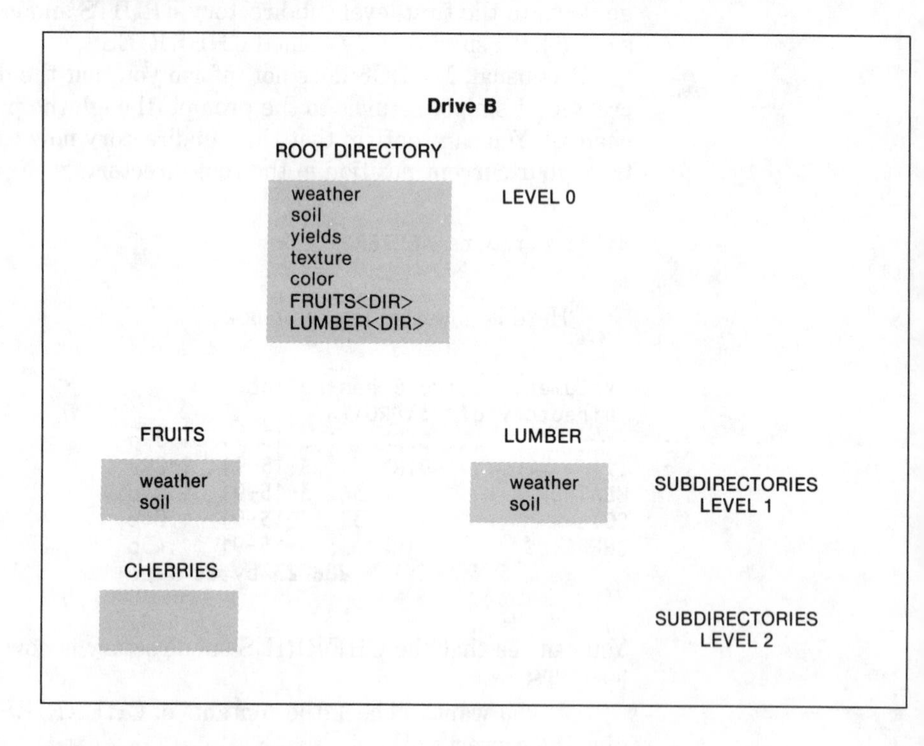

Figure 7-6. A Sample Directory Structure

Establishing Paths

Almost any MS-DOS command can be used on any file in a subdirectory. The only secret is to establish the correct path to the file. The CHERRIES subdirectory in the FRUITS subdirectory is empty. Copy the "yields" file, currently in the root directory, into this new subdirectory. Make sure root is your current directory before attempting this.

```
B:\>copy yields fruits\cherries <ENTER>
```

If you want, check the contents of this subdirectory with DIR.

```
B:\>dir fruits\cherries <ENTER>
 Volume in drive B has no label
 Directory of B:\FRUITS\CHERRIES
```

```
.              <DIR>      3-15-91   1:45p
..             <DIR>      3-15-91   1:45p
YIELDS                31  3-15-91   1:05p
        3 File(s)   286999 bytes free
```

Or you can specify the file itself.

```
B:\>dir fruits\cherries\yields <ENTER>
 Volume in drive B has no label
 Directory of B:\FRUITS\CHERRIES
YIELDS                31  3-15-91   1:05p
        1 File(s)   285975 bytes free
```

When you are tracing a path to a file, first list the intervening subdirectories (separated by slashes). The filename comes last. This illustrates how you move down through a directory. But you can also move up in the tree structure. To move up one level, just change the directory to the parent directory.

```
B:\>cd fruits\cherries <ENTER>
```

Your current directory is now the subdirectory CHERRIES. Use DIR to be sure you are in the correct subdirectory.

```
B:\>dir <ENTER>
 Volume in drive B has no label
 Directory of B:\FRUITS\CHERRIES
.              <DIR>      3-15-91   1:45p
..             <DIR>      3-15-91   1:45p
YIELDS                31  3-15-91   1:05p
        3 File(s)   285975 bytes free
```

A Shortcut

The special symbols . and .. shown in subdirectories represent special instructions for moving around in the directory structure.

Now you are finally going to find out the meaning of the . (period) and .. (double period) directory entries.

In the preceding example, you moved up in the directory structure by using the CHDIR command and listing the name of the parent directory. This is a valid way to move up in a directory; however, MS-DOS has given us a shortcut for moving up one level while not affecting the current directory.

Be sure your current directory is still CHERRIES. Enter this command, leaving a space between DIR and the periods.

```
B:\>dir .. <ENTER>
```

MS-DOS will respond with a display.

```
 Volume in drive B has no label
 Directory of B:\FRUITS
.            <DIR>        3-15-91  1:29p
..           <DIR>        3-15-91  1:29p
WEATHER              36   3-15-91  1:04p
SOIL                 31   3-15-91  1:04p
CHERRIES     <DIR>        3-15-91  1:45p
        5 File(s)    285975 bytes free
```

How did you get back to FRUITS? You moved up one level.

The double period symbol tells MS-DOS: "Move me to the current directory's parent directory." As long as you are not in the root directory, you can use the .. convention to move up one level without specifying the directory's name. This does not affect the status of your current directory (unless you use it with the CHDIR command).

Now issue the DIR command with a single period, leaving a space between DIR and the period.

```
B:\>dir . <ENTER>
 Volume in drive B has no label
 Directory of B:\FRUITS
.            <DIR>        3-15-91  1:29p
..           <DIR>        3-15-91  1:29p
YIELDS              31    3-15-91  1:05p
        3 File(s)    285975 bytes free
```

The CHERRIES subdirectory is listed. The single period tells MS-DOS: "Apply this command to me, the current directory." Notice that using the period conventions does not change the current directory. These conventions are used only in subdirectories; they do not appear in root directories. You don't have to use these symbols, and don't do so at first if they confuse you. But gradually, as you become more familiar with tree-structured directories, try experimenting with their use again. They may save you a lot of time.

MOVING AROUND IN A TREE-STRUCTURED DIRECTORY

To understand the usefulness of the tree-structured directory system, you need to practice moving around in the structure. To do this, you use the COPY command.

First, let's add a little complexity to the tree. You now want to enter your records on a second crop, peaches. The logical place for this new data is a subdirectory under FRUITS. Move back to the root directory using CHDIR\ (assuming you are still in the FRUITS/CHERRIES subdirectory).

```
B:\>mkdir \fruits\peaches <ENTER>
```

The information that you want to store in this subdirectory is in the file "color," which is in the root directory.

```
B:\>copy color fruits\peaches <ENTER>
```

The system replies:

```
1 File(s) copied
```

To illustrate a point, assume that the file you want to include in this directory is on another disk. You would have to use a different command.

```
B:\>copy a:color fruits\peaches <ENTER>
```

MS-DOS allows you to copy information from a file on one disk to a directory or subdirectory on a disk in another drive. All you need to do is include the drive indicator.

There is one more file in the root directory that you want to include in this PEACHES subdirectory. It is called "texture."

```
B:\>copy texture fruits\peaches <ENTER>
```

If you want to, use the DIR command now to verify the new subdirectory and its contents.

```
B:\>dir fruits\peaches <ENTER>
 Volume in drive B has no label
 Directory of B:\FRUITS\PEACHES
.            <DIR>      3-15-91   1:53p
..           <DIR>      3-15-91   1:53p
COLOR               23  3-15-91   1:06p
TEXTURE             25  3-15-91   1:05p
        4 File(s)   283927 bytes free
```

As a final step, we are going to create a new subdirectory in LUMBER called REDWOOD.

```
B:\>mkdir lumber\redwood <ENTER>
```

Figure 7-7 is a map of the complete tree-structured directory.

Figure 7-7.
The Completed Directory Structure

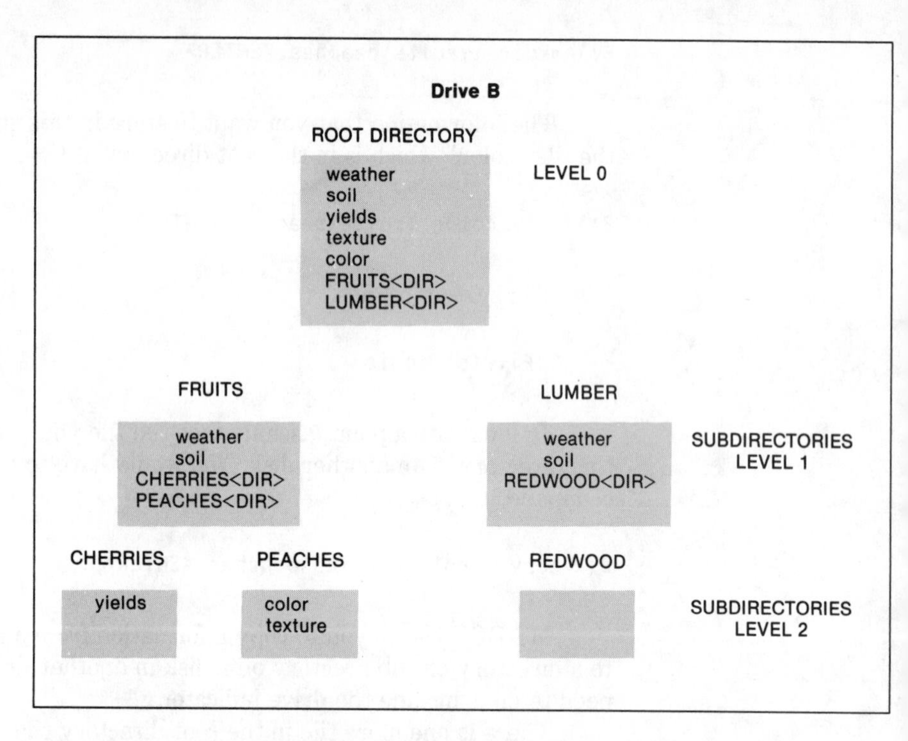

Within the CHERRIES subdirectory is a file called "yields." Now you want to use the same general contents in your REDWOOD subdirectory. Here are the steps you take to transfer "yields" from one subdirectory to another. The path is illustrated in *Figure 7-8*.

Figure 7-8.
Moving Around Subdirectories

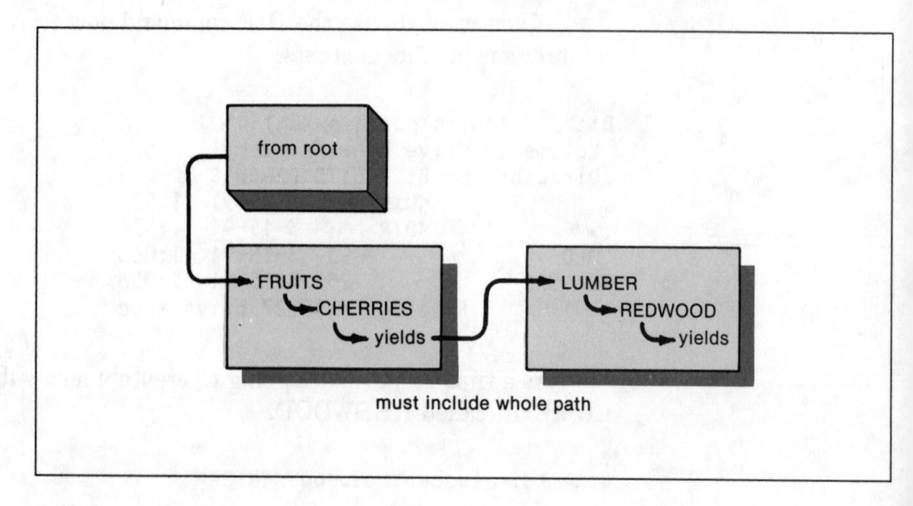

First, make sure you are in the root directory. Because you are dealing with second-level directories, you must go up to the root and then down into the subdirectories. You can't go across to level-one or level-two subdirectories; the path must go through the common link, the root.

```
B:\>copy fruits\cherries\yields lumber\redwood <ENTER>
        1 File(s) copied
```

A DIR command confirms the copy.

```
B:\>dir lumber\redwood <ENTER>
 Volume in drive B has no label
 Directory of B:\LUMBER\REDWOOD
.            <DIR>     3-15-91  1:56p
..           <DIR>     3-15-91  1:56p
YIELDS              31  3-15-91  1:05p
        3 File(s)   281879 bytes free
```

With tree-structured directories, you can move quickly within a complex structure. This is essential when you are dealing with a large number of files on a fixed disk. But using the COPY command in this way also demonstrates the importance of clear, easily defined paths. You can see that if you create too many subdirectories within subdirectories, you could easily get lost in the resulting maze. Keep the paths simple.

MAINTAINING YOUR FILES

All of the rules normally associated with the COPY command are in effect when you are working with subdirectories. Suppose, for instance, that you want to copy the contents of the subdirectory PEACHES into REDWOOD. You want to copy all the files in the subdirectory, so the easiest method is to use a wildcard with the COPY command. PEACHES contains two files, "color" and "texture."

```
B:\>copy \fruits\peaches\*.* \lumber\redwood <ENTER>
```

MS-DOS will tell you what is going on.

```
B:\FRUITS\PEACHES\COLOR
B:\FRUITS\PEACHES\TEXTURE
        2 File(s) copied
```

Both files in PEACHES are now also in REDWOOD.

The usual caution when using wildcards applies: make sure you want all the files, or a number of files that are similar, to be copied before becoming involved with wildcards.

Now check the contents of LUMBER/REDWOOD with the DIR command.

```
B:\>dir \lumber\redwood <ENTER>
 Volume in drive B has no label
 Directory of B:\LUMBER\REDWOOD
.            <DIR>       3-15-91   1:56p
..           <DIR>       3-15-91   1:56p
YIELDS                31 3-15-91   1:05p
COLOR                 23 3-15-91   1:06p
TEXTURE               25 3-15-91   1:05p
        5 File(s)   279831 bytes free
```

After you have worked to build a beautiful, well-designed tree-structured directory, you have reason to be proud. But eventually some of your directories will become obsolete. If you just go on building bigger and better directories, you will make path finding both confusing and time-consuming.

Just as MS-DOS provides DEL (or ERASE) to eliminate no-longer-needed files, it also has a command to rid you of unnecessary directories.

The RMDIR Command

The internal command RMDIR (or RD) is used to remove a subdirectory. A subdirectory can be erased, however, only if it is empty of files or other subdirectories.

The RMDIR (ReMove DIRectory) command helps you with the housekeeping chores in your directory structure. But before you can eliminate a directory, you must first provide for the files inside it. This is a safety feature that MS-DOS builds into the directory structure. It can prevent you from accidentally erasing a file while eliminating a directory.

Suppose that halfway through the growing season there is a terrible infestation of Tasmanian peach flies. Your entire peach crop is down the drain, and you destroy all your peach trees. You no longer need your PEACHES subdirectory cluttering up your directory structure. To remove this directory you must first get to the correct subdirectory.

```
B:\>chdir fruits\peaches <ENTER>
B:\>dir <ENTER>
```

As with all erase functions, be careful. Be sure you are in the correct subdirectory.

```
 Volume in drive B has no label
 Directory of B:\FRUITS\PEACHES
.            <DIR>       3-15-91   1:53p
```

```
..              <DIR>     3-15-91  1:53p
COLOR                 23  3-15-91  1:06p
TEXTURE               25  3-15-91  1:05p
         4 File(s)   279831 bytes free
```

Be sure you don't need any of the files in the subdirectory before you erase them.

```
B:\>erase *.* <ENTER>
Are you sure (Y/N)? y <ENTER>
```

You answer *y*.

With the files gone, you can erase the subdirectory. You must be one level up from the subdirectory you want to erase. Move up to the FRUITS subdirectory.

```
B:\>cd .. <ENTER>
```

Now remove the subdirectory.

```
B:\>rmdir peaches <ENTER>
```

It is a good idea to use DIR to be sure the subdirectory is gone.

```
B:\>dir <ENTER>
 Volume in drive B has no label
 Directory of B:\FRUITS
.               <DIR>     3-15-91  1:29p
..              <DIR>     3-15-91  1:29p
WEATHER               36  3-15-91  1:04p
SOIL                  33  3-15-91  1:04p
CHERRIES        <DIR>     3-15-91  1:45p
         5 File(s)   282903 bytes free
```

COPYING DIRECTORY TREES WITH XCOPY

Starting with MS-DOS 3.2, you have available a powerful new version of the COPY command, called XCOPY (for "extended COPY"). Thus far you have only been copying one (or a few) files at a time. You can copy a whole directory to another directory using wildcards, for example:

```
B:\>copy fruits\*.* lumber <ENTER>
```

copies everything in the FRUITS directory to the LUMBER directory (perhaps all you have left is fruit trees, and the fruit isn't doing well this year . . .).

But suppose you want to duplicate a whole set of directories and subdirectories, perhaps as a backup on another disk. With COPY, you would first have to use MKDIR to make each of the directories on the destination disk. Then you would have to copy each directory to the corresponding directory on the other disk. For example, suppose you want to copy the whole directory structure that you've created on drive B to your hard disk, under the directory FARMING. Here's how you might do it.

First, change to your hard disk and make the directories and subdirectories:

```
B:\>c:
C:\>mkdir farming <ENTER>
C:\>mkdir farming\fruits <ENTER>
C:\>mkdir farming\fruits\cherries <ENTER>
C:\>mkdir farming\fruits\peaches <ENTER>
C:\>mkdir farming\lumber\redwood <ENTER>
```

That's a lot of typing! Now you have to copy all of the contents of these directories from drive B to drive C. You might try to do it this way.

```
C:\>copy b:\*.* farming <ENTER>
```

Using the wildcard ought to tell MS-DOS to copy all of the files in the root directory of B to the FARMING directory on drive C. In fact, it does copy all of the ordinary files in the root directory of drive B.

```
C:\>dir farming <ENTER>
 Volume of drive C has no label
 Directory of  C:\FARMING
.             <DIR>     3-15-91  4:13p
..            <DIR>     3-15-91  4:13p
WEATHER             36  3-15-91  1:29p
SOIL                31  3-15-91  1:04p
        4 File(s)  1456128 bytes free
```

But where are the subdirectories FRUITS and LUMBER, and their subdirectories? Unfortunately, COPY copies only *files* in the specified directory, not subdirectories, or the files in subdirectories.

Now try doing the job with XCOPY. First, remove the directories you created on drive C. (This isn't really necessary, but it helps demonstrate how XCOPY will create subdirectories.)

```
C:\>rmdir farming <ENTER>
C:\>rmdir farming\fruits <ENTER>
```

```
C:\>rmdir farming\fruits\cherries <ENTER>
C:\>rmdir farming\fruits\peaches <ENTER>
C:\>rmdir farming\lumber\redwood <ENTER>
```

Now you can copy the whole directory structure from drive B to the FARMING directory on drive C, with just one command:

```
C:\>xcopy b: \farming /s <ENTER>
Does FARMING specify a file name
or directory name on the target disk d
Reading source file(s)
                    ← path for each file copied is listed
```

Your command tells XCOPY to copy everything on drive B—files, subdirectories, and files in subdirectories—to the FARMING directory on drive C. The /s switch is necessary to specify that subdirectories as well as the root directory be copied. It doesn't matter that you haven't created any of the subdirectories for FARMING on drive C, because XCOPY will create any subdirectories that have files on the source disk. (If you want it to create empty subdirectories on the destination as well, you can add the /e switch.)

Why does MS-DOS ask you whether the destination refers to a directory or a file? It makes a big difference: if FARMING is intended to be a destination *file*, then everything on drive B will be copied to this file, with each copy overwriting the previous one. You will end up with a file called "farming" that will be a copy of the last file found on drive B! Therefore it is very important to type a 'd' to tell XCOPY that the destination is a directory. As you recall, when the destination of a copy operation is a directory, the source files are copied into the directory—they don't replace the directory.

To be on the safe side, you can create the destination directory with the MKDIR command before you give the XCOPY command. (You don't have to create the subdirectories, just the main directory.)

It is a good idea to check the results of any COPY or XCOPY command with the DIR command. When you get a directory listing of \FARMING, you will find that all of the subdirectories, as well as the files, from drive B have been copied there.

```
 Volume in drive C has no label
 Directory of  C:\FARMING
.             <DIR>      3-15-91   4:13p
..            <DIR>      3-15-91   4:13p
WEATHER             36   3-15-91   1:29p
SOIL                31   3-15-91   1:04p
FRUIT         <DIR>      3-15-91   4:13p
LUMBER        <DIR>      3-15-91   4:13p
        4 File(s)  1357824 bytes free
```

And if you look at the directories of FRUIT and LUMBER, you will find that all of *their* files have also been copied!

You can see that XCOPY can be very useful. Besides copying the directory structure from a floppy disk to your hard disk, you can also copy a set of directories from your hard disk to a floppy for backup or exchange with another user.

XCOPY has a variety of other switches, many of which work like the BACKUP command, discussed in Chapter 8. After you have read that chapter, check the entry on XCOPY in your MS-DOS manual and do some experimenting.

When you modify your tree structure frequently, it is often difficult to keep track of exactly which files and subdirectories belong where. How can you quickly get an overview of the tree structure on a disk?

One way is to use DIR and note all the files with the <DIR> extension. Then you can use CHDIR to reach each of these subdirectories and then use DIR again, noting which are <DIR> files here and so on. This is time-consuming and frustrating. Once again, MS-DOS has anticipated this need and provides a command to give you a guide to your overall directory.

The TREE Command

The external command TREE is used to display the entire directory structure of a disk, including all files stored in each subdirectory.

TREE is an external command that displays every pathname on a disk. Make sure you are in the root directory when you issue this command. Include the /f switch to get a listing of files in each subdirectory.

```
B:\>tree /f <ENTER>
```

Here is the TREE display for our example disk.

```
DIRECTORY PATH LISTING FOR VOLUME ???????????

Path: \FRUITS
Sub-directories:    CHERRIES
Files:              WEATHER
                    SOIL

Path: \FRUITS\CHERRIES
Sub-directories:    None
Files:              YIELDS

Path: \LUMBER
Sub-directories:    REDWOOD
Files:              WEATHER
                    SOIL
```

```
Path: \LUMBER\REDWOOD
Sub-directories:    None
Files:              YIELDS
                    COLOR
                    TEXTURE
```

The appearance of the tree display will vary somewhat with your version of MS-DOS, but the same information will be shown. In MS-DOS 4.0, by the way, you can get a tree display that starts at any directory or subdirectory—you don't have to start from the root directory.

MS-DOS looks for files you request in only one location. When you call for a file, MS-DOS only looks for it in the current directory. While if you specify a pathname, then MS-DOS only looks there. This is true whether you are using an MS-DOS command, such as COPY, or executing a program that needs a data file. Only one directory is searched, either the current one or the one specified in a path. This is also true of your program files. When you call for a program, MS-DOS immediately searches for it in the current directory. If it is not found, it won't be executed.

The PATH Command

The internal command PATH is used to establish a search path for external commands, program files, and batch files. When a command is entered at the MS-DOS prompt, and a search path has been defined, MS-DOS will first search the current directory on the current disk drive. If the file is not found, MS-DOS will continue searching according to the guidelines established by PATH.

You are now developing quite an elaborate directory structure. One problem you may encounter is that you want to run an external MS-DOS command, but MS-DOS can't find it because you are in a different directory (or even on a different drive). When you installed MS-DOS it may have already helped you with this problem by including a PATH command.

The PATH command does not have anything to do with the use of pathnames in general. It is only used to search for DOS commands, programs, files, and batch files not found in the current directory. The names in a PATH command must be separated by semicolons.

Because you don't have any program files or batch files in your directory, you will have to abandon the orchards for a moment. Imagine that you are in a subdirectory on drive C that is called \NEWPROGS. You're looking for a program called RUNSUM.EXE. Here is how you tell MS-DOS where to look for the program.

```
C:\>path \ACCTING;\PROGS\MISC;\ <ENTER>
```

Then, when you enter the program name RUNSUM.EXE, MS-DOS searches for the program in four places:

- The current directory (this is automatic).
- The ACCTING directory under the root.
- The MISC directory under the PROGS directory under the root.
- The root itself (indicated by \).

The PATH command can also search in directories on other drives. Just include the drive designator in the PATH command.

```
C:\>path \ACCTING;\PROGS\MISC;A:\OLDPROGS <ENTER>
```

If you enter PATH without any other information, MS-DOS will search the last path it was given. To discontinue this extensive searching feature, enter PATH with a single semicolon.

```
C:\>path ; <ENTER>
```

By the way, some programs have to find special "overlay" files in order to work properly. PATH searches only for executable files, but the APPEND command (introduced with MS-DOS 3.3) may allow your program to find the files it needs. You use the APPEND command in the same way as the PATH command.

```
C:\>append \progs\misc <ENTER>
```

tells programs to look in the PROGS and MISC directory to find their overlays or special data files. To remove the APPEND feature, follow APPEND with just a semicolon:

```
C:\>append ; <ENTER>
```

After this command, the search reverts to the current directory only.

SOME GUIDELINES

Like many tools in MS-DOS, tree-structured directories can be useful or mystifying. The idea is to start slowly and build as you go. As long as your directory structure makes sense to you and is logical for your needs, it will save you time and energy.

Don't get carried away creating a new subdirectory for every file. For one thing, if you create too many directories and subdirectories, you will have a hard time finding anything on the disk. It would be like an office that had a separate file folder for every single incoming letter. MS-DOS, too, slows down when it has to search too many directories or too many layers of directories. Most users have no need to go further down than three levels: root, subdirectories of the root, and their subdirectories.

Although the search path established by the PATH command can be changed at any time, a standard search path can be defined in your AUTOEXEC.BAT file so that it is automatically defined when the system is powered up or is reset.

When creating directories, keep in mind the mechanics of moving around inside them. While it is easy to move up and down a limb, it is impossible to swing between limbs. Make sure that your levels contain logical subdirectories and that you eliminate the need to go up and down again to get to a file you use frequently.

On floppy-disk systems it is a good idea to keep all your subdirectories in the root. This makes it easy for you to find exactly what you need without time-consuming searches. If possible, keep data files that run with specific programs in the same directory. Then, when a program needs a data file, it can find it right in the current directory.

Keep in the root directory all utilities and command files that you use frequently. This will save you time and make them available for all files in the directories under the root.

You can even keep most of your programs in the root directory. Once you have established a home for your programs, use PATH to keep these programs readily available.

Give your subdirectories distinct names.

Remember that subdirectory files also occupy space on a disk and grow larger as more files are stored in them. It is therefore wise to keep the number of subdirectories to a minimum when using floppy disks. A complex directory structure on a hard disk does not require as much attention to disk space, however, because of the much larger storage capacities.

SUMMARY

This concludes your introduction to tree-structured directories. Using this tool, with restraint, on floppy-disk systems is a convenience. But using this tool on fixed-disk systems is a necessity. In this chapter you have learned about root directories and subdirectories, traveling along the path to better file organization. In addition to learning how to put files in a subdirectory, you have moved around inside the tree-structured directory to create pathnames to find and store your files. Finally, you have become familiar with the directory commands: MKDIR, CHDIR, RMDIR, XCOPY, TREE, PATH, and APPEND.

REVIEW

1. Tree-structured directories include a main, or root, directory and sets of subdirectories related through paths.
2. Subdirectories allow you to group files and even other subdirectories into categories.
3. A pathname specifies the straight-line path through names of upper- and lower-level directories, separated by backslashes, to get to a filename; MS-DOS commands will work with pathnames as if they were extended filenames.
4. The MKDIR command lets you create a subdirectory.
5. The CHDIR command (same as CD) followed by a pathname lets you change from one directory or subdirectory to another; used by itself, it tells you the name of the current directory.
6. The period and double period (. ..) are shortcut conventions that direct commands to operate on the current and parent directories, respectively.
7. The XCOPY command can be used to copy whole sets of directories and subdirectories from one disk to another.
8. The RMDIR command lets you remove subdirectories, but only after you move or erase all files within it.
9. The TREE command displays every pathname on the disk; the /f switch lists all files in each subdirectory.
10. The PATH command specifies a list of directories that MS-DOS can search in order to find the command or program that you want to run. The APPEND command provides a similar list that programs can use to find their overlay files.

Quiz for Chapter 7

1. Tree-structured directories allow you to:
   a. create structures of directories on disks that resemble the structure of a tree (root, trunk, and branches).
   b. create subdirectories.
   c. create subdirectories within subdirectories.
   d. any of the above.
   e. none of the above.
2. The directory that is always created after a disk is formatted with the FORMAT command is called the:
   a. ground.
   b. root.
   c. branch.
   d. leaf.
3. Is the root directory always the parent directory for the entire directory structure on a disk?
   a. Yes.
   b. Sometimes.
   c. No.
   d. Never.
4. A subdirectory is, in fact, a special type of:
   a. disk drive.
   b. file.
   c. key.
   d. display.
5. Can subdirectories be named following the same rules used for normal files?
   a. No.
   b. Only if the parent directory is the root.
   c. Yes.
   d. Only if the subdirectory does not contain other subdirectories.
6. A subdirectory, or a file, within a subdirectory can be referenced by an MS-DOS command anywhere within the directory structure by using:
   a. pathnames.
   b. branchnames.
   c. maps.
   d. diagrams.

7. A pathname can consist of:
   a. a single \ to refer to the root directory.
   b. a single subdirectory name with or without a preceding \.
   c. a string of consecutive subdirectory names, each separated by a \.
   d. any of the above.
8. A subdirectory is created using the:
   a. EDLIN command.
   b. CHDIR (or CD) command.
   c. MKDIR (or MD) command.
   d. RMDIR (or RD) command.
   e. COPY command.
9. To change the current, or default, directory, the following command is used:
   a. COPY.
   b. CHDIR (or CD for short).
   c. MODE.
   d. EDLIN.
10. A directory pathname can be used with:
    a. any MS-DOS command that deals with files.
    b. any MS-DOS command that doesn't deal with files.
    c. either of the above.
    d. none of the above.
11. A subdirectory can be deleted (by using RMDIR or RD) only if it:
    a. contains files.
    b. contains subdirectories.
    c. has no files or subdirectories in it.
    d. none of the above.
12. The parent directory of the current subdirectory can be referenced, or accessed, by using what symbol with an MS-DOS command:
    a. . (one period).
    b. .. (two periods).
    c. ... (three periods).
    d. any number of periods.
13. The XCOPY command is most useful for:
    a. copying a single file to another drive.
    b. making a copy of a whole floppy disk on another floppy drive.
    c. copying all of the files in a directory to another directory.
    d. copying a directory and its files and subdirectories.

14. The TREE command is used to display the entire directory structure of a disk. What switch is required if you also want TREE to display all the files contained in each subdirectory?
    a. None.
    b. /f.
    c. A disk drive identifier.
    d. A filename.

15. The search path established when using the internal command PATH can include:
    a. more than one disk drive identifier.
    b. more than one directory path.
    c. both a and b.
    d. none of the above.

Housekeeping

ABOUT THIS CHAPTER

With the increased use of a computer, the need to expand disk storage space often arises. Hard disks are often considered to be the next logical step to expanding your system's on-line storage capability. Hard disks are particularly useful in cases where large amounts of data are being handled, making the constant changing of floppy disks bothersome and time-consuming.

Most serious PC users today have hard disks—even many laptop computers now come with hard disks. If you don't have a hard disk, you should definitely consider adding one. Many application programs sold today will run on a floppy-based system with difficulty, if at all.

You can buy an external or internal hard disk that plugs into a controller card in one of your system's expansion slots. Even more convenient is the "disk on a card," where not just the disk controller but the disk itself is built into an expansion card. Many hard disks come preformatted. Check the documentation or ask the dealer what, if anything, you must do to prepare the disk for use with MS-DOS. If you need to format or partition your hard disk, see Appendix B.

This chapter builds on the knowledge of directories, subdirectories, and paths you gained in Chapter 7. In that chapter you ran MS-DOS commands from your hard disk (if available), but you didn't look closely at its directory structure.

While tree-structured directories are useful on floppy disks, they are virtually essential on a hard disk, which can hold dozens of directories and thousands of files. Making backups of all that valuable data is also essential, so you'll learn how to use the BACKUP and RESTORE commands and perform other housekeeping tasks.

Before learning how to use your hard disk, it is useful to take a look at the differences between hard disk drives and the floppy disks that you learned how to use in Chapter 5.

Hard disks are so named because they are solid disks, magnetically coated like floppies and sealed in a container that is never opened. Hard disks are very sensitive to smoke and other forms of damage. Compared with hard disks, floppies are indestructible. For this reason, many hard-disk systems are sealed inside the computer unit where they can never get dirty, lost, nor need to reside in smoke-filled rooms. Even when hard disks are not actually located inside the computer, they are still permanently sealed in a protective case.

Is Your Hard Disk Ready?

Your hard disk normally has the drive letter C. Try to get a directory of your hard disk by typing *DIR C:*. If you get a directory, you're all set. If you get the error message

```
Invalid drive specification
```

or

```
Error reading drive C:
```

or something similar, your hard disk isn't ready for use with MS-DOS. See Appendix B for information on partitioning and formatting your hard disk. You may want to have your dealer do this for you.

In some ways it is inconvenient not to be able to get the disk out of the drive. It means that information you want to share must be copied to floppies. And the sheer volume of data does make backing it up more inconvenient. But because of its enormous storage capacity and greater speed of access, the hard disk more than compensates for its disadvantages.

This capacity means that you can have all your programs and data on tap practically all the time. Accessing programs and files is much simpler than with floppies: no more inserting and removing disks, no more lost information because of unlabeled or missing disks. This is a real savings in your time and frustration.

You don't have to be concerned about running out of room. Even if you manage to fill up your hard disk to its maximum capacity, (20, 30, or more megabytes) you don't need to worry. You can transfer any information on a hard disk to a floppy for storage, simply by using the COPY command; it's not as if you have to go out and buy a new hard disk when you reach 30MB—though you eventually may. Of course, you can also put the information from the storage floppies back on the hard disk. This chapter discusses the commands that accomplish these transfers.

The second great thing about hard disks is that they are fast, often more than ten times as fast as floppy disks.

Although hard disks are often considered the ultimate in data storage, many of them are fragile devices and vulnerable to certain environmental conditions. The risk of a hard disk malfunctioning is relatively high, and it is therefore important to back up your data regularly.

Before you start to think that hard disks are all you'll ever need, let's look at the major disadvantage of hard disks. Surprisingly, the same thing that makes the disk so convenient—all your files in one place—is also a hazard. With all your information stored in one place, you must be doubly diligent about making backups. And backing up files from hard disk files is time-consuming. It can take more than a half hour to copy all the files on a full hard disk to thirty floppies.

You may ask, what's the point in copying to floppies? The reasons why you need backups for files stored on a hard disk are even more compelling than those for floppies. Remember, all your files are in one place, and they are inside the machine. This means that they are vulnerable to power failures or power surges. One of these, and you could lose some or all of the data stored on your hard disk. The heads that read the information from the disk can cause damage to the disk's surface if dust or dirt gets into the system—and you are looking at potential catastrophe. So don't "put all your eggs in one basket"; make backups of your hard-disk files.

HARD-DISK INSURANCE

MS-DOS makes protecting your files easier with two commands, BACKUP and RESTORE. Use BACKUP to copy files from the hard disk to floppies and RESTORE to return the files to the hard disk. Be sure your hard disk is ready to go before you begin using these commands.

The BACKUP Command

The BACKUP command provides various options in the way your hard disk is backed up. It can back up the entire hard disk, back up only certain subdirectories, or back up only files that have changed since the last backup operation took place.

The BACKUP program works a lot like the COPY command. That is, it copies the files from one device to the other; in this case, from the hard disk to a floppy. BACKUP has several useful switches that allow you to precisely define the files to be backed up.

Remember that when you use a hard disk, it is generally referred to as the C drive. Most hard-disk systems also include at least one floppy-disk drive. This floppy is referred to as drive A. You follow a pattern with BACKUP similar to that you use with COPY. In response to the DOS prompt C:\>, you first indicate the name of the file (with appropriate slashes if it is not part of the root directory) and then give the letter of the target disk. You must use FORMAT to prepare the target disk before issuing the command, unless you have MS-DOS 4.0 BACKUP, which automatically formats the disk if necessary. (In any case, be careful—BACKUP will write over any existing data unless you use the /a switch, discussed later.)

For the next few examples, you'll use the directories that you copied to the hard disk using the XCOPY command in Chapter 7. If you don't have these directories on your hard disk, don't worry—you can use any other directory for practice, though it would be better not to use the root directory or any DOS directory (just in case . . .).

Assuming your hard disk (drive C) is the current drive, use the command

```
C:\>backup \farming a: <ENTER>
```

to back up all of the files in the FARMING directory to the disk in drive A. This just backs up files, however—not subdirectories. Add the /s switch to back up subdirectories as well:

```
C:\>backup \farming /s a: <ENTER>
```

This will back up all of the subdirectories and files (FRUIT and LUMBER and FRUIT's subdirectory CHERRIES, and so on). You actually don't have to include the backslash (\) indicating the root directory, since MS-DOS starts paths at the root directory, and FARMING is a subdirectory of the root directory.

All the files in FRUITS are now copied to the floppy disk in drive A.

If you want to copy all the files in FRUITS and include its subdirectories, you also use the /s switch.

```
C:\>backup\farming\fruits a: /s <ENTER>
```

This command copies the files in FRUITS ("weather" and "soil") and the contents of CHERRIES—the "yields" file—which is the only subdirectory in FRUITS.

You can also use BACKUP to copy only the files in a subdirectory of a subdirectory. To copy only the contents of FRUITS\CHERRIES, you issue this command:

```
C:\>backup fruits\cherries a: <ENTER>
```

This copies all of the files in the CHERRIES subdirectory.

A Pathname Refresher

Recall that you can either specify a complete pathname to a file or directory, or you can make the directory your current directory. When you are copying a whole directory (and perhaps its subdirectories) with a command like BACKUP or XCOPY, it is usually better to stay "outside" the directory. Compare what these commands do:

```
C:\FARMING>backup cherries /s a:
```
← You're in the FARMING directory and backing up the CHERRIES subdirectory and its files and subdirectories

```
C:\>backup farming /s a:
```
← Here you're in the root directory and you're backing up the FARMING directory and its subdirectories (including CHERRIES)

```
C:\FARMING\CHERRIES> backup *.* a:
```
← Here you're in the CHERRIES subdirectory, and you're backing up only the files in that subdirectory (notice that there's no /s switch).

It's important to check where you are in your tree-structured directories before you issue a BACKUP or XCOPY command. Having issued the PROMPT PG command (perhaps in your AUTOEXEC.BAT file) enables you to just glance at the MS-DOS prompt to know your current location. Check, too, the results of the BACKUP or XCOPY command: what was copied to the destination disk?

Remember, if there are subdirectories in the specified subdirectory and you want them included, you must indicate this by including the /s switch.

You may also use the BACKUP command to copy the entire contents of the hard disk (like using *.* to copy all the files on a disk). When you want to copy all the files and their associated subdirectories on a hard disk you enter this command:

```
C:\>backup c: a: /s <ENTER>
```

With this command, you are instructing MS-DOS to copy everything on the hard disk (indicated by the c: drive designator) to the floppy in drive A. Of course, if you have lots of files, you will have to keep inserting new floppies until the entire copying procedure is completed. DOS will prompt you when a new disk is needed.

Mapping Your Hard Disk

It is useful to use the TREE command (introduced in Chapter 7) before beginning a hard-disk backup session. If you type

```
C:\>tree c: /f > diskmap <ENTER>
```

all of the directories, subdirectories, and files on your hard disk will be listed in the file diskmap. To send the output to the printer instead, turn on the printer and then type:

```
C:\>tree c: /f > prn <ENTER>
```

After consulting your diskmap, you can decide which directories to back up or copy to floppies. Of course, the ultimate security is to back up the whole hard disk. (See the redirection discussion in Chapter 9.)

To figure out how many formatted disks you need to have ready in order to copy the entire hard disk, you can use CHKDSK to find the total number of bytes that you have used on your hard disk. Divide that number of bytes by the number of bytes that a floppy can hold to find out how many floppies are needed. Of course, you'll need fewer floppies if you have the appropriate disk drives to use the higher capacity disks—1.2MB 5¼″ and 1.44MB 3½″. As mentioned earlier, backing up an entire hard disk can be very time-consuming. If you make periodic backups, it is only necessary to back up files you have created since the last backup. This is where the /m and /d switches come in handy.

The /m Switch

The /m option lets you back up only those files that you have modified since the last BACKUP session. This can save you lots of time. Luckily, you don't have to remember the last time you used a file (you could get this information from the DIR command, but that could take a long time). Built into MS-DOS is an internal marker that tells DOS if you have modified a file since your last BACKUP.

To copy only those files in the \CHERRIES directory and its subdirectories that have been changed since the last BACKUP, use this command:

```
C:\>backup farming\fruits\cherries a: /s /m <ENTER>
```

The /d Switch

Another way to back up new and modified files is to use the /d switch. This copies only files that were modified after a certain date. For example, you last backed up your files on August 1, 1991. You want to back up any files in the FRUITS directory that were created or modified since that date.

```
C:\>backup farming\fruits\cherries a: /d:08-01-91 <ENTER>
```

The /s Switch

If you want to back up files created after a specific date and any files that have been modified in any way (not necessarily related to a particular date), you add the /s switch:

```
C:\>backup farming\fruits a: /d:08-01-91 /s <ENTER>
```

Of course, you can use these switches to copy all modified files on the entire hard disk by using the C: drive designator. But, in practice, it is probably better to copy modified files in smaller increments, such as subdirectories, so that you can assign certain subdirectories to specific floppies. If you just back up all your files in one move, it may be difficult to find specific files when you want to use the backup.

The /a Switch

The /a switch tells MS-DOS to add the backup files to any files already on the disk in the designated drive.

```
C:\>backup farming\fruits\cherries a: /a <ENTER>
```

If you issue this command, all the files in FRUITS\CHERRIES will be added to the files on the disk in drive A. Of course, you'll use this switch only if you want to save the files on the disk.

If you do not specify the /a switch in the command, MS-DOS will prompt you to insert a formatted disk. When you do not include /a in the command, all the files on the disk in the designated drive are erased before any new files are written.

BACKUP helpfully displays the name of the files it is copying. You can get a printout of the files you are backing up by using the control-key combination ^P. This is a handy way to document the backup session. If you write the number of the floppy that contains the files on the printout, it can provide a quick reference to the location of your backup files.

The /l Switch

Starting with MS-DOS 3.3, you can use the /l switch to have BACKUP make a *log file*, which lists all of the backup floppies made, with the complete paths for all of the files backed up.

```
C:\>backup c: a: /s /l <ENTER>
```

makes the backup log file "backup.log" in the root directory of drive C:. The command

```
C:\>backup c: a: /s /l:bk120989.log <ENTER>
```

also makes a backup file, but names it "bk120989.log."

A review of the BACKUP command and its switches is provided in *Figure 8-1.*

Figure 8-1. The BACKUP Command

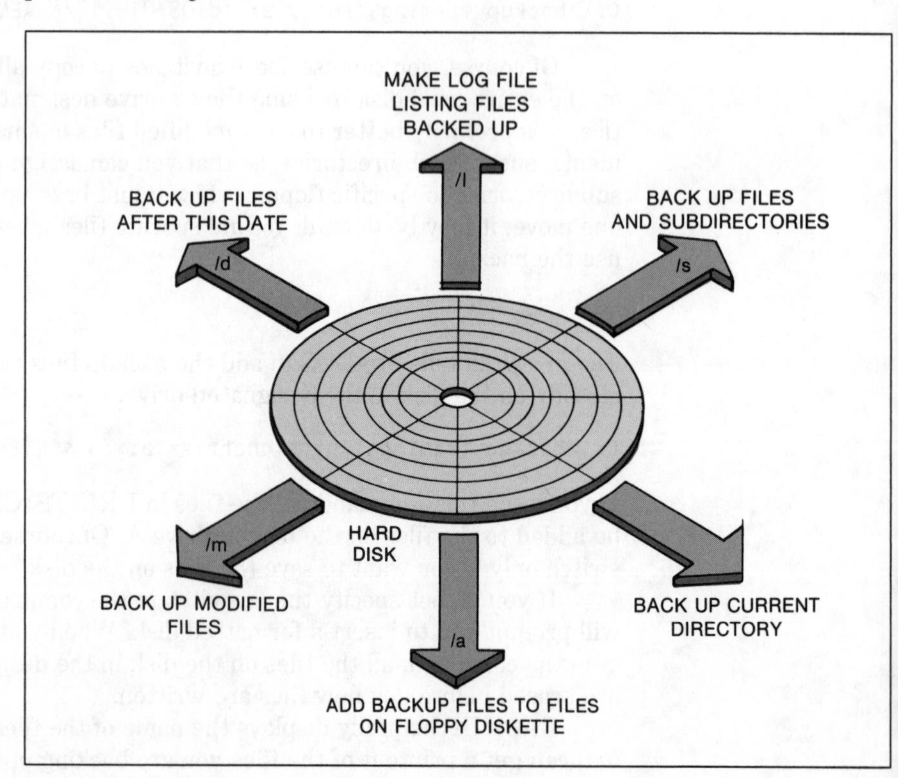

BACKUP or XCOPY?

In Chapter 7 you learned how to use XCOPY to copy a directory and its files and subdirectories to another disk. BACKUP and XCOPY are similar in several ways—they can both copy subdirectories, and they have similar options. (The /s, /a, /m, and /d switches mean the same thing for both commands.)

There are some differences, however. BACKUP can copy a whole hard disk to a series of floppy disks, but XCOPY will stop when it has filled one floppy disk. (You can use the /m switch and repeat the XCOPY command with fresh floppies, but this isn't as convenient.) XCOPY cannot copy a file that is too large to fit on one floppy disk (this is often the case with large database files).

BACKUP stores files in a special format that only RESTORE can read, while XCOPY, like its cousin COPY, stores files in the usual format, so you can use other MS-DOS commands with the backup disk as usual.

In general, you can probably use either XCOPY or BACKUP to back up one or a few directories, but you should use BACKUP to back up a whole hard disk. (You can also buy special backup utility programs that are faster and more convenient to use than BACKUP.)

The RESTORE Command

As a complement to the BACKUP command, the RESTORE command is provided to retrieve files from the backup disks and store them again on the hard disk.

When you restore something you return it to its original condition, such as restoring furniture (or attempting to restore hair). But "restore" might also mean "store again." Both of these meanings tell you what this command does: it copies back your files from the disk to the hard disk in the same form as they were when you last backed them up.

You can use RESTORE only with files that have been copied with the BACKUP command. Files you copied using COPY won't work with this command. You provide the same information in the RESTORE command as you do in BACKUP: the source disk, the target disk, and the name of the files to be copied. To restore all of the files in the FRUITS directory, you enter this command:

```
C:\>restore a: c:farming\fruits <ENTER>
```

Once again, if you want to copy all the files and any subdirectories in the directory, you must include the /s switch.

```
C:\>restore a: c:farming\fruits /s <ENTER>
```

The RESTORE command can be used in a variety of ways, such as to restore all subdirectories and files, only the current directory, or only certain files.

RESTORE also has another switch, /p. Include /p when you want to see if the files you are restoring have changed since they were last backed up. This prevents you from restoring a copy of the files that does not include recent modifications. (Of course, if you have not made a backup since modifying the file, and something happens to your hard disk, you are out of luck. This is another good reason to make frequent backups.) Including /p verifies the files to be sure they are the latest version.

```
C:\>restore a: c:farming\fruits\cherries /p <ENTER>
```

The uses of RESTORE are illustrated in *Figure 8-2.*

Figure 8-2. The RESTORE Command

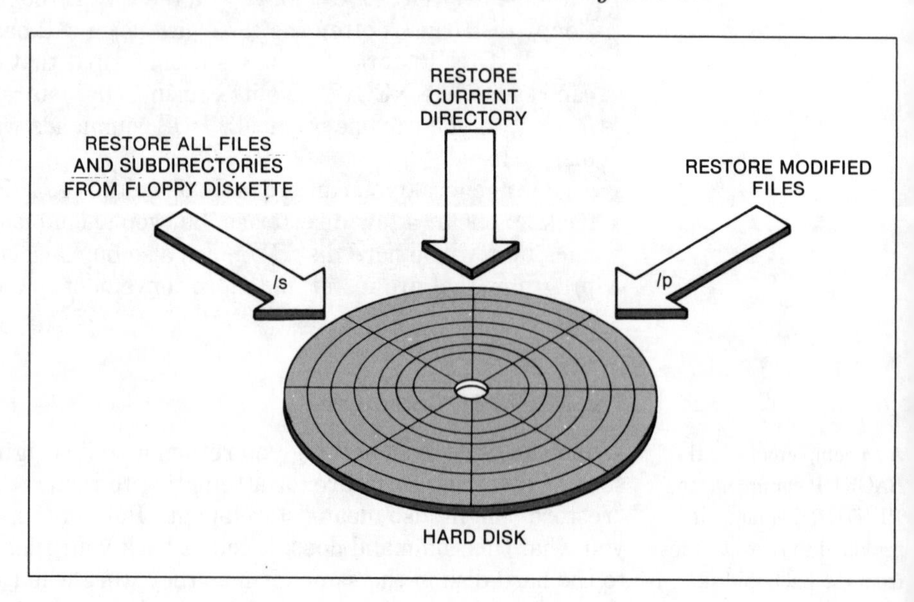

MORE HARD-DISK HOUSEKEEPING

Hard-disk housekeeping also includes keeping track of how much of your hard disk is in use and whether any problems have developed with it. You can use the CHKDSK command to check the status of your hard disk (or floppy disk, for that matter). CHKDSK and another command, RECOVER, can also be used to repair problems with the disk's directory structure or to recover files that are no longer properly listed in the directory.

Getting Information about Your Hard Disk

Every time you use the DIR command, MS-DOS provides a little information about your hard disk. For example, when you use the DIR command in the root directory of drive C, you'll see a display similar to the following:

```
C:\>dir
Volume in drive C is DOSDISK
Directory of C:\
.             <DIR>      1-31-91    9:41a
..            <DIR>      1-31-91    9:41a
COMMAND  COM    23791    1-31-91   12:00p
AUTOEXEC BAT      404    1-31-91   10:32a
CONFIG   SYS       99    1-31-91    2:22p
       <more files...>
DOS           <DIR>      1-31-91   11:34a
WORDPROC      <DIR>      1-31-91    3:29p
       <more directories...>
        17 File(s)  18031040 bytes free
```

Besides the list of filenames in a directory, their sizes, and their date of creation or alteration, the DIR command displays such information about the hard disk as its name and the amount of free space available. However, the DIR command does not provide a complete picture of what is on your hard disk. What if you need to find out such information as the number of files on the hard disk, the number of directories, the space occupied by hidden files, or how much of the disk consists of bad sectors? In these cases, the DIR command is of little help. Instead, you can use the CHKDSK command to get such additional information about the disk.

From the root directory of drive C, type the CHKDSK command:

```
C:\>chkdsk <ENTER>
 Volume DOSDISK          created Dec 31, 1990 3:01p
 21309440 bytes total disk space
    45056 bytes in 3 hidden files
   296960 bytes in 138 directories
 17840128 bytes in 1760 user files
    81920 bytes in bad sectors
  3041280 bytes available on disk
   655360 bytes total memory
   494960 bytes free
```

CHKDSK first displays the volume label and the date on which the volume label was assigned to the disk; in this case, the volume name is DOSDISK, created on December 31, 1990 at 3:01 P.M. (You may recall that you can use the LABEL command to display and change the volume label.) Next, CHKDSK displays the total storage capacity of your disk—in this case, 21309440 bytes.

But what are three "hidden" files? Each time you create a bootable MS-DOS disk, floppy or hard (with FORMAT /s), MS-DOS creates on the disk two hidden system files that it uses during system initialization. Since these files do not appear in your directory listings, they are hidden. MS-DOS hides them to prevent you from inadvertently deleting or renaming them. When you assign a volume name to a disk, MS-DOS creates a third hidden file. All these files show up in the output of the CHKDSK command:

```
45056 bytes in 3 hidden files
```

CHKDSK then displays the number of subdirectories and files that reside on your hard disk:

```
   296960 bytes in 138 directories
 17840128 bytes in 1760 user files
```

In addition to the number of directories, the CHKDSK command also shows the amount of storage used by the subdirectories themselves. The directory files use this space to store information about files such as filenames, their attributes, and their location in the hard disk. The CHKDSK command then displays the number of files and the space used by the files.

If the FORMAT command locates damaged sectors in your disk, it marks them as bad to prevent their use by MS-DOS. If damaged sectors exist in your disk, CHKDSK will display the number of bytes of damaged disk space:

```
81920 bytes in bad sectors
```

MS-DOS "locks out" these sectors so they can't be used to store files. It is normal for a hard disk to have a few tens of thousands of bytes in bad sectors. Given that the disk holds tens of megabytes, this is no problem.

Next, CHKDSK displays the amount of space available on the disk:

```
3041280 bytes available on disk
```

To determine the amount of space that you are actually using, subtract this value from the total disk space:

Actual space used = total disk space − bytes available
= 21,309,440 − 3,041,280
= 18,268,160 bytes

Finally, the CHKDSK command displays the memory utilization in your computer:

```
655360 bytes total memory
496960 bytes free
```

The first number tells you the amount of memory present in your system. When MS-DOS starts running, it occupies some memory; in addition, if you install some memory-resident programs, such as the APPEND command, they also use up some memory. That is why the amount of free memory in the second line is less than the first number. (Chapter 12 explains more about how MS-DOS commands and programs use memory.)

The MS-DOS 4.0 version of CHKDSK also displays the size of each allocation unit used on the disk. This is the smallest amount of space that can be used for a file. The number of allocation units on the disk and the units available are also displayed. For example:

```
 2048 bytes in each allocation unit
10337 total allocation units on disk
 1359 available allocation units on disk
```

Running a CHKDSK command every week or so will help you keep track of how much space is left on your hard disk. If space starts to run low and the number of files is increasing rapidly, it may be time for some housecleaning. You may want to use XCOPY or BACKUP to copy infrequently used directories to floppy disks. You also may want to use the TYPE command or a word processor to check text files and then eliminate duplicates and copy old files to an "archive" disk.

Recovering Damaged Files Using CHKDSK and RECOVER

There's another potential use for CHKDSK. Modern hard disks are remarkably reliable, but they can and do fail. If the disk or disk controller card fails, you will probably have to have a technician make repairs. A less grave problem is getting "bad sectors"—disk sectors where the recording media has been damaged, perhaps by a sudden power failure.

A bad sector is signaled when you use an MS-DOS command or program to access a file and get this error message:

```
C:\>type c:\farming\beans <ENTER>
Data error reading drive C
Abort, Retry, or Ignore?
```

In this case, you should try "retry" a few times. Sometimes the file will be read correctly on the second or third try. If so, it is a good idea to back up that file to a floppy—a sector problem may be developing on the hard disk. If you keep getting the error message after several tries, you should press *a* for Abort, and consider how to recover the file.

You can use the RECOVER command in this situation to extract as much data belonging to the file as possible. RECOVER makes a copy of the original file as far as possible, and writes the file in new sectors. It may leave gaps between parts of the file, where the original file occupied bad sectors. In this process, RECOVER automatically marks all the bad sectors it encounters in the disk's file allocation table (FAT), so that these bad sectors won't be allocated to other files in the future. If you are recovering a text file, you can use a word processor or text editor to see whether any data has been lost. For other types of files, use the corresponding application program to see if you have lost data; e.g., use the spreadsheet program for inspecting spreadsheet files. (However, you cannot use a partial copy of a program file—an .EXE or .COM file. You'll have to copy the program from a floppy back to your hard disk, or run the RESTORE command if you have used BACKUP on the hard disk.)

```
C:\>recover c:\farming\beans <ENTER>
Press any key to begin recovery of the
file(s) on drive C:
872 of 1435 bytes recovered
```

Notice that RECOVER displays the number of bytes recovered for the file. The file is given an arbitrary name such as "file0001.rec." After recovering a file, you can rename it, copy it elsewhere, modify its contents, or use it as a normal file.

Recovering "Lost" Clusters

MS-DOS uses a part of the FAT to keep track of which file each cluster (group of disk sectors) belongs to. Normally every cluster is either unused or accounted for as part of a file.

However, if you restart MS-DOS or turn off your system while a program is running, or terminate a program with <Ctrl> <Break>, a link in this chain of clusters could be broken. If this

Use RECOVER for Only a Few Files at a Time

Do not use RECOVER for recovering all files in a disk—especially your hard disk. By just giving the drive name, you could use RECOVER to recover all files on a disk, but this command will recover *all* files specified, not just the ones with damaged sectors. Your hard disk will end up with a root directory full of files numbered from file0001.rec to perhaps file0349.rec. (Actually, the RECOVER program may abort when it has exceeded the number of files allowed in the root directory.) All of your directory structure will be lost, and you won't know what is in any of your files! Your only recourse would be to RESTORE from your last BACKUP.

happens, the pointer to the cluster chain will be lost, and the data in these clusters will be unavailable to MS-DOS. To recover the file, and to fix the FAT, use the CHKDSK command with the /f option. CHKDSK checks the FAT to see if there are any lost clusters. Usually there are not, in which case it displays the hard disk statistics.

If CHKDSK discovers some lost clusters, it will display a message such as:

```
C:\>chkdsk /f
009 lost clusters found in 003 chains
Convert lost clusters to files (Y/N) ?
```

(You must use the /f switch. If you don't, CHKDSK will still ask you if you want to convert the clusters to files, but it won't actually do it, regardless of whether you type *y*.)

CHKDSK has no way of knowing to which files those lost clusters originally belonged. So it cannot attach them to their original files. If you type *y* for the above question, CHKDSK will convert these lost clusters into separate new files and place them under the root directory. Each cluster replaced by CHKDSK will be identified as a file with the name "FILEnnnn.CHK" under the root directory. The first cluster is named "FILE0000.CHK," the next one is named "FILE0001.CHK," and so on. If you already have files with similar names under the root directory (e.g., if you have "FILE0001.CHK" and "FILE0002.CHK" under the root), CHKDSK will start naming files from the next number on.

Later you can inspect these files with the TYPE command, or by whatever method, and if the information is important, you can save those files. At the worst, you can simply delete the files, thus reclaiming the storage space occupied by the lost clusters.

For Floppies, Too

Remember that all of the features of the CHKDSK and RECOVER commands work with floppy disks as well as hard disks.

Defragmenting (Optimizing) Your Disk

The final housekeeping problem is less serious, because it doesn't involve loss of data. You will probably notice that access to your hard disk slows down as you continue to create, copy, and delete files. When MS-DOS first starts putting files on your hard disk, there is space to make the files contiguous—that is, with one file following the next on the disk. When you delete files, however, their space is marked as "unused," creating "holes" between files on the disk. Also, if you add to a file, MS-DOS often won't be able to just tack the new data onto the end of the old, because a new file will already have been saved there. The result is that files start to get scattered—fragmented around your hard disk as MS-DOS uses the "holes" to store parts of newly created files.

The greater the fragmentation of files, the further the hard disk performance drops and the slower it gets. For reading or writing to a file, the read/write head has to move to all the tracks in the disk where pieces of the file are. This additional movement increases the access time and slows down the overall system performance. You can diagnose the problem of file fragmentation by seeing that the time MS-DOS takes for loading and executing programs is longer than normal. You can also note that with file fragmentation, your database search programs and spreadsheets take longer to read data files. To see whether files are fragmented, you can use the CHKDSK command. If you want to see whether a file, say ADDRESS.DAT, is stored contiguously, use the name of the file with the CHKDSK command.

```
C:\>chkdsk address.dat <ENTER>
All specified file(s) are contiguous
```

If the file is contiguous, CHKDSK displays the above message. If the file is fragmented (i.e., stored in two or more noncontiguous clusters), MS-DOS will display a message such as

```
C:\>chkdsk address.dat <ENTER>
C:\ADDRESS.DAT
     Contains 5 non-contiguous blocks
```

To inspect the contiguity of more than one file, use the wildcard characters in the place of filenames. For example, to check contiguity of all the files in the current directory, type

```
C:\>chkdsk *.* <ENTER>
C:\ADDRESS.DAT
     Contains 5 non-contiguous blocks
C:\CUSTOMER.DOC
     Contains 3 non-contiguous blocks
C:\SALES.DOC
     Contains 2 non-contiguous blocks
C:\EMPLOYEE.DAT
     Contains 2 non-contiguous blocks
```

Unfortunately, CHKDSK won't do anything to unfragment your disk. The best solution is to buy one of the commercial "disk optimization" programs. (Many utility packages such as the Norton or Mace utilities, include disk optimizers that you can use to check your disk regularly for fragmentation and to rearrange files so they are contiguous. Many of these programs are designed so that you need run them only a few minutes a week.)

A more cumbersome alternative is to use the BACKUP, FORMAT, and RESTORE commands. First, you make one (preferably, two) complete backups of your hard disk. You then reformat your hard disk (see Appendix B for how to do this), using the /s switch so the hidden files will be copied to your reformatted disk. You then use RESTORE to put all of your data back on the hard disk.

SUMMARY

This chapter presented some of the advantages and disadvantages of hard disks (the former outweigh the latter). You learned how to use the BACKUP and RESTORE commands to transfer files from hard disks to floppies and vice versa.

You also learned how to play "disk doctor," inspecting your hard disk with CHKDSK, and how to recover from some common problems—bad sectors, missing sectors, and fragmented sectors.

REVIEW

1. Hard disk drives include a sealed, built-in disk that holds many times the information of a floppy disk and allows much faster access.
2. It is very important to back up your hard-disk files onto floppy disks; power failures, power surges, and misalignment can destroy your files or your ability to access them.
3. The BACKUP command copies files from a hard disk to floppy disks.
4. Use the /s switch to back up all files and subdirectories.
5. Use the /m switch to back up all files modified since the last backup.
6. Use the /d switch to back up all files modified since a specific date.
7. Use the /a switch to back up files onto a floppy disk and save any existing files on that floppy disk.
8. Use the /l switch to make a log file that lists what was backed up.
9. The RESTORE command copies one or more files from floppy disks to a hard disk.
10. The RESTORE command has two switches; the /s switch includes all subdirectories in the restoration; the /p switch checks to see if files being restored have been modified since they were last backed up.
11. You can use CHKDSK to learn how many directories and files are on your hard disk, how much space they take up, and how much space is available.
12. You can also use CHKDSK to detect disk fragmentation and to find and recover "lost" sectors.
13. You can use the RECOVER command to recover the good part of a file that has bad sectors.

Quiz for Chapter 8

1. The advantages of using a hard disk instead of floppy disks are that it:
   a. has a higher storage capacity.
   b. stores data faster.
   c. retrieves data faster.
   d. all of the above.

2. A 30-megabyte hard disk is capable of storing:
   a. 3,000 bytes.
   b. 30 million words.
   c. approximately 30 million characters worth of data or the equivalent of about 90 floppy disks.
   d. none of the above.

3. Are hard disks more sturdy than floppy disk drives?
   a. Always.
   b. Never.
   c. Sometimes, depending on type of hard disk and the environmental conditions to which it is subjected.
   d. None of the above.

4. Regularly backing up a hard disk is important because:
   a. the large amount of stored data represents a considerable investment of your time.
   b. many types of hard disks are prone to damage under certain conditions.
   c. the collective amount of time taken to back up a hard disk regularly can be insignificant compared with what can be required to reconstruct the files on a damaged hard disk.
   d. all of the above.

5. The command provided with MS-DOS with the specific purpose of backing up a hard disk is called:
   a. XCOPY.
   b. BACKUP.
   c. COPY.
   d. TYPE.

6. The BACKUP command can be used in a variety of ways to back up a hard disk, including:
   a. backing up the entire hard disk.
   b. only backing up certain subdirectories.
   c. only backing up files that have changed since the last backup.

d. only backing up files created or modified after a certain date.
e. any of the above.
f. none of the above.

7. To retrieve backed up files from the backup floppy disks, which MS-DOS command should be used?
   a. COPY.
   b. CHKDSK.
   c. RESTORE.
   d. DIR.

8. Disk-related problems that can be detected by CHKDSK include:
   a. accidentally deleted files.
   b. missing directories.
   c. files that haven't been backed up yet.
   d. lost or damaged sectors.

9. The RECOVER command is used to:
   a. save as much as possible of a file with bad sectors.
   b. copy files from a backup disk to the hard disk.
   c. restore files that had been erased.
   d. bring back the old version of an accidentally changed file.
   e. all of the above.

10. The purpose of a disk optimizer program is to:
    a. speed up the disk drive head.
    b. increase the total capacity of a hard disk.
    c. make fragmented files contiguous again.
    d. rearrange the directory tree structure.

Advanced File Manipulation

ABOUT THIS CHAPTER

In this chapter, we will discuss pipes, filters, and redirection: sophisticated data management commands. These commands give you choices in determining where your information comes from (input) and where it goes after you're finished with it (output). They are the frosting on the cake in allowing you to make the most of your MS-DOS operating system.

STANDARD INPUT AND OUTPUT DEVICES

You know from your own computer use that you normally enter information from your keyboard. The keyboard is the standard input device in personal computer systems. When you want to look at your input or see the results of programs, you usually use your display screen. The screen, or monitor, is the standard output device in personal computer systems. These two devices are shown in *Figure 9-1*. It is possible to use other devices for input and output, however. For example, a file can be the source of input and a second file can be the destination of the output.

This is possible because in many ways MS-DOS treats the devices connected to your PC like ordinary disk files. You have already seen how you can use the COPY command to create a text file:

```
C:\>copy con: memo
      ← enter some lines of text
      ← Press F6 or Ctrl-Z
      <ENTER>
      1 file(s) copied
C:\>
```

The COPY command is copying from the con "file"—the keyboard—to the memo file on disk. If you type

```
C:\>copy con: prn:
```

The lines you type now go to the printer "file" rather than to the screen "file."

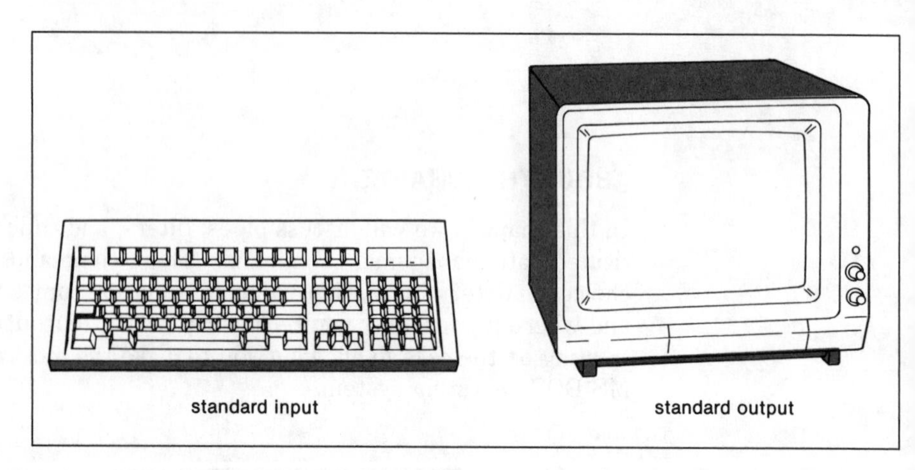

Figure 9-1. Keyboard and Display

MS-DOS allows input and output to and from commands to be optionally modified using special characters.

DOS sees things in black and white. There is a standard input device and a standard output device. By default these are the keyboard and display screen. But DOS doesn't really care what provides the input and output as long as you label them as the standard input and output devices when issuing commands. When you designate files, programs, or other devices as the means of input and/or output, you are using the concept of redirection.

REDIRECTING STANDARD OUTPUT

The output generated by a command, which normally is displayed on the screen of your computer's monitor, can be redirected to another device, such as a file on a disk or the printer. The > character, when used with a command, always means "redirect output to the following device."

The reasons why you might want to redirect output are numerous. Perhaps a specific program or command results in a new version of your data; you would like to keep this information in a separate file. Or you may want to have data automatically output to the printer. Perhaps you want to add output information to an existing file.

No doubt you recognize the > symbol from your high school math classes. It means "greater than." But in MS-DOS this symbol indicates the redirection of output. Think of it as standing for "send to this place," with the arrow pointing the way to the file or device to receive the information. Here is how you might redirect the output of a DIR command:

```
C:\>dir >a:listing <ENTER>
```

As a result of this command, the directory listing of drive C is sent to a newly created disk file called "listing" on drive A. The > character before the filename reassigns this file as the standard output device. Because the disk file is now the standard output device, you will not see the information on the screen (it hasn't been sent there). This process is illustrated in *Figure 9-2.*

Figure 9-2. Redirection of Output

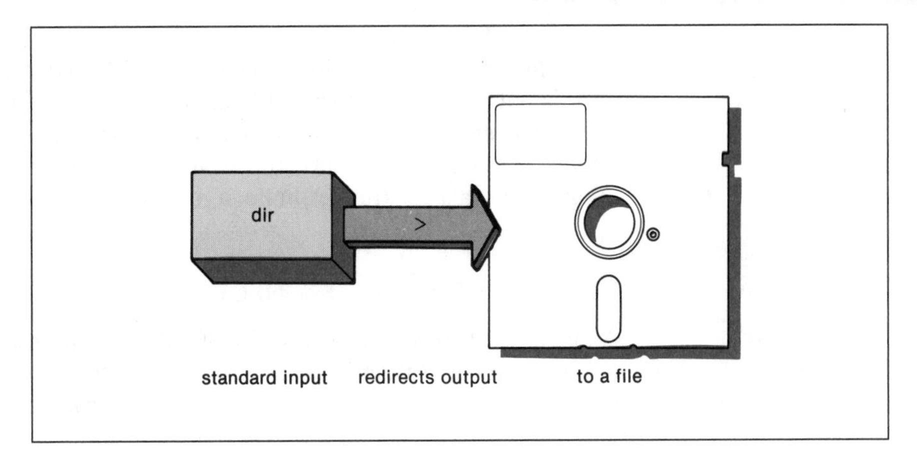

When you execute the command, the screen will show nothing, but the drives will whirr and the indicator lights will come on. After the information is transferred to the file, the standard output reverts to the display screen. If you want to change the destination of the next command, you must include a redirection marker in the command.

You haven't actually seen anything on the screen to tell you that the operation has been completed but you can check the new file by using the TYPE command.

```
C:\>type a:listing <ENTER>
```

The contents of the file "listing" will appear on the screen.

You can use directories and subdirectories in redirecting output.

```
C:\>dir farming\fruits\cherries >fruitdir <ENTER>
```

This puts the directory listing of the FARMING-FRUITS-CHERRIES subdirectory into a file called "fruitdir."

When a single > character is used to redirect output to a file, a new file is always created, overwriting any file by the same name if it exists. When the >> symbol is used, MS-DOS is instructed to append the output data to an existing file.

One thing to keep in mind as you redirect output to files: if you redirect to an already existing file, the contents of the file will be wiped out. But there is a simple solution to this problem: when you want to append the new output to the end of an already existing file you include >> in the command.

```
C:\>dir >>fruitdir <ENTER>
```

With this command, the directory listing of the current directory (C:\) is put into the "fruitdir" file at the end of the file.

Redirection using >> is a handy and safe way of keeping updated listings of your directories all in one file or for updating information in a file (for example, a mailing list).

REDIRECTING STANDARD INPUT

The < character is used to redirect input to a file rather than accept input from the keyboard. For example, a command that normally displays a series of prompts requesting your input on the keyboard could have all of its prompts automatically answered by redirecting, as input to the command, a text file containing all the answers.

As you might expect, the opposite of output redirection is input redirection. This operation is symbolized by the "less-than" character (<). Think of this symbol as saying "take the content from this file and use it as input." Using this option you can make the standard input device a file instead of the keyboard. The uses for input redirection are more obscure than for output redirection, but one common use is to relieve yourself of the need to make the repetitious entries needed to start up a program. Simply include the responses necessary in a file named, for instance, "answers." Then redirect the input using this file. By far the most frequent use of redirected input, however, is with the use of filters in piping information.

Piping

Although there are no real pipes involved, the analogy of a pipeline is a useful tool for understanding the flow of information from input to output devices.

When a water department constructs a pipeline, it lays sections of pipe in a line to form one long conduit. The pipeline takes water from its source and pipes it to a water-storage area. Along the way, there are reservoirs that store the water temporarily. The water is then sent to a purification plant, where it is filtered before it is piped to its final destination, your home.

A more sophisticated method of using the redirection of input and output is the use of filters in piping information. Piping is a method of chaining together an MS-DOS command with other special commands to modify the flow of input and output information.

When you construct an MS-DOS pipeline, you do very much the same thing. The data you are going to put into the pipeline are stored in a source file or program. You want to use the output of this program or file as the input to the next program or command. In this way, you can hook commands, programs, and files together in a long chain, much as illustrated in *Figure 9-3.*

The data, however, do not go directly from the input file to the output file. If they did, you could accomplish the same goal by simply copying the file. Instead, in piping, the data are fed in from the input file, go through a filtering process where they are modified, and then go to their destination in the output file.

When you use piping, it appears to MS-DOS that the input is the same as if it were typed in from the keyboard. But in reality, MS-DOS creates internal temporary files, like reservoirs, to hold the data as they are being piped. You may encounter some of these temporary files as you work your way through the examples in this chapter. They would appear in your directory like this:

Figure 9-3. Piping

```
%PIPEx.$$$
```

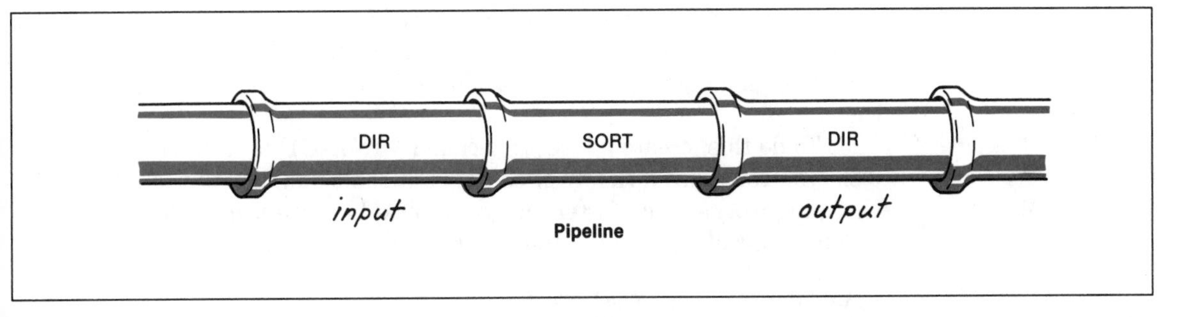

where x is an integer to distinguish different PIPE files.

Data within the pipeline can be modified by the use of filters.

Filters

Filters are special commands or programs used to modify input data in some manner and then output it again to an output device or to another command.

Filters are DOS commands or programs that read in data from the designated standard input device, modify the data in some way, and then output the modified data to the designated standard output device. Thus, by its position in the middle of the process (as shown in *Figure 9-4*), this command works to filter the data.

Filters allow us to use a program, command, or file as the standard input device. Filters output to files. MS-DOS contains three filters: SORT, FIND, and MORE.

Figure 9-4.
Filtering

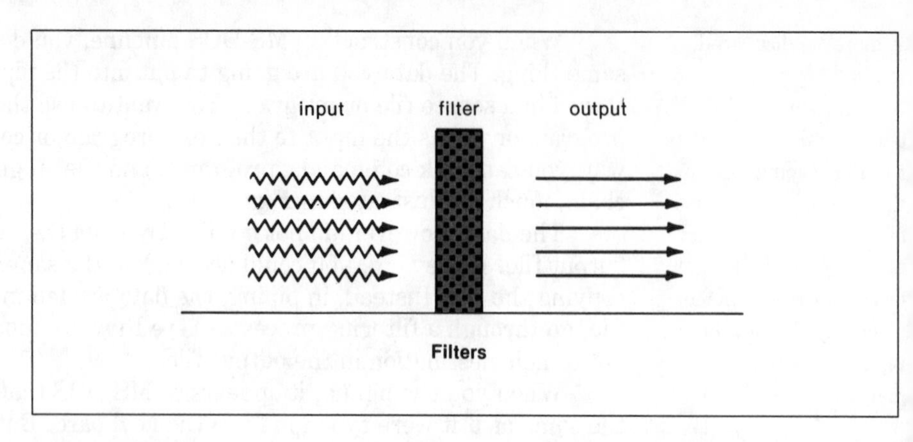

The SORT Filter

The SORT command is a filter designed to sort text in a variety of ways. SORT can be executed as a normal command, or it can be piped with other commands.

This filter sorts file contents either alphabetically or by column number. Learning to use SORT is like learning how to drive. You know you existed without it, but it's hard to imagine how. To experience the real pleasure of using SORT, you have to try it on some actual data. So you are going to create a file to play SORT with.

Assume that you are a connoisseur of fine wines and have a respectable wine cellar. The only way to keep up with its contents is to catalog immediately all new purchases before you taste any of them.

The current directory for these examples is C:\VINTAGE.

To do this, create a directory called VINTAGE on your hard disk (you could use a floppy of course, but the example will use drive C. Piping works much faster on a hard disk, because it doesn't take as long to create or use the temporary files.)

```
C:\>mkdir vintage <ENTER>
C:\>cd vintage <ENTER>
```

Now you're in the VINTAGE directory.

The first thing you need is a list of your new bottles of wine. Create a file called "wines" in this directory on drive C. The name goes in column 1, the year in column 23, the appellation in column 28, and the country in column 50.

You must create this file as an ASCII text file (see Chapter 6). That means you should use EDLIN or COPY CON: to enter the text. Also do not use the <TAB> key to space between columns because SORT cannot handle this character.

```
C:\VINTAGE>copy con: wines <ENTER>

Lafite                      45  Bordeaux            France
Phelps Insignia             74  Cabernet Sauvignon  U.S.A.
Ridge Gyserville            73  Zinfandel           U.S.A.
La Mission Haut Brion       64  Bordeaux            France
Y'Quem                      58  Sauterne            France
^Z <ENTER>
```

You can use the TYPE command to check the contents of your list.

```
C:\VINTAGE>type wines <ENTER>
```

The first thing you want is an alphabetical listing of the names of the new bottles to make it easier to enter them into your master file. This means that you want to SORT on the first column. (An alphabetical sort on the first column is the default condition of SORT.)

SORT accepts input from another program, command, or file. But you must include the reassignment character as part of the statement.

```
C:\VINTAGE>sort < wines <ENTER>
```

With this command you have told MS-DOS to sort the contents of the file "wines." Now watch the screen.

```
La Mission Haut Brion       64  Bordeaux            France
Lafite                      45  Bordeaux            France
Phelps Insignia             74  Cabernet Sauvignon  U.S.A.
Ridge Gyserville            73  Zinfandel           U.S.A.
Y'Quem                      58  Sauterne            France
```

SORT will also sort by reverse alphabetical order. To perform a sort so that the end of the alphabet tops the list, you use the /r option.

```
C:\VINTAGE>sort /r < wines <ENTER>
```

MS-DOS responds with your list in reverse order.

```
Y'Quem                      58  Sauterne            France
Ridge Gyserville            73  Zinfandel           U.S.A.
Phelps Insignia             74  Cabernet Sauvignon  U.S.A.
Lafite                      45  Bordeaux            France
La Mission Haut Brion       64  Bordeaux            France
```

But SORT can do more. Suppose you want to list your acquisitions by year, from oldest to newest, to help plan storage. To do this, use the /+n option. This switch allows you to sort by any column (indicated by the n in the command). You want to sort by year, which begins in column 23.

```
C:\VINTAGE>sort /+23 < wines <ENTER>
```

Immediately you have your new listing.

```
Lafite                 45  Bordeaux             France
Y'Quem                 58  Sauterne             France
La Mission Haut Brion  64  Bordeaux             France
Ridge Gyserville       73  Zinfandel            U.S.A.
Phelps Insignia        74  Cabernet Sauvignon   U.S.A.
```

You may also want to keep a listing of your wines by appellation. That's the information that begins in column 28. Again, you use the /+n switch.

```
C:\VINTAGE>sort /+28 < wines <ENTER>
Lafite                 45  Bordeaux             France
La Mission Haut Brion  64  Bordeaux             France
Phelps Insignia        74  Cabernet Sauvignon   U.S.A.
Y'Quem                 58  Sauterne             France
Ridge Gyserville       73  Zinfandel            U.S.A.
```

Would you like a list by country?

```
C:\VINTAGE>sort /+50 < wines <ENTER>
Lafite                 45  Bordeaux             France
La Mission Haut Brion  64  Bordeaux             France
Y'Quem                 58  Sauterne             France
Phelps Insignia        74  Cabernet Sauvignon   U.S.A.
Ridge Gyserville       73  Zinfandel            U.S.A.
```

Just as you can use a file as the input for the SORT command, you can also redirect the output to a file. For clarity's sake you would like to keep each sort in a separate file. This lets you reference your collection quickly. To output the results of a sort to a file, just include the output redirection character > in the command.

```
C:\VINTAGE>sort > vintners <ENTER>
```

This command tells DOS to sort on column 1 the information in the "wines" file and put the output in a file called "vintners." When you perform a sort that redirects the output, you have assigned a new standard output device. Therefore, it follows that you will no longer see the sort on your standard output device, the screen. When SORT has transferred the results to a file, it returns you to the prompt.

```
C:\VINTAGE>
```

You can verify the new file by using DIR.

```
C:\VINTAGE>dir vintners <ENTER>
 Volume in drive C is MSDOSDISK
 Directory of C:\VINTAGE
VINTNERS          290    3-15-91   2:15p
        1 File(s)  2360443 bytes free
```

Remember, the next time you want to add information to this "vintners" file you will need to use >> so that the output of the new SORT is appended to the contents of the file.

```
C:\VINTAGE>sort < wines >> vintners <ENTER>
```

Using redirection, you can also create individual files to hold your other sorts.

```
C:\VINTAGE>sort /+23 < wines >b:years <ENTER>
C:\VINTAGE>sort /+28 < wines >b:type <ENTER>
C:\VINTAGE>sort /+52 < wines >b:country <ENTER>
```

When you have done all this your directory will look like this:

```
C:\VINTAGE>dir <ENTER>
 Volume in drive C is MSDOSDISK
 Directory of C:\VINTAGE
.             <DIR>      3-15-91   2:05p
..            <DIR>      3-15-91   2:05p
WINES            290     3-15-91   2:07p
VINTNERS         580     3-15-91   2:16p
YEARS            290     3-15-91   2:16p
TYPE             290     3-15-91   2:16p
COUNTRY          290     3-15-91   2:17p
        5 File(s)  2357376 bytes free
```

SORT not only rearranges your data quickly but in conjunction with input and output redirection, becomes a powerful tool as well. You don't have to limit your use of SORT to files. Like all filters, it is really the most useful in piping. You can use the output of a command as input into the SORT filter. You create a piping sequence by separating the various commands, filters, and files with the vertical bar character (¦).

```
C:\>dir ¦ sort >alphadir
```

When piping several commands together, the ¦ character is always used to separate the commands on one line.

When using piping, you leave a space before and after each vertical bar. The above command goes to the current directory, sorts the directory alphabetically on the first column (because no options are included in the SORT command), and then puts the sorted directory into a file called "alphadir" on the disk in drive B.

Try using the DOS subdirectory on drive C:

```
C:\DOS>dir ¦ sort >alphadir <ENTER>
```

The directory won't be listed on the screen, but you'll hear the drive working, and the indicator light will be on. This is MS-DOS creating the temporary pipe "reservoir" file that holds the output of DIR and the output of SORT. When the sorted directory is complete, it will be redirected to the file "alphadir." If you want to see the sorted display, enter the command without output redirection.

```
C:\DOS>dir ¦ sort <ENTER>
```

In a few minutes the sorted listing will appear on the screen.

```
          47 File(s)    2870400 bytes free
 Directory of C:\DOS
 Volume in drive C is MSDOSDISK
 Volume Serial Number is 1454-3E20
.            <DIR>       1-31-91  11:15a
..           <DIR>       1-31-91  11:15a
APPEND   EXE     11186   1-31-91  12:00p
ASSIGN   COM      5785   1-31-91  12:00p
ATTRIB   EXE     18247   1-31-91  12:00p
BACKUP   COM     33754   1-31-91  12:00p
BASIC    COM      1065   1-31-91  12:00p
BASICA   COM     36285   1-31-91  12:00p
CHKDSK   COM     17771   1-31-91  12:00p
COMMAND  COM     37637   1-31-91  12:00p
COMP     COM      9491   1-31-91  12:00p
DEBUG    COM     21606   1-31-91  12:00p
DISKCOMP COM      9889   1-31-91  12:00p
DISKCOPY COM     10428   1-31-91  12:00p
DOSSHELL GRA       213   1-31-91   3:56p
DOSUTIL  MEU      9768   1-31-91   3:38p
EDLIN    COM     14249   1-31-91  12:00p
FASTOPEN EXE     16302   1-31-91  12:00p
FDISK    COM     70151   1-31-91  12:00p
```

```
FILESYS  EXE     11125  1-31-91  12:00p
FIND     EXE      5983  1-31-91  12:00p
FORMAT   COM     22923  1-31-91  12:00p
GRAFTABL COM     10271  1-31-91  12:00p
GRAPHICS COM     16733  1-31-91  12:00p
GRAPHICS PRO      9413  1-31-91  12:00p
IFSFUNC  EXE     21653  1-31-91  12:00p
JOIN     EXE     17457  1-31-91  12:00p
KEYB     COM     14759  1-31-91  12:00p
LABEL    COM      4490  1-31-91  12:00p
MEM      EXE     20133  1-31-91  12:00p
MODE     COM     23056  1-31-91  12:00p
MORE     COM      2166  1-31-91  12:00p
NLSFUNC  EXE      6910  1-31-91  12:00p
PCIBMDRV MOS       295  1-31-91  12:00p
PCMSDRV  MOS       961  1-31-91  12:00p
PCMSPDRV MOS       801  1-31-91  12:00p
PRINT    COM     14024  1-31-91  12:00p
RECOVER  COM     10732  1-31-91  12:00p
REPLACE  EXE     17199  1-31-91  12:00p
RESTORE  COM     40030  1-31-91  12:00p
SHARE    EXE     10301  1-31-91  12:00p
SORT     EXE      5914  1-31-91  12:00p
SUBST    EXE     18143  1-31-91  12:00p
SYS      COM     11472  1-31-91  12:00p
TEST     EXE     20133  1-31-91  12:00p
TREE     COM      6334  1-31-91  12:00p
XCOPY    EXE     17087  1-31-91  12:00p
```

It is important to remember that when you SORT a file the contents of the file are not changed. The file remains in the same order as before the sort. For instance, if you performed the above sort on your system disk, the sorted listing would not appear the next time you entered DIR. Instead, you would get the normal directory listing. This is why it is valuable to redirect the output of a SORT to a file if you want to use the sorted information again.

The FIND Filter

The FIND command is a filter that is used to search for and output specified text. It can be used as a standard command, or it can be piped with other commands and filters.

FIND is a fast and easy way to locate specific items in a file. FIND works by finding strings. A string is a group of characters enclosed in quotation marks. Like the SORT filter, FIND can receive input from a file or command and send it to any designated standard output device, such as the screen, another file or program, or the printer. FIND's functions are illustrated in *Figure 9-5*.

One note of caution about the use of strings: strings will be found only when they exactly match the enclosed string in the command. This includes the use of upper- and lowercase letters and all punctuation marks.

Suppose you want to find out which of your recent purchases were from France.

```
C:\VINTAGE>find "France" wines <ENTER>
```

Notice that you enter the command first, followed by the string, which must be enclosed in quotation marks. The name of the file to search is entered last. Every line containing the string will appear on the screen.

```
---------------- wines
Lafite                    45  Bordeaux        France
La Mission Haut Brion     64  Boudeaux        France
Y'Quem                    58  Sauterne        France
```

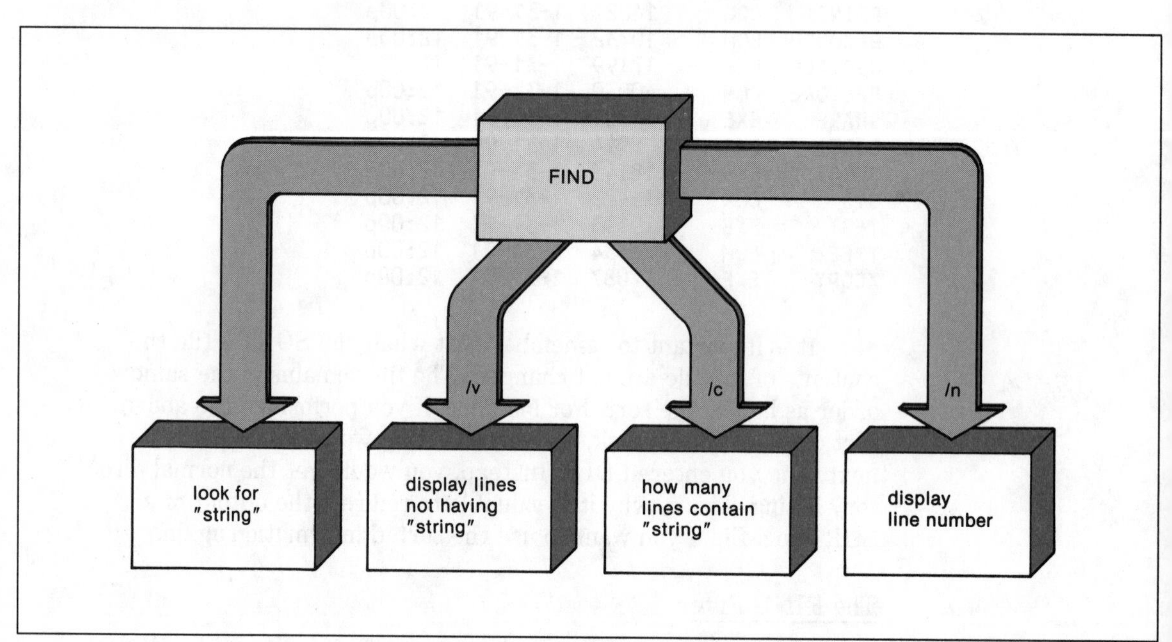

Figure 9-5. The Find Command

Suppose you want a list of French wines, but you want it in alphabetical order. Then simply combine FIND in a pipeline with SORT.

```
C:\VINTAGE>find "France" wines | sort <ENTER>
---------------- wines
La Mission Haut Brion     64  Bordeaux        France
Lafite                    45  Bordeaux        France
Y'Quem                    58  Sauterne        France
```

If you wish, you can put this sorted French list into its own file on your B drive for later reference. Be sure to put a formatted floppy disk in drive B.

```
C:\VINTAGE>find "France" wines | sort b:French <ENTER>
```

The last command would not produce any display, of course, because you reassigned the output to be sent to the file "French" on your B drive.

There may be times when you want to FIND lines in a file that do not contain a specified string. For example, you want to list your American purchase returning to the VINTAGE directory on your C drive. FIND allows you to do this with the /v switch.

```
C:\VINTAGE>find /v "France" wines <ENTER>
```

FIND works for a few seconds.

```
- - - - - - - - - - - - - - - wines
Phelps Insignia              74  Cabernet Sauvignon  U.S.A.
Ridge Gyserville             73  Zinfandel           U.S.A.
```

Now you want all non-French wines, and you want them in alphabetical order.

```
C:\VINTAGE>sort < wines | find /v "France" <ENTER>
```

Don't let the length of this command confuse you; just take it one step at a time. It tells DOS to sort the items in the "wines" file (on the first column because no column is listed) and then to find all lines that do not display the string "France."

Now let's suppose you are not particularly interested in the names of the French wines, you just want to know how many are in the file. Then you would use FIND with the /c switch. The /c switch returns a count of the lines containing the string.

```
C:\VINTAGE>find /c "France" wines <ENTER>
```

The response is the name of the file, followed by a number.

```
- - - - - - - - - - - - - - - wines: 3
```

The final FIND option allows you to locate occurrences of the string very precisely. The /n switch displays the line number followed by the line itself, for every instance of the indicated string.

```
C:\VINTAGE>find /n "France" wines <ENTER>
---------------- wines

[1]Lafite                    45  Bordeaux        France
[4]La Mission Haut Brion     64  Bordeaux        France
[5]Y'Quem                    58  Sauterne        France
```

The line numbers indicate the position of the entries in the original file. For example, there are only three items in our display. Yet Y'Quem is assigned a line number of 5. This is because Y'Quem was the fifth entry in the original "wines" file. Locating a string by line number can be useful in large files.

You don't need to limit the use of FIND to a display on the screen or a redirection to a file. You can also use it with commands. Try this combination:

```
C:\>dir \dos | find "EXE" <ENTER>
```

MS-DOS responds.

```
XCOPY    EXE     17087  1-31-91  12:00p
FASTOPEN EXE     16302  1-31-91  12:00p
IFSFUNC  EXE     21653  1-31-91  12:00p
SHARE    EXE     10301  1-31-91  12:00p
APPEND   EXE     11186  1-31-91  12:00p
ATTRIB   EXE     18247  1-31-91  12:00p
FILESYS  EXE     11125  1-31-91  12:00p
FIND     EXE      5983  1-31-91  12:00p
JOIN     EXE     17457  1-31-91  12:00p
MEM      EXE     20133  1-31-91  12:00p
TEST     EXE     20133  1-31-91  12:00p
NLSFUNC  EXE      6910  1-31-91  12:00p
REPLACE  EXE     17199  1-31-91  12:00p
SORT     EXE      5914  1-31-91  12:00p
SUBST    EXE     18143  1-31-91  12:00p
```

FIND will take your request literally. It will list not only the files with the extension EXE, but also any files that contain the string "EXE" within their filenames (e.g., AUTOEXEC.BAT).

Because the SORT and FIND command filters require very specific input they can't be used with global characters (wildcards).

Neither the SORT nor the FIND filter allows the use of global characters (wildcards). In addition, in FIND, a quotation mark (") is interpreted as a search for an apostrophe (').

You may remember the MORE command, which you used in Chapter 6 to look at text files. This command is also a filter: it normally takes its input from a file and shows it on the screen. To look at your wine list with MORE, type:

```
C:\VINTAGE>more < wines <ENTER>
```

The big thing to remember with MORE is to include the < symbol to redirect input. If you don't, MORE will wait for input from the standard input device—the keyboard. It will display everything you type on the screen. You can "break out" of this situation by typing <Ctrl>C or <Ctrl><Break>.

Combining FIND, SORT, and MORE

By combining the FIND, SORT, and MORE filters on a single command line, you can enhance the operation of standard MS-DOS commands.

Now that you've learned about the FIND, SORT, and MORE filters and have examples of their use in piping and redirection, let's use them as building blocks to show how they can interact. You may have come to the conclusion that it would really be easier to read your DOS directory if the files were listed alphabetically and the display stopped scrolling automatically when the page was full. This is a reasonable request.

When the piping of MS-DOS commands and filters is used, temporary files are created on the current disk that contain information needed by the various commands and filters. While a piping operation is in effect, you may see these files in a directory listing. However, these files are automatically deleted when the piping operation is completed.

```
C:\>dir | sort | more <ENTER>

       47 File(s)     2870400 bytes free
 Directory of C:\DOS
 Volume in drive C is MSDOSDISK
 Volume Serial Number is 1454-3E20
.            <DIR>      1-31-91   11:15a
..           <DIR>      1-31-91   11:15a
APPEND   EXE     11186  1-31-91   12:00p
ASSIGN   COM      5785  1-31-91   12:00p
ATTRIB   EXE     18247  1-31-91   12:00p
BACKUP   COM     33754  1-31-91   12:00p
BASIC    COM      1065  1-31-91   12:00p
BASICA   COM     36285  1-31-91   12:00p
CHKDSK   COM     17771  1-31-91   12:00p
COMMAND  COM     37637  1-31-91   12:00p
COMP     COM      9491  1-31-91   12:00p
DEBUG    COM     21606  1-31-91   12:00p
DISKCOMP COM      9889  1-31-91   12:00p
DISKCOPY COM     10428  1-31-91   12:00p
DOSSHELL GRA       213  1-31-91    3:56p
DOSUTIL  MEU      9768  1-31-91    3:38p
EDLIN    COM     14249  1-31-91   12:00p
--MORE--           ← press a key to continue
FASTOPEN EXE     16302  1-31-91   12:00p
FDISK    COM     70151  1-31-91   12:00p
FILESYS  EXE     11125  1-31-91   12:00p
FIND     EXE      5983  1-31-91   12:00p
FORMAT   COM     22923  1-31-91   12:00p
GRAFTABL COM     10271  1-31-91   12:00p
GRAPHICS COM     16733  1-31-91   12:00p
GRAPHICS PRO      9413  1-31-91   12:00p
```

```
IFSFUNC  EXE     21653  1-31-91  12:00p
JOIN     EXE     17457  1-31-91  12:00p
KEYB     COM     14759  1-31-91  12:00p
LABEL    COM      4490  1-31-91  12:00p
MEM      EXE     20133  1-31-91  12:00p
MODE     COM     23056  1-31-91  12:00p
MORE     COM      2166  1-31-91  12:00p
NLSFUNC  EXE      6910  1-31-91  12:00p
PCIBMDRV MOS       295  1-31-91  12:00p
PCMSDRV  MOS       961  1-31-91  12:00p
PCMSPDRV MOS       801  1-31-91  12:00p
PRINT    COM     14024  1-31-91  12:00p
RECOVER  COM     10732  1-31-91  12:00p
REPLACE  EXE     17199  1-31-91  12:00p
RESTORE  COM     40030  1-31-91  12:00p
SHARE    EXE     10301  1-31-91  12:00p
--MORE--         ← press a key to continue
SORT     EXE      5914  1-31-91  12:00p
SUBST    EXE     18143  1-31-91  12:00p
SYS      COM     11472  1-31-91  12:00p
TEST     EXE     20133  1-31-91  12:00p
TREE     COM      6334  1-31-91  12:00p
XCOPY    EXE     17087  1-31-91  12:00p
C:\>
```

Another way to redesign the directory is to group all the same files together and then list them with the extensions in alphabetical order. To do this you need to know that the extension designation begins in column 10.

```
C:\>dir \dos | sort /+10 | more <ENTER>
.             <DIR>      1-31-91  11:15a
..            <DIR>      1-31-91  11:15a
         47 File(s)   2868352 bytes free
BASIC    COM      1065  1-31-91  12:00p
MORE     COM      2166  1-31-91  12:00p
LABEL    COM      4490  1-31-91  12:00p
ASSIGN   COM      5785  1-31-91  12:00p
TREE     COM      6334  1-31-91  12:00p
COMP     COM      9491  1-31-91  12:00p
DISKCOMP COM      9889  1-31-91  12:00p
GRAFTABL COM     10271  1-31-91  12:00p
DISKCOPY COM     10428  1-31-91  12:00p
RECOVER  COM     10732  1-31-91  12:00p
SYS      COM     11472  1-31-91  12:00p
PRINT    COM     14024  1-31-91  12:00p
EDLIN    COM     14249  1-31-91  12:00p
KEYB     COM     14759  1-31-91  12:00p
GRAPHICS COM     16733  1-31-91  12:00p
CHKDSK   COM     17771  1-31-91  12:00p
DEBUG    COM     21606  1-31-91  12:00p
```

```
FORMAT   COM     22923  1-31-91  12:00p
MODE     COM     23056  1-31-91  12:00p
BACKUP   COM     33754  1-31-91  12:00p
BASICA   COM     36285  1-31-91  12:00p
--MORE--             ← press a key to continue
COMMAND  COM     37637  1-31-91  12:00p
RESTORE  COM     40030  1-31-91  12:00p
FDISK    COM     70151  1-31-91  12:00p
 Volume Serial Number is 1454-3E20
SORT     EXE      5914  1-31-91  12:00p
FIND     EXE      5983  1-31-91  12:00p
NLSFUNC  EXE      6910  1-31-91  12:00p
SHARE    EXE     10301  1-31-91  12:00p
FILESYS  EXE     11125  1-31-91  12:00p
APPEND   EXE     11186  1-31-91  12:00p
FASTOPEN EXE     16302  1-31-91  12:00p
XCOPY    EXE     17087  1-31-91  12:00p
REPLACE  EXE     17199  1-31-91  12:00p
JOIN     EXE     17457  1-31-91  12:00p
SUBST    EXE     18143  1-31-91  12:00p
ATTRIB   EXE     18247  1-31-91  12:00p
MEM      EXE     20133  1-31-91  12:00p
TEST     EXE     20133  1-31-91  12:00p
IFSFUNC  EXE     21653  1-31-91  12:00p
DOSSHELL GRA       213  1-31-91   3:56p
DOSUTIL  MEU      9768  1-31-91   3:38p
PCIBMDRV MOS       295  1-31-91  12:00p
PCMSPDRV MOS       801  1-31-91  12:00p
PCMSDRV  MOS       961  1-31-91  12:00p
--MORE--             ← press a key to continue
 Volume in drive C is MSDOSDISK
GRAPHICS PRO      9413  1-31-91  12:00p
 Directory of C:\DOS
```

You could SORT by date and/or time, but because SORT is very literal, this is useless. If SORT were presented with these three dates:

9-05-90   5-02-93   7-16-92

it would sort them like this:

5-02-93   7-16-92   9-05-90

In other words, SORT interprets 9-05-90 as greater than 5-02-93 (since 9 is greater than 5), so it puts it at the bottom of the list. As you saw when sorting the "wines" file by year, you can successfully use numbers to SORT, but they must run consecutively.

Finally, you could also sort the DOS directory by file size, if you wished.

```
C:\>dir\dos ¦ sort /+17 ¦ more <ENTER>
```

SUMMARY

In this chapter you learned about the standard input and output recognized by MS-DOS commands and many other programs. You then learned how to redirect input and output to alternative files and devices. You also saw how a pipe creates a link between two commands so that the output of the first command becomes the input of the second. You then learned how to use the three MS-DOS "filter" commands—SORT, FIND, and MORE—with piping and redirection.

REVIEW

1. The keyboard is the standard input device; the screen is the standard output device.
2. MS-DOS treats devices such as the keyboard and printer as files. This means that most commands you can use with ordinary files you can also use with devices—for example, COPY CON.
3. The "greater-than" and "less-than" symbols (> <) are redirection commands. Use them to redirect the output or input of MS-DOS commands to files.
4. The SORT filter sorts the contents of a file in alphabetical or reverse alphabetical order. It can also sort starting at a specified column.
5. The FIND filter locates strings of alphanumeric characters within a file.
6. The MORE filter displays the contents of a file, pausing between each screenful.

Quiz for Chapter 9

1. The redirection of output to a device other than the monitor screen is accomplished by following an MS-DOS command with:
   - **a.** the > character followed by a device name or filename.
   - **b.** the >> character followed by a filename that is to be appended with the output information.
   - **c.** either a or b.
   - **d.** the < character.
2. The redirection of input to an MS-DOS command other than the keyboard is accomplished by following the command with:
   - **a.** the * character.
   - **b.** the < character and a device name or filename.
   - **c.** the \ character.
   - **d.** the > character.
3. Can both input and output redirection be used at the same time with a command?
   - **a.** Yes, always.
   - **b.** Yes, but an input device or file cannot be the same as the output device or file.
   - **c.** No, never.
4. An MS-DOS pipeline is:
   - **a.** an interface between computer and monitor.
   - **b.** a tool used to modify the flow of input and output information to and from MS-DOS commands.
   - **c.** a method of sequencing filenames.
5. An MS-DOS filter is:
   - **a.** a device for filtering "bugs" from your system.
   - **b.** a program used to smooth out power surges.
   - **c.** a special command designed to modify the input and output generated by other MS-DOS commands.
   - **d.** none of the above.
6. Filters are used in which of the following ways?
   - **a.** As a filter to another MS-DOS command.
   - **b.** Some filters can be used as regular commands.
   - **c.** As a filter to another MS-DOS command, combined with the use of other filters.
   - **d.** Any of the above.
   - **e.** None of the above.

7. The SORT filter can sort text in a variety of ways from:
   a. a file.
   b. output from another command.
   c. output from another filter.
   d. any of the above.

8. When an MS-DOS command is piped with one or more filters, each command or filter must be separated from another by which character?
   a. ¦
   b. *
   c. ?
   d. \

9. The ¦ piping separator and the < and >redirection symbols can be used within the same pipe:
   a. always.
   b. if needed, but only if there are no conflicts.
   c. sometimes.
   d. never.

10. The FIND filter is used to search for and display specified text:
    a. found in a file.
    b. found in output from another command.
    c. found in output from another filter.
    d. any of the above.
    e. none of the above.

11. The MORE filter can be used:
    a. as a command to display the contents of a file and pause when the screen is full.
    b. as a filter to cause displayed text output by another command to pause when the screen is full.
    c. as a filter to cause displayed text output by another filter to pause when the screen is full.
    d. any of the above.
    e. none of the above.

12. Can the SORT, FIND, and MORE filters be used together within a single piping operation?
    a. No.
    b. Yes.

Using Batch Files

ABOUT THIS CHAPTER

As you become more familiar with MS-DOS commands, you gain an understanding of how, when, and why to use specific commands. In fact, what you may have found at first difficult becomes increasingly routine as you employ these commands more often.

The fact is that many of the operations you perform with the computer are repetitive. You probably find yourself using certain sequences of commands, in the same pattern, over and over again. Just as the editing keys gave you one shortcut to avoid useless repetition, MS-DOS has another helpmate to save you time and frustration. This new tool is called a batch file, and in this chapter you'll see how batch files can make your computing more efficient.

WHAT ARE BATCH FILES?

A batch file is a special type of file that contains a series of commands that can be automatically executed by MS-DOS. As viewed by MS-DOS, a batch file is in fact a command that contains a series of other commands in text form.

Batch files are something like a cookbook for commands. They contain lists of steps in the form of MS-DOS commands that combine to produce one result. After this recipe is established, the batch file gives you the same result every time you run it. The ingredients in a batch file are data files. These may change from time to time, but the product of the batch file is still the same. An example from the kitchen may help to explain this.

Bread is really a combination of grain, liquid, and flavoring. When you make bread, the ingredients may vary. You can use whole wheat or white flour; you can include water or milk; you can add raisins or caraway seeds. The steps in making bread always follow a specific pattern, however. First you measure, then you combine, then you knead, and finally you bake. The result is bread. A recipe for bread is a shortcut most cooks use because it defines what and how much and in what order. Not only does this reduce mistakes, it makes the process go faster because the procedure is already laid out; you just follow the instructions. Having made the bread, when you want to eat a piece, you just cut off a slice; you don't have to go out and cut the wheat, grind the flour, and so on.

Batch files perform a similar service for MS-DOS users. You enter a series of commands that, when executed in order, provide specific results. The product is always the same because you follow the same steps each time. Even if you enter different filenames, the commands still perform in the same order. And because all of these commands are stored in one file, identified by a batch filename, you can use this formula over and over again, simply by entering the batch filename. This is faster than entering each of the commands separately and eliminates mistakes, since the commands are already correctly entered in the batch file. The batch file is already made up.

Batch files are ASCII text files, just like the files you use when you work with EDLIN or your word processor. The files you use most frequently hold various kinds of information, data, programs, or operating system commands. Batch files contain commands and some explanatory statements. How much a batch file can do is dependent on how many commands you enter. Batch files are most useful when they perform a sequence of commands that you use quite frequently.

Here's one example of the convenience of batch files. You may find that you frequently perform the following sequence of events. First you format a disk, then you copy files to it, then you ask for a directory of the disk, and finally you look at one or more of the files to check the contents. This procedure can be done by entering four commands: FORMAT, COPY, DIR, and TYPE. You could enter each of these commands separately, repeating the drive designations and filenames each time. But you can save yourself time and eliminate the inevitable typing errors by putting all these commands in a batch file. To execute this batch file, all you do is enter one command: the name of the batch file. Let's review your normal procedure.

First you enter the FORMAT command.

```
format b:
```

After the disk is formatted you enter a second command.

```
copy a:datafile b:
```

When the copy is made you ask for a directory.

```
dir b:
```

And finally, you list the contents of the file.

```
type b:datafile
```

Now let's see how you can put all these commands in one batch file.

CREATING A BATCH FILE

Batch files can be easily created by using any text editor, such as EDLIN or a word processor.

Before you can follow a recipe it has to be written down. Putting a series of commands in a batch file is simple. The rules for a batch filename are the same as for other filenames, but in a batch file you must include the extension .BAT.

To run through this exercise on batch files, you are going to create a practice file called "datafile." For brevity's sake, this file will contain only one line: "This is a demonstration batch file." Because this is an ASCII file, you can use EDLIN to create this data file.

EDLIN is on your hard disk as the file "EDLIN.COM." Your "datafile" will be created on drive A. Put a formatted disk in drive A and call up EDLIN, which is described in detail in Appendix A. If you don't wish to use it, use another text editor, or a word processor in ASCII text mode. You can even use the COPY CON method that you've already learned.

```
C:\>edlin a:datafile <ENTER>
New file
*i <ENTER>
     1:*This is a demonstration batch file. <ENTER>
     2:*^C <ENTER>

*e <ENTER>
```

This file is going to be the generic data file in the example. It stands for any files you might want to use in the batch file.

Now you can create a batch file "copydata.bat," which will perform the steps previously discussed concerning making a new data disk in drive B:. Here's how you can do it with EDLIN.

Enter one command per line.

```
C:\>edlin copydata.bat
New file
*i <ENTER>
     1:*format b: <ENTER>
     2:*copy a:datafile b: <ENTER>
     3:*dir b: <ENTER>
     4:*type b:datafile <ENTER>
     5:*^C

*e <ENTER>
```

Each command contained in a batch file must be on a line of its own.

Enter each command on a separate line. This is the standard EDLIN procedure. The only difference is that your filename contains the .BAT extension. This batch file assumes that the disk in drive B is unformatted (line 1). It "believes" that the data you want to copy ("datafile") is on the disk in drive A, and that you want to copy this file to the disk on drive B (line 2). You then want to check the directory for the existence of the file (line 3) and type out the contents of the file (line 4).

An alternative method (and often the quickest way) of creating a batch file is to use the COPY command to copy what is typed on the keyboard to the batch file. A special device name (CON:) is used to represent the console (the console always means the "keyboard for input" and "monitor screen for output").

To create "copydata.bat" using COPY CON:, enter the commands in sequence. There are no line numbers when using COPY CON:. Again, enter one command per line.

```
C:\>copy con: copydata.bat <ENTER>
format b: <ENTER>
copy a:datafile b: <ENTER>
dir b: <ENTER>
type b:datafile <ENTER>
^Z <ENTER>
```

^Z (<Ctrl>Z) is the end-of-file marker. After you enter it, MS-DOS responds.

```
1 File(s) copied
```

Note that creating a batch file using COPY does not cause any of the commands within the file to be executed. To MS-DOS they are just like any other text. The "1 File(s) copied" message means that this created file is now stored on the hard disk (drive C).

USING A BATCH FILE

Starting a Batch File

Because a batch file is considered to be a command to MS-DOS, it is executed by simply entering the batch file's name without the .BAT extension. Once a batch file has started execution, all text normally displayed by the commands within the batch file will be displayed, as if the commands had been entered individually.

From now on, anytime you want to perform the FORMAT-COPY-DIR-TYPE sequence, you simply type in the name of the batch file in response to the MS-DOS prompt. Of course, you must have the source and destination disks in the correct drives. The sequence of commands is executed automatically. MS-DOS shows you each command as it is processed. The appearance is the same as if you were entering each command separately. Enter the batch filename. You do not need to include the extension.

```
C:\>copydata <ENTER>
```

The batch file begins executing.

```
A>format B:
```

This is the first command in your batch file.

```
Insert new diskette for drive b:
and strike any key when ready
```

All messages associated with the FORMAT command appear automatically. You must strike a key here for the file to continue processing.

```
Formatting....Format complete
362496 bytes total disk space
362496 bytes available on disk
Format another (Y/N)?n
```

Again, you must respond to all command requests for input. Next, MS-DOS copies the file.

```
C:\>copy a:datafile b:
1 File(s) copied
```

MS-DOS automatically continues with the third command in the batch file.

```
C:\>dir b:
```

The normal messages associated with DIR are displayed.

```
Volume in drive B has no label
Directory of B:\
DATAFILE            38  4-22-91  11:35a
          1 File(s)    361472 bytes free
```

MS-DOS now executes the fourth command in the batch file.

```
C:\>type b:datafile
```

Here are the contents of "datafile":

```
This is a demonstration batch file.
```

When the batch file is finished, MS-DOS returns to the prompt.

```
C:\>
```

Running a Batch File

When you run your first batch file you will be amazed at how quickly the commands happen. You may even feel a lack of control watching messages and commands appear on the screen. But MS-DOS keeps you informed of what it is doing each step of the way. Each command is displayed as the batch file reaches it, and all messages and queries associated with the command are displayed during processing. You can just sit back and observe.

This is the wonder of batch processing. With the simple input of one filename and a response to the "strike key" and "FORMAT another" queries, you have formatted a disk, copied a file, displayed a directory, and typed out the contents of the file. And MS-DOS has returned to await your next command.

You can execute several batch files in a row. To do this, simply make the last command in a batch file the name of another batch file. For example, suppose you had two batch files: "copydata" and "erasedat." "Erasedat" might be a batch file to clean up a disk after all the needed files had been copied. The last command line of "copydata" would contain the name "erasedat."

```
format b:
copy a:datafile b:
dir b:
type b:datafile
erasedat.bat
```

When you call another batch file from within a file, the processing continues with the first command in the new file, as depicted in *Figure 10-1*. This is a one-way street, however. You can't return to "copydata" once you begin processing "erasedat." These files are chained one to the other.

Figure 10-1. Superbatch

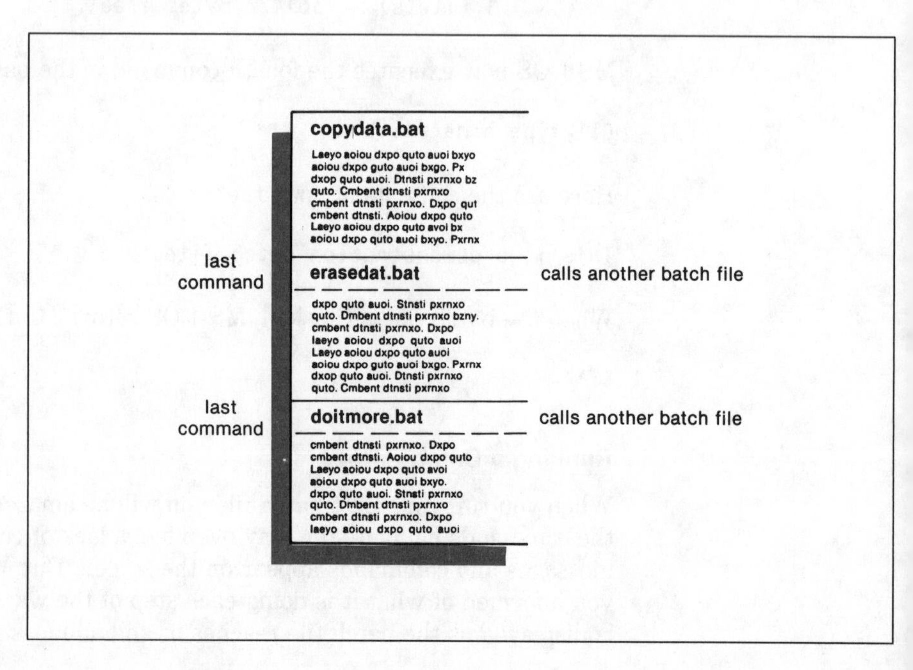

This example is a simple illustration of how useful batch files can be. You are probably already planning to fashion your own batch files to eliminate the drudgery of certain sequences of operations you perform quite frequently.

Stopping a Batch File

To stop a batch file before it finishes normally, use the <Ctrl>C or <Ctrl><Break> functions. MS-DOS will display a prompt asking you if you indeed want to stop the batch process or whether it should continue.

Occasionally you may want to stop the processing in the middle of a batch file. Perhaps you realize that you don't have time to complete the batch file, or you want to use different data disks, or you don't want a series of chained batch files to execute. Whatever the reason, MS-DOS allows you to do this. You stop batch processing just like you interrupt any on-going operation on the computer: you press ^C or <Ctrl><Break>. When a batch file is processing and you press ^C, MS-DOS displays the message:

```
Terminate batch job (Y/N)?
```

A *y* answer tells DOS to ignore the rest of the commands in the batch file and return you to the DOS prompt. An *n* answer tells DOS to terminate processing of the current command but to continue processing with the next command in the batch file. Guidelines for this procedure appear in *Figure 10-2*.

For example, while processing the "copydata" file, you might not want to see the entire directory of the disk. Therefore, you would press <Ctrl><Break> while the DIR command was processing and then type *n* in response to the terminate question. Processing would continue with the TYPE command.

REPLACEABLE PARAMETERS

Often you may want to perform the same sequence of commands on different sets of files. In the initial version of "copydata," you were able to copy only one specific file, "datafile." But this situation is very limiting. It means that whenever you want to copy some other file besides "datafile," you need to create a new batch file containing the new filename. Obviously this limits the timesaving capabilities of batch files.

A parameter is the part of a command that indicates what the command is to be performed on. Usually this is the name of the file that will be affected by the command. The command "copy a:datafile b:" consists of the actual command name "copy" and the parameters that identify what the command is to operate on: the file in drive A called "datafile." "Datafile" is a parameter of this command.

Figure 10-2.
Stopping a Batch File

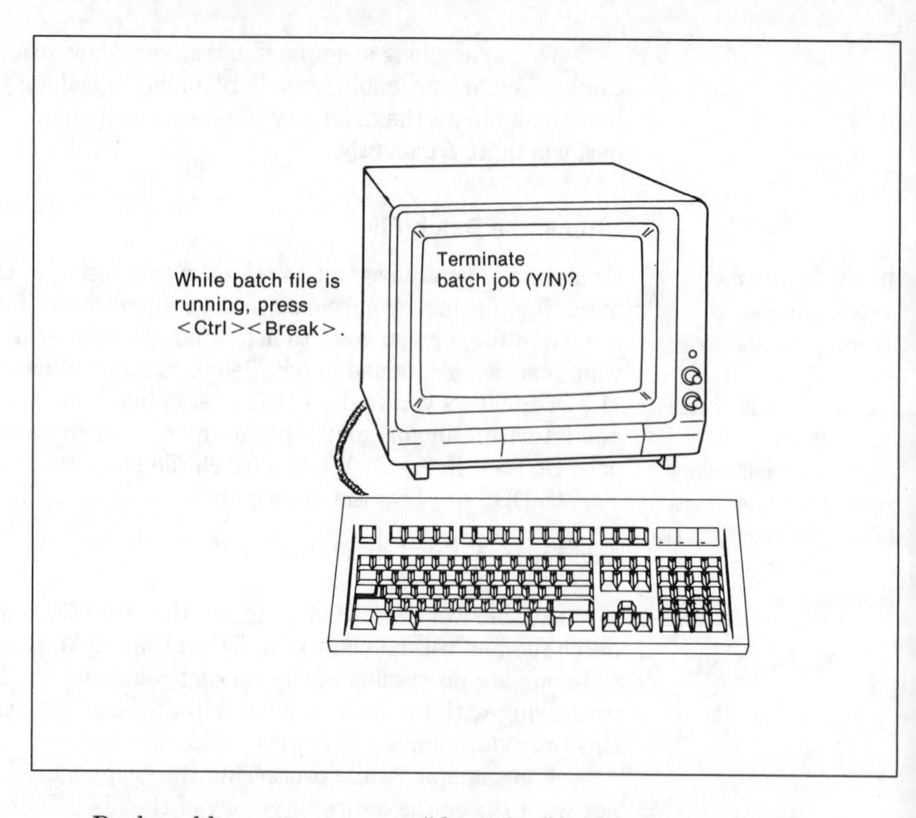
While batch file is
running, press
<Ctrl><Break>.
Terminate
batch job (Y/N)?

A batch file can be written in such a way that when it is typed at the MS-DOS prompt you can specify optional parameters that are subsequently used as parameters to any of the MS-DOS commands contained within the batch file. These optional parameters are called replaceable parameters.

Replaceable parameters are "dummies," which means that they are symbols that stand for the actual names of real files. In batch files, replaceable parameters are indicated by the percent sign (%) followed by a number, for example, %1 or %2. The actual files that replace these symbols are specified when you call the batch file. The name of the file to replace %1 follows the batch filename; the file to replace %2 comes next on the command line.

Imagine that you have created a batch file to display the contents of several files. You want to use this file over and over again, but you will type out different files each time, so you create the batch file using replaceable parameters. The name of this file is "typeit.bat." Within the file are three commands.

```
type %1
type %2
type %3
```

When you call the file you indicate the files to be substituted for the %1, %2, and %3 parameters by listing them in order on the command line. Leave a space between parameters.

```
typeit chap1 chap2 chap3
```

When MS-DOS encounters the first dummy parameter, %1, it substitutes chap1 for this parameter. Then chap2 is substituted for %2, and chap3 for %3. If the file also contained another command using these parameters, then chap1, chap2, and chap3 would again be substituted.

```
copy %1
copy %2
copy %3
```

The replaceable parameters will have the same values throughout the batch file.

The parameters listed after the filename are substituted whenever %1, %2, or %3 are called for in the batch file.

```
type %1
type %2
type %3
copy %1
copy %2
copy %3
```

You can have up to ten replaceable parameters (%0–%9) in a batch file. It is possible to have more; see the SHIFT command later in this chapter for ways to get around this limitation. The %0 is reserved for the name of the batch file itself. Thus, typing %0 in the file above would cause MS-DOS to type out the "typeit" file itself.

Replaceable parameters can be used in any batch file. Just remember that you must specify what files are to be substituted for the dummy parameters when you call the file.

You can use all of the MS-DOS commands in a batch file. But, in addition, there are specific batch commands (or subcommands) that are only used in batch files.

COMMANDS IN BATCH PROCESSING

The ECHO Command

The ECHO command is a special command used to turn on or off the echoing (display) of the individual commands contained in a batch file as they are being executed.

The concept of echoing is not new to you. We discussed echoing in a different context earlier when we used the editing keys ^P and ^N to control the echoing of the screen to the printer. Here the same type of echoing is meant, but we are talking about echoing the commands within a batch file to the screen.

Normally, the ECHO command is in the ON mode. In the ON mode, each command is echoed (displayed) on the screen as that command is processing. The display of each command can be useful when you want to keep close track of what is happening inside a batch file. But this echoing feature can also be bothersome when you don't need it, cluttering up the screen with useless information.

If you don't want to see each command displayed on the screen, you can set ECHO to the OFF mode. When ECHO is OFF, the commands themselves do not appear on the screen, but all messages associated with the commands are still displayed. To eliminate echoing, enter this command before any commands you don't want to see. For example, if you wanted to include ECHO OFF in the "copydata" file, you would enter it first.

```
C:\>copy con: copydata.bat <ENTER>
echo off <ENTER>
format b: <ENTER>
copy a:datafile b: <ENTER>
dir b: <ENTER>
type b:datafile <ENTER>
^Z <ENTER>
1 File(s) copied
```

When you run this version of "copydata" you will not see any command lines on the screen after the initial ECHO OFF command.

```
C:\>copydata <ENTER>
C:\>echo off
```

This first command tells you ECHO is OFF. Messages displayed by MS-DOS commands still appear.

```
Insert new diskette for drive B:
and strike any key when ready
```

Press a key to continue.

```
Formatting....Format complete

362496 bytes total disk space
362496 bytes available on disk

Format another (Y/N)?n
```

You answer *n*.

```
1 File(s) copied
  Volume in drive B has no label
  Directory of B:\
```

The DIR output is displayed.

```
DATAFILE            38  4-22-91   11:49a
         1 File(s)    361472 bytes free
This is a demonstration batch file.
C:\>
```

Starting in MS-DOS 3.3, you can put an "at" sign (@) in front of any batch file command to turn off the echoing of that line. Thus, if you use the line @ECHO OFF, not only is echoing turned off, but not even the ECHO OFF line is echoed.

If at some point in the batch file you again wanted to see the echoing of each command as it was processed, you would enter a new ECHO command, ECHO ON. All subsequent commands would then appear on the screen.

The ECHO command can also be used to cause any text you desire to be displayed on the screen while echoing has been turned off (by a previous ECHO OFF command). To echo text to the screen, simply insert ECHO followed by the text to be displayed at the point in the batch file where you want the text display to occur.

ECHO has another option that allows you to put messages on the screen, even when ECHO is in the OFF mode. Although you will not see the commands, you will see the message. Let's set the ECHO OFF in the "copydata" batch file, but include a message we do want to see displayed.

```
C:\>copy con: copydata.bat <ENTER>
echo off <ENTER>
format b: <ENTER>
copy a:datafile b: <ENTER>
dir b: <ENTER>
echo Here are the contents of datafile: <ENTER>
type b:datafile <ENTER>
^Z <ENTER>
```

The results of this batch file are exactly the same as those of the last example until the DIR listing has been displayed. Then our message is echoed.

```
DATAFILE          38  4-22-91  11:49a
         1 File(s)    361472 bytes free
Here are the contents of datafile:
This is a demonstration batch file.
C:\>
```

If you enter ECHO with no parameters, MS-DOS displays the current status of ECHO (ON or OFF). Use ECHO to decide which commands you want to see during batch file processing and to give yourself helpful messages regardless of the status of the ECHO command.

The REM Command

The REM command is used in batch files to insert text that is not to be treated as a command by MS-DOS. REM is useful for inserting text that describes the function of a batch file or that describes a specific batch command line. If an ECHO OFF command has been previously executed, the line containing the REM command will not be displayed when the batch file executes.

The REM (REMark) command is used, like the ECHO command, to put comments into a batch file. These can be reminders to you (or any other user of the batch file) that explain what the file does or what is happening at a specific moment. REM statements are affected by the status of ECHO. When ECHO is in the OFF mode, REM statements are not displayed in the same way that commands are not displayed. The ECHO and REM commands are compared in *Table 10-1*.

REM commands can contain any information you think will help you understand the batch file better. You can also use REM to insert blank lines in a file. The following batch file, “newdisk,” formats new disks and puts the system on them. It then checks the condition of the disk.

```
C:\> copy con: newdisk.bat <ENTER>
rem This file formats and checks new disks. <ENTER>
rem The system will be put on the diskette. <ENTER>
format b:/s <ENTER>
dir b: <ENTER>
rem Here is the condition of this diskette. <ENTER>
chkdsk b: <ENTER>
rem This diskette is ready to use, don't forget to label it!
 <ENTER>
^Z <ENTER>
 1 File(s) copied
```

To run “newdisk,” enter the filename.

```
C:\>        <ENTER>
```

This is what you will see on the screen:

Table 10-1. Comparison of ECHO and REMark

	ECHO		REMark
ON	Commands are displayed.	ECHO ON	REM statements are displayed.
OFF	Commands are not displayed but messages still appear.	ECHO OFF	REM statements are not displayed.

```
C:\>rem This file formats and checks new disks.

C:\>rem The system will be put on the diskette.

C:\>format b:/s
Insert new diskette for drive B:
and strike any key when ready
```

You then press a key.

```
Formatting....Format complete
System transferred

362496 bytes total disk space
 40960 bytes used by system
321536 bytes available on disk

Format another (Y/N)?n
C:\>dir b:

Volume in drive B has no label
Directory of B:\

COMMAND  COM:    17664 4-22-91  12:00p
         1 File(s)   321536 bytes free

C:\>rem Here is the condition of this diskette.

C:\>chkdsk b:
362496 bytes total disk space
 22528 bytes in 2 hidden files
 18432 bytes in 1 user files
321536 bytes available on disk

262144 bytes total memory
237456 bytes free
```

```
C:\>rem This diskette is ready to use, don't forget to label it!
C:\>
```

You can see from this example how the addition of REM statements can help clarify the contents and operations of a batch file. If you wish, you can use the ECHO OFF mode to eliminate the display of all command lines, but remember this will also eliminate the display of all REM statements.

The PAUSE Command

The PAUSE command is used to cause a batch file to pause at a specific point in a batch file while it is executing. When any key is pressed after a batch file has paused as a result of a PAUSE command, MS-DOS resumes executing the batch file from the point it halted. Alternatively, the <Ctrl>C or <Ctrl><Break> keys can be pressed to abort the batch file while it has paused.

The PAUSE command puts a built-in stop into a batch file. You use this command when you need to do something before the next command is executed, such as change a disk or turn on the printer. You might also use PAUSE to allow a full screen to be read before proceeding to the next screen.

Because you stop processing with the PAUSE command, you must then press a key to continue the batch file. As part of the PAUSE command, MS-DOS has an automatic message that appears after the PAUSE command— "Strike any key when ready." You don't need to add this message, because it will always appear after a PAUSE command. PAUSE could be incorporated into the "newdisk" batch file.

```
C:\>copy con: newdisk.bat <ENTER>
rem This file formats and checks new disks. <ENTER>
pause Remove the diskette currently in drive B. <ENTER>
rem The system will be put on the diskette. <ENTER>
format b:/s <ENTER>
dir b: <ENTER>
rem Here is the condition of this diskette. <ENTER>
chkdsk b: <ENTER>
rem This diskette is ready to use. Don't forget to label it!
 <ENTER>
^Z <ENTER>

1 File(s) copied
```

A new version of "newdisk" would be created.

```
C:\>rem This file formats and checks new disks.

C:\>pause Remove the diskette currently in drive B.
Strike a key when ready....
```

You press a key.

```
C:\>rem The system will be put on the diskette.

C:\>format b:/s
Insert new diskette for drive B:
and strike any key when ready

Formatting....Format complete
System transferred

362496 bytes total disk space
 40960 bytes used by system
321536 bytes available on disk

Format another (Y/N)?n
```

You answer *n*.

```
C:\>dir b:

Volume in drive B has no label
Directory of B:\

COMMAND  COM:    17664 4-22-91  12:00p
         1 File(s)   321536 bytes free

C:\>rem Here is the condition of this diskette.

C:\>chkdsk b:
362496 bytes total disk space
 22528 bytes in 2 hidden files
 18432 bytes in 1 user files
321536 bytes available on disk

262144 bytes total memory
237456 bytes free

C:\>rem This diskette is ready to use. Don't forget to label it!
C:\>
```

PAUSE is a useful safety device within a batch file. In this case, you use it as a warning, so you will be sure not to format over a disk that contains data. This warning can be very effective in helping you avoid those errors everyone makes at one time or another. For example, if you have included in a batch file the command to erase all old files, inserting a PAUSE could save you from a frustrating mistake.

```
dir b:
pause Make sure all desired files have been copied, or break.
del oldfiles
```

The GOTO Command

A batch file can be constructed in such a way so that it behaves like a program written in BASIC or another programming language by using GOTO commands to branch to specific parts within a batch file or to create repeating loops.

The GOTO command works in conjunction with a label. The label is any name you choose that identifies a location in a batch file, rather like the way a line number in EDLIN indicates a location. The label is preceded by a colon (:). GOTO transfers control of the processing to the line after the label.

GOTO is a convenient command when you want to keep repeating a certain activity without changing any parameters. Suppose you had a letter and needed several duplicates made. Using GOTO, you could set up a batch file to type out as many duplicates as you needed.

When you use GOTO and refer to a label that precedes the GOTO line, you create a *loop*. A loop is an operation that will keep repeating until you stop it. To escape from a loop in a batch file, use ^C or <Ctrl><Break> to terminate the job. The loop itself is not displayed on the screen. A GOTO loop is illustrated in *Figure 10-3*.

Figure 10-3.
The GOTO Command

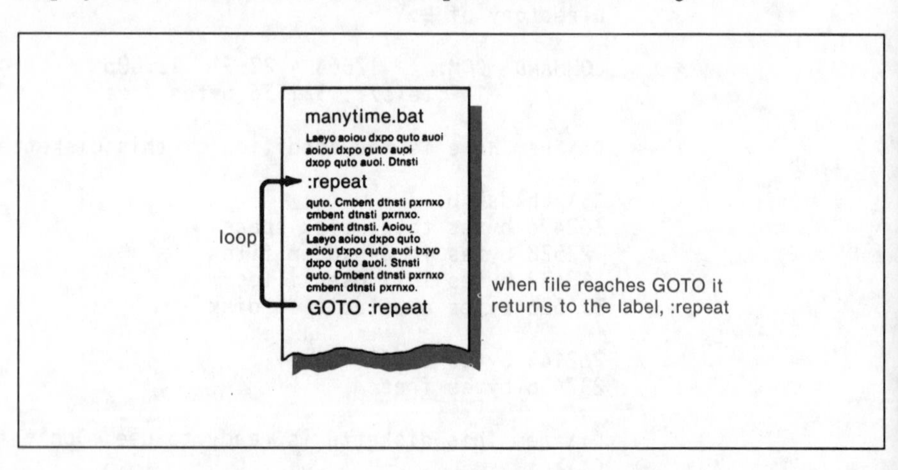

The name of the batch file in *Figure 10-3* is "manytime.bat." The label that defines where the command returns is called ":repeat."

```
C:\>copy con: manytime.bat <ENTER>
rem This file makes duplicate copies of a letter. <ENTER>
echo off <ENTER>
echo Put a new disk in drive B:
pause
copy a:letter b: <ENTER>
:repeat <ENTER>
type b:letter <ENTER>
echo Press CTRL BREAK to stop this batch file. <ENTER>
goto :repeat <ENTER>
^Z <ENTER>

1 File(s) copied
```

To run this batch file, you must have the file "letter" on the disk in drive A. For our example, the file "letter" contains one line, "This is a sample for the goto command." To execute "manytime," enter its name.

```
c:\>manytime <ENTER>
```

"Manytime" results in this display:

```
C:\>rem This file makes duplicate copies of a letter.
Put a new disk in drive B:
Strike a key when ready...
C:\> echo off
        1 File(s) copied
This is a sample for the goto command.
Put a new disk in drive B:
Strike a key when ready...
Press CTRL BREAK to stop this batch file.
This is a sample for the goto command.
Put a new disk in drive B:
Strike a key when ready...
        .
        .
        .
```

These messages continue to be displayed until you stop processing by pressing <Ctrl><Break>.

The IF Command

command is ovided so that within a batch file, you can check and compare strings of text, check for the existence of specified files, or check for errors and cause the batch file to behave in certain ways according to the results.

The IF command tells the batch file to continue processing the next command if a certain condition is true. As illustrated in *Figure 10-4*, the condition can be one of three options: IF exist, IF string, and IF ERRORLEVEL.

IF Exist

IF exist uses a file specification as the test. If the file exists (the condition is true), then processing passes to the specified GOTO location. If the file does not exist (the condition is false), then batch processing continues with the next command.

Figure 10-4. The IF Command

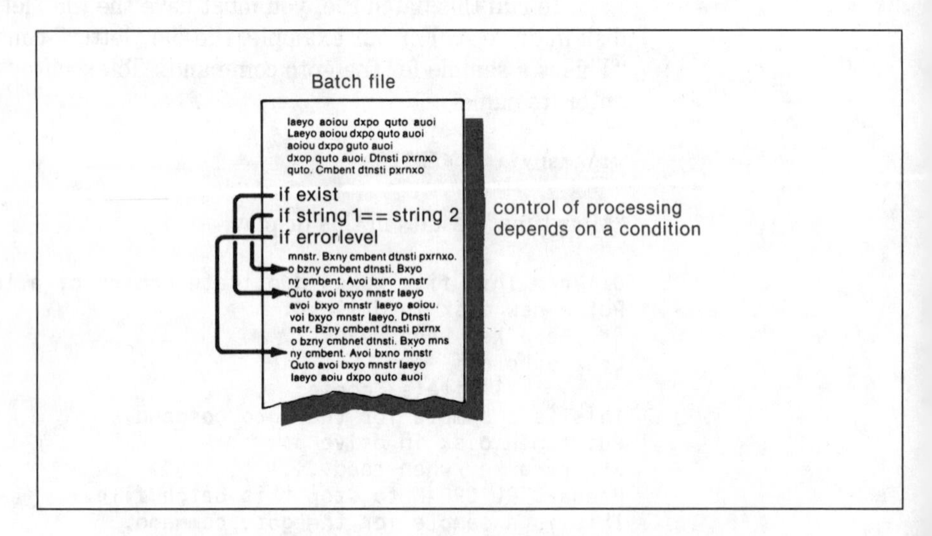

For an IF exist example, let's create a batch file that prints a letter until it is instructed to stop. (PRINT is a new MS-DOS command that sends a file to the printer. Make sure your printer is on before running the batch file.) This batch file contains another instruction. It tells MS-DOS to check first to see if the letter has already been copied from A to B. If the letter does not exist on B, the batch file formats the disk in B, copies the file to B, and makes sure the file is on B by listing a directory. Then it starts printing. If the file already exists on B, the letter has been copied and printing begins immediately. Here are the contents of the "copylet" batch file:

```
C:\>copy con: copylet.bat <ENTER>
echo off <ENTER>
if exist b:letter goto :exists <ENTER>
format b: <ENTER>
```

```
copy a:letter b: <ENTER>
dir b: <ENTER>
:exists <ENTER>
print b:letter <ENTER>
echo Press CTRL BREAK to stop this batch file. <ENTER>
goto :exists <ENTER>
^Z <ENTER>

1 File(s) copied
```

Here are the results of the first run of "copylet":

```
C:\>copylet <ENTER>

C:\>echo off
Insert new diskette for drive B:
and strike any key when ready
```

The "letter" file was not found on the B disk so formatting begins.

```
Formatting....Format complete

362496 bytes total disk space
362496 bytes available on disk

Format another (Y/N)?n          1 File(s) copied
```

You answer *n*; MS-DOS proceeds to copy the file to B.

```
Volume in drive B has no label
Directory of B:\
```

MS-DOS lists the directory.

```
LETTER              40  4-22-91   12:54p
         1 File(s)    361472 bytes free
```

```
This is a sample for the goto command.
```

← This goes to the printer thanks to the PRINT command.

```
Press CTRL BREAK to stop this batch file.
This is a sample for the goto command.
Press CTRL BREAK to stop this batch file.
This is a sample for the goto command.
Press CTRL BREAK to stop this batch file.
This is a sample for the goto command.
Press CTRL BREAK to stop this batch file.
This is a sample for the goto command.
Press CTRL BREAK to stop this batch file.
This is a sample ....
```

The file is now in the exists loop.

The first time you run "copylet," the "letter" file will not be found on the B disk unless it had been copied previously. The batch file checks for this condition. Not finding the file on the indicated disk, it proceeds to format the disk, copy the file, and give you a directory. Printing then begins and continues until you halt the batch file.

Provided you use the same disk in drive B, the results will be different the second time you run "copylet."

```
C:\>copylet <ENTER>

C:\>echo off
This is a sample for the goto command.          ← This goes to the
                                                   printer.
Press CTRL BREAK to stop this batch file.
This is a sample for the goto command.
Press CTRL BREAK to stop this batch file.
This is ....
```

On all consequent runs of "copylet," the condition is true (the "letter" file already exists on drive B). Therefore, the batch file skips directly to the exists loop and begins printing the letter. This continues until you terminate the batch file.

IF String

The IF command can also be used to compare any replaceable parameters that are specified against specific text strings or other parameters.

The second IF option uses a string as a test. A string is simply computereze for a group of characters. In this IF command you tell DOS to go to a specific location or to perform a certain operation when the strings match (the condition is true). When you enter the strings in the command, they are separated by two equal signs (==). For example, you might have a batch file with replaceable parameters. It contains this command:

```
IF %1 == Seamus echo Seamus is ready.
```

Whenever Seamus was entered as the %1 parameter, this condition would be true, and the echo command "Seamus is ready" would be displayed. However, if Matt was entered as the %1 parameter, then the condition would be false and the echo message would not appear.

IF ERRORLEVEL

The third IF option uses ERRORLEVEL as the test. ERRORLEVEL is an indicator (sometimes called a "flag") that signals the status of a certain condition. ERRORLEVEL is internally set as a part of certain MS-DOS commands. It indicates whether an operation was successfully performed. Usually ERRORLEVEL 1 indicates failure of the operation; ERRORLEVEL 0 indicates successful completion of the command.

Imagine that you had a program that copied all files from one disk to another. This "copyall" file includes three commands.

```
copy a:*.* b:
if errorlevel 1 echo copyall failure
dir b:
```

The message "copyall failure" appears on the screen if all the files are not successfully copied. Non-completion of the operation in this case makes the condition true. The message does not appear when all the files are copied, because this results in an ERRORLEVEL of 0 and the IF condition is false.

These IF commands may seem a bit complicated at first. Take your time and go slowly as you begin to use this command. A few practice sessions will increase your confidence. You will quickly discover how useful the IF command can be in making your batch commands do exactly what you need them to do.

Using Batch Files to Simplify Backup

Your regular backup operation can be greatly enhanced by using a batch file containing the BACKUP command to check for such things as error conditions or to select backup options.

Batch files can make the hard-disk backup procedure easier for you. Batch files contain MS-DOS commands, including the commands used with the hard disk. One of the features of BACKUP is that it sets up an exit code value (a numerical marker that is MS-DOS's version of tying a string to its finger) when it is finished copying. This code ranges from 0 to 4:

0 Indicates that everything was completed normally.

1 Indicates that DOS found no files to backup.

2 This value is not used.

3 Indicates that the user terminated the backup procedure.

4 Indicates that the backup was terminated by an error.

As you know, IF can be used with ERRORLEVEL to cause a certain action to occur. By using IF in a batch file, you can automate the backup procedure and reduce the chance of making errors when performing backups. Using IF with BACKUP in a batch file is a good example of how useful and rewarding batch files can be. Here is how using ERRORLEVEL might clarify the operations going on in a batch file:

```
copy con: backall.bat
backup c: a/s
if errorlevel 0 echo backall completed
if errorlevel 1 echo backall failure
if errorlevel 3 echo you've terminated backall
if errorlevel 4 echo an error has terminated backall
```

The SHIFT Command

The SHIFT command is used to move the contents of any specific replaceable parameters downward: parameter %1 is transferred to %0, %2 to %1, %3 to %2, and so on. (The old %0 is lost.) This command allows you not only to check all parameters initially specified with the batch file by doing continual shifts so that only %0 needs to be checked but also to specify more than ten parameters on the batch file's command line.

After you have developed some of your own batch files and have seen just how timesaving they can be, you may want to use more than ten replaceable parameters. You may want to type out twelve files or copy fifteen files. The SHIFT command enables you to solve this dilemma by exceeding ten replaceable parameters. You can't just add %11, %12, and so on. Instead, after you have substituted the first ten parameters, your %1 parameter drops off the list and all the remaining parameters shift one position to the left.

Suppose that for some obscure reason you want to create a batch file to display the letters of the alphabet up to and including the letter L. This means there are twelve parameters you want substituted into the file. This is how the contents of "alphabet" appear:

```
echo off
echo %0 %1 %2 %3 %4 %5 %6 %7 %8 %9
SHIFT
echo %0 %1 %2 %3 %4 %5 %6 %7 %8 %9
SHIFT
echo %0 %1 %2 %3 %4 %5 %6 %7 %8 %9
SHIFT
echo %0 %1 %2 %3 %4 %5 %6 %7 %8 %9
SHIFT
```

You execute this file by calling the batch file.

```
C:\>alphabet A B C D E F G H I J K L <ENTER>
```

The first time you use parameters in your batch file, the first ten parameters are substituted just as they were entered. But after the SHIFT command, all the parameters move over one space to the left. The leftmost parameter is dropped, and the new parameter (number 10 in the list) is moved into the %9 position. This move to the left continues each time you issue the SHIFT command.

The output of "alphabet" looks like this:

```
C:\>echo off
alphabet A B C D E F G H I
A B C D E F G H I J
B C D E F G H I J K
C D E F G H I J K L
```

You can easily see how you could continue substituting parameters until all that you included have been displayed. Once there are fewer than ten parameters left, the spaces to the right will be left blank.

The FOR Command

The FOR command provides a function called FOR-LOOP, frequently found in programming languages. The FOR command allows you to examine a series of parameters to a specific MS-DOS command and cause that command to execute repeatedly, each time with a different parameter, until all parameters have been used.

As illustrated in *Figure 10-5*, this batch command allows repetition of the same command on a series of files and uses a few new concepts. The first is the concept of a *set*, a group of files that follows the "in" portion of the FOR command. Thus, the set in the following example is chap1.txt, chap2.txt, and chap3.txt. Immediately following the FOR command is a variable, designated by two percent signs (%%) and a name. This variable also follows the "do" section of the command. The FOR command allows you to repeat an action or operation for each of the files contained in the set.

Suppose you want to create a batch file to check for the existence of files on a disk, in this case, three files named chap1, chap2, and chap3. The FOR command can accomplish this.

```
for %%A in (chap1.txt chap2.txt chap3.txt) do dir %%A
```

Figure 10-5.
The FOR Command

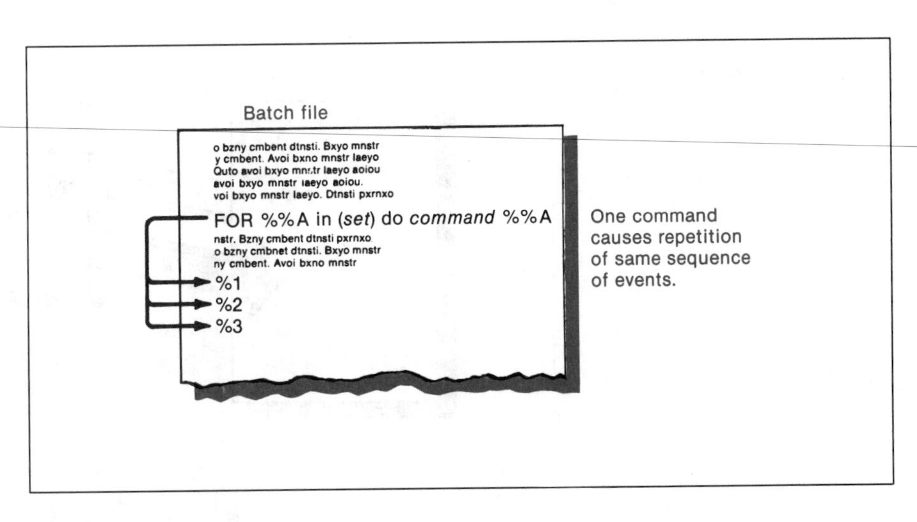

If the files are found, three results are displayed.

```
dir chap1.txt
dir chap2.txt
dir chap3.txt
```

You can make this command even more powerful by using wildcards for the set. Here is an easy, fast way to copy all the files on a disk:

```
for %%B in (*.*) do copy %% b:
```

The CALL Command

Programmers often divide their programs into short, logically connected sets of program statements called "subroutines." They then write a main program that calls subroutines as needed. When a subroutine is finished executing, control returns to the main program, which continues until it calls the next subroutine, which then executes and returns and so on.

The CALL command, shown in *Figure 10-6*, lets you do this with batch files. When your batch file has a line like:

```
call otherbat
```

the batch file "otherbat" will start to execute. (Note that you don't need to specify the .BAT extension, though you can if you wish.)

Figure 10-6. The CALL Command

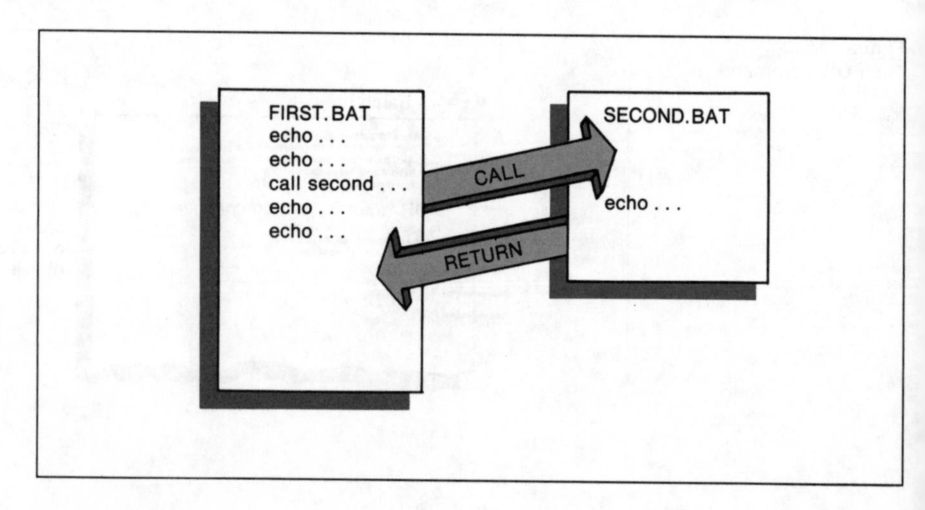

When "otherbat" is done, control returns to the next line in the original batch file.

To test the CALL command, create the file first.bat

```
C:\>copy con: first.bat
@echo off
echo This is the first batch file
echo calling the second batch file
call second                              ← this calls the file
                                           second.bat
echo now back in the first batch file
                                         ← press F6 or Ctrl-Z
     1 file(s) copied
```

Now create second.bat:

```
C:\>copy con second.bat
echo This is the second batch file <ENTER>
```

Execute the first batch file and see the results:

```
C:\>first
This is the first batch file
calling the second batch file
This is the second batch file
now back in the first batch file
```

For MS-DOS versions earlier than 3.3, you can use the Command /C command to call a second batch file. In the preceding example, you would replace the line CALL SECOND with the line COMMAND /C SECOND. This command runs a copy of COMMAND.COM, the MS-DOS command processor, and tells it to run the batch file "second.bat" and then exit. When it exits, the original batch file continues. This method is less elegant than CALL, and uses some extra memory to run the second copy of COMMAND.COM, but it does the job.

SUMMARY

In this chapter you were introduced to batch files and batch processing. You learned that you can create files using both the EDLIN program and the COPY CON: command. Each of the batch commands, ECHO, REM, PAUSE, GOTO, IF, SHIFT, FOR, and CALL was explained. Batch processing is a method that you will continue to develop as you find your own uses for this special feature of MS-DOS.

REVIEW

1. Batch files contain MS-DOS commands, filenames, and a few special commands; names of batch files always end with the extension .BAT. To create a batch file, use EDLIN or use the command COPY CON: and end by entering <Ctrl>Z alone on the last line.
2. To run a batch file, type its name at the prompt. To interrupt the operation of a batch file, type <Ctrl>C or <Ctrl><Break>.
3. You can include replaceable parameters (%1, %2, and so on) in a batch file; to invoke the batch file, type in the names of the files you wish the batch file to operate on.
4. The ECHO command can be set to ECHO ON or ECHO OFF and display or inhibit displaying the batch file commands on the screen as the file executes.
5. The REM command is used to begin a line of explanatory comments.
6. Place the PAUSE command in a batch file at a point where you intend the operation to pause for you to do something, such as swap disks.
7. The GOTO command runs the batch file instruction sequence from whatever label, preceded by a colon, you specify. GOTO is often used to create a repeating sequence, or loop.
8. The IF command allows GOTO branching to a label, depending on the existence of a file or a complete match of two strings or an error indication.
9. The SHIFT command allows reuse of replaceable parameters %0 to %9 to increase the total number of substitutions.
10. The FOR command allows you to execute a DOS command on a group of files.
11. The CALL command is used to call another batch file, execute it, and then return to the current batch file. COMMAND /C is a way to do this for versions of MS-DOS before 3.3.

Quiz for Chapter 10

1. The MS-DOS batch function is used to:
   - a. automatically execute a series of MS-DOS commands contained within a batch file.
   - b. execute a file that is somewhat like a cookbook of commands.
   - c. execute a file that has the extension .BAT.
   - d. all of the above.
2. Batch files always contain:
   - a. binary-coded data.
   - b. ASCII text.
   - c. encrypted data.
   - d. none of the above.
3. A batch file can be created using:
   - a. a text editor such as EDLIN.
   - b. a word processing program.
   - c. the "COPY CON: filename" command sequence, where "filename" is the name of the batch file.
   - d. any of the above.
   - e. none of the above.
4. A batch filename must contain:
   - a. the extension .BAT.
   - b. any extension.
   - c. no extension.
5. A batch file is executed by MS-DOS by entering the filename:
   - a. with the extension .BAT.
   - b. without the extension .BAT.
   - c. either of the above.
   - d. none of the above.
6. The execution of a batch file can be prematurely stopped by:
   - a. pressing <Ctrl>B.
   - b. pressing <Ctrl>C.
   - c. pressing <Ctrl>D.
   - d. pressing <Ctrl>G.
7. Up to how many replaceable parameters may be checked within a batch file when it is executed?
   - a. 2
   - b. 5
   - c. 10
   - d. 20

8. The special batch ECHO command is used for:
   a. turning off echoing of text to the display.
   b. turning on echoing of text to the display.
   c. echoing specified text to the display.
   d. any of the above.
   e. none of the above.

9. The REM command is used to:
   a. insert commands in a batch file.
   b. remove text from a batch file.
   c. insert in a batch file remarks or comments that are not to be treated as commands by MS-DOS.
   d. none of the above.

10. To cause the batch file to pause at a specific point while it is executing, you should insert which command at the point where you want the pause to occur:
    a. STOP command.
    b. PAUSE command.
    c. <Ctrl>S command.
    d. <Ctrl>Z command.

11. The GOTO command is used in batch files to:
    a. cause a branch to another part of the batch file.
    b. branch so that a repetitive loop occurs.
    c. either a or b.
    d. none of the above.

12. The IF command is used to:
    a. check the existence of a specified file on a disk.
    b. check and compare two text strings.
    c. check for an error condition.
    d. any of the above.
    e. none of the above.

13. The SHIFT command is used to:
    a. shift the contents of each replaceable parameter downward.
    b. allow the use of more than ten replaceable parameters.
    c. shift the screen sideways.
    d. shift the definition of the keys on the keyboard over by one position.
    e. a and b.

14. The FOR command is used to execute the same command repeatedly, each time with a different parameter, until:
    a. some of the specified parameters have been covered.

b. the second parameter has been covered.
c. all specified parameters have been covered.
d. any of the above.
e. none of the above.

15. The CALL command is used when you need to:
a. call a machine-language subroutine from a batch file.
b. execute another batch file and then return.
c. dial a phone number on a modem
d. immediately terminate the batch file.

11

Using DOSSHELL

ABOUT THIS CHAPTER

You now have learned many things that you can do with MS-DOS commands and option switches. You've also probably made your share of mistakes, and perhaps you've wondered if there is an easier way to deal with MS-DOS than having to remember exactly how to type everything at the command prompt. In this chapter you'll learn about an alternative way to use MS-DOS: the DOSSHELL utility, which is provided in MS-DOS version 4.

DOSSHELL offers pull-down menus with which you select what part of the shell you wish to work with. You can use the keyboard or a mouse to select programs, files, and command options.

DOSSHELL makes MS-DOS easier to use, particularly for beginners. DOSSHELL uses windows (areas of the screen) to list your programs and files. You can use either the keyboard or a mouse (a pointing device) to run programs or manipulate files. DOSSHELL streamlines many routine operations by letting you point to things on screen instead of typing commands. You'll see how easy it is to select options from pull-down menus, run commands and application programs, and add new programs to the menu list.

You may be perfectly happy typing commands such as DIR WORDPROC to get a quick listing of the files in your directory. You also know that it's not hard to use the COPY, DEL, and TYPE commands to work with the files in your directory. Why wait extra seconds to load DOSSHELL? Why learn how to navigate through a series of menus and windows to do something as simple as DEL LETTER1?

You can run many commands such as COPY and DISKCOPY from the shell. Other commands, such as DIR and CD are built into the operation of the shell's File System display.

These are good questions. DOSSHELL provides some real advantages, as you will see, but it isn't the best tool for every kind of PC housekeeping task. So DOSSHELL also provides you with quick access to the traditional command-line prompt for those occasions when it is easier to type in the command you want. In order to appreciate the value of DOSSHELL, you should first review how the basic command-line interface to MS-DOS works.

THE COMMAND-LINE INTERFACE

Most users think that the command prompt (such as C:\>) is part of MS-DOS itself. Actually, this prompt is generated by a separate program called COMMAND.COM. MS-DOS is always running one program or another, and when it isn't running something that you've told it to run (such as your word processor), it loads and runs COMMAND.COM, which just waits for your next command. Basically the COMMAND.COM program allows you to do three things:

- Run internal MS-DOS commands, such as DIR to list directories or COPY to copy files.
- Run external MS-DOS commands or utilities, such as CHKDSK to get a summary of disk usage or FORMAT to prepare a disk.
- Run other programs, such as Lotus 1-2-3 or a MS-DOS batch file.

COMMAND.COM is the program that provides the MS-DOS command-line interface and prompt. COMMAND.COM interprets your commands. If the command is an external MS-DOS utility program (such as XCOPY) or an application program, MS-DOS removes most of itself from memory and runs the program. When the program is terminated, MS-DOS reloads COMMAND.COM.

When it is told to run a program, COMMAND.COM removes most of itself from memory and transfers control to the other program. When the other program stops running, the part of COMMAND.COM remaining in memory reloads the rest of COMMAND.COM. (Chapter 12 explains how you can use the COMSPEC variable to help MS-DOS "find itself.")

In other words, COMMAND.COM is the MS-DOS–user interface. In addition to running your application programs, it allows you to enter commands that resemble English words rather than having to communicate directly with low-level machine routines. Traditionally, MS-DOS users type commands such as COPY LETTER A:LETTER.BAK or FORMAT A: /F:720 to a prompt such as C:\>. After they press the <ENTER> key, MS-DOS responds to the request.

The advantage of typing commands directly at the command line is that MS-DOS will do exactly what you tell it to do, and do it immediately, without requiring a series of menu selections. You can also put commands, one per line, in a batch file to have them executed automatically. (See Chapter 10 for more about this powerful feature.)

The disadvantage of working at the command prompt is that you must know *exactly* how to tell MS-DOS what you want to do. If you make a mistake, you may get a not-very-helpful error message, such as "too many parameters." If the command is correct but has a potentially dangerous effect (such as erasing all of the files in a directory), MS-DOS will ask you for confirmation. But otherwise, you're on your own. Sometimes MS-DOS will do what you *told* it to do rather than what you *wanted* it to do! Learning to use the command line effectively requires becoming familiar with the syntax and rules for using a variety of MS-DOS commands. This can be a tedious process, though a comprehensive encyclopedia (such as *The Waite*

Group's Using PC DOS or *The Waite Group's MS-DOS Bible)* can help you get the most out of MS-DOS.

Another problem with using the command line is that often you don't have easy access to the information you need for the next step. Suppose, for example, you want to back up the file LETTER1 from your hard disk to a floppy. Fine, but where *is* LETTER1? Is it in the WordPerfect directory? The customer contacts directory? The accounting directory? Before you can copy the file, you often have to issue a series of DIR commands in order to find the file. This lack of easily accessible information about directories and files frustrates many beginning MS-DOS users.

DOSSHELL is a useful tool, but it can't do everything that you can do from the command line. You can develop batch files to automate more complicated tasks, as explained in Chapter 10. You can install these batch files (as with other programs) and run them from DOSSHELL.

DOSSHELL: A GRAPHICAL USER INTERFACE

Rather than just giving you a bare prompt on the screen, DOSSHELL makes sure that the information you need to complete your tasks will usually be on the screen when you need it. When you want to copy a file, for example, there will be a list of directories and files that you can browse through until you find the file you want. You don't have to try to think of all the directories the file might be in and type a DIR command to look at each one. Other information about your files and directories is made available when you select reports from a menu.

When DOSSHELL asks you for something and you're not sure what it wants, a key-press brings up a "help" box. Many frequently used MS-DOS commands, such as COPY, DISKCOPY, and DEL, are already packaged for you into menu selections. You don't have to remember the exact name of the command that you need.

Because DOSSHELL uses windows to present (and ask for) information, and allows you to select commands from menus rather than typing them in, it is an example of a *graphical user interface.* It isn't as fancy as Microsoft Windows or the Macintosh desktop, because it relies mainly on text rather than graphic symbols (icons). This can be an advantage, because a text-based program can run faster and use less memory than a fully graphics-based program.

INSIDE DOSSHELL

Now that you're aware of the reasons for using DOSSHELL, you're ready to look at the anatomy of DOSSHELL. Where does it reside and how does it work? How do the facilities offered by DOSSHELL fit into the structure of standard MS-DOS? How is DOSSHELL installed in your system?

DOSSHELL doesn't actually replace COMMAND.COM. Rather it runs as a separate program over it, providing menus, dialog boxes, and window displays, and calling upon COMMAND.COM or external MS-DOS commands to carry out the operations you select. In this way it provides all the functions of COMMAND.COM and simplifies many of the MS-DOS commands, but you don't need to memorize the syntax or details of usage required by the traditional command line. (Although DOSSHELL is available only with MS-DOS version 4, a variety of third-party shell programs provide a similar range of functions to users of earlier MS-DOS versions.)

How DOSSHELL Runs

Since DOSSHELL is a regular MS-DOS utility program, you can run it automatically on startup by placing the name DOSSHELL in the AUTOEXEC.BAT file, or you can type *dosshell* at the regular command prompt. The MS-DOS version 4 installation program, SELECT, provides the appropriate AUTOEXEC.BAT commands for you, according to your disk configuration and your responses to the questions it has asked you about how you want to run the shell.

(If you have not yet installed MS-DOS version 4 and DOSSHELL, please read the section on MS-DOS version 4 in Appendix B. Then after you have installed the shell, continue here. You'll get more out of this chapter if you can try out the DOSSHELL features and commands on your own PC.)

DOSSHELL is actually run from a batch file (DOSSHELL.BAT) that in turn runs setup programs. DOSSHELL has a number of settings that specify the screen display, the use of a mouse, the features to be included, and so on. You probably won't have to change any of the settings that MS-DOS version 4 installs for you. They are explained in your MS-DOS manual.

DOSSHELL Menus

DOSSHELL has a *hierarchical*, or layered, *menu system*. This means that you start with general menus and, as necessary, make more specific selections from successive submenus or pop-up boxes until you have selected the actual task that you want to perform.

The Start Programs screen is the "master menu" for DOSSHELL. From it, you can select from among a group of programs including MS-DOS Utilities. You can also select the File System program in order to perform file housekeeping.

The highest-level menu, the Start Programs screen, shown in *Figure 11-1*, enables you to set up or revise menus of programs that can be run from the shell. Related programs, such as a word processor, printer control program, file converter, and spelling checker, can be grouped together, and you can switch back and forth among these program groups. It's important to realize, however, that unlike the case with Microsoft Windows or OS/2, you can run only one program at a time.

Program Groups

The default list of programs shown on the Start Programs screen is called the *Main Group*. A program group is a list of programs related by function. The Main Group is special in that it can contain other groups as well as programs, just as a directory can contain subdirectories. The Main Group is the only group that can contain other groups, which are also called *subgroups*.

Figure 11-1. The Start Programs Screen

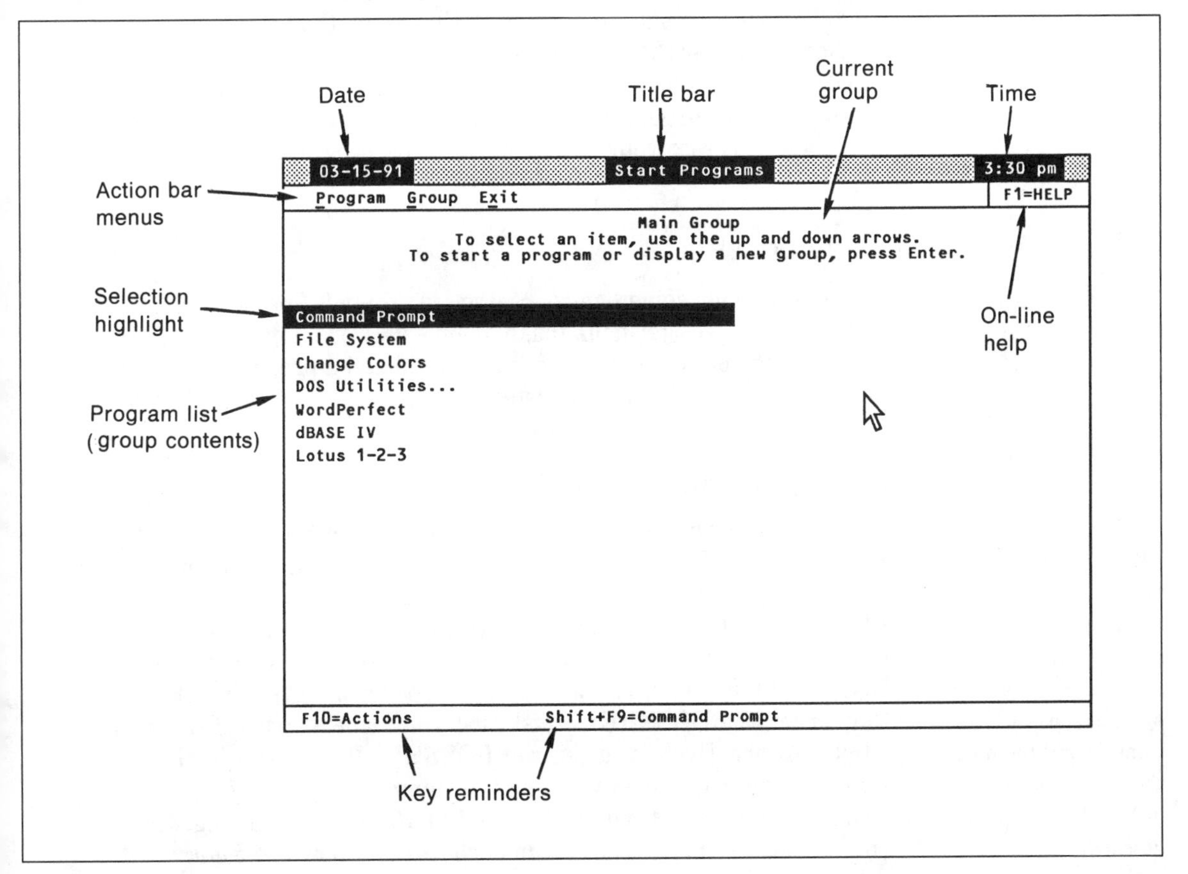

In *Figure 11-1*, the application programs WordPerfect, Lotus 1-2-3, and dBASE IV have been added to the Main Group menu. You will learn later how to add your applications to the program selection menus.

The Main Group also contains some built-in groups and programs, including a group of MS-DOS Utilities (time, date, copy, compare, backup/restore, and format), a program that you can use to change the colors used by the shell, and the program COMMAND.COM described as "command prompt," which gives you access to the traditional MS-DOS command line.

One of the options under Main Group is the File System program. This in turn provides a set of menus enabling you to manipulate files, control the way file information is displayed, and set various options. *Figure 11-2* shows how the supplied and user-defined groups and programs fit together in DOSSHELL's Main Group structure. In the figure, Command Prompt, File System, and Change Colors are programs supplied with the shell. DOS Utilities . . . , also supplied with the shell, is a subgroup of the Main Group. (You can tell that it is a subgroup rather than a program because it ends with ellipses, or three dots.) The subgroups Spreadsheet, Database, and Writing are user-defined subgroups containing application programs. (You'll soon learn how to create your own group and add programs to it.)

USING DOSSHELL

Now it's time for some hands-on practice. You will see how to start and exit the shell, get help, make menu selections, run an MS-DOS utility command, manage your files, and install a program and a program group in the menu system.

Starting and Exiting DOSSHELL

If you have a hard disk with MS-DOS 4.0, DOSSHELL will start automatically when you boot the system. If you have a floppy-only system, start MS-DOS from the startup disk, then insert your shell disk in drive A and type *dosshell*.

How you start DOSSHELL depends on how you have installed it. Recall that DOSSHELL can be run in one of two ways. In one way, you place a line with the word *DOSSHELL* in your AUTOEXEC.BAT file, and DOSSHELL then runs automatically when the system is started from the hard disk. (For some floppy-based configurations, you will have to boot from a system disk and then insert the DOSSHELL disk that you made as part of the installation.) Alternatively, you can run DOSSHELL from the regular MS-DOS command line by typing the command DOSSHELL. Whichever way you start it, you will know DOSSHELL is running when you see a Start Programs screen such as that shown in *Figure 11-1*.

Figure 11-2.
Structure of DOSSHELL

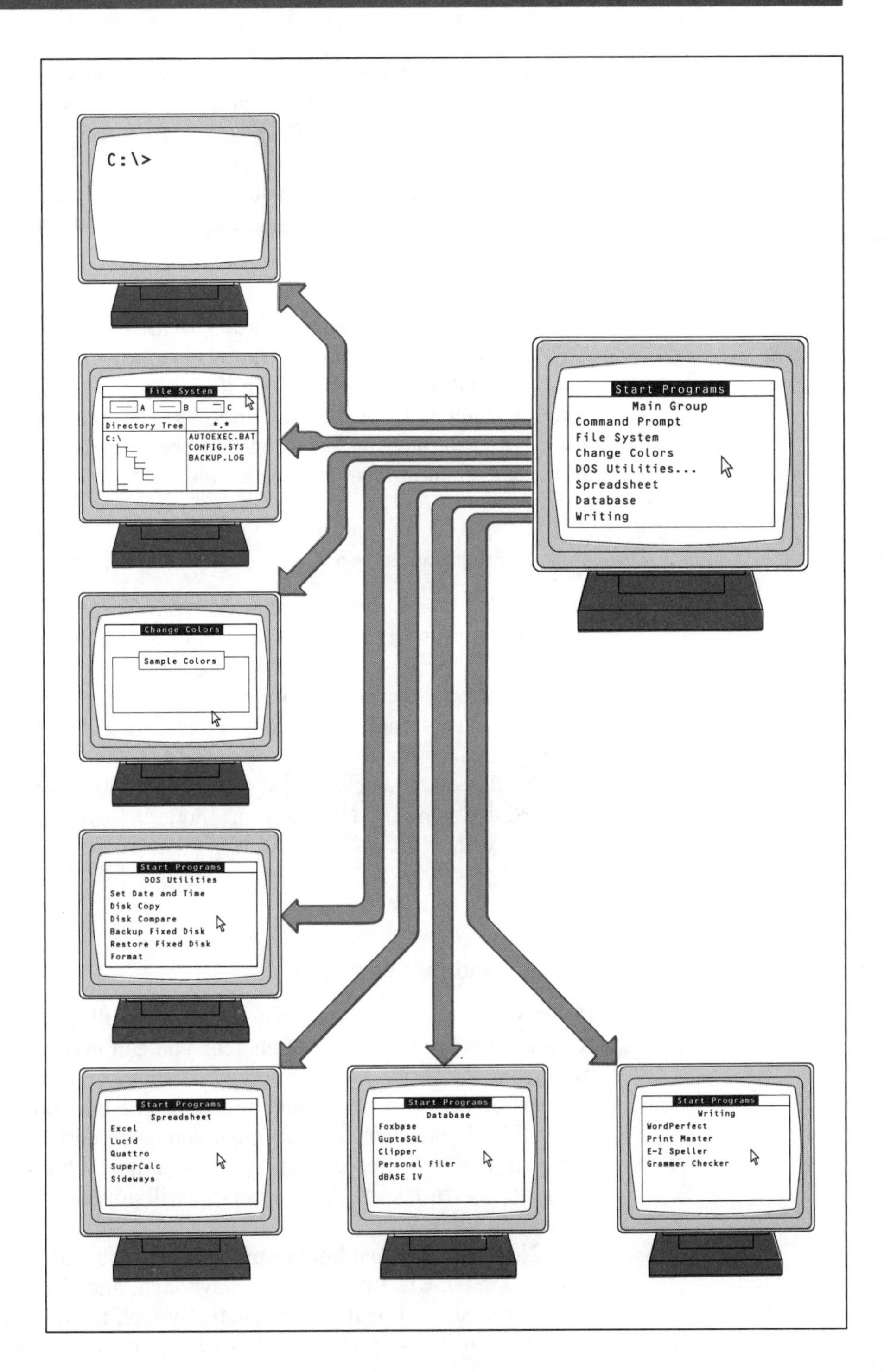

When you are running the shell, you can exit from it in two ways: you can press <F3>, or you can select Exit from the action bar at the top of the Start Programs screen (refer to *Figure 11-1*) and then select Exit Shell from the pull-down menu that appears. You will soon learn all of the methods for selecting items in the shell.

The Start Programs Screen

If you haven't done so already, start DOSSHELL. You should be looking at a screen similar to that shown in *Figure 11-1*. DOSSHELL can run in either "text mode" or, if you have a suitable display adapter (such as EGA), it can run in "graphics mode." This figure shows the graphics-mode screen, but the text-mode screen is similar and those small differences will be noted.

Start Programs Screen

The *title line*, with Start Programs at the top center, includes the current date at the left end and the current time at the right end.

Just below this line on the left is the *action bar*, a menu from which you can make selections. In this case, it offers three selections: Program, Group, and Exit.

The main part of the screen shows the group of programs currently selected. Normally, as shown here, this is the Main Group. When you select a subgroup, it is shown instead of the Main Group.

Pop-Ups and Pull-Downs

If you select an item from the action bar, a pull-down menu appears. A *pull-down menu* is a list of choices you can make after selecting an item from the action bar. Some menu choices present a pop-up box. A *pop-up box* requests additional information from you so that DOSSHELL can carry out the task you selected from a pull-down menu. If you see ellipses (. . .) next to a menu choice (as in DOS Utilities . . . in *Figure 11-1*), a pop-up will appear when you choose that menu item.

Next, you'll learn how to make selections and run programs from DOSSHELL, first with the keyboard, and then with the mouse. While DOSSHELL can be run perfectly well from the keyboard, many people find the mouse easier to use for many operations.

Making Selections from the Keyboard

To select a program or group by using the keyboard, move the selection cursor (the highlighted bar over a line of text) up and down with the arrow keys and then select the desired item by pressing <ENTER>. On the action bar, you can use the left-arrow and right-arrow keys to move the cursor, and then press <ENTER> to select the highlighted item. Alternatively, to make a selection, press the key corresponding to the underlined letter in the item you want. Use the <F10> key to switch between the program list and the action bar.

Running a Program

When the Start Programs screen comes up, the cursor (a shaded bar) will highlight the Command Prompt selection. Use the down-arrow key to move the cursor until it is over Change Colors. Press <ENTER> to run the Change Colors program. Now press <Esc>. The <Esc> key generally returns you to where you were before you made the last selection. In this case, it returns you to the Main Group on the Start Programs screen.

You can run programs by selecting them from a program list (if the program has been installed in a program group). You can also run programs from the File System by selecting the program's filename from a file list. Finally, if you press <SHIFT><F9> to get a command-line prompt, you can run programs from the command line as usual.

Selecting a Program Group

Move the selection cursor with the up- or down-arrow key until it is over *DOS Utilities*. Press <ENTER>, and the list of programs in the DOS Utilities group will be shown. You can run any of these programs by using the arrow keys to move the cursor atop the desired program and then pressing <ENTER>. For now, press <Esc>, and you will be returned to the Main Group on the Start Programs screen. You will learn how to use the DOS Utilities program later.

Using Pull-Down Menus

Press <F10> to switch the selection cursor from the list of items in the Main Group to the row of items on the action bar: Program, Group, and Exit. (<F10> is a *toggle*: typing it again returns the selection cursor to the list of items in the center of the screen.) You can now move the selection cursor from left to right and back again by using the left-arrow and right-arrow keys. Use the right-arrow key to move the cursor over the Exit item. Press <ENTER> to select Exit. The pull-down menu shown in *Figure 11-3* will appear. For now, press <Esc> to return to the action bar.

Figure 11-3. Pull-Down Menu

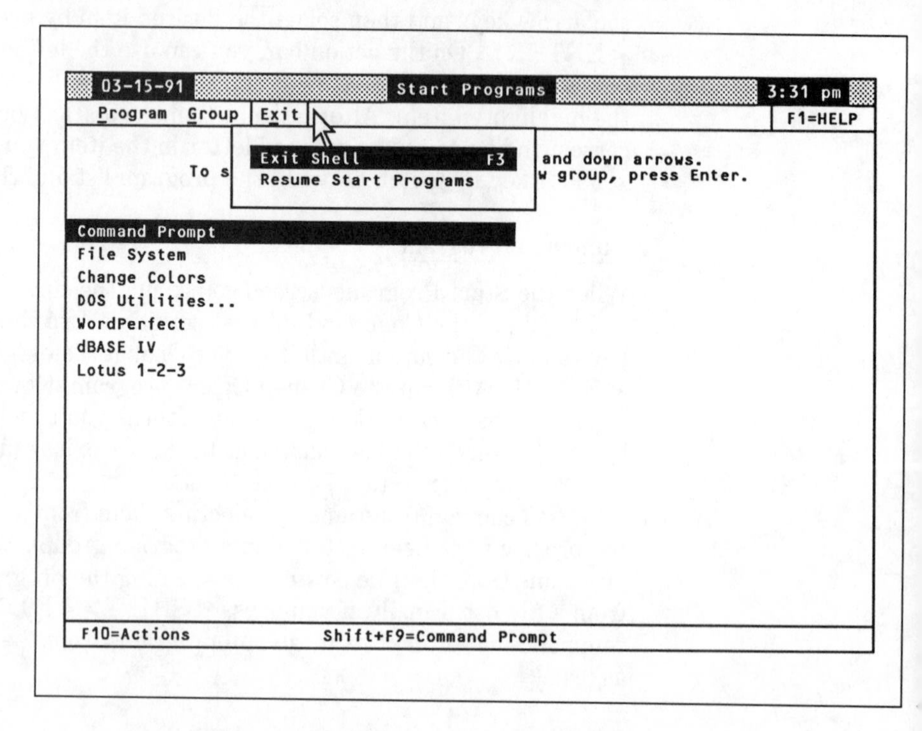

As an alternative, with the cursor on the action bar, type *x*. The Exit menu will appear. Press <Esc> to return to the action bar.

On pull-down menus, items that are not applicable to your work appear dim in graphics mode, or the first letter appears as an asterisk in text mode. For example, if the highlight is on one of the built-in programs (such as DOS Utilities) and you select the Program menu, you'll find that the Delete, Change, and Copy selections are dimmed. This is because these selections aren't used with built-in programs.

Making Selections with a Mouse

With a mouse, making selections is even simpler. On text-mode screens, a small shaded rectangle represents the mouse position—it moves in the direction that you slide the mouse on your desk. On graphics-mode screens, an arrow-shaped pointer is used, as shown in *Figure 11-3*.

Although many mice have two or more buttons, DOSSHELL uses only one. This is normally the left-hand button, but left-handed users may find it more comfortable to have DOSSHELL recognize the right-hand button instead. You can do this by adding the /LF option switch to the DOSSHELL.BAT file, as explained in your MS-DOS manual.

Mouse Maneuvers: Single-Clicking, Double-Clicking, and Dragging

Click the mouse by pressing the left-hand mouse button (unless your mouse is set up for left-hand use). When a double-click is called for, press the button quickly, twice. To drag the mouse, hold the button down while moving the mouse in the desired direction.

On a pull-down menu, when you press the mouse button once, the menu item under the mouse pointer is selected. Pressing the mouse button once is called *single-clicking*, or just *clicking*. When you single-click on an item in a list (such as a file or program name), it is highlighted, indicating that it has been selected as the current item. It is not run immediately, however.

Pressing the mouse button twice in rapid succession is called *double-clicking*. When you double-click on the name of a program in a program list or file list, the program is run.

Holding the mouse button down while moving the mouse is called *dragging*. Dragging is not used often with DOSSHELL, but it can be used to move (scroll) text inside a window.

Running a Program

Move the mouse until the mouse pointer (the arrow or small shaded box) is over Change Colors and double-click. The Change Colors program will run. Move the mouse pointer until it is in the small rectangle marked "Esc=Cancel" and click. You'll be returned to the Start Programs screen. Note that you can also press the <Esc> key to cancel the program. In general, you can mix mouse and keyboard commands, using whichever method is most convenient.

Selecting a Program Group

Move the mouse pointer until it is over DOS Utilities. Double-click, and the list of programs in the group appears. You can run any of these programs by double-clicking on its name. For now, click in the Esc=Cancel rectangle (or just press the <Esc> key) and you will be returned to the Main Group on the Start Programs screen. (You'll learn how to use some of the DOS Utilities programs later in this chapter.)

Using Pull-Down Menus

Move the mouse pointer to Exit on the action bar (with the mouse, you don't need to use <F10> to switch from the program list to the action bar). Click and the Exit menu will drop down. Move the pointer to Resume shell and click (or press the <Esc> key) to return to the Start Programs screen.

To exit from a pull-down menu without choosing anything from it, press <Esc> or click with the mouse anywhere outside the menu.

Getting Help

To get help with your current activity, press <F1> or click on F1=Help with the mouse.

When you're running DOSSHELL, help is only a keystroke or mouse-click away. Move the selection cursor over File System, or click once with the mouse to highlight this item. Press the <F1> key, or click with the mouse over the F1=Help rectangle. You'll see the help window, shown in *Figure 11-4*, whose text describes the File System (which you will be working with in detail later in this chapter).

Figure 11-4. Context-Sensitive Help Window.

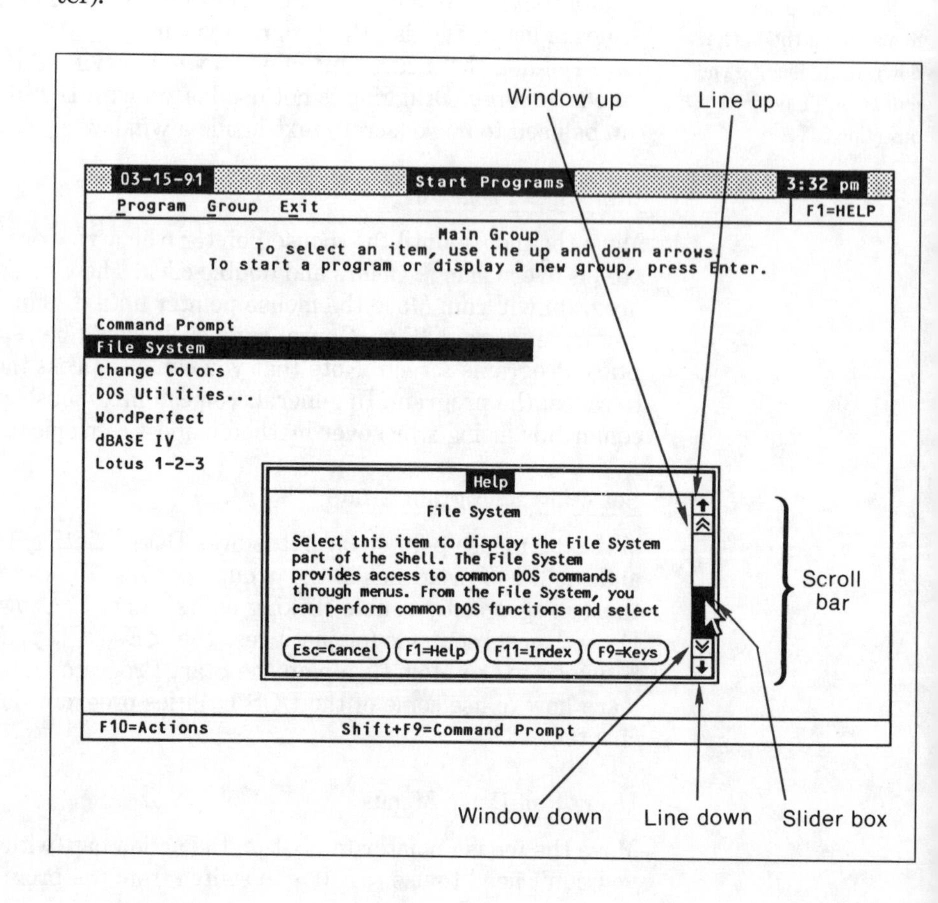

Scrolling Text in Windows

Scrolling text is moving the visible portion of the text up or down in the window. You can scroll text a line at a time with the up-arrow and down-arrow keys or a windowful at a time with the <PgUp> and <PgDn> keys.

Only a small part of the help text is visible in the window. To continue reading, you can use the keyboard to scroll: press the up- and down-arrow keys to scroll (move) the text up and down one line, or click on the up- and down-arrow symbols with the mouse.

Press the <PgUp> and <PgDn> keys to scroll the text up and down a window at a time. The arrows will appear shaded when no more scrolling in either direction is possible.

If the shell is in graphics mode and you have a mouse, you can use the scroll bar features on the right side of the window as shown in *Figure 11-4*. Click on the single arrows at the top and bottom of the bar to scroll the text up or down by one line. (When an arrow is shaded, it means that you cannot scroll in that direction.)

With the mouse, you can drag the slider bar to move a proportional distance up or down in the window text.

Click on the double arrows just inside the single arrows to scroll the text up or down one windowful. Place the mouse pointer over the shaded rectangular *slider box*, and drag the box up or down to scroll the window text. (Remember that dragging means moving the mouse with the button held down.) When you move the slider box, the text is moved relative to the position of the slider. For example, if you drag the slider until it is three-fourths of the way to the bottom of the scroll bar, the text will scroll to a position approximately three-fourths of the way to the end.

Practice scrolling the text with the keyboard and mouse. Note that although you can use all of the mouse selection methods when the shell is in text mode, the scroll bar feature does not appear, so you must use the keyboard methods for scrolling text in windows.

You can use the keyboard scrolling, scroll bar, and slider techniques with any window that has more text than can be displayed at once.

Getting Help on a Topic

Notice that the help window shown in *Figure 11-4* offers, in addition to the Escape option, the options F1=Help, F11=Index, and F9=Keys. Here, the F1 option provides "help on help"; that is, it brings up a help window that describes the use of the help facility itself.

To get help on a particular topic, press or select <F11>, and then select the desired topic from the list.

If you press <F11> (or click it with the mouse), you'll see another type of help window called Indexed Help Selections, shown in *Figure 11-5*. The previous help window (*Figure 11-4*) was context-specific; it referred to the currently selected item (in that case, the File System). Indexed Help, on the other hand, allows you to get help on any topic you care to select with the selection cursor or mouse. The window shows only the first five topics. To see more, scroll by using any of the methods discussed earlier.

Figure 11-5. Indexed Help Window

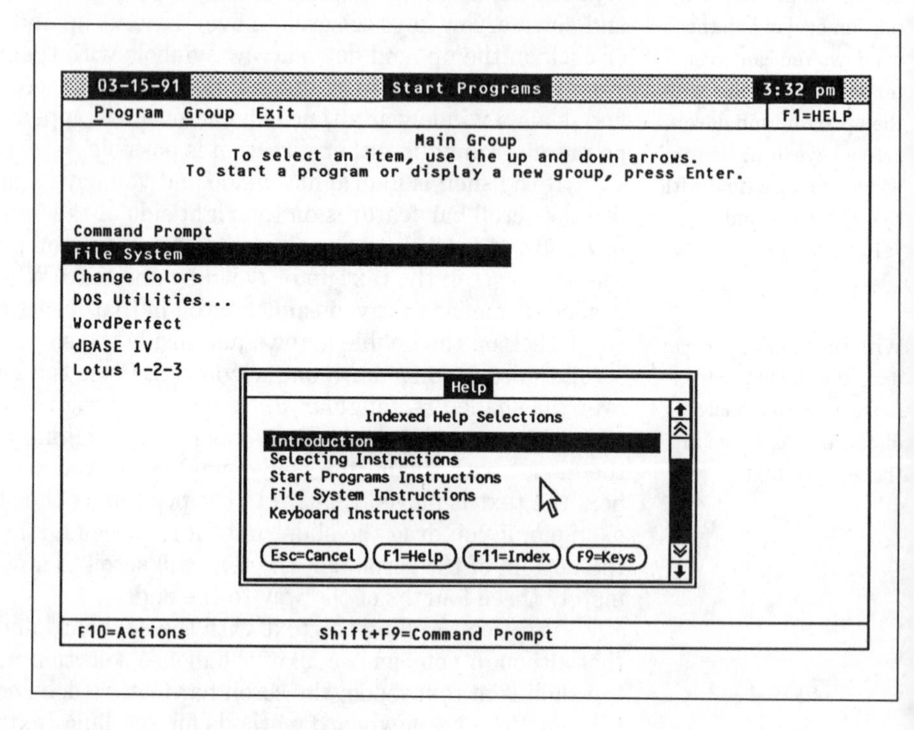

Getting a Summary of Special Keys

For a reminder of what the special keys do in DOSSHELL, press or select <F9>.

If you press <F9> (or click it with the mouse), you will see yet another type of help window, shown in *Figure 11-6*. This window describes each of the keys having special meaning to DOSSHELL. Again, you can scroll to see the rest of the list.

To close the help window and resume operations, press the <Esc> key or click Esc=Cancel with the mouse.

Table 11-1 summarizes the special functions that the shell assigns to certain keys to help you manipulate the menus and the information on the screen. It lists some techniques that you have not seen yet—such as moving through the File System screen and selecting files there—but you will see how to do this when the File System is discussed. Also, remember that you can use the mouse, if you have one, to make selections instead of using these special keys.

Figure 11-6.
Key Assignments
Help Window

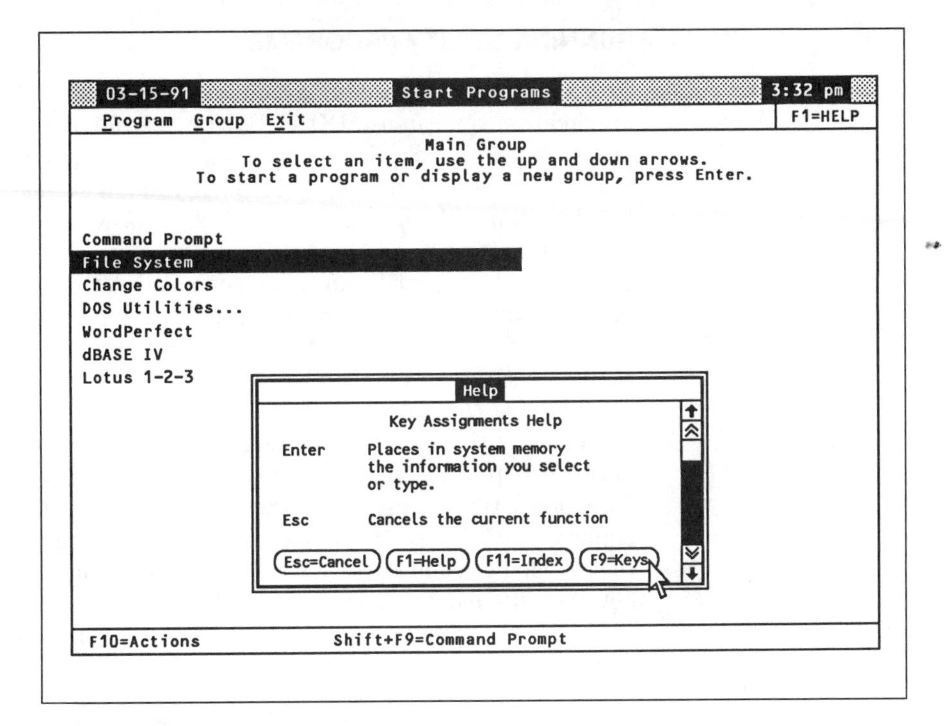

Table 11-1.
Using Special Keys
in the Shell

Key	Function
<ENTER>	Make a selection
Highlighted letter key	Make a selection
<F10>	Switch to action bar
Arrow key	Move the cursor
<F1>	Get help
<F9>	Get help on key assignments
<F11>	Get indexed help
<Esc>	Back out of a menu or close a window
<F3>	Exit from the shell or return to Start Programs
Arrow keys, <PgUp>, <PgDn>	Scroll text in a window
<SHIFT><F9>	Get command-line prompt
<TAB>, <SHIFT><TAB>	Move around the File System screen
Space bar	Select and deselect a file in the File System

RUNNING UTILITY PROGRAMS

Now that you know how to get on-line help and how to move around in windows, you can use DOSSHELL to perform a common task—copying a disk. Suppose you have a disk in drive A, and you need to copy it to a disk in drive B. (If you have a disk handy for copying, and a blank or unneeded disk to copy to, try these steps as you read.)

From the Start Programs screen, select DOS Utilities. Remember that you can use either the cursor bar or the mouse to make selections from the current list of programs or groups in the center of the screen.

Figure 11-7 shows the DOS Utilities group. Notice that there is a new list in the center of the screen, showing the programs available in this group. Now select Disk Copy. The startup window for the Diskcopy Utility pops up. This window, shown in *Figure 11-8*, is the equivalent of the command line: it allows you to provide the information needed to complete the command. Unlike the command line, however, the most commonly needed information is already provided. In this case, the source drive is specified as a, and the destination drive as b.

Figure 11-7. The DOS Utilities Program Group

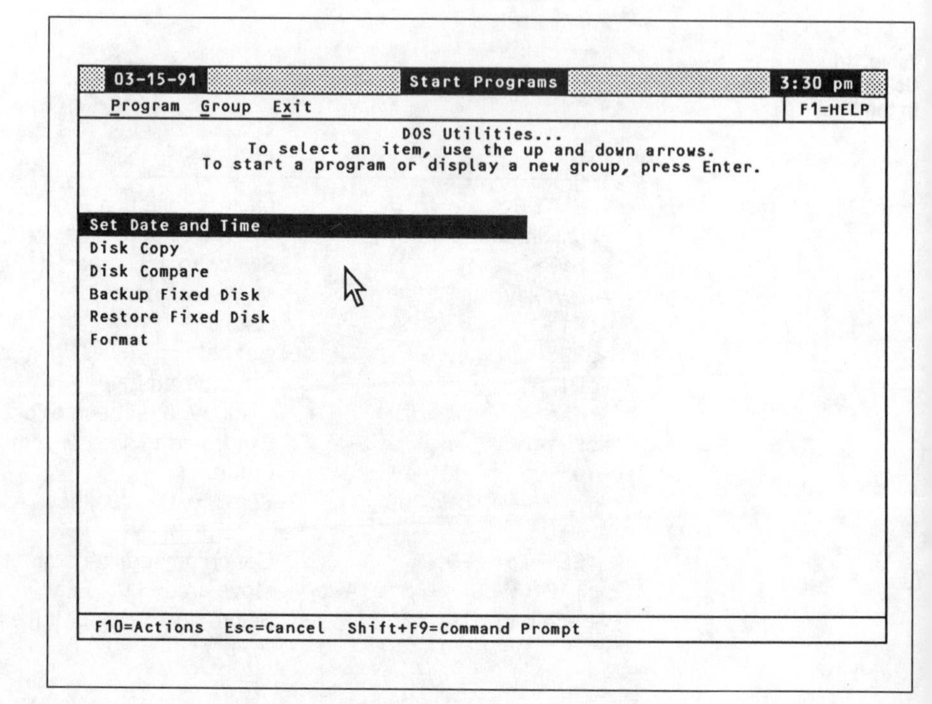

Figure 11-8. The Diskcopy Program Prompt Window

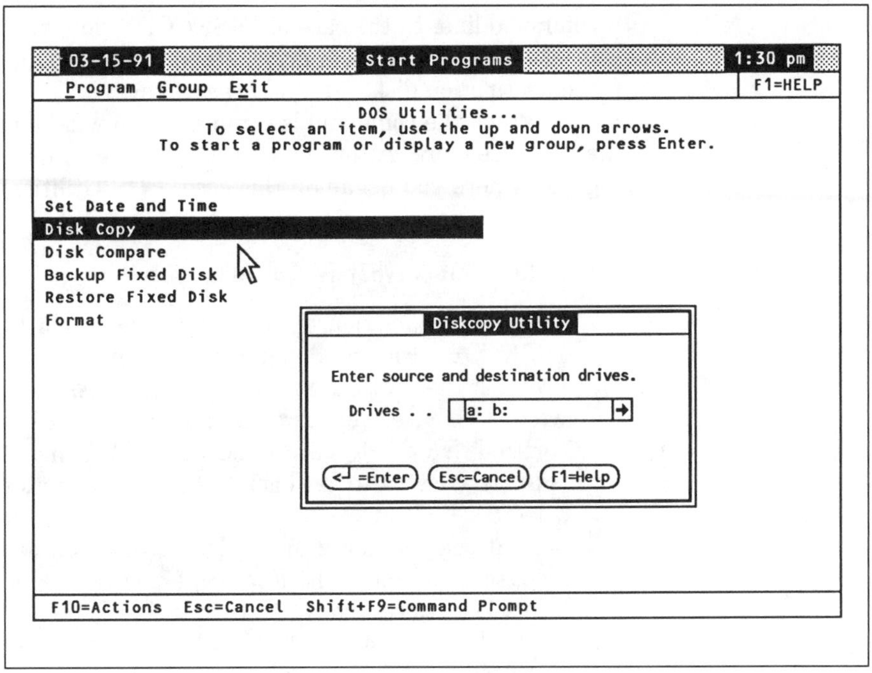

```
03-15-91          Start Programs          1:30 pm
Program  Group  Exit                      F1=HELP
                 DOS Utilities...
        To select an item, use the up and down arrows.
     To start a program or display a new group, press Enter.

Set Date and Time
Disk Copy
Disk Compare
Backup Fixed Disk
Restore Fixed Disk
Format
                        Diskcopy Utility

               Enter source and destination drives.

                 Drives . .  a: b:

               <┘ =Enter   Esc=Cancel   F1=Help

F10=Actions  Esc=Cancel  Shift+F9=Command Prompt
```

Suppose you want to switch drives, copying B to A? Just use the right-arrow and left-arrow keys to move the cursor to the part of the command line you want to change (in this case, the names of the source and destination drives), and type the appropriate drive letters. Note that the mouse cannot be used to move the insertion point. You either must use the arrow keys or start typing at the current cursor location.

Many MS-DOS commands and other programs require the names of one or more files that will be manipulated. When the pop-up window for a program appears, a cursor indicates where the text you type will appear. Type any necessary filenames or command switches, and then press or select <ENTER> to run the program.

Suppose you don't know what to do next? For example, you may not be sure how to specify the drive letters. To invoke ever-present help, press the <F1> key (or click the F1 box with the mouse), and a help window will pop up. This help is context-specific, giving the information you need to complete your data entry. Here, it briefly explains the purpose of the DISKCOPY command and tells you how to specify the drive letters. (Note that these help screens don't describe all the options that can be used with each command. They refer you to the MS-DOS 4.0 manual, *Using DOS*.)

To execute the disk copy (DISKCOPY A: B:), press <ENTER> or click on Enter with the mouse. You do not have to type "diskcopy a: b:."

When the DISKCOPY command runs, the screen will be switched to text mode, and you'll see the same messages and prompts that you would if you were running the command from the command line. In the case of DISKCOPY, you will be prompted to insert the source disk in drive A and press a key and then to insert the destination disk in B and press a key.

When the command is complete, you will be prompted to press a key once more. After you do this, you are returned to the program group where you began (in this case, DOS Utilities).

Getting Out of Whatever You're In . . .

Remember that up to the time you are actually running the DISKCOPY command, you can back out of what you are doing by pressing the <Esc> key or, if the word Esc is shown, by clicking it with the mouse. For example, if you selected Disk Copy and then realized that what you wanted was Disk Compare, all you have to do is press <Esc> to get back to the DOS Utilities group and then select Disk Compare.

If you keep pressing <Esc>, you eventually end up at a top-level screen such as the File System screen. From such a screen, select Exit to return to the highest-level screen: Start Programs. From there, <F3> or Exit will allow you to exit the shell itself and go to the MS-DOS prompt. If you just want to go to the command prompt temporarily (without terminating the shell), press <SHIFT><F9>. When you are finished with the command line, type *exit* to return to the shell.

Once a command such as DISKCOPY has started to run, however, you cannot get out of it by pressing <Esc>. Press <Ctrl>C instead, once for each disk insertion prompt. When you are asked "Terminate Batch File (Y/N)?", type *y*.

WORKING WITH YOUR FILES

In the traditional command-line mode, it is hard to visualize the full structure of your file system, particularly on a hard disk. By using one of the more informative versions of the MS-DOS prompt (such as PROMPT pg, which shows the current drive and directory) or by issuing the CD command by itself, you can determine the current directory. You can use the DIR command to view the current directory, listing files and subdirectories. You can also use it to view another directory, but only if you know the correct pathname. The TREE command can be used to get a complete listing of the file system structure, but you can't scroll around in the resulting list or make selections from it directly.

When you are in the File System display, the directory window on the left shows the tree structure of your current disk. The file window on the right gives a list of files in the current directory.

In contrast to the traditional command-line mode, DOSSHELL gives you an active, movable window on your file system. To see how it works, select File System from the Main Group. There will be a pause while DOSSHELL loads your directory and file structure into memory. You will see a display similar to that in *Figure 11-9.* (The directories and files listed will of course be different.)

Notice that the File System screen is divided into the following areas:

- The title line (here, it displays File System)
- The action bar, with the menus File, Options, Arrange, and Exit
- The drive selection area for selecting the current drive. You can select the drive with the mouse or you can press <Ctrl> plus the key corresponding to the drive letter.

Figure 11-9. File System Default Display

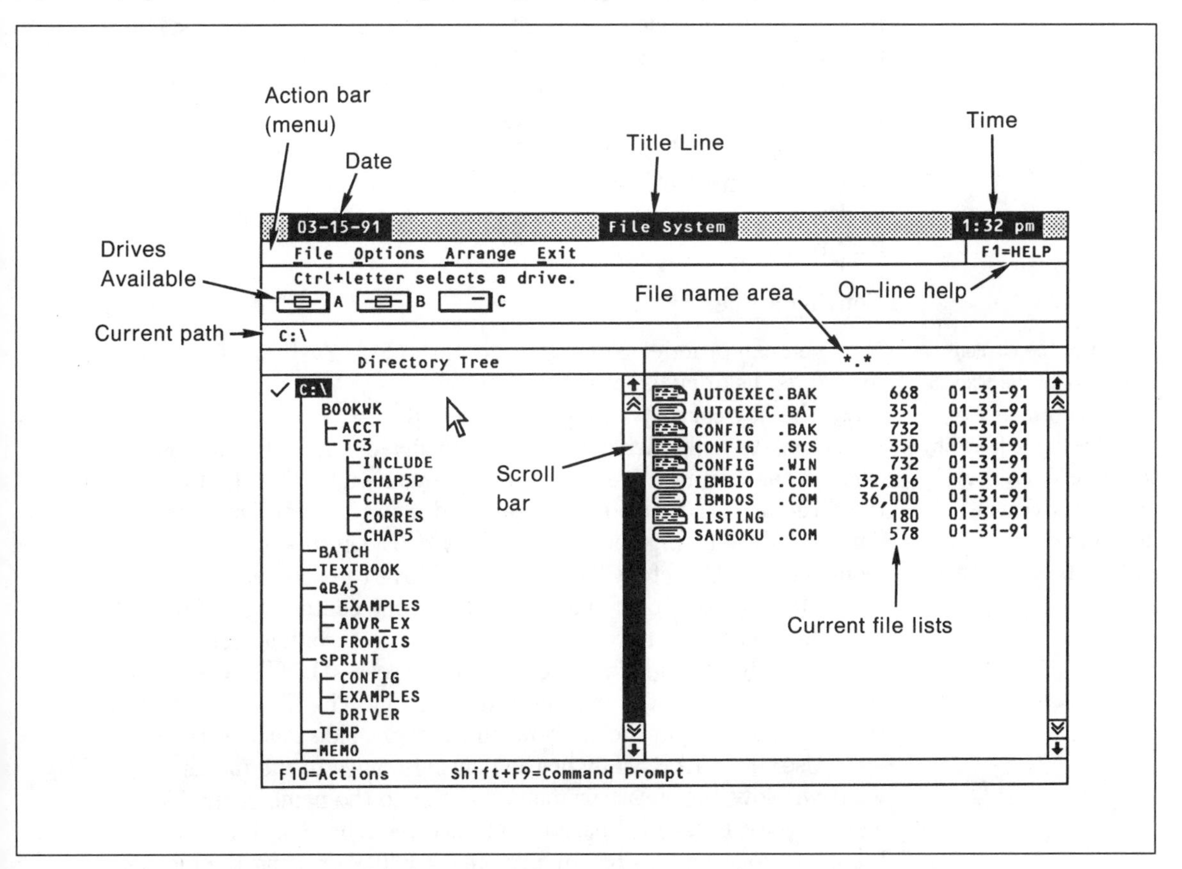

- The path area, showing the current path (in this case, C:\, which represents the root directory of drive C). For more on pathnames, see Chapter 6.
- The Directory Tree (on the left side of the main part of the screen). This listing shows the directories and subdirectories (here, those on drive C), with subdirectories indented under their parent directories. Thus, you can see at a glance that SYS is a subdirectory of INCLUDE, which in turn is a subdirectory of TC.
- The filename area, or file list, a display of files in the currently selected directory (on the right side of the main part of the screen).

Press the <TAB> or a backtab (<SHIFT> <TAB>) keys to move among the action bar, the drive selection area, the Directory Tree, and the file list. Or use the mouse to move the pointer directly to the area from which you want to make a selection. Press <F10> at any time to make a selection from the action bar.

You can scroll through both the Directory Tree and the file list portions of the window independently, using the up- or down-arrow keys or the <PgUp> or <PgDn> keys, as discussed earlier in connection with Help text windows. With the mouse, click on the up- or down-arrow key or, in graphics mode, use the various scroll bar features.

Copying a File

To change the current disk drive in the File System, press the <Ctrl> key followed by the drive letter. For example, to change to drive B, press <Ctrl>B.

Now you can practice copying a file in the File System. If you need to change disk drives, press the <Ctrl> key. While holding it down, press the key corresponding to the new drive. For example, press <Ctrl>A to make drive A the current drive. Or, with the mouse, click on the icon representing the drive you want. The shell will load the directory structure for the selected drive into the Directory Tree window. Move (using the <TAB> key or Backtab keys or the mouse) to the Directory Tree window. Move the selection cursor or the mouse pointer to the name of a directory containing a file that you wish to copy. If necessary, use one of the scrolling methods to move quickly through the directory list. Press <ENTER> or click the mouse to select the highlighted directory. The files in that directory will be listed in the window on the right side of the screen.

Use the <TAB> key or the mouse to move to the file list window. Move the cursor or mouse pointer to the name of the file you want to copy. Press the space bar or click the mouse once to select the file. Move to the action bar by pressing <F10> or using the mouse. Select the File option. When the menu drops down, select Copy.

A window appears with the name of the source file already filled in. You are prompted for the destination filename. Type the filename (or a full pathname if you are copying to another directory). Press <ENTER> or click the Enter box, and the file will be copied.

Use this same technique for the other options that manipulate files, such as deleting, viewing, or printing files. Try out some of these options, using a file that doesn't contain important data—just in case you make a mistake.

Selecting Multiple Files

When you're in the file list, you can select more than one file simply by repeatedly pressing the space bar or by clicking with the mouse on each file. Each file you select is marked by a symbol placed in front of its name: a checkmark in graphics mode or a > in text mode.

Running a Program from the File System

To run a program from the File System, find its filename, select it, and press <ENTER> (or double-click with the mouse).

If a file in the file list is an executable program (if its extension is .COM, .EXE, or .BAT), you can run it by moving the selection cursor to it (or moving the mouse pointer), and either pressing <ENTER> or double-clicking with the mouse. An Open File window will pop up, allowing you to specify any options or filenames that the program needs. Pressing or clicking on Enter runs the program.

You can try this by finding one of your favorite programs in the file list and pressing <ENTER> or double-clicking on the program name. When you have exited the program in the usual way, you'll be returned to the File System screen.

Associating a file extension with an application program allows you to run the application by selecting one of its data files. For example, if you associate WordPerfect with the .WP extension, you can run WordPerfect by selecting any file that has the .WP extension.

You can also run an application program by opening one of its data files. To do this, press <ENTER> or double-click on the filename. For this technique to work, you must have used the Associate function to associate an application program with a particular file extension. For example, .WKS can be associated with Lotus 1-2-3.

Using the MS-DOS Command Prompt

If you wish to use the traditional methods for working with files or running programs, you can press <SHIFT><F9> at any of the shell's main screens. This option switches the system into text mode and provides a standard MS-DOS prompt—the basic command line you have been using throughout this book. The facility for easy access to the standard prompt is useful when you need to perform MS-DOS commands that are not presented as menu items in DOSSHELL, such as MODE or XCOPY. You can also run any program from the command prompt as usual, as long as there is enough memory available. (Remember that the shell is still reserving some memory for itself.) When you're ready to return to DOSSHELL, type *exit* at the MS-DOS prompt and then press <ENTER>.

MORE FILE OPTIONS

The Options menu in the File System lets you control which files will be shown in the file list and how they will be sorted. You can also get a status report on the currently selected drive and directory.

Selecting and Sorting Files

First, select Display Options from the Options menu. This function has two parts, as shown in the pop-up in *Figure 11-10*. First, it allows you to use a name with wildcards to select files from the current directory to be shown in the file list. Second, it gives you control over the order in which the files in the file list will be displayed. Try typing *.TXT into the file selection pop-up. The result will look like *Figure 11.10*, assuming that you have some files with the *.TXT extension in the current directory. This pop-up also asks you how you want to sort the selected files.

Figure 11-10. File Display Options Box

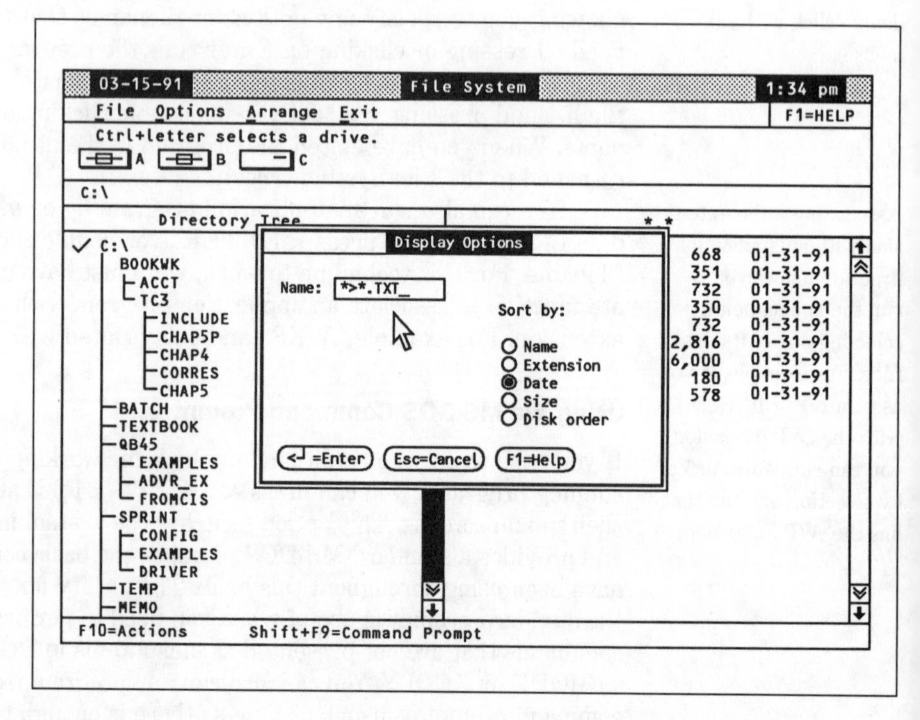

Files can be sorted by:

- Name: alphabetical order by name (the default).
- Extension: alphabetical order by extension. The files are not alphabetized by name within each extension group, however.
- Date: in order of date, from most recent to oldest. The date used is the date the file was created or last modified.
- Size: from largest (in number of bytes) to smallest.
- Disk order: the actual order in which the files appear on the disk. Note that sorting a large directory by this method can speed up shell operations with the files.

In *Figure 11-10*, the Date option was selected. Press <ENTER> or click on it to confirm the name selection and sorting option. Until you restart the shell or change the specifications, all file lists will be displayed in the way you selected, even if you select a different directory.

You don't have to worry about damaging your files or disk when using these file options. The files are sorted only in the buffers that the shell uses to keep track of directory and file information. The actual directory on disk is not affected by any of these operations.

Selecting the File List Format

By selecting the Arrange menu from the File System action bar, you can control how the file lists on the right side of the screen will be displayed. There are three selections:

- Single File List shows a single list of all files in the current directory (as modified by any display options you've set). This is the default that has been shown in the examples.
- Multiple File List shows two file lists, one for each of the two most recently selected directories. *Figure 11-11* shows one use for this option. Here you can view the contents of the \PCDOSBIB\NOTES directory on drive C. Then, by selecting drive A and the NOTES directory, you can also display the list for A:\NOTES to see if you have backed up everything to the floppy.

To find a file regardless of where it is on your disk, select System File List from the Arrange menu in the File System. All files on the disk will be listed, and you can use wildcards in the File Display options box to find the file.

- System File List shows every file on the selected disk (see *Figure 11-12*). This is useful because you can then use Options/Display Options, type the name of a file, and find the file, regardless of where it is on the disk. Note that the Show Information display discussed earlier is automatically given for the last selected file.

When you next start the shell, the default Single File List is restored.

Getting Information about Your Disk

You can also get a summary of statistics about the current disk, directory, or file, without having to run a command such as CHKDSK. Select Show Information from the Options menu. This function displays information about the currently selected file, drive, and directory. If you select the System File List display under the Arrange option, the Show Information display for the currently selected file is provided automatically at the left, as shown in *Figure 11-12*. The following information is displayed:

- The last file selected and its attributes (*a* is archive, *r* is read-only, *h* is hidden)
- The currently selected drive
- The number of files selected and their total size
- The currently selected directory, the number of files in it, and the total size of the files in the directory
- The currently selected disk volume name, the capacity of the disk, the amount of unused storage, and the number of files and directories on the disk

Associating a File Extension with an Application

It was mentioned that you can, for example, arrange things so that Lotus 1-2-3 is run whenever you select a .WKS file in the File System. Here's how to do it. Select Associate from the File menu in the File System. In the pop-up window, type the extension .WKS and supply the filename of the application to be associated (in this case, the Lotus program). That's all there is to it!

Figure 11-11.
Multiple File Lists

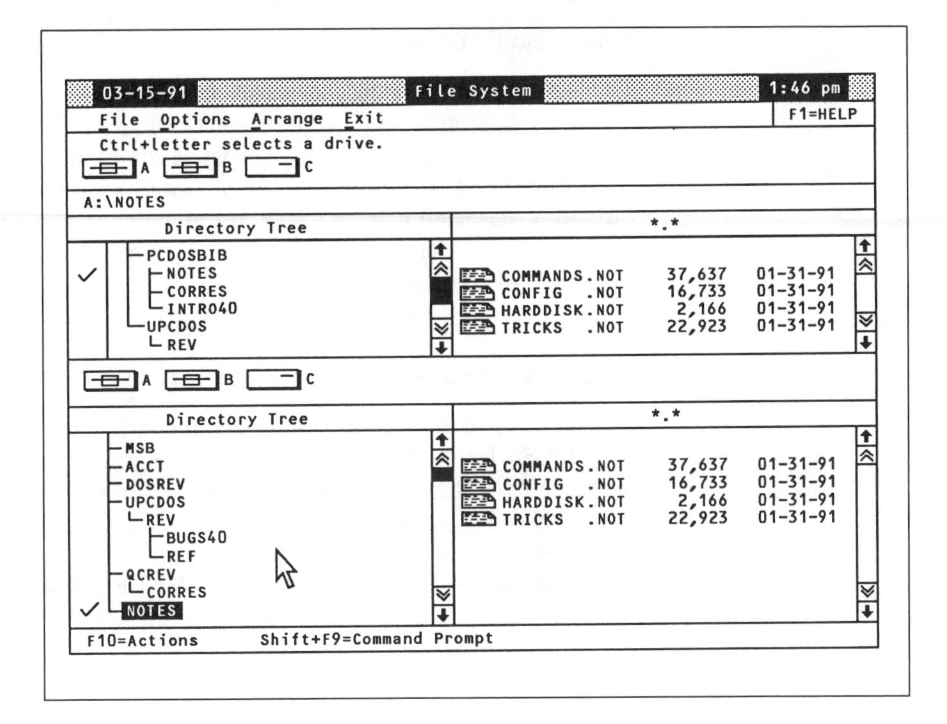

Figure 11-12.
System File List

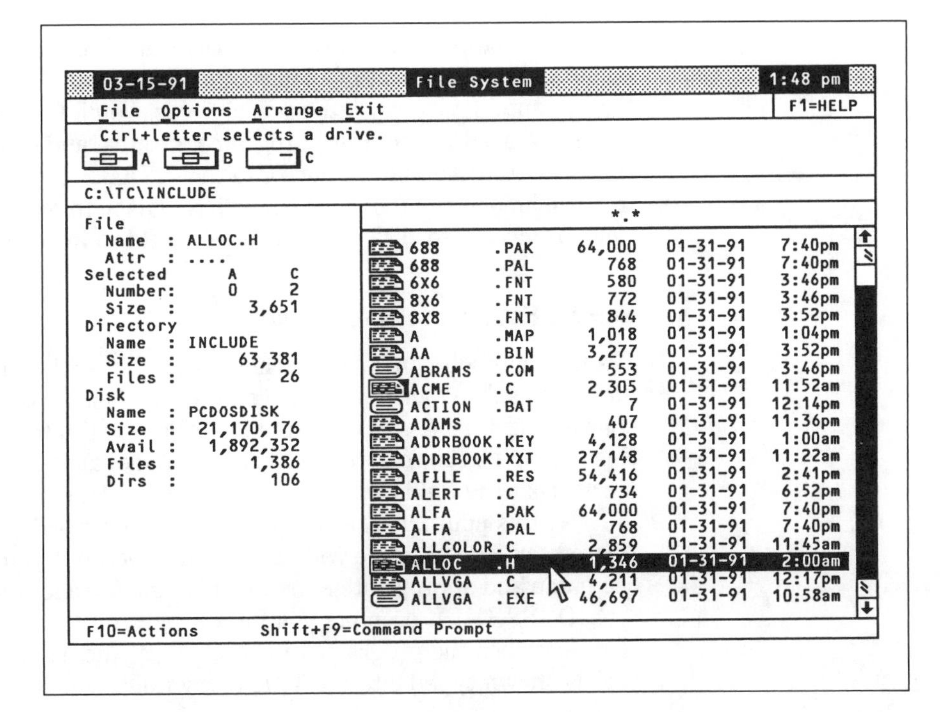

Other File Options

Explore the other menu options in the File System. On the File menu, for example, you'll find options to Print a file, as well as Move or Rename it. (Move is handy because it combines in one step what is traditionally a two-step process in MS-DOS—copying a file to a new directory and then deleting it from the original directory.) Remember that you can get on-line help about any menu option simply by pressing <F1> or clicking on it.

CREATING A CUSTOM MENU SELECTION

As you have seen, you can run programs either by selecting them in the File System or by getting an MS-DOS prompt and typing the program's filename there. The easiest way to run applications, however, is for you to provide them as menu selections in the Main Group or another program group.

You should now be back at the Start Programs screen. If you are in the File System screen, use the Exit option from the action bar to return to Start Programs.

From the action bar, select Program and then Add. (By now you should know how to select items, so the details will no longer be repeated.)

A box appears requesting information about the program to be installed (see *Figure 11-13*). This box is an example of a pop-up box that accepts data entry into several fields. You'll find that these boxes are used to configure programs, groups, and other items that require extensive information. Use the <TAB> key or Backtab keys to move among the fields, or use <ENTER> to move to the next field. You can also click the mouse on a field to insert data in it.

Making Entries in Pop-Up Boxes

If a field has solid ends, or brackets (< >), in text mode, you are limited to a fixed amount of space for entry. The Password field, shown in *Figure 11-13*, is an example. The other data entry fields in this pop-up box have arrows (> in text mode) at the end. The arrow means that the fields will scroll as you enter data.

At this point, you're ready to install your word processor or text editor. The example will use WordPerfect, but you can substitute the name and appropriate startup command for another program.

DOSSHELL prompts you for a program title. Type a name that describes the program. In *Figure 11-13*, the name "Word Processor" is shown typed into the Title entry field.

Figure 11-13. Add Program Box

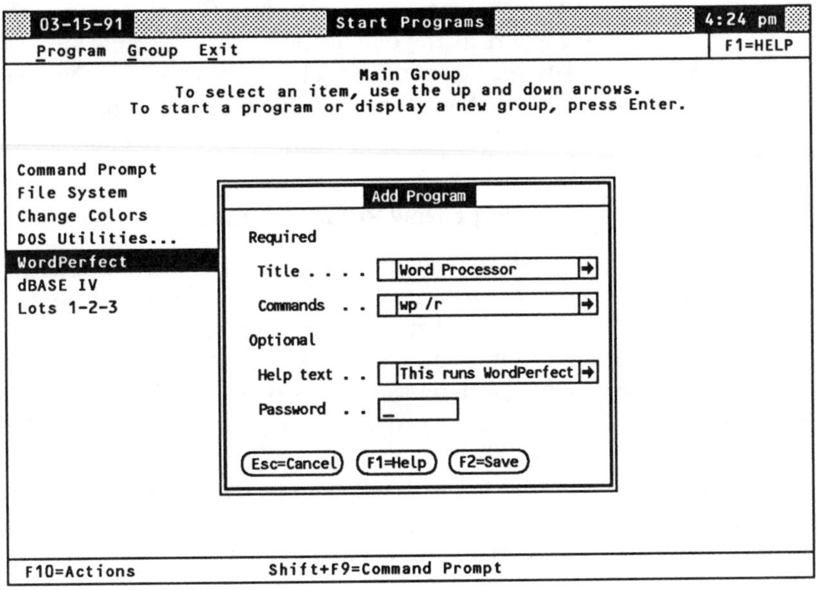

```
03-15-91              Start Programs               4:24 pm
 Program  Group  Exit                              F1=HELP
                         Main Group
            To select an item, use the up and down arrows.
        To start a program or display a new group, press Enter.

Command Prompt
File System                    Add Program
Change Colors
DOS Utilities...      Required
WordPerfect            Title . . . .   Word Processor
dBASE IV
Lots 1-2-3             Commands  . .   wp /r
                      Optional
                       Help text . .   This runs WordPerfect
                       Password  . .   _

                      Esc=Cancel  F1=Help  F2=Save

F10=Actions         Shift+F9=Command Prompt
```

Editing Text in Pop-Up Boxes

Adding a program puts it on the list of programs in a program group. When you add the program, you can specify what information will be requested from the user, and you can store user input in variable placeholders that can be used by the program or batch file.

Within a data entry field like the Title field shown in *Figure 11-13*, you can use the left- and right-arrow keys to move the insertion point. If you want to insert characters in front of existing text, press the <Ins> key and type the new characters. Use the <Del> key to delete existing characters that you no longer want.

Move to the Commands field, where you give the actual command used to run the program from the command line. In the case of WordPerfect, you use the command wp /r. Note that you can add whatever command-line options the program ordinarily accepts. In this case, the /r option tells WordPerfect to use expanded memory.

Move to the Help text field, where you enter the text that will be displayed if the user presses the <F1> key to ask for help. You can also move to the Password field. In this example, no value was supplied for a password, so you are not asked for one. Press <F2> or click on it to save the new program specifications.

You should now be back at the Main Group screen. A new item with the name you have given (Word Processor in this example) appears at the end of the list of programs and groups in the Main Group. You can now select this application and run it as you run the File System menu, for example. See your MS-DOS manual or *The Waite Group's Using PC DOS* for more information.

Creating a New Program Group

Creating new program groups allows you to group your application programs to suit a particular purpose, such as including a word processor, spelling checker, and printer-control program together. You can also set up program groups for different users in your office. You can also control which shell features and program groups are available to a particular user by assigning passwords, as explained in your MS-DOS manual.

Recall that several program groups can reside within the Main Group (see the earlier *Figure 11-2*). You have just added the WordPerfect program (or another program of your own choice) to the Main Group. But suppose that you use your system for three areas of activity: writing, database, and spreadsheet. The logical thing to do is to create three program groups within the Main Group, one for each area. This is easy to do. Adding a group requires information similar to that used for adding a program, as you will see in the following steps.

From the Group menu, select Add. Type a descriptive name for the group into the Title field. In the Filename group, give the name of a data file that MS-DOS will use to contain information about the group. DOSSHELL will create this file with the extension .MEU (for menu).

Type some descriptive text in the Help text field to explain the purpose of the program group you are installing. Optionally, type a password into the Password field. The user will now have to enter this password to use the program group. Press <F2> or click on it to save the new group.

Suppose that you've created a new program group called Writing. It would be logical to have the word processor (such as WordPerfect, in the example) in the Writing group rather than in the Main Group, which is cluttered with such built-in programs as File System.

Select the program file Word Processor from the Main Group. Use the arrow keys to move the highlight over the name of the program, or click *once* with the mouse. (Don't press Enter or click twice—you want to select the program, not run it.) Select Copy from the Program menu. Select the new group, Writing. Press <F2> or click on it. Your word processing program will now be copied to the Writing group. Select Delete from the Program menu to remove the Writing program from the Main Group.

As you can see, you have the flexibility to set up menus for each kind of work you do. If several people use the system, each person could have his or her own menu by creating a group with the person's name as the title. If you wanted, you could provide a password for each group so that only the rightful owner could access it.

SUMMARY

As you have seen, DOSSHELL is a versatile interface that gives easy access to your files and programs and provides powerful housekeeping functions. In addition, DOSSHELL can provide a friendlier working environment for less experienced users.

To make DOSSHELL work for you, start by setting up program groups based on your main work activities. Then install your favorite application programs with appropriate options. If other people also use the machine, you can set up groups and program lists for them. You can even use DOSSHELL on a network. (For a discussion of this, see your MS-DOS manual.)

If you are an experienced user, you may find in the end that all the menus and boxes get in your way—so be it. You'll still have learned how to provide greater ease of use for the casual or less experienced user. Reducing the intimidation factor in your workplace is no small thing.

Learning about DOSSHELL has also helped you learn more about how MS-DOS works. This will help you in Chapter 12, where you will learn how to configure many aspects of the MS-DOS operation to suit your needs.

REVIEW

1. You can run DOSSHELL automatically from your AUTOEXEC.BAT file, or you can run it by typing *dosshell* at the command-line prompt.

2. DOSSHELL's main menu screen, Start Programs, allows you to select DOSSHELL functions from pull-down menus or to select programs to run. By selecting a program group, you get a list of programs in that group that you can run.

3. You can use either the keyboard or a mouse to make selections. If you are not sure how to proceed, press <F1> to get help.

4. Several important MS-DOS Utility commands, such as DISKCOPY, FORMAT, and BACKUP can be run from the DOS Utilities program group.
5. The File System display enables you to view your files and directories. Select a directory to view files in that directory. Choose files from the file list for copying, viewing, or other operations.
6. If you need to do something that you can't do from within DOSSHELL, press <SHIFT><F9> to get an MS-DOS command-line prompt.
7. Use the "Add Programs" feature on the Start Programs screen to add programs to a program list. Use the "Add Group" feature to create a new group of programs.

Quiz for Chapter 11

1. DOSSHELL is a:
   a. new version of MS-DOS.
   b. program that makes MS-DOS easier to use.
   c. command prompt.
   d. disk utility program.
   e. multitasking operating system.
2. The program that accepts your MS-DOS commands is called:
   a. COMMAND.COM.
   b. DOSSHELL.
   c. AUTOEXEC.BAT.
   d. MSDOS.SYS.
   e. SELECT.
3. DOSSHELL presents information mainly in the form of:
   a. icons (symbols).
   b. charts.
   c. menus and lists.
   d. color graphics.
4. The "main menu" screen presented by DOSSHELL is called:
   a. File System.
   b. Utilities.
   c. Program List.
   d. Start Programs.
   e. Command Line.
5. Program groups are used for:
   a. putting all of the files used by a program in one place.
   b. presenting a menu of related programs.
   c. finding all files that have a particular extension.
   d. adding commands to your application programs.
6. With DOSSHELL, the mouse:
   a. can be used at any time as an alternative to the keyboard.
   b. can only be used inside windows.
   c. replaces the keyboard.
   d. can be used to draw pictures.
   e. can only be used in graphics mode.
7. In DOSSHELL, the <F1> key is used to:
   a. stop the current program.
   b. get an MS-DOS prompt.
   c. open the current window.

d. get help related to your current selection.
e. get indexed help.

8. If you are running DOSSHELL and want to use the DISKCOPY command, you can:
   a. press <SHIFT><F9> and then type the DISKCOPY command at the prompt.
   b. select Disk Copy from the DOS Utilities group
   c. drag the A drive icon over to the B drive icon.
   d. both a and b.
   e. all of the above.

9. On the File System screen, you can view a list of:
   a. all of the files on the current drive.
   b. all files with a particular extension.
   c. all of the files in two different directories.
   d. files sorted according to date.
   e. all of the above.
   f. none of the above.

10. DOSSHELL helps beginning MS-DOS users mainly by:
    a. running all of the programs they need automatically.
    b. making it easy to select programs and find information.
    c. speeding up the operation of MS-DOS.
    d. showing users how to write their own programs.
    e. fixing disk problems.

Configuring Your System

ABOUT THIS CHAPTER

Configuring MS-DOS involves allocating memory among MS-DOS features and your application programs.

This chapter is about configuring MS-DOS and your application programs. *Configuration* means specifying what features and functions will be used and to what extent. Configuration is mainly about how to allocate your system's memory in order to let MS-DOS and your application programs run as fast and efficiently as possible. For example, MS-DOS has features that can considerably speed up the loading of files from disk, but these features require that an additional portion of your memory be reserved for MS-DOS. This memory will not be available for your application programs, and, as a result, these programs won't be able to hold as much data in memory at one time. This in turn may mean that the program spends more time moving data to and from the disk, and that can slow down your application.

In addition, you may want to run one or more of the popular memory-resident utility programs (such as SideKick and Memory Mate). These programs provide pop-up convenience for making notes, keeping a calendar, dialing a phone, and other functions. Each of these programs, however, uses up more of your precious memory, making less available for your main application program.

You'll learn how to find out how much memory each of the MS-DOS features and utility programs running in your system uses, and how to make tradeoffs involving your memory. You'll also learn how you can use expanded memory in some cases to ease the "memory crunch." In addition, you'll learn how to change other MS-DOS settings as needed in certain circumstances, how to install a new software package, and how to use a system feature called the *environment* to control your application programs.

The very power and flexibility of the modern PC requires that you spend some time and effort if you are going to get the most out of it. Because a PC is such a general-purpose tool, its manufacturer and the creators of MS-DOS can only do part of the work of configuration. They can't know whether you have 640K of memory or several megabytes, or what might be the best way to allocate that memory. They don't know how many disk drives you have, or what useful devices you want to plug into your PC's expansion slots, or exactly how a new scanner, mouse, or CD-ROM drive will work. That's all right, however, because MS-DOS is designed to be easily configurable to your needs.

You'll learn how to complete the configuration process and customize your system using these tools:

- CONFIG.SYS, a text file that you create, giving instructions that tell MS-DOS what MS-DOS features and special device-control programs to install.
- device drivers, which are special programs (usually with a .SYS file extension) that allow MS-DOS and your applications program to access disk drives, mice, video displays, and other devices.
- AUTOEXEC.BAT, another text file that you create, giving the names of MS-DOS commands and other programs to be run at startup.
- MS-DOS commands and other programs that load themselves into memory and remain there, waiting to be activated as needed.
- the environment, an area of memory that serves as a kind of "bulletin board" containing information that can be used by MS-DOS and your application programs.

You may find this material to be a little tougher going than the rest of the book, but you don't have to learn (or use) all of it at once. As you learn about these tools and MS-DOS features, don't be afraid to experiment. Observe whether a particular operation (such as moving through a large file in your word processor) speeds up or slows down. Think about how you want your software to behave. Remember that what ultimately counts is what works best for you.

WHAT YOU SHOULD KNOW BEFORE YOU BEGIN

This chapter is last in this book because it looks behind the scenes at what is going on in your system when you start MS-DOS and run your programs. Ideally, you should have read all the preceding chapters before starting this one. You should be familiar with entering MS-DOS commands. You should know how to create and edit a text file (Chapter 6), because the two key files used in this chapter (CONFIG.SYS and AUTOEXEC.BAT) are text files.

HOW MS-DOS WORKS (AN OVERVIEW)

In order to be able to configure your system you need to know something about how the various parts of MS-DOS work together. How do you and your application programs interact with MS-DOS? How does MS-DOS find out what devices are connected to your system? How can you tell MS-DOS how you want to divide your available memory between system features and your running programs? The best way to find out is to observe what happens when your system starts up.

How MS-DOS is Loaded

MS-DOS has three parts: the BIOS, the kernel, and the command processor, or shell.

System startup goes through several stages, and MS-DOS has three major parts (or modules) that come into play before you finally see that C:\> prompt on your screen.

When you turn on the power to your PC, an automatic hardware test called the POST (Power-On Self-Test) runs. The details vary with the model of PC, but usually a running total of how much memory has been checked is displayed. If any chips are found to be bad, a code number is displayed indicating the row and column position of the problem chip (which may be on the main system board or an expansion card), and the system stops until the problem is corrected. The documentation provided by your computer's manufacturer should list the meanings of the codes used for bad chips and other system problems.

Assuming the hardware checks out OK, control is passed to a small program stored in ROM. This "ROM bootstrap" code directs the first disk drive (A) to try to read the information needed for loading MS-DOS. If you have a properly formatted system disk in drive A, MS-DOS will start to load. If you don't have a disk in drive A, the bootstrap program will try to read the information from drive C (the hard disk). Most users these days start their system directly from the hard disk. Because the system always checks drive A first, however, you can always override your hard disk and start from a floppy. You will have to do this if something has damaged the system files on your hard disk or the hard disk itself.

The BIOS: Built-In Device Control

The bootstrap program first reads a file called IO.SYS (or IBMBIO.COM in IBM PC DOS) into memory. This file contains the *BIOS* (Basic Input/Output System), a collection of "primitive" hardware-oriented routines that control the standard built-in devices—the keyboard, clock, internal disk drive, video display, and printer output.

The BIOS is used to control hardware devices.

> The BIOS is the hardware-specific part of MS-DOS, because it has to control devices directly. Several manufacturers in addition to IBM have designed ROM chips from which all or part of the BIOS is loaded. Occasionally incompatibilities between IBM and non-IBM BIOS chips turn up, though this is much less of a problem today.

The MS-DOS Kernel: Functions at Your Service

The MS-DOS kernel provides system functions used by MS-DOS commands and application program.

After the BIOS is loaded, the MS-DOS *kernel* is loaded from a file called MSDOS.SYS (IBMDOS.COM in PC DOS). The kernel is a standard set of program routines called "system functions" that can be called on by any MS-DOS program as needed. (For example, your word processor will call on a particular service to open a file for your resume and another service to send the characters you have written to the disk.) In addition to managing files, code in the MS-DOS kernel manages memory (allocating it to a program or releasing it when no longer needed), handles input and output of characters, obtains the time from the system clock, and so on.

Some of the kernel routines that were loaded are then used to compile lists of information about the devices connected to the system. First, the information that MS-DOS already "knows" about—the built-in devices, such as the keyboard and clock—is stored in tables, together with a list containing the address (location in memory) of each table. This information includes the type of device, whether it reads data as text or binary values, the size of sectors used, and so on, as appropriate to the particular device.

The CONFIG.SYS File and Installable Device Drivers

Device drivers mediate between MS-DOS (or an application program) and hardware devices. Some device drivers are built into MS-DOS; you can install others in your CONFIG.SYS file.

One of the main tasks of the CONFIG.SYS file, mentioned earlier, is to load *device drivers*. What is a device driver? It is a program that knows how to control a particular device and how to receive information from it. An application program (and its programmer) doesn't have to deal with the low-level details of the device directly. When the MS-DOS input/output functions are called, codes are sent to the driver which in turn sends out the signals that control the device. If the device needs to get the system's attention (for example, a printer may signal that its buffer is full and it cannot accept any more characters), a message is returned by the driver to indicate a change in the device's status. The device driver is thus a sort of intermediary or interpreter between software and hardware (see *Figure 12-1*).

Thanks to the BIOS, MS-DOS has drivers for the standard built-in devices, such as the keyboard, printer, and serial ports, but what about your extra disk drive, mouse, EGA card, scanner, computer fax board, or whatever? How does MS-DOS find out what else it will have to deal with?

The answer is that MS-DOS provides for the manufacturers of devices to supply their own "custom" device drivers. By convention, device driver files have the extension .SYS. If you have a mouse, for example, chances are that you received with it a disk containing (among other things) a file called MOUSE.SYS—that's the device driver for the mouse.

After the kernel is loaded, MS-DOS looks in the root directory of your boot drive for a file called CONFIG.SYS. This text file that you create can contain a number of different commands and settings that will be discussed later in detail. One of the commands used, DEVICE, tells MS-DOS to install the specified device driver: for example, DEVICE=C:\SYS\MOUSE.SYS might be used to install a mouse driver. When a device driver is installed from the CONFIG.SYS file, the same sort of information used for the built-in devices is added to the lists kept by MS-DOS.

Figure 12-1. MS-DOS, Device Drivers, and Devices

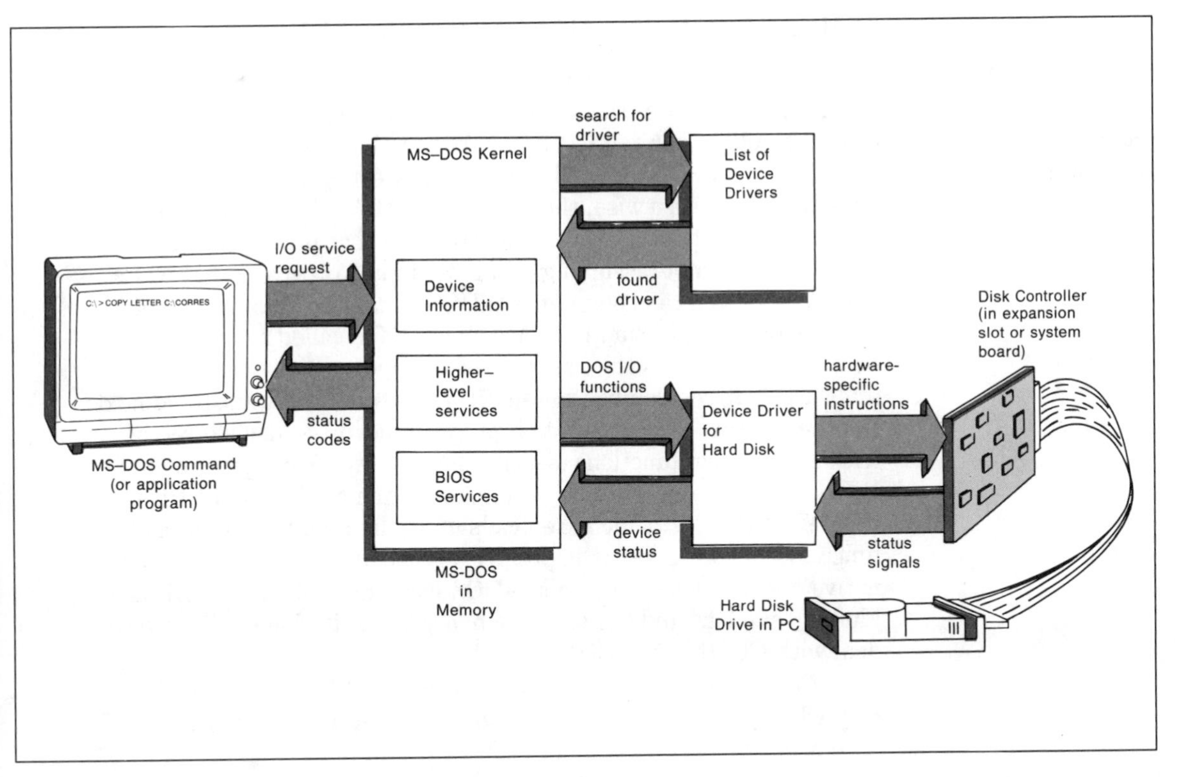

The AUTOEXEC.BAT File

The AUTOEXEC.BAT file runs a series of MS-DOS commands when you start your system.

After the contents of the CONFIG.SYS file have been acted upon, MS-DOS looks for a file called AUTOEXEC.BAT in the root directory of your boot drive. AUTOEXEC.BAT, is, as the .BAT extension indicates, a batch file. It works just like the batch files discussed in Chapter 10, except that it is run automatically at startup. Nearly all users have an AUTOEXEC.BAT: if nothing else, having an AUTOEXEC.BAT file prevents MS-DOS from presenting you with the annoying TIME and DATE prompts at the start of each session. The function of the AUTOEXEC.BAT file is simple: it is a list of commands that are run every time you start your system.

In fact, as with any batch file, anything you can type at the C:\> prompt can be included as an automatic command in your AUTOEXEC.BAT file. This can include MS-DOS commands (such as MODE or PRINT), memory-resident utility programs (such as Sidekick–SK.COM), or an application program (such as WordPerfect) that you want to use first in every session. The programs often include command-line switches to specify details of operation.

COMMAND.COM, Your User Interface, the C> Prompt

COMMAND.COM provides the C:\> prompt and interprets your commands.

If your AUTOEXEC.BAT file specified that an application program be run at the start of the session, then that program is now running. (For example, if you put C:\WP50\WP at the end of your AUTOEXEC.BAT, you will be in WordPerfect and can proceed with your writing.) Otherwise, the program COMMAND.COM is now running. COMMAND.COM is the program that provides you with your C:\> prompt (assuming you have a hard disk) and that waits patiently for you to type in an MS-DOS command or the name of another program to run. COMMAND.COM is called a "shell" because it surrounds the internals of the operating system with an interface that you can use to tell MS-DOS what you want to do next. In other words, your application program normally deals directly with the internal functions (services) in the MS-DOS kernel or the BIOS, but you send MS-DOS commands such as DIR or TYPE to COMMAND.COM, which then calls upon the appropriate internal functions to do the job. (Chapter 11 described DOSSHELL, an alternative way for you to access MS-DOS commands. DOSSHELL is a kind of "shell around the shell": when you use it, you don't have to deal with COMMAND.COM directly unless you want to.)

Figure 12-2 summarizes how the parts of MS-DOS come into play when you start your system and how you interact with MS-DOS once it is running.

The Environment

The MS-DOS environment is a list of information that can be used by MS-DOS commands or other programs.

The third main tool for configuring MS-DOS and application programs is the environment, a block of memory containing information that can be accessed by MS-DOS or any program. You have already seen one important piece of information stored there: the PATH specified using the PATH command, for example:

```
PATH C:\WP;C:\123;C:\DBASE;C:\UTILS;
```

The PATH is the list of directories to be searched for an executable program. An "environmental variable" is a label that refers to a piece of information in the environment: for example, the PATH

Figure 12-2. How MS-DOS Works

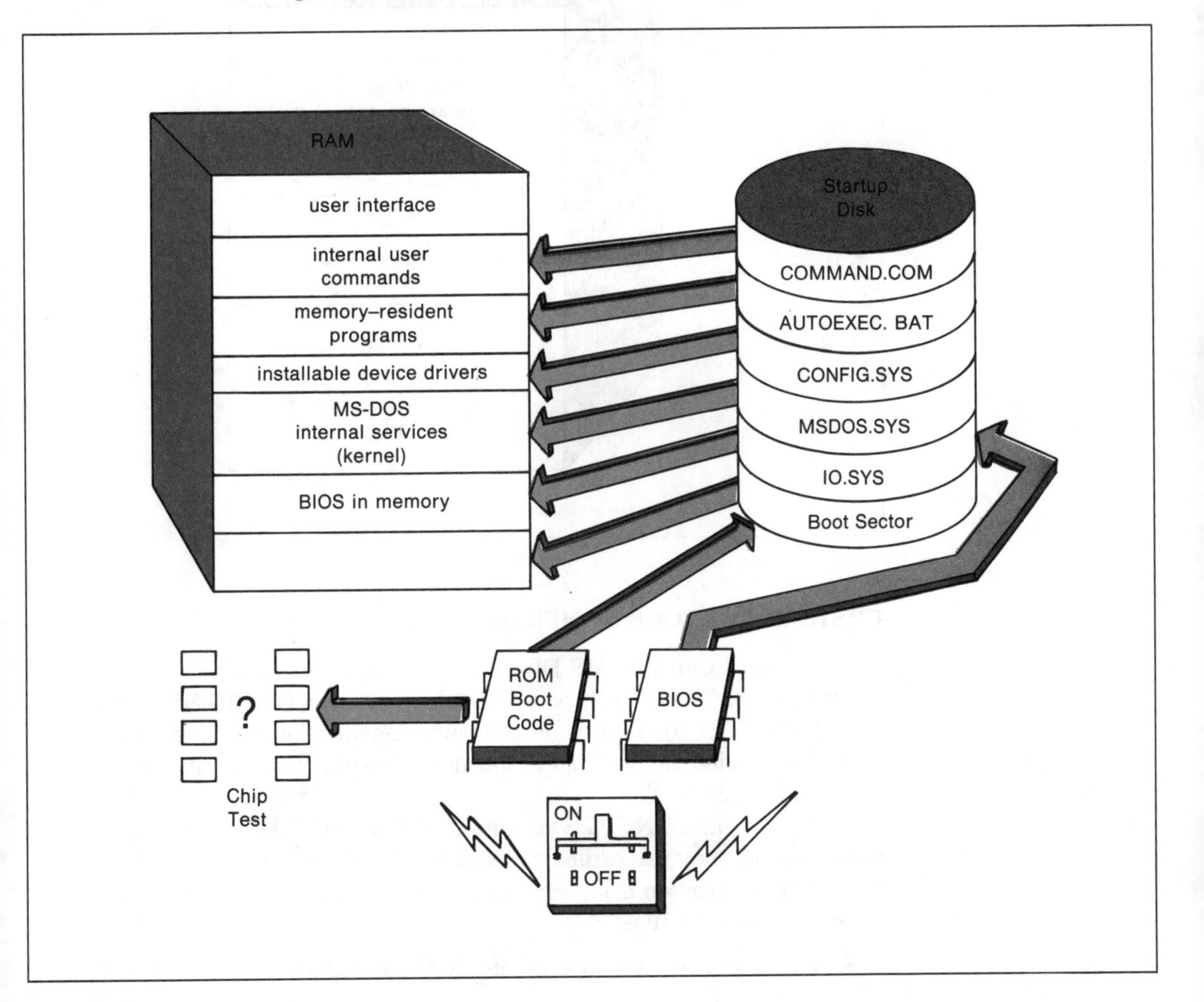

variable. Some other MS-DOS commands (APPEND, for example) also create environmental variables. You can specify additional variables using the SET command, which will be discussed later in the chapter. An application program can be designed to look for certain variables to tell it where to find files that it needs, the kind of screen display to use, and so on. *Figure 12-3* shows how programs can use variables.

Figure 12-3. Programs and Environmental Variables

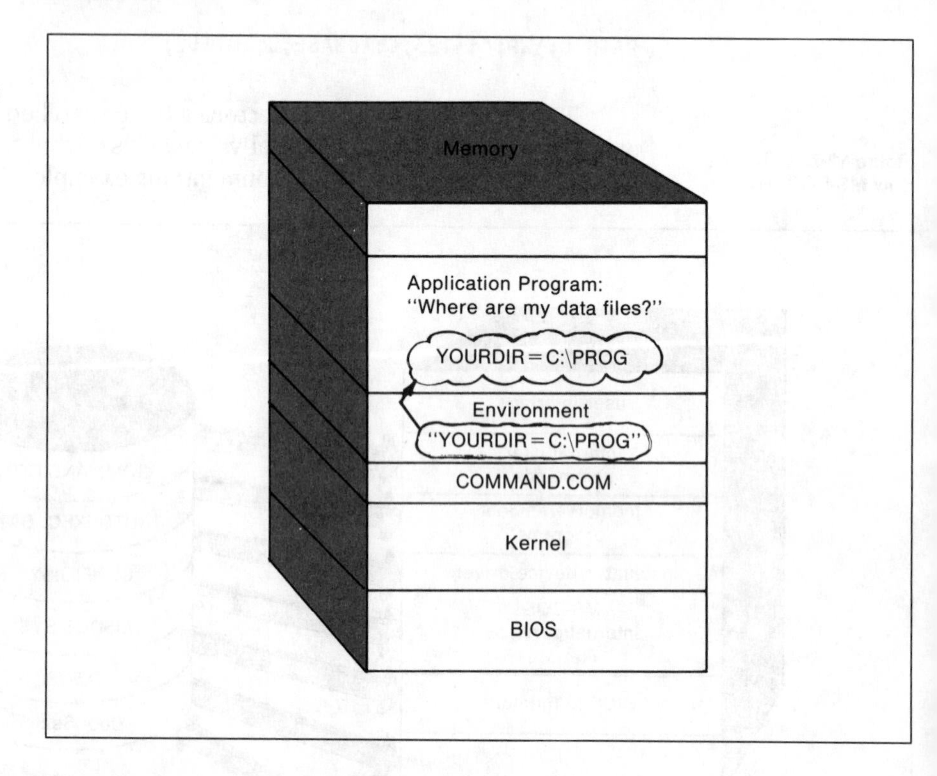

CUSTOMIZING YOUR CONFIG.SYS FILE

You have now seen that MS-DOS (and your program) can be controlled or affected in three principal ways: the CONFIG.SYS file, the AUTOEXEC.BAT file, and the environment. Now that you've seen the big picture, it's time to get down to specifics, starting with the CONFIG.SYS file.

Recall that CONFIG.SYS (and AUTOEXEC.BAT) are text files. That is, they use ordinary characters that you can type at the keyboard. You saw in Chapter 6 that there are several ways you can create or edit text files:

- With a text editor, such as SideKick's notepad

- With a word processor, making sure it is in "ASCII text" mode
- With EDLIN (see Appendix A)
- By typing COPY CON: FILENAME at the MS-DOS prompt

While you can use the COPY CON method to create a *new* AUTOEXEC.BAT file, you probably already have an AUTOEXEC.BAT file. Later versions of MS-DOS (especially DOS 4) create an AUTOEXEC.BAT and a CONFIG.SYS file for you when you run the DOS installation program. Typing COPY CON: CONFIG.SYS will *erase* your CONFIG.SYS and start over. You don't want to do this because you'll lose any settings that MS-DOS has already made for you.

Change to your root directory if necessary (by typing CD C:\), then type:

```
C:\>type config.sys
```

If you get a listing, you already have a CONFIG.SYS file. Type

```
C:\>copy config.sys config.bak
```

to make a backup copy. If you get confused or something doesn't work right, use the COPY command to copy CONFIG.BAK to CONFIG.SYS and reboot the system. (It is also a good idea to copy your current CONFIG.SYS and AUTOEXEC.BAT files to an "emergency floppy," a safety precaution that is discussed at the end of this chapter.)

CONFIG.SYS commands can be grouped according to the function they serve:

- Installing device drivers
- Controlling how programs are run
- Fine-tuning file and disk operations
- Specifying the command processor and environment

AN EXAMPLE CONFIG.SYS FILE

The functions of CONFIG.SYS will be demonstrated by showing a CONFIG.SYS file from a working MS-DOS system, one part at a time. Here's the first part:

```
DEVICE=C:\DOS\SYS\EMM.SYS 208,00
DEVICE=C:\DOS\SYS\IBMCACHE.SYS
```

```
DEVICE=C:\DOS\SYS\MOUSE.SYS
DEVICE=C:\DOS\SYS\ANSI.SYS
INSTALL=C:\DOS\FASTOPEN.EXE C:=(50,25)
```

(The commands in this CONFIG.SYS file will be shown in uppercase, which is traditional in MS-DOS documentation, but you can type them in lowercase if you wish.)

Installing Device Drivers (*.SYS Files)

Device drivers usually have a .SYS extension. You can install them with a DEVICE= statement in your CONFIG.SYS file.

The statements that begin with DEVICE= are used to load into memory the installable device drivers mentioned eariler. You can recognize device drivers because their file names end with .SYS.

In the sample CONFIG.SYS file, there are four DEVICE statements. They load the following device drivers:

- EMM.SYS, which provides control for an expanded memory board
- IBMCACHE.SYS, which provides a disk cache (a way to speed up disk access, which will be discussed later)
- MOUSE.SYS, which (as you might expect) allows use of a mouse
- ANSI.SYS, which provides enhanced MS-DOS display and keyboard functions needed by some programs

In the sample CONFIG.SYS file, the DEVICE statements have been put together at the beginning of the list to make it easier to find them. Some device drivers (such as ANSI.SYS) are provided with MS-DOS, while others (MOUSE.SYS and IBMCACHE.SYS) are provided by hardware manufacturers. MS-DOS loads device drivers in the order that it finds them in the CONFIG.SYS file. (A few device drivers require that some other driver be loaded first, and you should watch for references to this in the driver documentation.) Otherwise, statements in your CONFIG.SYS file can be in any order.

Notice that the device drivers shown here are in the directory C:\DOS\SYS. Putting them in a separate directory makes it simpler to find them among all of the other DOS-related files. You do have to remember to specify the correct directory in your DEVICE statements.

The fifth line in the CONFIG.SYS file includes the INSTALL command. This is new with MS-DOS 4.0, and it allows certain MS-DOS commands to be run from CONFIG.SYS instead of from AUTOEXEC.BAT. The FASTOPEN command, which will be discussed later, helps speed access to disk files. For those programs that support it, you should use INSTALL in the CONFIG.SYS file rather than using the AUOTEXEC.BAT file, because programs mentioned in the CONFIG.SYS file are loaded more efficiently into memory.

To use a device driver, you should check its documentation. The device drivers listed in *Table 12-1* are provided with MS-DOS (most of them are found only in the later versions).

Table 12-1. MS-DOS Device Drivers

Driver	Use for	DOS Version
ANSI.SYS	Screen and keyboard functions	2.0 and later
DISPLAY.SYS	Screen (for foreign languages)	3.3 and later
DRIVER.SYS	Add-on disk drives	3.2 and later
PRINTER.SYS	Printer (for foreign languages)	3.3 and later
VDISK.SYS	Create in-memory disk drive	2.0 and later
XMAEM.SYS	Expanded memory (80386 machines)	4.0
XMA2EMS.SYS	Expanded memory (80286 and 80386 machines)	4.0

EXTENDED AND EXPANDED MEMORY

Many PCs today have 1MB or more of memory, but MS-DOS can only use 640K to load or run programs directly. There are two ways that you can use additional memory: one is called *extended memory* and the other *expanded memory*. These sound similar, but they're quite different.

Extended and expanded memory are different ways of letting your PC use more than 640K of memory. Some MS-DOS 4.0 commands and many application programs can use expanded memory; fewer can use extended memory.

Extended memory is available on any system that uses the 80286, 80386, or higher-model processor. Examples of such systems are the IBM PC/AT and most models of the IBM PS/2 (except for the model 25 and the older model 30). Extended memory "extends" the range of memory addresses that can be directly accessed by the processor. Because it uses the processor in a different way from the way MS-DOS uses it, it isn't used widely in MS-DOS systems. (Two possible uses are discussed later.)

Expanded memory uses a different way to get at the extra memory: it uses a portion of the standard (below 604K) memory as a "window" into which it copies data stored in the extra memory on your memory expansion card. MS-DOS 4.0 provides two device drivers for handling expanded memory: XMAEMS.SYS and XMA2EMS.SYS. These drivers allow certain commands (such as BUFFERS, FASTOPEN, and VDISK.SYS) to use expanded memory. However, most users with non-IBM memory expansion boards (as well as users of earlier versions of MS-DOS) will have to use the device drivers provided by the memory board manufacturer. These drivers will work with those application programs that know how to use expanded memory, but they won't work with MS-DOS commands.

For example, if you have a PS/2 with 1MB memory, you have 640K of standard MS-DOS memory plus 384K of additional memory, much of which can be used as either extended or expanded memory. With MS-DOS 4.0, specifying

```
DEVICE=XMA2EMS.SYS /X:16
```

allocates 256K (16 times 16K) of expanded memory. If you have a system with an 80386 processor, you need to use this statement *first:*

```
DEVICE=XMAEMS.SYS
```

Depending on your expansion memory hardware, you may have to use additional switches with these drivers. These switches are described in your MS-DOS manual.

Using an In-Memory "Disk Drive": VDISK.SYS

Use VDISK.SYS to install a virtual (in-memory) disk drive.

A *virtual disk* (often called a RAM disk) is an area of memory that MS-DOS treats like a disk drive. Once you have installed the VDISK.SYS driver, you can copy files to and from this memory, use DIR to list the names of files stored there, and in most ways treat the memory just like a disk drive.

There are two big differences between a virtual disk drive and a physical one, however. First, the virtual drive is much faster than a physical floppy drive (or even a hard drive) because it has no physical parts like motors, switches, or read/write heads, only electronic signals. The other difference is that the virtual drive, unlike the physical drive, doesn't store its contents permanently. When the power is turned off or your system is rebooted, everything in the virtual drive is lost. Therefore, you have to make sure that you save any changed files to a physical disk before ending your session!

To create a virtual disk, put a statement like this in your CONFIG.SYS file:

```
DEVICE=C:\DOS\SYS\VDISK.SYS 360 512
```

This specifies that the virtual drive will hold up to 360K worth of files, and that it will use a sector size of 512 bytes. (The default sector size is 128 bytes. If you are going to use a large number of files with your virtual disk, a value like 128 is better, because it reduces the minimum file size.)

VDISK.SYS may also give you an opportunity to take advantage of your extended or expanded memory. Starting with DOS 3.0, you can use extended memory by adding the /E switch to VDISK.SYS as follows:

```
DEVICE=C:\DOS\SYS\VDISK.SYS 360 /E:360
```

With DOS 4.0, you can also use expanded memory for a virtual disk:

```
DEVICE=C:\DOS\SYS\VDISK.SYS 512 /X:512
```

This allocates 512K of expanded memory to your virtual disk. Remember that before you use expanded memory for MS-DOS commands you must install the XMAEMS.SYS driver (and the XMA2EMS.SYS driver if you have an 80386 machine).

What is the bottom line on virtual disks? If your system has only floppy disk drives, copying programs and files to a virtual disk will speed things up immensely—if you can spare the memory. Most applications use 400K or more, so you'll probably need expanded or extended memory. If you have a hard disk, however, the gain in speed probably doesn't justify using memory for a virtual disk. That same memory can be used for BUFFERS, FASTOPEN, and a disk cache (all discussed later), with the rest of the expanded memory being used directly by your applications where possible. This strategy gives you an impressive increase in speed plus the security of keeping all data on physical disks.

Using DISKCACHE.SYS (and others) for Increased Speed

Another use for a device driver is to set up an area of memory to be used to hold data that has been read from the disk or that will eventually be written to the disk. This area of memory is called a *cache*. Like the virtual disk, it takes advantage of the fact that operations performed within memory are much faster than operations involving physical disk drives. Unlike the virtual disk, however, the disk cache works automatically as your MS-DOS commands or other programs access the disk. There is no need to copy files back and forth to memory and less chance of losing data in a power failure.

When your program asks MS-DOS to read 128 bytes from the disk, for example, MS-DOS has to read a whole sector (512 bytes) because of the way the disk drive controller is designed. If there is no provision for saving the whole sector in memory, and the program requests the next 128 bytes of data, the whole sector has to be read again. This means time wasted positioning the recording head, waiting for the sector to arrive at the head, and rereading the data. With a cache, however, a whole 512-byte sector (or more) is stored in memory the first time it is requested. On later requests, the driver first checks memory to see if the sectors containing the needed data are already there. If they are, the data is transferred from memory rather than reading the disk again. Similarly, data to be written can be accumulated and then written all at once (see *Figure 12-4*). (Not all cache software does "write caching," and it isn't a good idea for some critical operations, since a power failure would lose your data waiting to be written. This could put your database "out of synch.")

Figure 12-4.
How a Disk Cache Works

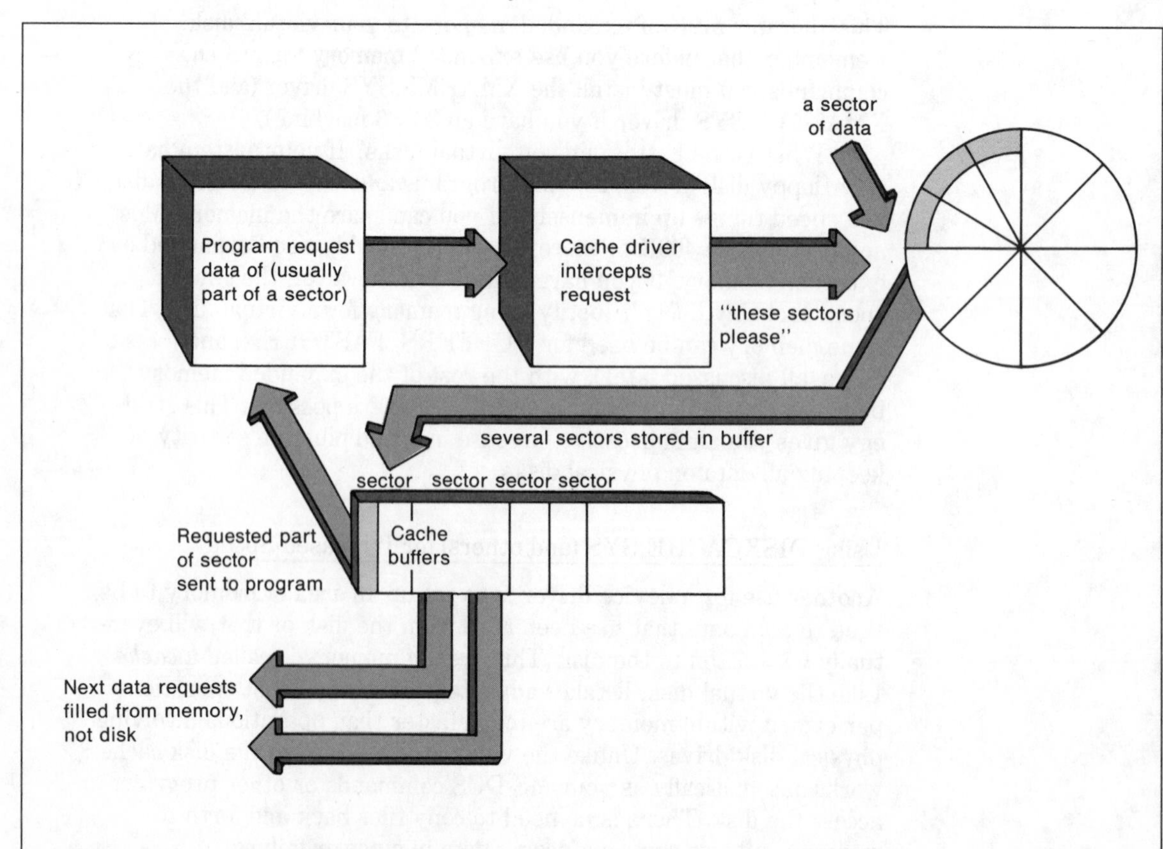

IBMCACHE and other disk-cache programs speed disk access by storing soon-to-be-needed data in memory.

IBM provides a cache driver called IBMCACHE.SYS with its PS/2 models, together with an installation program that asks you whether you want to put it in regular or extended memory. (The IBMCACHE.SYS file is hidden on your system disk, and the program IBMCACHE.COM has to be run from there. This installation program creates the correct CONFIG.SYS statement automatically.) If you have a PS/2, you have at least 384K of extended memory, which can't be used for much else when running MS-DOS (except for a virtual disk, perhaps), and you should choose to put IBMCACHE.SYS in extended memory and allocate all 384K to the disk cache. You can also specify the number of sectors to be read at a time by the driver (2, 4, or 8). If your application reads a lot of files in which the data is arranged in sequence (for example, word processor or spreadsheet files), try 8 and see what happens as you decrease it. If your application reads data records that can be anywhere in the file ("random access"—used by most database programs), try setting it to 2 sectors and see what happens as you increase it. The best way to calibrate things is to try loading the same file three times into your application program, and use a stopwatch to see how long it takes—then change the number of sectors, reboot, and try again.

If you don't have an IBM PS/2, don't feel left out. Many other companies make disk-caching software, some of which works better or is more flexible than IBMCACHE. While the principles of operation will be the same, you will have to run the product's installation program and follow the manufacturer's directions.

Making It Easier to Bail Out: the BREAK Command

Now that the DEVICE and INSTALL commands have been covered, it's time to continue to the next part of the example CONFIG.SYS file:

```
BREAK=ON
```

The BREAK command can make it easier to stop "runaway" programs.

In addition to the DEVICE driver installation command, you can use a number of other useful commands in your CONFIG.SYS file. The BREAK command can be useful for "bailing out" of certain programs that are caught in a loop or misbehaving in some other way. You may remember that you can press <Ctrl><Break> (or <Ctrl>C) to stop the currently running program. How rapidly a program will respond to your break key depends on whether BREAK is on or off. When it is off (the default), the system responds to <Ctrl><Break> only while an operation involving the keyboard, screen, printer, or auxiliary device is being performed.

This means that a program cannot be interrupted by <Ctrl><Break> while it is performing calculations or doing disk I/O, for example.

When BREAK is on, the check for <Ctrl><Break> is done whenever a call to a system function is being performed by the running program, including disk access. This means that when BREAK is on, you can interrupt the running program at almost any time, unless the program has made other provisions for handling user breaks.

To turn BREAK on, simply put the line BREAK=ON in your CONFIG.SYS file. (You can also run the BREAK command by putting the line BREAK ON in your AUTOEXEC.BAT file, or by typing BREAK ON at the command prompt.) If you are running commercial software you shouldn't need to "break out" of the program, and should leave BREAK off. Having BREAK on slows your programs somewhat because MS-DOS has to stop and check the keyboard more often.

Specifying Internal Resources: the FILES, FCBS, LASTDRIVE, and STACKS Commands

The next part of the example CONFIG.SYS file uses some commands that specify "how many of something" MS-DOS should provide:

```
FILES=20
FCBS=12,6
LASTDRIVE=G
STACKS=12
```

The FILES, FCBS, LASTDRIVE, and STACKS commands can increase the capacity of MS-DOS in various areas. Use them if you get an appropriate error message.

MS-DOS is designed to provide enough room to store information about files and disk drives sufficient for "normal" use. But as people run more and bigger programs, these built-in limits may be exceeded. When the default settings provided by MS-DOS don't give your applications programs or MS-DOS commands as many file handles, file-control blocks, drive information blocks, or memory stacks as they need, you can increase them. In most cases, your application's documentation will tell you what to put in your CONFIG.SYS file.

The FILES Command

MS-DOS keeps information about all open files in memory. By default, MS-DOS allows up to 8 files to be open at one time. Many applications (especially data bases) need to have more files open. If you have programs such as SideKick resident in memory or run the

PRINT command "in background," you'll need additional files. If you get an error such as "unable to open file," put a statement such as FILES=20 in your CONFIG.SYS. You can use a number up to 255, though a single program cannot use more than 20 files.

The FCBS Command

You probably don't need the FCBS command unless you are running an older program that uses something called a *file-control block* to keep track of its files. (Most programs use *file handles* instead, and these are taken care of by the FILES command.) If you get error messages referring to FCBS, try a statement such as FCBS 12,6. This means "allow space for up to 12 file-control blocks, and don't close the first 6 of these to make room for new files." You may have to experiment with this setting. Up to 255 FCBS can be specified, but check your program documentation.

The LASTDRIVE Command

The LASTDRIVE command is needed if you have more than five disk drives or more than five letters that you can use to refer to disk drives. You probably don't have five physical disk drives attached to your PC, but don't forget to count "logical drives" created with the FDISK utility when your hard disk was partitioned, virtual disks created with VDISK.SYS, or drives created with the ASSIGN and SUBST commands. If, as a result of using these commands, you expect to be able to access a drive G, for example, but get an error message, include a command such as LASTDRIVE=G in your CONFIG.SYS. (This allows for 7 drives with letters A through G.) You can have up to 26 drives (LASTDRIVE=Z).

The STACKS Command

The STACKS setting refers to memory stacks, which are blocks of memory that the processor uses to temporarily store information when it has been interrupted (for example, by a signal sent by a hardware device). Some devices interrupt the processor so frequently that it runs out of stacks and you get a message referring to "internal stack failure," the system is halted, and you have to reboot. If this happens, try a statement such as STACKS=16 in your CONFIG.SYS. (The STACKS command is available starting with MS-DOS 3.2.) You can also specify a second number that increases the size of each stack from its default (usually 128 bytes). Thus STACKS=12,256 means up to 12 stacks of up to 256 bytes each. You probably won't have to specify the stack size unless told to by your hardware documentation.

The FILES, FCBS, LASTDRIVE, and STACKS commands all consume memory according to how many of each you specify. While in most cases the amount of memory involved is small, it is a good idea to set these and other settings no higher than is needed by your applications. While this requires some experimentation, it means that more of that precious 640K of MS-DOS memory will be available for processing your data. That often translates to speed.

The BUFFERS Command and Disk Performance

```
BUFFERS=3
```

Our example CONFIG.SYS file also includes a BUFFERS command. This command allocates the specified number of buffers (512-byte memory areas) to store information being read from disk. Buffers work basically in the same way as the disk cache discussed earlier: they allow repeated access to data from memory rather than from rereading the disk. The BUFFERS statement in the example CONFIG.SYS file, BUFFERS=3, specifies 3 buffers (or about 1.5K of memory). The value used here is actually quite low, because the IBMCACHE.SYS disk-cache driver has also been installed. If you will be using a disk cache there is no need for a high BUFFERS setting because the cache does the same job as BUFFERS (and usually does it better). But if you don't have disk cache, and you use applications that mainly read sequential data (word processors and spreadsheets, for example), you can try 15, 20, 30, or even more buffers, checking performance by timing file access as discussed earlier. Since each 2 buffers uses 1K of memory, you don't want to use more buffers than you need.

MS-DOS 4.0 adds two useful features to the BUFFERS command. First, if you have expanded memory, you can add the /X switch to your BUFFERS setting to have the buffers allocated from expanded memory. (You must have the XMAEM.SYS driver installed first, however.) If you have enough expanded memory you can allocate up to 10,000 buffers (instead of up to 99), though a more modest 50 to 100 is better.

The BUFFERS command is similar to a disk cache. In MS-DOS 4.0, you can add read-ahead buffers and use expanded memory to hold disk data.

Second, you can allocate "read-ahead buffers." Normally, only one disk sector is read into the buffer when the data is needed for the first time. Because much of the overhead in using the disk comes from the initial head positioning, it is more efficient to read several sectors at a time, particularly if the additional data is likely to be needed soon (this is usually the case with a word processor, for example). Up to 8 read-ahead buffers can be specified. Thus an

MS-DOS 4.0 user with expanded memory might use this statement: BUFFERS=50,8 /X. This says to allocate 50 buffers, read 8 sectors at a time, and use expanded memory for the buffers.

Using FASTOPEN to Speed File Access

```
INSTALL=C:\DOS\FASTOPEN.EXE C:=50
```

FASTOPEN is another useful addition to your CONFIG.SYS file if you have MS-DOS 4.0. (Remember that when you use the INSTALL command you must specify the full path, filename *and* extension of the program being installed.)

If you have MS-DOS 3.3, you use your AUTOEXEC.BAT file instead, without the INSTALL command. The MS-DOS 3.3, AUTOEXEC.BAT version of the example command would be:

```
FASTOPEN C:=50
```

The FASTOPEN command sets up a buffer that holds information about the location of directories or files. This speeds access to frequently used files.

FASTOPEN specifies buffers will be used to hold file directory information. Every time MS-DOS is asked to find a file, it must search directories on the disk. On a hard disk, where a file may have a path such as C:\OFFICE\CORRES\JULY\LETTER4, this means searching the root directory for the location of the OFFICE directory, searching that directory for the CORRES subdirectory, then searching that subdirectory for the JULY subdirectory, and finally finding the entry for the file LETTER4 and noting which *cluster* (group of disk sectors) contains the beginning of the file's data. If you are are working with that file in your word processor, you may be accessing it repeatedly during a session in order to save it to disk or view another part of it.

When FASTOPEN is installed and MS-DOS is asked to find a particular file, the actual location of the first cluster for each directory along the path to the file is stored in a *file information buffer*. When the file is needed again, FASTOPEN searches to see if its "address" is already in a buffer, and if so, it can go directly to the file on the disk, bypassing all of the directories and subdirectories. If the file hasn't been referred to before in the current session, some of the directories on its path may have already been used, and FASTOPEN can take a shortcut to the last remembered directory in the path.

The example FASTOPEN command sets up the FASTOPEN buffer for drive C (you must specify a hard drive: FASTOPEN won't work with floppies), with room for 50 pieces of file or directory information. This should be enough for most users, though if you work with a lot of files (or have many deeply nested subdirectories), you might try 100. Using too many FASTOPEN buffers ties up memory and may slow your system because of the time needed to search through all the buffers.

In MS-DOS 4.0, FASTOPEN has two new features. You can use a FASTOPEN command like this in your CONFIG.SYS file:

```
INSTALL=C:\DOS\FASTOPEN.EXE C:=(100,200) /X
```

to specify 100 file information buffers and 200 cluster information buffers; the /X specifies that expanded memory will be used for these buffers. (Again, you must have installed the XMAEMS.SYS driver before you can use expanded memory with MS-DOS commands.)

What is a *cluster information buffer*? Each disk has a table listing which clusters (usually groups of 4 disk sectors) contain the information for a particular file. If there is enough continuous space available on the disk, a new file will be stored in consecutive clusters, but as disk space is used, and existing files are expanded, many files end up being stored in a series of groups of clusters (something like 1–40, 83–92, 101–105, 120–121).

When the second number is used with FASTOPEN, a number of buffers (200 in the example) are reserved to hold the starting and ending cluster numbers for each segment of the file. As with the directory information, this means that FASTOPEN can often take a shortcut to find the next part of the file needed. (See *Figure 12-5*.)

Your disk cache or BUFFERS setting and FASTOPEN make up your fast disk-access team. The cache or BUFFERS settings stores the actual file data, while FASTOPEN stores the information needed to get at that data. This increases the effective speed of your hard disk considerably.

RUNNING PROGRAMS FROM YOUR AUTOEXEC.BAT FILE

Once MS-DOS has been loaded and has read the CONFIG.SYS file, it looks for AUTOEXEC.BAT in your root directory (C:\ on a hard disk). If it finds it, it reads it a line at a time, running whatever commands or other programs are specified. You don't have to have an AUTOEXEC.BAT file, but most people do. At minimum, having one means that you don't have to answer the TIME and DATE prompts. Here's an example AUTOEXEC.BAT file which, as with the example CONFIG.SYS file, will be presented a bit at a time:

```
@ECHO OFF
VERIFY OFF
```

Figure 12-5. Finding File Location and Clusters

```
PATH C:\DOS;C:\WP50\WP;C:\MEMO;C:\QC;
APPEND C:\DOS;C:\WP50
PROMPT $P$G
```

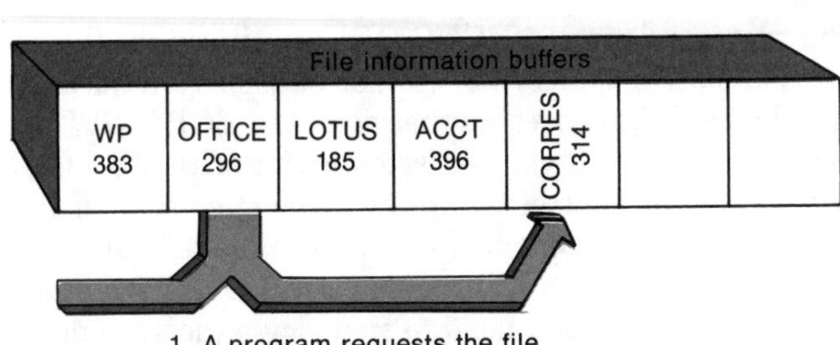

Disk

1. A program requests the file C:\OFFICE\CORRES\JULY\LETTER4
2. FASTOPEN intercepts the request. It searches the buffer and finds C:\OFRICE\CORRES in cluster 314
3. The disk is read starting with cluster 314, bypassing the C:\OFFICE directory
4. JULY (cluster 391) and LETTER4 (cluster 115) are found by searching directories
5. This information is added to the File information buffers

314

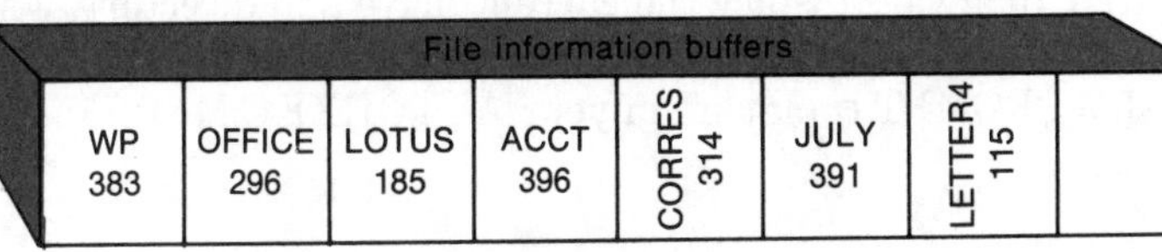

Cluster 115 LETTER4

6. In DOS 4.0, the file data cluster ranges can be stored to speed data access

Cluster information buffers

116 118 135 138 291 294

Groups of clusters holding data for LETTER4

Starting Cluster

MS-DOS Commands Run from AUTOEXEC.BAT

Any MS-DOS command or other program that can be run from the command line can also be run automatically from your AUTOEXEC.BAT file.

A number of MS-DOS commands set up features that you will want to be available for the whole session. It makes sense to put these commands in your AUTOEXEC.BAT file so that they'll be executed automatically.

In the example listing, @ECHO OFF specifies that the statements in this and other batch files will not be displayed during execution. (The "at" sign specifies that even the ECHO OFF statement won't be displayed. It can be used starting with MS-DOS 3.3.) The purpose is to avoid cluttering up the screen and confusing users.

The VERIFY OFF command in the example tells MS-DOS not to check the accuracy of data written on the disk. Modern disk drives are very reliable, so you don't need to slow down the system by having VERIFY on. It is, however, a good idea to type *verify on* at the command line before backing up your hard disk or copying floppies, and then type *verify off* to turn it off again.

You encountered the PATH and APPEND commands in Chapter 7. They tell MS-DOS where to search for executable programs and non-executable "overlay" files, respectively. You may not need APPEND, but PATH is virtually mandatory. Without it, you will have to type long pathnames or frequently change directories in order to run many programs.

The PROMPT command is strongly recommended. It specifies a string to be displayed as the MS-DOS prompt. The PG tells PROMPT to always display the current drive and directory, which makes it easy to tell where you are in the file system. (MS-DOS 4.0 puts this PROMPT command in your AUTOEXEC.BAT file during installation.)

Utility Commands in AUTOEXEC.BAT

The next example AUTOEXEC.BAT commands control devices and perform utility functions. Their operation is in many ways similar to device drivers.

```
C:\DOS\MODE CON LINES=50
C:\DOS\PRINT
SET COMSPEC=C:\DOS\COMMAND.COM
SET MEMO_DIR=C:\MEMO
SET MEMO_FILE=DOSNOTES
C:\MEMO\MEMO /R /X
```

The MODE command has many options for controlling the screen, printer, serial port, and other devices. The PRINT command lets you print a file while you do other work.

The MODE command performs a number of useful functions involving the printer, screen, keyboard, and other devices, which will be discussed later. Note that the MODE command, unlike the preceding three commands, is an external command: that is, it is run from a file on disk (MODE.COM) rather than being part of COMMAND.COM. When you run an external command from AUTOEXEC.BAT, that command is probably not stored in the root directory (if you have followed our advice about having a separate DOS directory for your MS-DOS command files). Therefore the full path (C:\DOS\MODE) is given.

The PRINT command allows you to send files to the printer while you continue to do other work. For example, you can now type *print letter* at the command prompt, and the file LETTER will be printed while you write your next document.

Also remember that if you have MS-DOS 3.3 rather than 4.0, you'll probably want to add a FASTOPEN command to AUTOEXEC.BAT. See the earlier discussion for an explanation of how FASTOPEN speeds file access.

The command C:\MEMO\MEMO /R /X runs the memory-resident Memory Mate program (a free-form notebook/database). Because this program (like the PRINT command) installs itself in memory and then returns control to MS-DOS, the next thing you will see is the C:\> prompt. If you want to run a program such as WordPerfect at the start of the session, just add a line like C:\WP50\WP to the end of the AUTOEXEC.BAT file.

Memory-Resident Utilities

Memory-resident (TSR) programs can be very convenient to use, but they take some memory away from your main application program.

The MS-DOS PRINT command and the MEMO (Memory Mate) program mentioned above both install themselves in memory for future use. The *memory-resident programs* (sometimes called TSR programs, for "Terminate and Stay Resident") are useful for two main reasons. Some, like the PRINT program, have the ability to perform a task "in the background" while you continue with your main application. While MS-DOS can actually run only one program at a time, the "foreground" program (such as your word processor) is often idle, waiting for you to type something. Certain programs like PRINT can take advantage of this idle time to get control of the processor and do a bit of work. Since the work is done a little bit at a time, the CPU is returned to the control of the foreground program quickly, so you usually won't notice your application being slowed down.

The second handy feature about most memory-resident programs is that you can trigger them by pressing a "hot key." Thus you can run a spreadsheet program and then "pop up" your memory-resident notepad program, make some notes, and return, without your spreadsheet being disturbed.

Memory-resident programs have two potential drawbacks, however. First, they use memory that won't be available for your main application program. (Some memory-resident programs can install most of themselves in expanded memory, minimzing the use of the 640K MS-DOS memory. Take advantage of this option wherever possible.) Second, memory-resident programs can sometimes interfere with other such programs or with application programs. You may have to read the documentation provided with the programs and experiment with the order in which the programs are loaded. As shown in the previous example, memory-resident programs that you always want available can be loaded from your AUTOEXEC.BAT file.

Configuring Devices with the MODE Command

You can use the MODE command mentioned above to configure a number of devices connected to your system. (Some of MODE's functions are actually small memory-resident programs, so MODE commands can use up a little memory.) Some useful examples will be given here, but you may wish to explore MODE in more detail by consulting *The Waite Group's Using PC DOS.*

The general form for a MODE command is:

MODE device-name specifications

and you can have as many MODE commands as you need.

Here are some examples of useful MODE commands:

`MODE LPT1 COLS=132 LINES=8`	← set parallel printer to print 32 columns, 8 lines per inch
`MODE BW80`	← set video display to black and white, 80 columns
`MODE CON CO80 LINES=50`	← set display to color, 80 columns, 50 lines (for VGA)
`MODE COM1 2400,N,8,1`	← set serial port (for modem) to 2400 baud, no parity, 8 data bits, stop bit
`MODE LPT2=COM1`	← redirect output from second parallel port to first serial port used to connect a serial printer to some MS-DOS applications)
`MODE COM1 /STA`	← display status of first serial port
`MODE /STA`	← display status of all devices

TAKING STOCK AND MAKING TRADEOFFS

You've now surveyed the CONFIG.SYS settings and device drivers and many of the useful commands you can run from your AUTOEXEC.BAT file. Each line you put in one of these files installs a useful feature, Otherwise, why would you put it there? At the same time, most of these features use some of your memory, which will not be available to your application program. This means that, like a kid with a dollar in a candy shop, you can't have everything. It's time to look at how to choose.

Examining and Prioritizing Items in CONFIG.SYS and AUTOEXEC.BAT

Any given feature implemented in your CONFIG.SYS or AUTOEXEC.BAT file can turn out to be one of the following:

- Unnecessary. For example, you don't have that old mouse any more, so you shouldn't be installing its driver from your CONFIG.SYS file. You don't need both BUFFERS=75 and a disk-cache program. If you haven't been using the virtual disk you installed in expanded memory, or your new word processor can use expanded memory directly, remove the DEVICE=VDISK.SYS line from your CONFIG.SYS file.
- Necessary but not adjustable. The BREAK setting is either on or off. Most device drivers are either installed or they aren't.
- Useful and adjustable. How many BUFFERS do you want? How large a virtual disk (VDISK) do you want in expanded memory? You will be spending most of your time configuring these settings, because you have to find out how much more performance you get when you increase them and how much memory it will cost you.

Finding Out How Much Memory Is Tied Up

Use the CHKDSK command (or, in MS-DOS 4, the MEM command) to see how much of your memory is available for use by your application programs.

To set priorities for the use of memory by system features, it is helpful to know how much memory is tied up in each feature. First, use the CHKDSK command (introduced in Chapter 8) to determine your total installed memory and memory actually available to your applications program. If you have MS-DOS version 4, you can type the MEM command to get a much quicker report on available memory. For example:

```
C:\>mem
    655360 bytes total memory
```

```
 654336 bytes available                          ← regular MS-DOS memory

 515528 largest executable program size
2097152 bytes total EMS memory                   ← expanded memory
2031616 bytes free EMS memory

 393216 bytes total extended memory
 262144 bytes available extended memory
```

Determining Tradeoffs (Application Memory vs. Buffers, Cache, etc.)

Use expanded memory where possible to conserve the 640K of main MS-DOS memory. Some application programs use expanded memory automatically, others can be told to do so.

If your program won't run at all with the amount of memory available, you'll have to recover some memory by adjusting your commands and configuration settings. Even if your program will run, however, it is a good idea to take inventory of your system every few months to review the features you are using, the amount of memory they use, and whether you are using your memory efficiently. Many application programs sold today are designed to run faster if you can give them more memory. (For one thing, if your word processor has enough memory to store the whole document in memory, it won't have to keep reading and saving parts of the document to disk when you make changes or move the cursor!) The following checklist may help:

- Do you have expanded memory? If so, check your programs' documentation to see if they can use it.
- Do you have MS-DOS 4.0? If so, use expanded memory for the BUFFERS and FASTOPEN commands.
- If you have installed a disk cache, lower your BUFFERS setting to 10 or so. If you have extended memory and the cache will use it, that will free expanded memory for other uses.
- Do you always need all of your memory-resident programs? Would it be better to install certain ones only when they are needed, and then remove them? Does your application program already provide functions similar to those provided by your memory-resident programs?
- Should you upgrade your MS-DOS version? Newer versions use somewhat more memory, but they also provide features (such as FASTOPEN) that can speed up your system. MS-DOS 4.0 can use expanded memory for disk buffers.

How Much Memory Does It Use?

You can use *Table 12-2* in conjunction with a listing of your CONFIG.SYS and AUTOEXEC.BAT files to determine how much memory is tied up by each statement or setting:

Table 12-2. Memory Usage for PC DOS Commands and Features

Feature	Approximate Memory Used (in K)
APPEND	7.5
ASSIGN	1.5
BUFFERS	0.5 per buffer
FASTOPEN	8.5 for FASTOPEN C: = (20,20) .5 per 10 additional directory buffers .5 per 32 additional cluster-list buffers
FCBS	.5 for about 18 file-control blocks
FILES	0.5 for 8 file handles
GRAFTABL	1.0
GRAPHICS	5.5
KEYB	.0
LASTDRIVE	0.5 for 6 drives (LASTDRIVE = F)
MODE	.5 (when resident for device control)
NLSFUNC	3.0
PRINT	6.0 (default; add 0.5 for every 3 files in queue after the first 10)
SHARE	5.5 (default; add 0.5 per every 32 file locks)
STACKS	0.5 for ten 32-byte stack frames
VDISK.SYS	1.0 (plus size of virtual disk)
XMA2EMS.SYS	0 (varies somewhat)

Taking a Memory "Snapshot" with MEM (DOS 4.0)

If you want to snoop even further into your system, and you have MS-DOS 4.0, try typing MEM /PROGRAM. You will get a listing like this (only part is shown:)

```
C:\>mem /program

Address     Name        Size      Type
000000                  000400    Interrupt Vector
000400                  000100    ROM Communication Area
000500                  000200    DOS Communication Area
```

```
000700      IBMBIO      002470      System Program

002B70      IBMDOS      0088A0      System Program

00B410      IBMBIO      008430      System Data
              DASDDRVR  0001E0        DEVICE=
              EMM       0029C0        DEVICE=
              IBMCACHE  003020        DEVICE=
                        000380        FILES=
                        000100        FCBS=
                        0014E0        BUFFERS=
                        0001C0        LASTDRIVE=
                        000CD0        STACKS=

013850      MEM         0000C0      Environment
013920      FASTOPEN    002720      Program
016050      COMMAND     001640      Program
0176A0      COMMAND     000200      Environment
0178B0      MOUSE       0000D0      Environment
017990      MOUSE       002960      Program
01A300      MEMO        0000D0      Environment
01A3E0      MEMO        008000      Program
0223F0      SP          0000D0      Environment
0224D0      SP          027740      Program
049C20      SP          010000      Data
059C30      COMMAND     0000D0      Data
059D10      COMMAND     001640      Program
05B360      COMMAND     0000B0      Environment
05B420      MEM         012F60      Program
06E390      IBMDOS      031860      -- Free --

  655360 bytes total memory
  654336 bytes available
  280528 largest executable program size

 2097152 bytes total EMS memory
 2031616 bytes free EMS memory

  393216 bytes total extended memory
  262144 bytes available extended memory
```

The main use of this listing is to show you every device driver and other program that you have currently installed in memory. Notice that the values for FILES, FCBS, BUFFERS, LASTDRIVE, and STACKS are given, too. The size is given in hexadecimal numbers; to convert hex to decimal, first, convert any digit other than 0–9 as follows: A = 10, B = 11, C = 12, D = 13, E = 14, and F = 15. Multiply each digit from right to left by its place value (1, 16, 256, 4096, 65536 . . .). Add the products together. (See *Figure 12-6.*) For a bit more detailed listing, try MEM /DEBUG.

Figure 12-6. Converting from Hexadecimal to Decimal

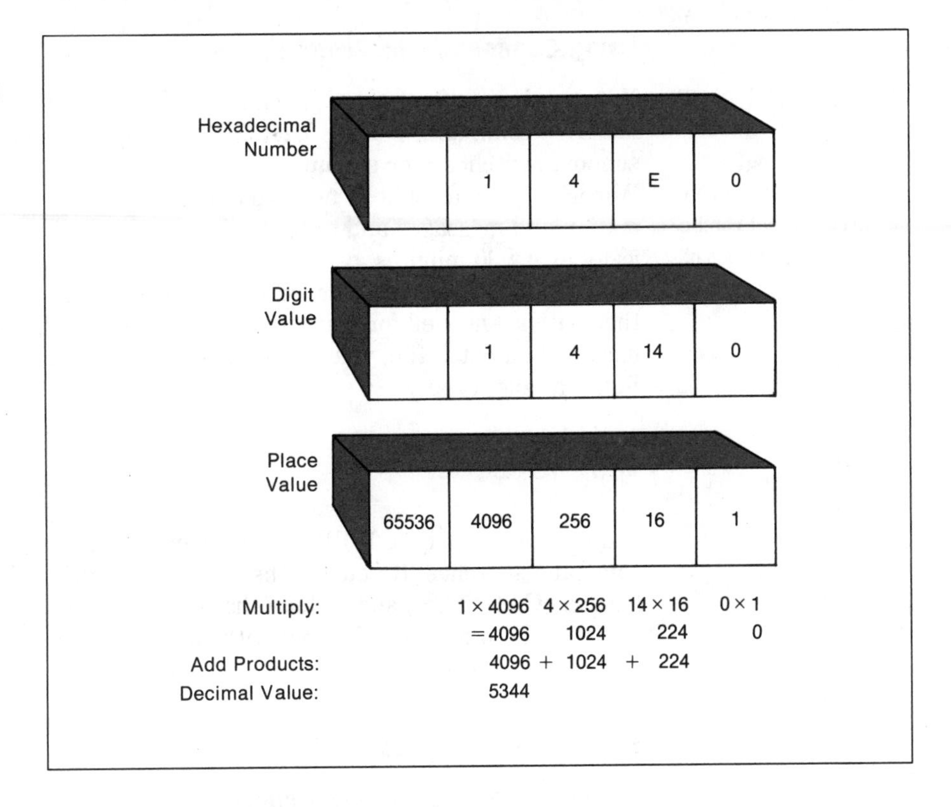

CUSTOMIZING YOUR APPLICATIONS

In configuring your system, don't overlook your main programs—those that you use to do the actual work for which you bought a PC. Modern word processors, spreadsheets, and data bases provide dozens of adjustable features. Many of them, such as the colors of menus and the values of page margins, aren't relevant to the overall performance of the program. Here the focus is on things that affect the speed of your application (for example, use of expanded memory), its use of system features (for example, using the Enhanced Graphics Adapter [EGA] to display 43 lines of text instead of 25), or its access to the disk (such as specifying where the program should find its configuration file). Since these features require the program to do things differently when it is loading and starting to access your system, they are usually implemented either as switches that you specify on the command line or as settings that you put in the environment before running the program (more on that a little later).

Using Command-Line Switches

Check your application program documentation for command-line switches or environmental variables that can be used to configure use of the display, memory, or disk.

You are already familiar with command-line switches used with MS-DOS commands such as DIR /W. Many application programs also support switches. For example, typing WP /R /B-30 will start WordPerfect and tell it to use expanded memory to hold menu information and messages and to back up the current file to disk automatically every 30 minutes.

In Chapter 10 you learned how to write batch files. If you put the switches needed for starting a program (and other useful information) in a batch file, you won't have to remember what to type. For example, type

```
C:\>copy con wpr.bat
wp /r /b-30
```

and now you just type WPR to start WordPerfect with the specified command switches. If you put the batch file WPR.BAT in a directory (such as C:\BATCH) and include that directory in your PATH, you will be able to run WordPerfect with these settings from anywhere on your hard disk.

Setting Environmental Variables

Earlier you learned the environment is a part of memory where MS-DOS keeps information such as the search path. Many programs will also look in the environment for information in addition to the search path. You can use the SET command to put information in the environment. Here are some SET commands to add to the example AUTOEXEC.BAT file:

```
SET COMSPEC=C:\DOS\COMMAND.COM
SET MEMO_DIR=C:\MEMO
SET MEMO_FILE=DOSNOTES
```

Use the SET command to list, set, change, or remove environmental variables. The SHELL command can be used to increase the size of the environment.

The word SET is followed by a label for the piece of information: COMSPEC, for example. Since you can change the information associated with a label (by using a different SET command), the label is a variable. Next comes an equals sign (=) and then the information to be stored in the variable: for example, the path C:\DOS\COMMAND.COM.

The second two SET statements in the example set variables used by the Memory Mate program: the first specifies the directory where it will look for its data files, while the second gives the name of the default data file it should use. You should check your program's documentation to see which environmental variables it needs (or which can be used optionally).

To find out what variables are currently defined, just type *set*:

```
C:\>set
MEMO_DIR=C:\MEMO
MEMO_FILE=DOSNOTES
COMSPEC=C:\DOS\COMMAND.COM
PATH C:\DOS;C:\WP50\WP;C:\MEMO;C:\QC;
PROMPT=$P$G
```

To remove a variable from the environment, type *set* by the variable name and an equals sign, like this

```
C:\>set memo_dir=
```

Changing the Size of the Environment and the Location of COMMAND.COM

The SHELL command can be used in your CONFIG.SYS file to increase the size of the MS-DOS environment. You need to do this if you put some SET commands in your AUTOEXEC.BAT file (or have defined a long PATH) and get the message "out of environment space." (Remember that the PATH command stores the path information in the environment.) You also use the SHELL command to specify a location for COMMAND.COM other than the root directory of the startup drive. For example, the statement

```
SHELL=C:\DOS\COMMAND.COM /P /E:512
```

can be used in the example CONFIG.SYS file to specify that COMMAND.COM should be loaded from the DOS directory on drive C, and remain in memory (you want COMMAND.COM to always come back for another command). The /E switch specifies the size of the environment in bytes. (In this case, 512 bytes. If you are using MS-DOS 3.1, the number you should use is the number of 16-byte blocks rather than the number of bytes, so you would use /E:32 rather than /E:512. You cannot set the environment size with the SHELL command in MS-DOS versions earlier than 3.1.)

When MS-DOS runs a program, it removes most of COMMAND.COM from memory in order to provide maximum memory for your program. When the program terminates, it must reload COMMAND.COM. While the SHELL command tells MS-DOS where it should load COMMAND.COM from at startup, the COMSPEC command (also used in the CONFIG.SYS file and shown in the SET examples above) specifies where COMMAND.COM should be reloaded from.

For example, suppose you want to be able to boot MS-DOS from a floppy disk. When you boot from a floppy, MS-DOS will sometimes need to reload the COMMAND.COM file from the floppy, which can require that you swap disks. To fix this, add a line like this to your CONFIG.SYS file:

```
COMSPEC=C:\COMMAND.COM
```

(Or, if you've moved COMMAND.COM to your DOS directory, use *COMSPEC=C:\DOS\COMMAND.COM.)* This tells MS-DOS to reload COMMAND.COM from your hard disk rather than the floppy.)

INSTALLING AN APPLICATION

You have been looking at many of the ways to help MS-DOS to perform better. You have learned how to make tradeoffs between MS-DOS memory and memory available to your application program. It is now time to look at how you can install an application program and customize it to take best advantage of your hardware and the program's features.

Selecting Software

When buying software, consider compatibility, ease of learning, ease of use, versatility, power, and expandability. Your priorities will probably change as you gain experience.

Given the limitations of the medium, no book can make specific recommendations about which word processor or spreadsheet program to buy. Numerous magazines offer comparative reviews that break applications down to various aspects and then score them. These reviews can be useful, but you should keep your own needs in mind. If you are a beginner, a program's "ease of use" and "ease of learning" score may be most important, and the presence of advanced features would be a bonus, but of secondary importance. When you have become an experienced user, the reverse is likely be true. Nevertheless, there are some very general criteria for choosing software that you should keep in mind:

- Compatibility—will it work with my hardware? Do I need to upgrade my MS-DOS version to use this product? (Upgrading is often a good idea.) Would I need to add more memory or a better graphics display in order to really enjoy using this product? Can this program use files from its competitors and export files that they can use? Can it produce output suitable for a variety of uses?

- Ease of learning—how good is the documentation? Are any books about this program available from third parties? Is there extensive on-line help?
- Ease of use—is the interface logical and intuitive? Is a mouse supported? Are commands consistent from one part of the application to another?
- Features and power—does it have the specific features that I need? Does it have other features that I might want to use eventually? Does the program get the job done in a reasonable amount of time?
- Expandability—can I upgrade to more advanced versions? Do third parties make add-on packages (such as macros) for this product?

Taking Inventory

Now you have made your choice and brought the box home. These days many software packages are hefty, filled with disks and manuals. Installing software is easier (and less prone to problems) if you do it systematically.

Most packages have a brief manual that explains the first steps you should take in installing and using the software. (It is often called "Quick Start" or "Installation.") Look it over for important information.

Use the DISKCOPY command to make a backup copy of all of the disks on which the software is distributed. Install from the backups, not the originals. That way if you do something wrong you always will be able to make a fresh, undamaged copy.

Look for a "packing list" in the documentation or on disk. Print it out for reference. It lists all of the files that should be on the distribution disks. For our example, we'll install the imaginary product "Unicorn Personal Information Manager."

```
C:\>print a:packing.lst
```

The printout might look like this:

```
***** Files in UNICORN version 1.0 Distribution *****

*** Disk 1 -- Installation and Program ***

README.CO        program to display README file
README.TX        text file with last-minute changes/additions
                 to UNICORN
```

```
INSTALLF.BAT   batch file to install UNICORN on floppy disks
INSTALLH.BAT   batch file to install UNICORN on hard disk
UNICORN.EXE    main UNICORN program
UNICORN.OVL    overlay file for UNICORN program

*** Disk 2 -- Help Files and Forms ***

MAINHELP.HLP   main online help for UNICORN
HELP1.OVL      overlay file for help
HELP2.OVL      overlay file for help
CONTACT.FRM    pre-designed forms for use with UNICORN
PHONE.FRM
ADDRESS.FRM
MEMO.FRM
BILL.FRM

*** Disk 3 -- Printer Drivers and Utilties ***

HPLJII.DRV    HP Laserjet driver
EPS80.DRV     Epson compatible driver
STAR.DRV      Star printer series driver
HPDJII.DRV    HP Deskjet driver

FNTLOAD.EXE   program to download HP Laserjet fonts from
              UNICORN
```

When installing software, read the README file and installation manual for instructions. Look for command-line switches and environmental variables that you can "package" into a batch file for running the program with your customized setup.

First look at the README file. Some programs let you look at the file by typing *readme* at the MS-DOS prompt—this runs a program that displays the file, as in the case of UNICORN. In other cases, there is just a text file, which you can print out by typing *print readme.txt* or view one screen at a time by typing *more < readme.txt*. (You could also do this with UNICORN, but you should use the "reader" program when available, since it usually lets you page back and forth through the file.)

Next, you install the program. The more elaborate programs have menu-driven installation programs that step you through all of the choices. They usually ask you what video display you have (or find out directly by asking your PC). They ask you what printer you have, so they can install the appropriate printer driver. Like the device drivers discussed earlier, a printer driver translates requests made by your application program to control codes for a device. In this case, when the program has marked text as boldface, for example, the "boldface" command is sent to the driver, which issues the appropriate string of control codes for the printer.

UNICORN is an example of a simpler program—it uses batch files for installation. The installation manual should tell you what information you need to supply on the command line when running the batch file. For UNICORN, you might type

```
A:\>installh c:\unicorn /e hpljii
```

meaning to install UNICORN on the hard disk in the C:\UNICORN directory, and include drivers for the EGA display and the HP Laserjet II printer.

Command-Line Switches

Once you have installed the program, check the documentation for command-line switches that you can use when running the program. Especially, look to see if there is a switch that tells the program to use expanded memory where possible. (Some programs use expanded memory automatically when they find it.) If you have expanded memory, there is usually no better use for it than letting your applications use it to speed up their processing.

If you find one or more switches you want to use, make a batch file "packaging" the switches so that you don't have to remember them:

```
C:\>copy con uni.bat
cd c:\unicorn
unicorn /x /l=50 /m=mymacros.mac
```

UNICORN now will run in expanded memory with 50 lines on the VGA display and will load macros (prerecorded command sequences) from the file MYMACROS.MAC.

Using the Environment

Some programs look for environmental variables. UNICORN, for example, recognizes three variables: MYDIR, which specifies the directory to be used for macros and personal preference files; MYFILE, which specifies which database to load automatically at the start of the session; and CALENDAR, which names the calendar file to use for appointments. You can establish these variables with SET commands:

```
SET MYDIR=C:\OFFICE\PLANS
SET MYFILE=C:\OFFICE\PLANS\GENERAL
SET CALENDAR=C:\OFFICE\PLANS\CAL1990.CAL
```

If you will always be using these settings, you can add them to your AUTOEXEC.BAT file so they will be put in the environment automatically at the start of every session. If you use many different application programs with their own variables, a cleaner way to handle variables would be to put them in your UNI.BAT file:

```
set mydir=c:\office\plans
set myfile=c:\office\plans\general
set calendar=c:\office\plans\cal1990.cal
cd c:\unicorn
unicorn /x /l=50 /m=mymacros.mac
set mydir=
set myfile=
set calendar=
```

This sets the variables, runs UNICORN, and then removes the variables from the environment when they are no longer needed.

Customization Menus

Finally, don't overlook the program's own built-in menus that may allow you to set many features such as foreground and background colors, how often data is to be saved to disk, fonts to be used to display text, default style settings for page formatting, and so on. Take the time to explore each menu item.

AN EMERGENCY FLOPPY

The best-laid plans . . . often go astray. You have invested a lot of time and energy in arranging programs on your hard disk and placing data files there. If you've read Chapters 4 and 8, you know about the importance of making backups of your floppy disks and hard disk.

Now assume the hard disk fails. You start your system and get an error message such as "drive C: not ready." The only way to get MS-DOS running in this situation is to boot your system from a floppy. Do you know where the floppy that came with your version of MS-DOS is? Did you copy it, or do you have only the original? Assuming you find it and start your system, will you have the utilities you need to begin to restore your hard disk?

By spending a few minutes preparing an "emergency floppy" now, you can save hours of frustration later.

Preparing an emergency floppy is simple. Start by taking the distribution floppy for your version of MS-DOS, and use the DISKCOPY command to copy it:

```
C:\>diskcopy a: b:
```

Later versions of MS-DOS, such as 3.3 and 4.0, have more than one distribution disk. You should always copy all of the disks for backup purposes anyway, but only one copy—usually marked "system disk"—will be bootable. With version 4.0, you can create a floppy-based copy by running the installation program and telling it to install to floppies (rather than your hard disk). Check your documentation for the number of blank formatted disks that you should have on hand.

The next step is to copy your AUTOEXEC.BAT and CONFIG.SYS files to the floppy from the hard disk, for example:

```
C:\>copy \autoexec.bat a:
C:\>copy \config.sys a:
```

You may need to edit the AUTOEXEC.BAT and CONFIG.SYS files on your floppy disk if any commands use *relative pathnames*. A relative pathname is one that is in relation to the current directory rather than giving an absolute location. For example, if you boot from drive C, the current directory will be C:\, and the pathname DOS\SYS will refer to the directory C:\DOS\SYS. If you boot from drive A, however, the pathname DOS\SYS will refer the SYS subdirectory of the DOS directory on drive A (and there probably won't be one). To fix this, always start pathnames in AUTOEXEC.BAT and CONFIG.SYS files with the root directory of C: for example, C:\DOS\SYS. This will work regardless of the drive you boot from.

Prepare two emergency floppies—one to start your system when the sysem files on the hard disk have been damaged, and one that doesn't use the hard disk at all.

This emergency floppy will enable you to run your system when a system file (such as one of the hidden files) on your hard disk has been damaged. You can then run the SYS command to copy fresh copies of the system files to the hard disk. Unfortunately, a more common problem is for the hard disk to fail. (Hard disks are pretty reliable, but it pays to be prepared. There is also the danger of a "virus" program destroying data on your hard disk.) You should prepare a second emergency floppy for such conditions. It is like the first one, except that it doesn't refer to anything on your hard disk. The AUTOEXEC.BAT file will be minimal (perhaps just PATH A:) and the CONFIG.SYS file might have just FILES=20 and BUFFERS=20. You should also copy your favorite text editor to this disk so you will have something to revise files with. (If you are using 360K floppies you may have to delete some little-used MS-DOS commands to make room for the editor.)

It may take you as long as half an hour to prepare these emergency disks, but, together with frequent backups of your hard disk, they provide insurance against a disaster.

VERSIONS OF MS-DOS

Major versions of MS-DOS added significant features. You can use the VER command to see which version you have. If you have MS-DOS 2.0 or 2.1, you can add many features at a modest cost in memory by upgrading to version 3.3 or 4.0.

If you type *ver* at the MS-DOS prompt, you will see a message describing the version of MS-DOS that you are running. For example:

```
C:\>ver

IBM DOS Version 4.00
```

(Many versions also announce themselves with a longer message when loaded.) The MS-DOS version number has a whole number part (the major version number—4, in this case); a decimal number, indicating a minor revision (such as 3.2); and, optionally, a second decimal place indicating a very minor revision (such as a bug fix or a version designed for a particular machine, such as Compaq). (By the way, this discussion refers to IBM PC-DOS as well as MS-DOS, but for convenience both will be referred to as "MS-DOS".)

Each version of MS-DOS added some new commands or capabilities. For example, MS-DOS 2.0 added support for hard disks, hierarchical (tree-structured) directories, installable device drivers, and the "handle" method for accessing files. It is considered the first "modern" version of MS-DOS (version 1.0 is considered obsolete). Version 3.0 added improved hard-disk facilities and support for networks. Version 3.2 added support for 720 K 3½″ disks, and 3.3 added support for 1.44MB 3½″ disks. Version 4.0 adds support for large (more than 32MB) hard disks in a single partition, as well as a new DOS Shell interface (see Chapter 11). These are just the broad outlines: most versions introduced new user commands or CONFIG.SYS settings.

Versions of MS-DOS are generally "upwardly compatible": a program that runs under one version will usually run on later versions. (There are occasional exceptions: when MS-DOS 4.0 was released, certain utility programs that dealt with the file allocation table for hard disks didn't work, because MS-DOS 4.0 made some changes in the table format to deal with disks larger than 32MB. These programs have since been revised to work with MS-DOS 4.0.) The reverse is not always true: some programs will not run with earlier versions of MS-DOS because an internal service they need isn't available. The program documentation should specify the minimum version of MS-DOS needed. If you have version 2.0 or 2.1, now is a good time to upgrade to version 3.3 or 4.0.

When you upgrade to a later version of MS-DOS, you copy all of the system files (including the hidden *.SYS files) to your hard disk, replacing those used by the earlier version. It is important to replace all of the existing files because a command (such as XCOPY.EXE) from one version of MS-DOS will not run with any other version—you will get the "incompatible DOS version" message. MS-DOS 4.0 is particularly easy to install because it has a menu-driven installation program that not only installs the necessary files but also creates many useful CONFIG.SYS settings and AUTOEXEC.BAT commands for you.

SUMMARY

You now have control over your MS-DOS system. You not only know how to use MS-DOS, but you also know how to configure it to your needs. If you wish to learn more tricks and useful techniques involving the many MS-DOS commands, see Appendix E for suggested reading.

REVIEW

1. CONFIG.SYS and AUTOEXEC.BAT are text files that you create to specify MS-DOS features and run programs.
2. MS-DOS has three basic parts: the BIOS, the kernel, and the user interface program COMMAND.COM.
3. The environment is an area in memory where you can put information that can be used by MS-DOS or your programs.
4. Device drivers are loaded through your CONFIG.SYS file. They enable MS-DOS to use add-on devices and additional features.
5. Expanded memory can let MS-DOS 4.0 and some programs use more than 640K of memory.
6. You put the name of an application program as the last line in your AUTOEXEC.BAT file, enabling you to begin each session with that program working.
7. You can find out how much memory each MS-DOS feature and memory-resident program uses and consider the tradeoffs involved.
8. When installing a new application program, check its documentation for such features as the ability to use expanded memory and the ability to use the MS-DOS environment to control the program.

9. Preparing an emergency floppy with essential MS-DOS files is good insurance. If your hard disk should fail, you can start the system from the floppy and may be able to access undamaged parts of the hard disk.
10. Most programs will run on all versions of MS-DOS after 2.0, but later versions add new commands and features.

Quiz for Chapter 12

1. The CONFIG.SYS and AUTOEXEC.BAT files are:
   - **a.** required in order for your PC to work at all.
   - **b.** very useful to most MS-DOS users.
   - **c.** printable text files.
   - **d.** both a and c.
   - **e.** both b and c.
   - **f.** none of the above.
2. You can install device drivers by using the:
   - **a.** MODE command.
   - **b.** SYS command.
   - **c.** DEVICE command.
   - **d.** COPY command.
3. The MS-DOS environment is used to:
   - **a.** speed loading of disk files.
   - **b.** specify information that can be used by MS-DOS or application programs.
   - **c.** interface MS-DOS with external devices.
   - **d.** load the BIOS into memory.
4. A portion of memory can be used like a disk drive after you run the:
   - **a.** MODE command.
   - **b.** XMAEM.SYS device driver.
   - **c.** FASTOPEN command.
   - **d.** VDISK.SYS device driver.
5. Expanded memory allows you to:
   - **a.** store more data in the same amount of memory.
   - **b.** run more than one program at a time.
   - **c.** keep programs and data in memory even when the power has been shut off.
   - **d.** access more than 640K of memory, depending on the command or program being used.
6. The BUFFERS setting and disk-caching programs speed disk access by:
   - **a.** storing disk sectors in memory, where they can be read as needed.
   - **b.** speeding up the disk drive motor.
   - **c.** storing the entire file directory from the disk in memory.
   - **d.** allowing you to store more data on the hard disk.

7. You know that you need the FILES, FCBS, LASTDRIVE, or STACKS commands when:
   a. you install an additional disk drive.
   b. you receive certain error messages referring to files, disk drives, or stack frames.
   c. your application program isn't running fast enough.
   d. the Power-On Self-Test (POST) indicates a problem.

8. Command-line switches can be used with:
   a. MS-DOS commands only.
   b. all MS-DOS commands and application programs.
   c. all programs except memory-resident programs.
   d. some MS-DOS commands and application programs.

9. The COMSPEC environmental variable is used to:
   a. specify which user interface to use with MS-DOS.
   b. specify the location of the command processor (shell).
   c. increase the size of the MS-DOS environment.
   d. both b and c.
   e. all of the above.

10. The various versions of MS-DOS since 2.0 are:
   a. downwardly compatible.
   b. incompatible.
   c. upwardly compatible.
   d. interchangeable.

EDLIN

Chapter 6 introduced methods for creating text files. This appendix shows you how to use EDLIN, a text editing program supplied with MS-DOS. If you have access to a word processor or "notepad" type program (such as SideKick), you are usually better off using it, since it is easier to use and more powerful than EDLIN. With a word processor or "full screen editor," all of your text is on the screen and you can move around in it with the cursor keys, inserting and deleting text as desired. EDLIN ("EDit LINes") is a "line editor," meaning that you have to work with each line of text separately, using line numbers for identification.

Learning EDLIN can still be useful, however, especially if you have to work on different PCs. Since EDLIN is distributed with MS-DOS, it is likely to be available on any PC. EDLIN also has the advantage that it automatically creates plain text (ASCII) files that are understandable by MS-DOS, while word processing programs usually must be specifically instructed to create such files.

LINE NUMBERS

As with all line-oriented text editors, EDLIN identifies with line numbers each line of text in a text file, numbering them sequentially from the beginning of the file to the end. When text is changed in a text file, EDLIN automatically renumbers the lines as necessary.

Because EDLIN is a line editor, it identifies all information in terms of line numbers. Line numbers are only reference points within the file; they are not part of the data contained in the file. You don't have to enter the line numbers as you enter text; they are automatically supplied by EDLIN.

```
1: This is the first line of text.
2: You do not enter the line number as part of the file.
3: The numbers are supplied automatically by EDLIN.
```

Lines within the file are numbered in sequence. When lines are inserted or deleted, EDLIN remembers the lines automatically. But it doesn't show you the renumbering until you ask to see the file again. This is a bit confusing at first.

Suppose you want to add a new line at the beginning of an existing file (you'll learn how to do this in just a minute). This is a file about computer history, and right now, the first line reads:

```
In the beginning there was ENIAC...
```

When you create or display this file using EDLIN, the first line begins with a number.

```
1: In the beginning there was ENIAC...
```

If you decide to change your opening and now want the first line to read: "And on the eighth day She created computers," the line number would change.

```
1: And on the eighth day She created computers.
2: In the beginning there was ENIAC...
```

Thereafter, if you wanted to modify "In the beginning there was ENIAC . . . ," you would need to refer to it as line 2.

GIVING COMMANDS

EDLIN accomplishes its editing tasks by receiving your instructions in the form of commands. Some commands are entered by themselves; others must be accompanied by a line number or range of line numbers.

EDLIN receives its instructions from you in the form of commands. Commands are indicated by one-letter abbreviations as shown in *Table A-1.* Many commands also require that you indicate which line or line numbers are to be affected by the command. The format of EDLIN commands is simple. First you enter the beginning line number, then the ending line number (line numbers in a range are separated by commas), and finally the single-letter abbreviation indicating the command. Here are examples of EDLIN commands:

Table A-1. Format of EDLIN Commands

Command	Meaning
1D	Delete line 1.
1,9L	List the file starting with line 1 and ending with line 9.
4I	Insert a new line before line 4.
E	End the editing session.

Each EDLIN command is discussed in detail in this appendix.

Current Lines

The line of text currently being worked on inside EDLIN is called the current line and is identified by an asterisk following the line number. When commands are entered that affect the current line, the current line number need not be entered.

A shortcut to referencing other line numbers from the current line is to use the plus symbol to refer to a number of lines after the current line or the minus symbol for a number of lines before the current line.

Inside EDLIN, the current line (the line you are working on or the last line you modified) is indicated by an asterisk (*) after the line number and preceding the text on that line. If line 2 is your current line, it appears like this:

```
2:*In the beginning there was ENIAC...
```

Using the current line as a marker can help you move through your file quickly. For instance, to make modifications to your current line you do not need to enter the current line number. Instead you enter a period. For example, *.d* tells EDLIN to delete the current line.

You can use the current line in place of a starting line number as a shortcut to get to a new location. To do this, you indicate the new location relative to the current line using a plus or minus sign and a number. So, *+35* refers to the line that is 35 lines after the current line, and *−54* refers to the line that is 54 lines before the current line.

Until you are more familiar with EDLIN, you should use actual line numbers to get to the line you want. Later you might find using the current line useful for moving faster in a large file.

Command Prompt

The EDLIN command prompt is identified by a single asterisk appearing on a line of its own on the far left of the screen. It is in response to this prompt that EDLIN commands are entered.

In addition to being a marker of the current line, the asterisk is used as a command prompt. When EDLIN is waiting for a command or for you to enter some information, the asterisk appears on the far left of the screen and is not associated with a line number. When the asterisk is located after a line number, it is indicating the current line.

STARTING EDLIN

Since EDLIN is an MS-DOS command, you simply type it at the command line, followed by the name of the file that you wish to create or revise. (If you have a floppy-only system, you will need to have your system disk or another disk containing EDLIN.COM in your current drive.)

```
C:\>edlin chores <ENTER>
```

EDLIN responds promptly with one of the messages listed in *Table A-2.*

```
New file
*
```

Table A-2. EDLIN's Opening Messages

IF EDLIN Displays:	It Means:
New file	There is no file by this name on the designated disk.
End of input file	The file has been loaded into memory.
*	The file is too large to fit into memory; memory is filled up to 75% capacity. The remainder of the file is still on the disk.

So far so good: this is a new file, and the asterisk is the EDLIN prompt, which tells you the program is waiting for further instructions.

EDLIN returns this new-file message after it searches the indicated drive and does not find an existing file with the entered filename. In other words, because there is no "chores" file on the disk, EDLIN assumes this is a new file.

If you enter the name of an existing file, EDLIN reads this file into memory, then returns a different message.

```
End of input file
```

There is only one instance in which you do not receive a message from EDLIN in response to entering a filename. This is when your file is so large that not all of it can fit into the computer's memory at one time. When this is the case, and it is rare that a beginner would have files this large, EDLIN reads in as much of the file as can fit, reserving 25% of the memory. EDLIN operates with this 25% safety reserve at all times. If this instance should occur, EDLIN will simply display the asterisk prompt with no additional message. Later we will describe some commands for creating space within memory and moving data around when your file is very large.

BACKUP FILES

One important feature of the EDLIN editor also found in many other MS-DOS programs is its built-in safety mechanism that automatically creates a backup file whenever a text file is modified.

One feature of the EDLIN editor is a built-in safety device. This feature automatically creates a backup file when you modify an EDLIN file. This backup has the same name and contents as your text file but is identifiable by a three-letter addition to the filename. Not surprisingly, this extension is .BAK. When you list your files using the DIR command, you will see these "insurance" files listed with the .BAK extension.

The .BAK file contains a duplicate version of the latest text in a file, not including changes made in the current editing session. Use a .BAK file if you lose the contents of an EDLIN file.

EDLIN also has another built-in safety feature. It won't let you edit a file with a .BAK extension. If you could get into the backup files and make changes to this last version, you wouldn't have that unedited copy when you needed it. To use a backup file, you must first use the RENAME command to give the file a new name, removing the .BAK designation. Once the file is no longer the backup, you can begin the editing process all over again.

Of course, if anything happens to your disk, your insurance is canceled because both the original and backup files are stored on the same disk. It's a good practice, therefore, to have reserve copies of your files on separate disks (Chapter 6 explains how to do this with the COPY command).

ENTERING INFORMATION

Now you are ready to type your list of chores into the file. You inform EDLIN that you want to begin entering text by typing in the letter I. As in MS-DOS commands, you can use upper- or lowercase letters to enter commands.

The I command is used to place EDLIN into insert mode. Once EDLIN is in insert mode, any text typed on the keyboard will be inserted into the text file.

I stands for insert. While you are not strictly "inserting" information into your new, empty file, this is the command that EDLIN uses to begin new files. As you might suspect, you also use the I command to insert information into existing files.

```
*i <ENTER>
```

EDLIN accepts your instructions and presents you with the first line number.

```
New file
*i
    1:*_____
```

Begin to type in your list of chores. The first line of your file is your title. You must indicate the end of every line with <ENTER>. Each time you press the <ENTER> key, EDLIN will automatically supply a new line number for the next entry.

```
1:*Chores <ENTER>
2:*
```

If you make typing mistakes, use the <BACKSPACE> key to erase the characters (before pressing <ENTER>) and type the entry again.

When you have entered all the items, you'll have nine lines of text. EDLIN will be waiting for line 10.

```
1:*Chores
2:*Jody's soccer game, 9:00
3:*Chad's Little League game, 12:00
4:*go to grocery store
5:*mow lawn
6:*put up hammock
7:*dog to vet
8:*get dog flea collar!
9:*tennis with Annie, 2:00
```

The <Ctrl>C function (or <Ctrl><Break>) is used while in insert mode to return to EDLIN's command mode.

After you have entered the last chore, you are ready to exit from the insert mode. To return to command mode (EDLIN is ready to receive commands), you use the ^C (<Ctrl>C) or <Ctrl><Break>. Enter this <Ctrl>C combination now in response to the prompt for line 10.

```
10:*^C
*
```

The asterisk, which has been keeping track of the current line, returns to the prompt position at the far left and you're back in the command mode.

EXITING EDLIN

There is one more step to take before leaving the EDLIN program completely. You must tell EDLIN that this is the end of the file. You do that by using the E (END) command.

The E (END) Command

To save all edited text to the file stored on disk, the E command must be entered. Once entered, the E command causes EDLIN to update the text file and then display the MS-DOS prompt. The DIR command can then be used to verify the existence of the newly created or updated text file.

This command indicates the conclusion of an editing session. When you finish entering text in an EDLIN file, you must first exit the insert mode (using ^C) and then give the end-of-the-file signal to EDLIN by entering the E command. End the "chores" file now.

```
*e <ENTER>
```

As soon as you enter this command, EDLIN returns control to the operating system (indicated by the C:\> prompt).

```
C:\>
```

Table A-3 lists the steps to take to go into EDLIN and to return again to MS-DOS at the completion of the EDLIN program.

Table A-3.
In and Out with EDLIN

You Enter	Result
C:\>	Start out in operating system.
EDLIN filename	Call the EDLIN program.
i	Enter the "insert" mode.
lines of text	Enter the content of the file.
^C	Exit the "insert" mode.
e	Exit the EDLIN program.
C:\>	Returned to operating system.

Now, use DIR to check for the present of a file named "chores."

```
C:\>dir chores <ENTER>
```

There is your "chores" list on the directory.

```
 Volume in drive C has no label
 Directory of C:\
CHORES            175  4-18-91   8:50a
      1 File(s)   18361472 bytes free
```

Checking File Contents

There are two ways to check the contents of an EDLIN file. The first requires the use of the MS-DOS TYPE command (discussed in

Use MS-DOS's TYPE command to display the contents of a text file created or modified by EDLIN. You can also display the contents of your file while in EDLIN by entering EDLIN's L command.

full in Chapter 6). Enter the TYPE command and watch what happens.

```
C:\>type chores <ENTER>

Chores
Jody's soccer game, 9:00
Chad's Little League game, 12:00
go to grocery store
mow lawn
put up hammock
dog to vet
get dog flea collar!
tennis with Annie, 2:00
```

There is your file, exactly as you entered it. But notice one thing: there are no line numbers. That's because line numbers are not part of the data in EDLIN files, but simply reference points to use when editing or creating EDLIN files.

The second way to see the contents of your file is to use the EDLIN L (List) command. There'll be more about this command a little later, but right now you'll learn another way to end an editing session.

The Q (Quit) Command

If, during the course of an editing session with EDLIN, you decide not to save any changes to the text file, you can enter EDLIN's Q (Quit) command instead of the E command to exit EDLIN.

In addition to the E command, there is another way to end an editing session using EDLIN: use the Q (Quit) command. Choose the Q command when you want to stop editing, but don't care about saving the new file or any changes you have made to an existing file. The Q command does not write your file back to the disk, it simply cancels the current editing session.

You might want to stop a session because you find that you don't really want to make any changes or because things have gotten very mixed up, and you just want to throw this session away. This is the time for the Q command.

> Don't confuse the E (End) and the Q (Quit) command.
> E is for END.
> Save for the next day.
> Q is for QUIT.
> Toss this #%&* thing away.

EDLIN provides a safeguard to prevent the loss of changes that you intend to keep. When you enter the Q command, EDLIN asks a question.

```
Abort edit (Y/N)?
```

This is your last chance. A *y* response destroys the information entered in this editing session. An *n* lets you continue with the edit.

MAKING CHANGES

Now that you have created a file and stored it, it's time to make changes in your EDLIN file.

```
C:\>edlin chores <ENTER>
```

Because the file named "chores" already exists, EDLIN responds with the appropriate message.

```
End of input file
*
```

The asterisk prompt indicates that EDLIN is waiting in the command mode. It's ready to make any required modification. There is one problem though: where is the text of the file?

You must remember that EDLIN moves one step at a time. All you requested was access to the file. Now EDLIN is waiting to find out which part of the file you want to see. You have to issue a command in order to look at your file.

LOOKING AT THE FIRST DRAFT

The L (List) Command

EDLIN's L command can be used to list the entire contents of the text file, a range of lines, or a specified number of lines after the current line.

The L command lists the contents of an EDLIN file and allows you to look at a file, or a section of a file, while the EDLIN program is in operation (TYPE lets you look at the contents from MS-DOS). As with many EDLIN commands, LIST requires the use of line numbers so that EDLIN can find the correct location in the file. Remember, EDLIN commands follow this pattern: starting line number, comma, ending line number, letter of the command (some commands—discussed later—require additional information).

Following this pattern, enter the L command to display the "chores" file.

```
*1,9L <ENTER>

1:*Chores
2: Jody's soccer game, 9:00
3: Chad's Little League game, 12:00
4: go to grocery store
5: mow lawn
6: put up hammock
7: dog to vet
8: get dog flea collar!
9: tennis with Annie, 2:00
*
```

The command told EDLIN to list lines 1 through 9 of the file. If you enter the L command without any line numbers, EDLIN lists the 23 lines centered on the current line number. (The asterisk indicates that line 1 is the current line, which makes sense since you have just opened the file.) Displaying the section immediately surrounding the current line makes working with large files easier when you want to see an overview of the section you are editing. Because "chores" is so short, you could have entered L without a line number, and the entire file would have been displayed. Longer files require that you limit your range of line numbers to 23, the maximum number of lines that can be displayed at one time.

There are other ways to use the L command. The L command with one line number lists the 23 lines starting with that line number, no matter what the current line number is. For example, *43L would list from line 43 through line 65.

Getting the Right Line

Okay, as the weekend moves closer, it's time to get those chores in order. Glancing over your list, you detect a few minor conflicts. You decide that while you can definitely go to the soccer game at 9:00 and, barring excessive overtimes, make the Little League at 12:00, there is no way you can play tennis at 2:00 and get anything else done. So you make a quick call, "Sorry Annie, how about a bit of twilight tennis?" Because it is forecast to be in the high 90s tomorrow afternoon, Annie quickly agrees, "Tennis at seven."

To edit a specific line within EDLIN, enter the number of the line in response to EDLIN's command prompt. To edit line 10, for instance, type 10 and press <ENTER>, and the contents of line 10 will be displayed, followed by a blank line in response to which new text can be entered.

Now it's time to update your file. To edit a specific line within an EDLIN file, enter the line number in response to the asterisk prompt. This command doesn't require a letter of the alphabet, but simply a single line number. Your tennis match is on line 9.

```
*9 <ENTER>
```

EDLIN immediately displays a copy of that line, in its current version. You are then offered a seemingly blank line, preceded by the same line number.

```
9:*tennis with Annie, 2:00
9:*
```

This new line will contain the edited version of the current line. To update your list, you want to change the time of this appointment to 7:00. Type in the line again, changing the time. (Many of the short-cuts discussed in the section on special keys in Chapter 7 also apply to EDLIN. You may want to review them and then try them on a practice file.)

```
9:*tennis with Annie, 7:00 <ENTER>
*
```

A newly edited line is not immediately displayed by EDLIN. The L command preceded by the line number of the newly edited line (or a range of lines) must be entered to display the new text.

This is all that EDLIN shows you, it doesn't show you the correction right now. To see how changes affect the contents of an EDLIN file, you must use L to list the file again.

```
*1,9L <ENTER>
1: Chores
2: Jody's soccer game, 9:00
3: Chad's Little League game, 12:00
4: go to grocery store
5: mow lawn
6: put up hammock
7: dog to vet
8: get dog flea collar!
9:*tennis with Annie, 7:00
*
```

If you don't want to make any changes in a line once you have called for it, press <Ctrl>C. The line remains unchanged, and you are returned to the prompt (*).

INSERTING MATERIAL

The I (Insert) Command Revisited

What if you remember another thing that you want to do this weekend—go to the computer store to get that hot new game your son was telling you about. Well, add it to the list. To add new lines in an EDLIN file, use the I command, the same one you use to create a new file.

Line numbers can also be specified with the I (Insert) command to instruct EDLIN to begin the insertion of text at a specific line regardless of the current number of the line.

You have to give some additional information to EDLIN when you use the I command to insert information into an existing file. You must tell EDLIN where to insert the new line. You indicate the line number before the line where you want to make the insertion.

Because your list shows you going out to the grocery store anyway, why not put the computer store right above the grocery store? As with other EDLIN commands, enter the line number first and then the command. You want to insert this new line before line 4.

```
*4i <ENTER>
```

The screen displays the line number and waits for the new line.

```
4:*
```

Now type in your addition.

```
4:* go to computer store <ENTER>
```

EDLIN will continue to supply you with new line numbers for insertions until you exit the insert mode by using the ^C keys.

```
5:* ^C
*
```

Use the L command to display the changes.

```
*L <ENTER>
1: Chores
2: Jody's soccer game, 9:00
3: Chad's Little League game, 12:00
4: go to computer store
5: *go to grocery store
6: mow lawn
7: put up hammock
8: dog to vet
9: get dog flea collar!
10: tennis with Annie, 7:00
*
```

The new line is line 4, and all the remaining items on the list have been moved down one line. There are now a total of ten items on the list.

The # character can be used with many of EDLIN's commands instead of a specific line number or range of numbers to indicate the end of the file. To begin inserting text at the end of the file, for example, enter #I in response to EDLIN's command prompt.

You may want to add information following the last line at the end of a file, but there's no line number that you can insert before. EDLIN solves this problem by providing the # symbol. The # in conjunction with an editing command means "do this operation at the end of the current file in memory." If you had wanted to add the store trip to the end of the file, you would have entered this command.

```
*#i <ENTER>
```

In response to this command, EDLIN presents a line number that is one higher then the current total number of lines in the file.

```
11:*
```

You would then type in the new line or lines. EDLIN keeps supplying line numbers after every <ENTER>. But you don't want this item on your list twice. So press ^C to tell EDLIN you are finished with entering new information. Line 11 will remain blank and will not be included in the file. If you are skeptical, check your file using the L command. If the line somehow is included, the next command tells you how to get rid of it.

DELETING LINES

The D (Delete) Command

Look over your list. Does it seem like things are beginning to pile up? After all, this is the weekend; you deserve some time off. Maybe you can get the kid next door to mow the lawn and put up the hammock. You're in luck, because your neighbor agrees to do those chores. That's two things you can eliminate from your list.

The D command is used to delete the current line, a specified line or number of lines, or a range of lines.

To delete lines in EDLIN, use the D command. This command deletes lines from an EDLIN file. Enter a starting line number and an ending line number. In effect, these two line numbers form a block of the information you want to eliminate. This concept is useful for performing several commands in EDLIN. A block can also be only one line, in which case the starting and ending line numbers are the same and need be entered only once.

First double-check the line numbers of the items you want to delete by displaying the file with the L command.

```
*L <ENTER>
1: Chores
2: Jody's soccer game, 9:00
3: Chad's Little League game, 12:00
4: go to computer store
5: go to grocery store
6: mow lawn
7: put up hammock
8: dog to vet
9: get dog flea collar!
10: tennis with Annie, 7:00
*
```

In the current version of the file (since you added the computer store), "mow lawn" and "put up hammock" are line numbers 6 and 7. Enter a command to delete these lines.

```
*6,7d <ENTER>
*
```

To check to see that they are really gone, use the L command.

```
*L <ENTER>
```

You will see your revised listing.

```
1: Chores
2: Jody's soccer game, 9:00
3: Chad's Little League game, 12:00
4: go to computer store
5: go to grocery store
6:*dog to vet
7: get dog flea collar!
8: tennis with Annie, 7:00
*
```

Notice that in this new listing your original items 6 and 7 are deleted and the remaining items have been renumbered.

Table A-4 is a comparison of the I and D commands.

Table A-4. Comparison of Insert and Delete

Insert		Delete	
i	Begin a new file	d	Delete the current line
6i	Insert a new line 6 Line 6 becomes line 7	6d	Delete line 6 Line 7 becomes line 6
#i	Add new lines at end	1,6d	Delete lines 1 through 6 Line 7 becomes line 1

SEARCHING FOR STRINGS

Strings

The S command is used to instruct EDLIN to search for a specified string of characters or words. The text that is to be searched for is entered after the S command, followed by <ENTER>.

Often when you are using EDLIN, you want to find a specific place in a file by searching for a string, a word or pattern of characters within the file. You might, for instance, want to edit a section of a file dealing with the string "Christmas," or you may want to check that you changed "Strong and Sons" to "Strong and Associates" in a letter. To do this, you use the S command.

In addition to the string, which tells EDLIN what it should search for, EDLIN also needs to know where to search. You provide this information by indicating the starting and ending line numbers of the block to be searched.

Because you have made several modifications to your "chores" file, you want to make sure that the trip to the vet is still on the agenda. You want to search the entire file (lines 1 through 8) for the string "dog."

The S (Search) Command

By preceding the S command with a line number, a range of line numbers, or the # character, EDLIN is instructed to search a specific line, a range of lines, or the entire file. If the string of text is found, the first line on which the string occurs becomes the current line. If the string is not found, EDLIN informs you of that fact. To continue searching through the text file for the same text string, simply enter the S command without any limits.

The S command, which searches for a string in an EDLIN file, follows this pattern: line number to begin the search, a comma, line number to end the search, the S command, and then the string to be searched for. Enter the S command to find "dog."

```
*1,8sdog <ENTER>
```

EDLIN begins searching at line 1 and reports the first match.

```
6:*dog to vet
*
```

If you want to continue the search for other occurrences of "dog," enter the S command again.

```
*s <ENTER>
```

EDLIN displays the next match.

```
7: get dog flea collar!
*
```

When you enter S without entering a new string, EDLIN uses the last string it was told to search for.

There is one catch with the S command. It finds only *exact* string matches. If "dog" appeared in our file as "Dog" or "DOG", these instances would not be reported by EDLIN ("dog" at the start of a word—for example, "dogmatic"—will be found, however).

Each time you enter the S command, EDLIN continues searching for string matches until it reaches the last line number entered. If it does not find the string, it sends a message that tells you so.

```
Not found
```

Global Search

The S command can be used to search for all occurrences of a particular text string by preceding the S command with a question mark—after any line numbers specified. At each occurrence of the specified text string, EDLIN displays a prompt asking you if the line number displayed is the one you want.

There is a variation to the S command that allows you to continue searching after each occurrence of the string without reentering the S command. To do this "global search," insert a question mark (?) in the initial S command. Try looking everywhere for "dog."

```
*1,8?sdog <ENTER>
```

Notice that the question mark is entered before the S command. Because you included a ? in the S command, EDLIN asks you if this is what you were looking for or if you want to continue searching.

```
6: dog to vet
O.K.?
```

If you answer *n*, EDLIN continues to make matches. A *y* answer indicates this is where you want to be, and the search ends.

The R (Replace) Command

The R command is related to the S command in that it too goes through the file searching for the specified pattern. R, however, allows you to replace every instance of your string and another string.

As you are reading over your list you realize that the cat needs a shot too, and she certainly needs a flea collar. To put this information on your list you want to search through "chores" for "dog" and replace it with "dog and cat."

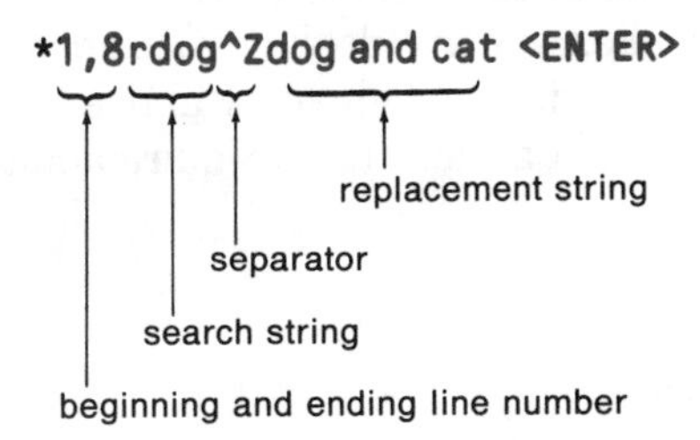

The R command performs the same function as the S command with the added capability of replacing the searched-for string of text with new text. The command is entered the same way as the S command except that the <Ctrl>Z function is pressed after the searched-for string, followed by the replacement text string. Use the question mark with the R command if you're not certain you want to replace all occurrences of a text string throughout the entire file or within a range of lines.

The beginning line number is followed by the ending line number. Then comes the R command preceding the string to be searched for. The R command requires one additional piece of information: the replacement string. A ^Z character separates the two strings. The R command automatically replaces every occurrence of the old string with the new string.

```
6: dog and cat to vet
7: get dog and cat flea collar!
*
```

As with the S command, you can use ? with the R command. This is useful if you are not certain you want to replace every occurrence of the string. When you include ? in the command, EDLIN asks if you want to make the replacement.

```
*1,8?rdog^Zdog and cat <ENTER>
6:*dog and cat to vet
O.K.?
```

Use *y* to approve the replacement and instruct EDLIN to continue with the search. It then displays the next occurrence of the string.

```
7: get dog and cat flea collar!
O.K.?
```

If you answer *n* to this query, no replacement occurs in this line, but the search continues until the ending line number is reached.

These commands, I(nsert), D(elete), S(earch), and R(eplace), are useful editing tools when you are dealing with small changes in just a few lines. But there are times when you will need to make changes involving large sections of a file. These require additional EDLIN commands.

MAJOR REVISIONS

The M (Move) Command

You use the M command when you want to relocate a block of information within an EDLIN file. Because you want to accomplish all your car-related chores at one time, you decide to move the animal items right up there with the store items. It's much more efficient to have your list in neat chronological order.

Entire lines or blocks of text can be moved within a file by using the M command. The command is entered by preceding the M command by the line or range of lines to be moved, a comma, and the line number before which the moved text is to be inserted.

The M command requires beginning and ending line numbers to define the block to be moved. You must also indicate the place to which you want the block moved. Just as in the I command, you indicate the line number before which you want the items to appear. Because the vet is farther away than the computer store, you move lines 6 and 7 to before line 4.

```
*6,7,4m <ENTER>
*
```

Notice that in addition to the comma separating the beginning and ending line numbers, you must also put a comma between the ending line number and the line number indicating the new location.

Now you have modified your list a lot. Time to see what the newest version looks like.

```
*L <ENTER>

1: Chores
2: Jody's soccer game, 9:00
3: Chad's Little League game, 12:00
4: *dog and cat to vet
5: get dog and cat flea collar!
6: go to computer store
7: go to grocery store
8: tennis with Annie, 7:00
*
```

The C (Copy) Command

Using the same rules for the M command, the C command can be used to copy, not move, a line or a range of lines to any part of the file.

Another useful way to move lines around inside an EDLIN file is with the C command, which duplicates lines within an EDLIN file. Just like the M command, the C command requires three line numbers: the starting and ending line numbers of the block and the line number before which the copied lines should appear.

In your "chores" file, there is really no need to put duplicate lines elsewhere in the file, but for practice copy lines 2 through 4 and put them before line 7.

```
*2,4,7c <ENTER>
*
```

The resulting list will have eleven items.

```
*L <ENTER>

1: Chores
```

```
2: Jody's soccer game, 9:00
3: Chad's Little League game, 12:00
4: dog and cat to vet
5: get dog and cat flea collar!
6: go to computer store
7:*Jody's soccer game, 9:00
8: Chad's Little League game, 12:00
9: dog and cat to vet
10: go to grocery store
11: tennis with Annie, 7:00
*
```

The three copied lines appear twice in the list, in their original location as lines 2, 3, and 4 and as new lines 7, 8 and 9. But this makes no sense, so you want to delete lines 7, 8, and 9.

Using the rules for specifying a number of lines or a range of lines with the D command, an entire block of text can be deleted.

```
*7,9d <ENTER>
*
```

OTHER EDITING COMMANDS

The remaining EDLIN commands require two files or one very large file, so you won't actually perform these commands. Be sure to read through the description of these three commands so that you will be familiar with their capabilities when you need to use them.

The T (Transfer) Command

A line or several lines can be transferred to another file by using the T command.

T is yet another line-moving EDLIN command, but in this case it moves lines from one EDLIN file to another, not to different locations within a file.

Here is a hypothetical situation where you would use this command. You have another file on the disk in drive B entitled "schedule." This contains a list of appointments that you want included in your "chores" file. You want to merge these two files.

You are going to add the contents of "schedule" to the "chores" file right before your tennis engagement, which is line 8. The T command requires you to give EDLIN these pieces of information: the line before which you want the transfer made, the drive containing the disk that holds the file, and the filename (with extension if necessary) of the file to be transferred. To merge these two files, you would use the following command:

```
*8tb:schedule
```

The contents of "schedule" would now appear in the "chores" file, located immediately before line 8.

The W (Write) Command

In cases where a file being edited by EDLIN has grown such that 75% of memory has been exceeded, the W command can be used to clear the memory for more text by writing (storing) the text currently in memory to the file.

As mentioned earlier, you may at some point be working with EDLIN files that are so large that they exceed the 75% memory capacity that EDLIN allocates for file size. In this case you'll need to work with your file in parts.

You know that an entire file is not in memory, because EDLIN does not return the "end of input file" message after you load a file. Instead only the asterisk appears. To access the part of your file that is still on the disk, you must first clear out some space in memory by writing lines back to a disk. This is the function of the W command. To use W, enter the number of lines that are to be written back to the disk followed by the command W.

```
*2222w
```

In response, EDLIN writes the first 2222 lines back to the disk. If you enter W without any line numbers, EDLIN writes back lines until memory is 25% full.

The A (Append) Command

After you have made room using the W command, you want to add the next section of your file to memory. The A command adds new text from a disk to the EDLIN file currently in memory. This command also uses the specified line numbers as a total count of lines to be moved. To add 2222 lines to the file, enter the number of lines to be appended followed by the command A.

```
*2222a
```

If you don't specify any line numbers here, EDLIN automatically fills memory up to its 75% working capacity.

It is unlikely that you will be using the W and A commands in the near future, as they are required only when editing very large files.

SUMMARY

In this appendix you have learned what an editor is and how to use the MS-DOS EDLIN editor. In addition to knowing how to create a new file, you now know how to use all the EDLIN commands: E, Q, L, I, D, S, R, M, C, T, W, and A. If you can make a word out of that, go to the head of the class!

Installing MS-DOS

Because of its "hands-on" nature, this book assumes that you already have MS-DOS installed on your system, so that you get a command prompt (such as C:\>) when you start the system. If you are just buying a new computer you should make sure that it includes a hard disk and the latest version of MS-DOS. Ask the dealer to install MS-DOS on the hard disk before you take delivery. That way you don't have to worry about partitioning or formatting the hard disk or transferring the MS-DOS files to it. Once you've unpacked the system and hooked it up, you just turn on the power, and MS-DOS is ready for you to use as you work with this book.

If your system didn't come with MS-DOS on the hard disk (or it doesn't have a hard disk) you should follow the installation instructions in your MS-DOS manual, together with the following guidelines and suggestions.

Having A Hard Disk Problem?

This appendix is intended mainly for preparing a hard disk for use with MS-DOS and installing MS-DOS on the hard disk.

If you are already running MS-DOS but are experiencing problems with your hard disk (you either can't access the disk at all or you get errors when you try to read certain files), you must be cautious. You should *not* use the FORMAT and FDISK commands discussed later if your hard disk has any data that you want to recover. The FORMAT and FDISK commands and the low-level format procedure will make it difficult if not impossible for you to recover existing data.

The best insurance against hard-disk trouble is to make frequent backups (see Chapter 8). There are also commercial programs available (and service bureaus) that may be able to recover data from a damaged hard disk.

INSTALLING MS-DOS 4.0

The latest version, MS-DOS 4.0, has the easiest and most complete installation procedure. When you start up the system using the disk marked "Installation," a menu-driven installation program called SELECT runs automatically. Press the <F1> key any time you want help with the current menu screen or the highlighted option. The MS-DOS manual also gives step-by-step instructions for users with hard or floppy-based systems, using 5¼″ or 3½″ floppy disks.

The most important menu presented by SELECT, which you see following the introductory screens, is entitled "Specify Function and Workspace." This allows you to choose one of the following:

- Minimum DOS function, maximum program workspace
- Balanced DOS function with program workspace
- Maximum DOS function, minimum program workspace

Here "DOS function" refers mainly to memory to be dedicated to optional MS-DOS features, notably the BUFFERS and FASTOPEN commands, which speed up disk performance, as explained in Chapter 12. "Program workspace" refers to the memory that is not used by MS-DOS and thus is available for your application program (and any memory-resident utility programs that you may wish to load).

If your application is one such as dBASE IV or LOTUS 1-2-3 that requires most of the available memory, or if you wish to use memory-resident programs such as SideKick, you may have to choose the first option, Minimum DOS function. You might try the second ("balanced") option first, and reinstall with the first option if you don't have enough memory to run your application. Many users will be able to use the third (Maximum DOS) option, however, and get faster disk performance.

When you see the screen called "Select Installation Drive," choose C if you have a hard disk. If your hard disk has not been prepared for use by MS-DOS, the installation program will lead you through the partitioning and formatting process that is discussed later. If the installation program doesn't recognize the hard disk at all, this may mean that the disk hasn't received a "low-level format"—the first step in preparing a disk for MS-DOS, which is usually done at the factory. See the later section on "Preparing Your Hard Disk."

If your system has expanded memory (see Chapter 12), make sure that "Expanded memory support" is listed as YES when you reach the "Review Selections" screen. This tells the installation program to prepare DEVICE statements for the MS-DOS 4.0 expanded memory drivers for your CONFIG.SYS file. This will allow some MS-DOS features (such as the BUFFERS and FASTOPEN commands) to use expanded memory. Unfortunately, the expanded memory drivers with IBM MS-DOS 4.0 work only with IBM expanded memory boards. You can still use the drivers provided with non-IBM memory boards with those of your application programs that support expanded memory, but you will not be able to use expanded memory with DOS commands. Some non-IBM versions of MS-DOS 4.0 may provide better support for non-IBM expanded memory hardware.

Once you've run the installation program, the remaining step is to set up your CONFIG.SYS and AUTOEXEC.BAT files. MS-DOS 4.0 prepares two files, CONFIG.400 and AUTOEXEC.400. First use the DIR command to see if there is an existing CONFIG.SYS or AUTOEXEC.BAT file. If there is, use a text editor (see Chapter 6) to merge the old and new files. If you don't have existing CONFIG.SYS or AUTOEXEC.BAT files, you can simply rename the files that the installation program had created:

```
C:\>ren config.400 config.sys
C:\>ren autoexec.400 autoexec.bat
```

Finally, reboot the system so the commands in these files will take effect. See Chapter 12 to learn more about the various commands and how to fine-tune them to suit your needs.

By default, MS-DOS 4.0 installs the DOSSHELL user interface program for you. (See Chapter 11 for an introduction and tutorial on using DOSSHELL.) If you decide that you don't want the shell to start up automatically, edit your AUTOEXEC.BAT file to remove the reference to DOSSHELL. Or you can place the word REM in front of it, which turns the line into a nonexecutable "remark." In this way, you can reinstall the shell simply by removing the REM later.

INSTALLING MS-DOS 3.3 AND EARLIER VERSIONS

Versions of MS-DOS prior to 4.0 do not have the extensive menu-driven installation program described in the previous section. Most of these versions of MS-DOS come with a single floppy disk containing the key system files (IBMBIO.COM, IBMDOS.COM, and COMMAND.COM), forty or so programs that run the external MS-DOS commands (such as CHKDSK and XCOPY), files that let you use the BASIC language, and an assortment of device drivers such as ANSI.SYS and DRIVER.SYS. Sometimes there is a second disk with less frequently used programs on it. Starting with MS-DOS 3.2, both 3½″and 5¼″ disk versions are available. Some packages have both sizes of disks. (If your version of MS-DOS is earlier than 3.3, consider upgrading to 4.0 so you can take advantage of the latest features.)

Backing Up Your MS-DOS Distribution Disks

Regardless of whether you are installing to your hard disk or will be using floppies only, your first step is to back up your MS-DOS distribution disk(s). Obtain a blank disk (or one with unneeded data) for each copy; these disks do not have to be formatted already—DISKCOPY will format them for you if necessary. Put the disk marked "System" or "Startup" in your drive A and start the system. When you see the MS-DOS prompt, type the following if you have only one floppy drive:

```
A:\>diskcopy a:
```

You will be prompted to exchange the MS-DOS disk and your blank disk until the copy is complete. When asked if you want to make another copy, you can reply *y* to make an extra copy of your master disk or if you want to copy any other disks in your MS-DOS package.

If you have two floppy drives of the same size (that is, both 5¼″ or both 3½″), you can put the disk to receive the copy in drive B and type this instead:

```
A:\>diskcopy a: b:
```

The copy will proceed without your having to swap disks. Again, you will be asked if you want to make more copies.

If you have a floppy-only system, you will use one of the copies of your distribution disk to start the system for each session. Generally, you will want to swap the disk in A then for one containing your application program. With some applications, you can erase all of the files containing MS-DOS commands that you don't use often and copy your application program to the disk. This may allow you to run your application without swapping disks.

Putting MS-DOS on Your Hard Disk

Users that have hard disks, however, have a bit more work to do. First, boot your system from a copy of your MS-DOS system disk, and type *dir c*: to see if the hard disk is recognized. (If it is, you will see an empty directory, unless someone has already installed MS-DOS on the disk. In the latter case, reboot from the hard disk, and type *ver* to check the MS-DOS version number. If the version is older than that on your MS-DOS system disks, install the later version to take advantage of new MS-DOS features.) If instead you get the "drive not ready" message, you will have to partition and format the hard disk before you can proceed. See the later section on "Preparing Your Hard Disk." With your MS-DOS system disk in drive A, you can transfer MS-DOS to your hard disk as follows:

```
A:\>sys c:
System transferred
     1 file(s) copied
```

This copies the two "hidden" MS-DOS system files to the root directory of your hard disk. It also copies the file COMMAND.COM. You can now create a DOS directory on your hard disk and copy the rest of the MS-DOS utility files to it:

```
A:\>md c:\dos
A:\>copy *.* c:\dos
```

If your distribution package for MS-DOS has more than one disk, simply put the next disk in drive A and repeat the COPY command.

You are now ready to use MS-DOS with this book. Remove the MS-DOS disk from drive A and restart the system: MS-DOS will be run from the hard disk. (If there is no AUTOEXEC.BAT file on the hard disk, you will be asked for the time and date each time you start the system. You can set the time and date by hand, or just press <ENTER> at each prompt. Once you learn how to create the AUTOEXEC.BAT and CONFIG.SYS files, you will no longer be pestered about the time and date.)

PREPARING YOUR HARD DISK

If you discovered earlier that your hard disk wasn't being recognized by MS-DOS, you can follow these steps to prepare the hard disk for use:

- Low-level formatting. This puts magnetic marks (tracks and sectors) on the disk so that the controller can find data.

- Partitioning. This divides the disk into one or more areas that will be treated as "logical drives" by MS-DOS, and referred to by such letters as C or D.
- High-level formatting. This uses the FORMAT command to set up the directory tables that MS-DOS needs to manage files on the disk.

Most disk drives come from the factory with the low-level formatting already done. This procedure is very technical, and it will destroy any existing data on the disk. Therefore it will be discussed last.

Partitioning the Disk with *FDISK*

Partitioning a hard disk means that you set up one or more areas of the hard disk, each of which is treated as an independent "logical drive" by MS-DOS and referred to using drive letters such as C or D.

Why would you want to do this? One reason is size: the versions of MS-DOS prior to 4.0 don't allow a partition larger than 32MB. If you have a hard disk with a capacity of 40MB, 60MB, or even more, and you are using a version of MS-DOS prior to 4.0, you must set up multiple partitions if you want to use all of your disk. (Of course, this is a good reason to consider upgrading to MS-DOS 4.0.)

Another reason for partitioning a hard disk is to allow for use of another operating system in addition to MS-DOS. While OS/2 can share partitions with MS-DOS, other operating systems such as XENIX and CP/M 86 cannot, so each operating system must have its own partition.

MS-DOS 4.0 allows partitions of virtually unlimited size. You must create at least one partition on your hard disk; you may create up to four separate partitions, if you decide you have the need. The first partition is called the primary DOS partition. The MS-DOS operating system starts up from this primary partition when you turn on the power. Additional partitions are called "extended" partitions.

With MS-DOS versions 3.3 and below, the largest allowable partition size is 32MB because this is the most disk space that can be mapped by the standard DOS file allocation table (FAT) in 2048-byte clusters. (There are special drivers you can get for earlier MS-DOS versions that can get around this limitation, but they are nonstandard.)

How to run FDISK

CAUTION: Changing Existing Partitions

If you run FDISK on a hard disk that is already partitioned, and you try to delete or change a partition, you will be warned that doing so will destroy any data in that partition. If you wish to repartition your hard disk, be sure to back up its data first (see Chapter 8 for more on the BACKUP command).

If you have MS-DOS 4.0 and your hard disk has been low-level formatted but not partitioned, put your Install disk in drive A and restart the system. The SELECT program will run FDISK for you. You should still read this section for general advice, but you can also get help from SELECT at any time by pressing the <F1> key. (See the section on "Installing MS-DOS 4.0" for more information about using SELECT.)

If you have an earlier version of MS-DOS, or you have already partitioned your hard disk and need for some reason to change the partitions, you must run FDISK directly from the command line. Here is how to partition a blank, low-level formatted hard disk using the FDISK utility, which is one of the MS-DOS external commands.

Use DIR to locate FDISK.COM on one of your MS-DOS operating system floppy disks. Load FDISK into your machine by typing:

```
A:\>fdisk
```

MS-DOS will load FDISK into memory and FDISK will present its first screen. Here is the FDISK screen for MS-DOS version 4.00.

```
IBM DOS Version 4.00
Fixed Disk Setup Program
(C) Copyright IBM Corp. 1983,1988
FDISK Options
Current fixed disk drive: 1
Choose one of the following:
    1. Create DOS Partition or Logical DOS Drive
    2. Set Active Partition
    3. Delete DOS Partition or Logical DOS Drive
    4. Display Partition Information
    5. Select next fixed disk drive
Enter choice: [ ]
Press Esc to exit FDISK
```

The first choice lets you create a DOS partition or create a logical DOS drive. Don't worry about what "logical DOS drive" means for now. You want to create a DOS Partition so you can use your blank hard disk, so enter 1 as your choice. FDISK will present this next screen:

```
Create DOS Partition or Logical DOS Drive
Current fixed disk drive: 1

Choose one of the following:

1. Create Primary DOS Partition
2. Create Extended DOS Partition
3. Create Logical DOS Drive(s) in the Extended DOS Partition

Enter choice: [ ]
```

Because your hard disk is completely blank, you want to create a primary DOS partition. The primary DOS partition is the one that the system will use when it starts up. It may be the only partition that you will use. Enter 1 as your choice. FDISK will present this screen:

```
 Create Primary DOS Partition
 Current fixed disk drive: 1

Do you wish to use the maximum available size for a Primary
DOS Partition and make the partition active?
(Y/N).......? [ ]
```

You can choose either Y (yes) or N (no). If you choose *n*, FDISK will let you set up part of your hard disk as the primary DOS partition and also let you create up to three additional extended partitions. Unless you are going to be using a non-DOS compatible operating system, there is little reason to do this with MS-DOS 4.0. All you need is to do is to create one partition that includes the entire hard disk space, so enter *y* as your choice. FDISK will present its last screen.

FDISK with Earlier MS-DOS Versions

If you are using MS-DOS 3.3 with a hard disk with a capacity of 30MB or less, you can follow the same procedure as above. If you are using a 40MB or higher-capacity hard disk, however, you will have to create multiple MS-DOS partitions, since no one partition can be larger than 32MB. On the first FDISK screen, choose 1 (Create DOS Partition) and then 1 again (Create Primary DOS partition). Then when you see this screen:

```
Create Primary DOS Partition
Current fixed disk drive: 1

Do you wish to use the maximum available size for a Primary
DOS Partition and make the partition active?
(Y/N).......? [ ]
```

Type *n*. You can then set the size of your primary and extended partitions up to the total capacity of your disk:

```
Create Primary DOS Partition
Current Fixed Disk Drive: 1

No partition defined

Total disk space is  305 cylinders.
Maximum space available for partition
is  305 cylinders.

Enter partition size...........:[    ]

Press ESC to return to FDISK options
```

The number of cylinders available will vary with the capacity of your hard disk. You don't have to worry about how large a "cylinder" is; just divide the total number to divide your disk proportionately. Thus if you have a 40MB hard disk that you want to divide into two equal 20MB partitions, just type in half the maximum number of cylinders. Now press <Esc> to return to the main FDISK menu and choose item 2 "Change Active Partition" to make this your active partition. Then go back and repeat the process to create your second partition. (When asked for the number of cylinders, this time you can just press <ENTER> to automatically allocate all of the remaining cylinders.) Remember that you don't make the second partition active; there can be only one active partition.

FDISK on MS-DOS Versions 3.2 or Earlier

These versions have no "extended DOS partitions." Here is the FDISK screen for MS-DOS 3.20.

```
IBM Personal Computer
Fixed Disk Setup Program Version 3.20
(C) Copyright IBM Corp. 1983,1986

FDISK Options

Choose one of the following:
    1. Create DOS Partition
```

```
    2. Change Active Partition
    3. Delete DOS Partition
    4. Display Partition Data
Enter choice: [ ]

Press Esc to return to DOS
```

To create a DOS Partition, choose item 1. The remainder of the partitioning process is similar to Version 4.0 presented above.

Once you have left FDISK, you get the following message:

```
You must restart your computer to continue
Press Ctrl+Alt+Del to continue with DOS installation
```

Make sure that your MS-DOS startup disk (or the Install disk if you are using MS-DOS 4.0 and running SELECT) is in drive A, and press <Ctrl> <Alt> <Del>. The computer will now reboot. After it has rebooted, it will now recognize the hard disk as your system's C drive.

High-Level Formatting (the FORMAT command)

CAUTION!

Running the FORMAT command destroys all existing data. MS-DOS will warn you of this fact. You should not normally have to format a hard disk that already contains data. Before doing a low-level format, changing a partition with FDISK, or running the FORMAT command, back up any existing valuable data.

Do not run FORMAT on a hard disk that has no existing partition. Create the partition(s) first with FDISK. FORMAT will not recognize a hard disk that is not partitioned, and it will instead attempt to format the *next* hard disk if any.

The last step in preparing your hard disk for MS-DOS is to do the high-level format.

If you are using MS-DOS Version 4.00, this will be done automatically by the SELECT program. See the section on Installing MS-DOS for more information about running SELECT.

If you have an earlier version of DOS, you will have to do the formatting manually. To do so, first put your MS-DOS distribution disk in drive A. Now type:

```
A:\>format c: /s
```

DOS will display the following message:

```
WARNING, ALL DATA ON NON-REMOVABLE DISK
DRIVE C: WILL BE LOST!
Proceed with Format (Y/N)?  y
```

MS-DOS will proceed to format the hard disk. The task is complete when the screen displays:

```
Format complete
System transferred
xxxxxxxxx bytes total disk space
xxxxxxxxx bytes available on disk
```

(The numbers shown will depend on the capacity of your hard disk. The second number will be a bit smaller than the first, since some space will have been taken by the system files.)

Your hard disk is now ready for MS-DOS installation, and you can return to the section on "Installing MS-DOS" to complete the process.

Low-Level Formatting

Finally, if FDISK or the MS-DOS 4.0 SELECT program don't recognize your hard disk at all, it may need low-level formatting.

CAUTION: BEFORE YOU BEGIN!

Low-level formatting destroys any existing data on the disk. If there are some files on your hard disk, it is already formatted, and you don't need (or want) to do a low-level format. The exception is if you have serious damage to the disk. In this case, you should attempt to back up as many files as possible before beginning the low-level format.

How to Do a Low-Level Format

If you need low-level formatting, how do you accomplish it? If you have a PS/2 or AT, check your system documentation: the Reference or Utility disks for many of these models have an option called "Prepare fixed disk for DOS" or something similar. Run this to take care of your low-level formatting. Other systems may also come with a low-level format utility. If you have bought a mail-order clone or you are installing a hard disk in an existing system, look for documentation accompanying the system or hard disk. You may have to call your dealer.

In some systems, the low-level formatting is performed automatically by a program in permanent memory on the controller. If you suspect this is the case, remove any disk from your floppy and restart the system. When the hard disk comes on, the display will indicate that low-level formatting is being done. (When it is over, you will have to restart the system from your MS-DOS floppy, since the hard disk won't be partitioned or high-level formatted yet.)

Using *DEBUG* to Do Low-Level Formatting

The last resort is to do low-formatting using the DEBUG utility of DOS to call the routine built into the controller ROM. You will need to know the manufacturer and model of the disk controller. What you type in after entering the DEBUG program depends upon the manufacturer and model of the disk controller. For example, type the *G=C800:5* command for the following controllers:

Western Digital	WD1002 WX2
Western Digital	WD1002 WX1
Western Digital	WD1002 27X
Seagate	ST01
Seagate	ST10
Seagate	ST11R

The following assumes that you have one of the above controllers. If you have another controller, please find the appropriate substitute for the G=C800:5 command. To start the process, type

```
A:\>debug
```

The monitor will display a dash

```
-
```

Type *G=C800:5<CR>* (or the equivalent if you are using another controller). The low-level format routine will request the technical data for your hard disk such as the number of cylinders, number of heads, interleave, reduced write current, write precomp., and ECC correction span. Most of the information required is very technical and beyond the scope of this book. You simply enter the value supplied with your disk controller and/or drive documentation.

Error Messages

As with all things you do, you learn to use MS-DOS by doing, by trial and error. No matter how conscientious you are, you will make mistakes. Making mistakes and correcting your mistakes is an effective way of learning. To make things easier, the designers of MS-DOS have documented many of the most common errors. That is why MS-DOS has error messages—to help you correct your mistakes.

There are many types of error messages. Those most frequently encountered are covered in this appendix. There are some messages that are not included. See your user's manual for a complete list of the messages to be found on your computer system.

This appendix divides error messages into two categories. The first covers error messages that refer to devices. The second lists messages that may or may not apply to a device but which refer to MS-DOS commands or MS-DOS itself. The messages are listed in alphabetical order.

DEVICE ERROR MESSAGES

Device error messages are displayed if MS-DOS finds an error when it tries to use a device attached to the computer. These messages have a common format. It's easy to understand the message when you understand the format.

This format has two variations. The first is displayed when MS-DOS has a problem reading (trying to get information) from a device.

```
type error reading device
Abort, Retry, Ignore?
```

The second variation is displayed when MS-DOS has a problem writing (trying to send information) to a device.

```
type error writing device
Abort, Retry, Ignore?
```

Type defines the nature of this specific error and will vary with the instance. *Device* refers to the piece of hardware involved in the error, such as a disk drive or a printer.

The second line of the format offers you three options to recover from the error: abort, retry, ignore. MS-DOS is waiting for you to enter one of these options from the keyboard.

Before responding, check the obvious causes for the error. For instance, if the error concerns a disk drive, you may have left the door open or failed to insert the correct disk. If the error indicates trouble with the printer, you may need to turn on the power or insert paper.

When you have checked all such obvious causes, enter one of the three options:

> *R* (Retry): Causes MS-DOS to try to perform the command or message again. This sometimes works even if you have not adjusted anything because the error might be minor and may not recur.
>
> *A* (Abort): Causes MS-DOS to stop the operation in progress. You should enter this response if *R* fails to correct the error.
>
> *I* (Ignore): Causes MS-DOS to retry the operation but ignore any errors it may encounter. It is not recommended that you use this response because it can result in losing data being read or written.

MS-DOS 4.0 adds a *Fail* option to some error messages. This option is similar to *Ignore*, and it sends an "error code" back to the running program. The program may be able to use this code to minimize damage caused by the error. When this option is presented, it is better to try *Retry* first, then *Fail*, and use *Abort* only when there is no other way to get out of the error message.

The following messages are those that might appear in the *type* section of the error message.

> *Bad call format*: A driver is a part of the operating system that controls a specific input/output device, for instance, a modem or printer. Each driver has specific codes in MS-DOS. One such identifier is a length request header. This message means an incorrect length request header was sent to the driver for the specified drive. Consult your dealer.
>
> *Bad command*: The command issued to a device is invalid.

Bad unit: An incorrect subunit number (driver code) was sent to the driver for the specified drive. Consult your dealer. (See "Bad call format.")

Data: An error was detected while reading or writing data. Use CHKDSK to see if your disk has a defective area.

Disk: After three tries, a disk read or write error is still occurring. You may have inserted the wrong type of disk (for example, 1.2MB disk in a 360K drive) or your disk may be inserted incorrectly. If neither is true, you may have a bad disk. If you receive this message, try the standard corrective procedures (such as the CHKDSK and RECOVER commands) before removing the disk. You may be able to salvage the data on the disk.

File allocation table bad, drive d: This message always refers to a specific disk drive. It tells you that the file allocation table (FAT) on the indicated drive is faulty. If you receive this error frequently, the disk is probably defective. You may be able to use a commercial utility program to recover the data.

No paper: This is an easy one to solve. There isn't any paper in your printer or the printer is not turned on. Correct the problem and press *r*.

Non-DOS disk: There is invalid data on the allocation table of the specified disk in the indicated device. The disk needs to be reformatted or the entire disk may be wiped out. (It may also be a disk for a non-MS-DOS computer system.)

Not ready: The device is not ready to read or write data. This may mean that the power is not turned on, the drive door is not closed, or there is no disk in the indicated drive.

Read fault: For some reason the device cannot receive or transmit data. The power may not be on, the drive may not contain a disk, or the device is not properly configured for MS-DOS use.

Sector not found: The sector holding the data you want cannot be located. The disk may be defective, or you may be using a single-sided disk in a double-sided drive.

Seek error: MS-DOS cannot locate the proper track on the disk in the indicated drive.

Write fault: For some reason, the device cannot receive or transmit data. The power may not be on, the drive may not contain a disk, or the device is not properly configured for MS-DOS use.

Write protect: You have instructed MS-DOS to write to a disk that is write-protected (either temporarily by you or permanently by the manufacturer). Either insert a new disk or remove the write-protect tab (or close the square window on a 3½″ disk) from this disk (be sure you want to write to it first). If there is no write-protect notch, you're out of luck.

ADDITIONAL ERROR MESSAGES

This is not a complete listing of all other error messages that you may receive from MS-DOS. Check your system manual if you cannot locate the message among the device error messages or in this section.

Some error messages are associated with a specific command. When this is the case, the command is shown following the error message.

All specified file(s) are contiguous: CHKDSK. All the files that you requested to write are on the disk sequentially.

Allocation error, size adjusted: CHKDSK. There was an invalid sector number in the file allocation table. The indicated filename was truncated at the end of the previous good sector.

Attempted write-protect violation: FORMAT. You attempted to FORMAT a write-protected disk. Remove the disk and insert a new one.

Bad command or filename: You entered the command or filename incorrectly. Check the spelling and punctuation and make sure the command or file you specified is on the disk in the indicated drive. You may be calling an external command from a disk that does not contain the command. Also check to see if your PATH includes the disk and directory containing the command or prompt.

Cannot edit .BAK file—rename file: To protect your data, EDLIN and some other programs won't let you access a backup file that has a .BAK extension. Rename the file using REN, or copy the file, giving it a new name.

Cannot load COMMAND, system halted: While attempting to load the command processor, MS-DOS found that the area in which it keeps track of available memory is destroyed. Try booting MS-DOS again.

Contains XXX non-contiguous blocks: CHKDSK. The indicated file has been written in sections on different areas on the disk (rather than in sequential blocks). See Chapter 8 for more information on "unfragmenting" files.

Disk boot failure: While trying to load MS-DOS, an error was encountered. If this continues, use a backup MS-DOS disk.

Disk error writing FAT x: CHKDSK. There was a disk error while CHKDSK was trying to update the FAT on the indicated drive. Depending on which of the allocation tables could not be written, *x* will be a 1 or a 2. If both are indicated, the disk is unusable.

Duplicate filename or file not found: RENAME. The name you indicated in a RENAME command already exists on the disk, or the file to be renamed is not on the disk in the specified drive.

Entry error: EDLIN. Your last command contains a syntax error.

Error loading operating system: An error was encountered while MS-DOS was trying to load from the fixed (hard) disk. If the problem persists, load MS-DOS from a disk and use SYS to copy MS-DOS to the fixed disk.

File cannot be copied onto itself: You tried to copy a file to the same name in the same directory.

File not found: The file named in a command parameter could not be found, or the command could not be found on the specified drive.

Incorrect DOS version: You attempted to run an MS-DOS command whose MS-DOS version is different from that of the main part of MS-DOS in memory. This may mean that you haven't completed an upgrade of MS-DOS on your hard disk and still have old versions of some commands. It can also happen if you try to run a command from a floppy disk that contains a different version of MS-DOS.

Insufficient disk space: There is not enough free space on the disk to hold the file you are writing. If you think there *should* be enough space, use CHKDSK to get a disk status report.

Intermediate file error during pipe: This message may mean that the intermediate files created during a piping procedure cannot be accommodated on the disk because the default drive's root directory is full. Your disk may also be too full to hold the data being piped or the piping files cannot be located on the disk. This probably will not happen if you run MS-DOS from a hard disk.

Invalid COMMAND.COM in drive d: While trying to reload the command processor, MS-DOS found that the copy of COMMAND.COM on the disk is a different version. Insert a disk containing the correct version of MS-DOS.

Invalid directory: One of the directories in the specified pathname does not exist.

Invalid number of parameters: The specified number of parameters does not agree with the number required by the command.

Label not found: GOTO #. You have named a label in a GOTO command that does not exist in the batch file. Use EDLIN to review GOTO and make sure all GOTO statements contain valid labels.

No room for system on diskette: SYS. The specified disk does not contain the required reserved space for the system. (Is the system already on the disk?) You can solve this problem by using FORMAT/s to format a new disk and then copying your files to this disk. (With MS-DOS 4.0, a particular area on the disk does not need to be available for the system files. You only need enough entries in the root directory and enough total space on the disk.)

Syntax error: The command was entered incorrectly. Check the format.

Terminate batch job (Y/N)?: You have pressed <Ctrl><Break> or <Ctrl>C during the processing of a batch file. Press *y* to end processing. Press *n* to stop the command that was executing when you pressed <Ctrl><Break> or <Ctrl>C; processing will continue with the next command.

Glossary

Adapter: A plug-in card containing circuits that provide additional memory, display capabilities, or other features. Often called *expansion card.*

Allocation Unit: The smallest number of magnetic disk sectors a file or a part of a file can occupy. Also called a *cluster*.

ANSI: An abbreviation for American National Standards Institute, an organization that has developed many standards for computer programming languages. Aspects of an ANSI screen-control standard were introduced in MS-DOS Version 2.00.

ASCII: An abbreviation for American Standard Code for Information Interchange, used to define the characters that are input (typed) and output (displayed) on most computers, including those with MS-DOS.

Backing Up: The making of duplicate copies of files or disks to provide access to data if the working copies are damaged or lost.

Batch: A computer process that automatically feeds commands to the computer one at a time from a file created by the user (called a "batch file").

Binary Code: A pattern of binary digits (0 and 1) used to represent information such as numbers or instructions to a computer.

BIOS: An acronym for Basic Input/Output System, a component of the MS-DOS operating system that handles input and output to devices attached to the computer. It is usually loaded from a ROM chip at startup.

Bit: An abbreviation for binary digit; the smallest piece of binary information; a specification of one of two alternatives.

Boot: The process of loading the operating system software after the computer has been powered up or reset.

Buffer: An area of memory used for temporary storage of data. In particular, an area of memory used to hold data that has been read from a disk. Use of buffers can speed disk access by reducing the number of times the disk must be physically read.

Byte: A group of 8 bits treated as a unit. Often equivalent to one alphabetic or numeric character.

CGA (Color Graphics Array): The lowest-resolution standard color graphics display adapter. Not suitable for text display.

Character: Any alphabetic, numeric, or symbolic character capable of being typed into or displayed by a computer.

Chip: A common word used to mean integrated circuit. The term was introduced because the first integrated circuits were fabricated using silicon chips.

Cluster: See *allocation unit.*

Command Line: The part of the screen where MS-DOS prompts you to enter your next command. Also, a complete line of command text including a command and possibly filenames or option switches.

Command-Line Option: See *switch.*

Command Processor: The part of an operating system that processes commands entered by the user. The command processor in MS-DOS is contained in a file called COMMAND.COM.

Command Prompt: Symbol indicating the current drive and often the current directory: for example, C:\>. The cursor is displayed just after the command prompt.

CPU: An acronym for central processing unit, the brain of a computer.

CRT: An acronym for cathode-ray tube, the primary element in a computer monitor, which projects information on the screen.

Cursor: The blinking or solid object displayed on monitors to denote the position on screen where the next character will appear when typed by the user or output by the computer.

Data Base: A collection of data elements stored in a file and organized in such a way as to facilitate the retrieval and update of data.

Device: A piece of equipment connected to a PC and used to receive, display, or store data. Keyboards, video displays, printers, mice, and disk drives are devices.

Device Driver: A special program that serves as an intermediary between MS-DOS and a device. It translates instruction from

MS-DOS or an application program into a form that is suitable for the particlar device.

Directory: A list of files stored on a magnetic disk.

Disk Cache: A program that sets up buffers for data being read from or written to a disk. This can speed disk access considerably.

Disk Optimization: The process of rearranging files so that all of their data is stored in the same part of the disk. This can speed disk access by reducing movement of the drive's read/write head. Sometimes called "defragmentation."

DOS: An acronym for disk operating system, the term given to any operating system designed for use in microcomputers equipped with magnetic storage disks.

DOS Shell (DOSSHELL): A program that provides a menu-driven, graphic user interface for MS-DOS 4.0. Also, a third-party program providing similar features for other versions of MS-DOS.

EGA (Enhanced Graphics Adapter): A higher-resolution color graphics display, suitable for both text and graphics applications.

Expanded Memory: Memory beyond the 640K that is directly usable by MS-DOS and application programs. Data is moved to and from expanded memory using a buffer in regular memory. A special device driver is necessary for using expanded memory, and application programs must be specifically designed to use it.

Expansion Card: See *adapter*.

Extended Memory: Memory beyond 640K that can be directly accessed by the CPU under certain circumstances, as opposed to expanded memory, which can be accessed only indirectly. Extended memory is not often used in MS-DOS systems, though it can be used for a virtual disk or with some disk-cache programs.

Extension: The part of a filename following a period. It is optional, and can have up to three characters. In the file LETTER.TXT, TXT is the extension.

External Command: In MS-DOS, external commands are stored in files, whereas built-in commands are stored within the operating system itself.

FAT: An acronym for file allocation table, a portion of a magnetic disk used by MS-DOS to store a file-storage map showing which parts of a disk are allocated to which file or part of a file.

File: A collection of data stored under a given name on a magnetic disk; a means of separating collections of data from each other on a disk.

Filter: A command that is designed to take data from a file or another command, process it in some way, and output it to another file, or command, or to the screen. The MORE and SORT commands are filters.

Fixed Disk: See *hard disk*.

Format: A term used to denote how data are arranged. Most commonly, it refers to how the characteristics of a magnetic storage disk are arranged, such as tracks, sectors, file allocation table, and directory.

Hard Disk: A fast, high-capacity disk drive—usually the disk is non-removable.

I/O: An abbreviation for input/output.

Input: The act of delivering information to a computer, such as typing on a keyboard.

Integrated Circuit: A circuit whose connections and components are fabricated into one structure on a certain material, such as silicon.

Interface: The link between two components of a computer, such as a disk drive and the computer, or a printer and the computer. Often used to denote the means by which the user and the computer communicate (called the "user interface").

Internal Command: A command that is contained within the operating system itself. In MS-DOS, all built-in commands are actually stored in the file called COMMAND.COM.

Kilobyte: 1024 bytes. Often expressed as K (2048 bytes = 2K, or 2 kilobytes).

Memory: The part of the computer other than disk storage media that is used for the temporary or permanent storage of data that are to be retrieved or manipulated by the computer.

Microcomputer: A computer that has its central processing unit (CPU) contained in a microprocessor integrated circuit.

Microfloppy: A hard-shelled 3½″ disk.

Microprocessor: An integrated circuit that contains a complete central processing unit (CPU).

Modem: An abbreviation for modulator/demodulator; used for the transmission and reception of computer data over telephone lines.

Monitor: A computer display device, monochrome or color, capable either of displaying only characters or of displaying graphics and characters.

Mouse: A hand-held pointing device that can be used instead of the keyboard to control DOSSHELL and certain other programs.

MS-DOS: An acronym for Microsoft Disk Operating System.

Non-Volatile Memory: Memory that is not erased when power is turned off.

Output: Information that is generated by a computer, such as information displayed on a monitor.

Parallel: A term commonly used to denote the sending, receiving, or processing of several data bits at once. For example, a "parallel interface" contains eight wires enabling the transmission of eight bits simultaneously.

Path: Indicates the series of subdirectories (route) needed to reach a given subdirectory or file. Also, a list of directories maintained by the PATH command. A program in a directory on this list can be run from any drive or directory.

Piping: Sending the data output by one command or program as input to another command or program. Indicated by the ¦ symbol.

Port: A part of a computer used to communicate with another device; usually contains a special interface and can handle input only, output only, or both input and output data according to the nature of the interface.

RAM: An acronym for random-access memory, a series of integrated-circuit memory devices used by a computer to temporarily store information that is to be processed. RAM is fully erased when power is removed from the system, except in some systems that contain RAM powered by batteries.

Redirection: The process of directing output generated by a command to a file or device instead of the normal output destination. Input to a command (normally the keyboard) can also be redirected so that it comes from a file or another command.

ROM: An acronym for read-only memory, an integrated circuit that contains permanent data that can be retrieved at any time by the computer. ROM is not erased when the computer's power is turned off.

Root: The main, or master, directory on a disk, from which all subdirectories originate.

RS-232: A serial communications interface standard, commonly used to send and receive data to and from other devices such as other computers, modems, and printers.

Sector: A division along a track of a magnetic storage disk. According to how floppy disks are formatted under MS-DOS, each track of a disk can contain eight, nine, or fifteen sectors per track.

Serial: A term commonly used to denote the sending, receiving, or processing of data bits successively, one bit at a time.

String: A group of characters treated as a single unit. Can correspond to a word, phrase, or sentence.

Subdirectory: A directory that originates from another directory (the root directory or another subdirectory). Subdirectories branch out from other directories much like the branches of a tree.

Switch: A slash (/) and letter following an MS-DOS command. A switch tells MS-DOS to include a particular optional feature. For example, DIR /W lists a directory in "wide" format.

Track: A circular one-bit-wide path on a magnetic storage disk on which data are stored. A magnetic disk contains a series of concentric tracks between the outer and inner edges. Floppy disks used with MS-DOS can have either forty or eighty tracks.

VGA (Video Graphics Array): The highest-resolution graphics adapter commonly used with PCs. Produces high-quality text and graphics.

Virtual Disk: An area of memory treated as though it were a disk drive. The VDISK.SYS device driver is used to create a virtual disk. Since it uses no mechanical parts, a virtual disk is considerably faster than an ordinary disk drive.

Volatile Memory: Memory that is erased when power is turned off.

Window: An area of the screen used to present or request information. DOSSHELL uses several kinds of windows.

Write-Protection: A method of preventing the storing of new data on a magnetic storage disk, thereby preventing the erasure of existing data. Under MS-DOS, specific files or entire floppy disks can be write-protected.

Related Waite Group Books

The Waite Group and Howard W. Sams & Co. have been providing tutorials and references on MS-DOS for just about as long as there has been a DOS. The following books can help you expand your understanding of MS-DOS whether you are a beginner, a power user, a casual programmer, or a software developer.

The Waite Group's Using PC DOS. (Indianapolis, IN: Howard W. Sams, 1989.)

This is the most comprehensive book available for PC DOS (MS-DOS) users. It includes complete tutorials on every aspect of using MS-DOS from basic commands to file management to customization and hardware installation. A detailed Command Reference section covers every version from 2.0 through 4.0 and gives dozens of tips and cautions.

The Waite Group's MS-DOS Bible, Third Edition. (Indianapolis, IN: Howard W. Sams, 1989)

This book is designed for users who want to learn more about MS-DOS features as well as explore the inner workings of DOS. It ranges from basic tutorials to the use of the DEBUG and LINK utilities. The introductory discussions of memory-resident programs and device drivers are good for beginning programmers. There is also a succinct Command Reference section.

Tricks of the MS-DOS Masters, Second Edition. (Indianapolis, IN: Howard W. Sams, due 1990)

With its dozens of commands and option switches, it isn't always obvious how you can use MS-DOS to perform a particular task. With this book, you'll find out. You can also discover many things that you hadn't thought you could do. Each "trick" is explained so you can understand why it works and how to apply it to varying situations.

The Waite Group's MS-DOS Developer's Guide, Second Edition. (Indianapolis, Howard W. Sams, 1989.)

This book is a resource for programmers who want to learn to write MS-DOS applications. Assuming you know C or assembly language, this book will show you how to call all of the MS-DOS system functions (including MS-DOS 4.0 features.) It demonstrates techniques of memory-resident and real-time programming. It shows you how to interface with expanded memory, the serial port, and EGA/VGA graphics. It also explains the low-level disk layout and techniques for file recovery.

The Waite Group's MS-DOS Papers. (Indianapolis, Howard W. Sams, 1988.)

A diverse collection of essays that combine theory and practice on important topics for MS-DOS users and programmers. The 14 papers are grouped into three sections: extending the MS-DOS user interface, programming tools and techniques, and working with the hardware interface. Highlights include a programmer's overview of MS-DOS; programming tools; access to undocumented MS-DOS functions; Microsoft Windows programming; and the theory and practice of device drivers, memory-resident programs, the EGA, the serial port, and expanded memory.

Answers to Quiz Questions

Chapter 1

1. a
2. d
3. b
4. e
5. b
6. c
7. a
8. c
9. a
10. c
11. d
12. e
13. e
14. b
15. e
16. d
17. e
18. d

Chapter 2

1. e
2. a
3. a
4. b
5. c
6. c
7. d
8. b

Chapter 3

1. b
2. b
3. c
4. f
5. b
6. c
7. c
8. e
9. a
10. c
11. c
12. b
13. f
14. b
15. a

Chapter 4

1. f
2. e
3. a
4. b
5. a
6. f
7. b
8. c
9. a
10. b
11. a
12. c

Chapter 5

1. a
2. c
3. b
4. a
5. d
6. a
7. e
8. b
9. b
10. e
11. b

Chapter 6

1. e
2. b
3. e
4. c
5. b
6. a
7. e
8. b
9. b
10. a

Chapter 7

1. d
2. d
3. a
4. b
5. c
6. a
7. d
8. c
9. b
10. a
11. c
12. b
13. d
14. b
15. c

Chapter 8

1. d
2. c
3. b
4. d
5. b
6. e
7. c
8. d
9. a
10. c

Chapter 9

1. c
2. b
3. b
4. b
5. c
6. d
7. d
8. a
9. b
10. d
11. d
12. b

Chapter 10

1. d
2. b
3. d
4. a
5. c
6. b
7. c
8. d
9. c
10. b
11. c
12. d
13. e
14. c
15. b

Chapter 11

1. b
2. a
3. c
4. d
5. b
6. a
7. d
8. d
9. e
10. b

Chapter 12

1. e
2. c
3. b
4. d
5. d
6. a
7. b
8. d
9. b
10. c

Index

The Waite Group

100 Shoreline Highway, Suite 285 | Mill Valley, CA 94941 | (415) 331-0575

Compuserve: 75146,3515 | usernet: hplabs!well!mitch | AppleLink: D2097

Dear Reader:

Thank you for considering the purchase of our book. Readers have come to know products from **The Waite Group** for the care and quality we put into them. Let me tell you a little about our group and how we make our books.

It started in 1976 when I could not find a computer book that really taught me anything. The books that were available talked down to people, lacked illustrations and examples, were poorly laid out, and were written as if you already understood all the terminology. So I set out to write a good book about microcomputers. This was to be a special book–very graphic, with a friendly and casual style, and filled with examples. The result was an instant best-seller.

Over the years, I developed this approach into a "formula" (nothing really secret here, just a lot of hard work—I am a crazy man about technical accuracy and high-quality illustrations). I began to find writers who wanted to write books in this way. This led to co-authoring and then to multiple-author books and many more titles (over seventy titles currently on the market). As The Waite Group author base grew, I trained a group of editors to manage our products. We now have a team devoted to putting together the best possible book package and maintaining the high standard of our existing books.

We greatly appreciate and use any advice our readers send us (and you send us a lot). We have discovered that our readers are detail nuts: you want indexes that really work, tables of contents that dig deeply into the subject, illustrations, tons of examples, reference cards, and more.

Understanding MS-DOS, Second Edition, updates the previous best-selling book to cover DOS 4 and the DOS shell. It melds The Waite Group's expertise and user-friendly style with the classic approach of Howard W. Sams & Company's Understanding Series. If you would like to explore MS-DOS/PC-DOS even further, look for our other DOS books. *The Waite Group's Using PC-DOS,* a comprehensive book for using DOS in a business environment, includes an extensive reference section, a Quick Primer, and tutorials. *The Waite Group's MS-DOS Bible,* Third Edition, combines a command reference section with tutorials. It covers introductory DOS topics for users and explores the inner workings of DOS for beginning programmers.

Power users will want to see *The Waite Group's Tricks of the MS-DOS Masters*, which covers advanced MS-DOS topics and little-known tricks. If you'd like to program in the MS-DOS environment, check out *The Waite Group's MS-DOS Developer's Guide*. Finally, *The Waite Group's MS-DOS Papers* is a diverse collection of essays for MS-DOS users and programmers. You can find a list of all our titles in the back of this book. In fact, let us know what you want and we'll try to write about it.

Thanks again for considering the purchase of this title. If you care to tell me anything you like (or don't like) about the book, please write or send email to the addresses on this letterhead.

Sincerely,

Mitchell Waite
The Waite Group

The Waite Group's MS-DOS® Papers
Edited by The Waite Group

IS-DOS Papers presents tutorials n fourteen of the most exciting ›pics in MS-DOS programming ›ritten by recognized experts and gurus" in the computer industry. 'he book offers a close look at uch important areas as the ex›anded memory specification (EMS), ›riting terminate and stay resident TSR) programs, undocumented MS-)OS functions, how to program the :nhanced Graphics Adapter (EGA), nd inner workings of MS-DOS sys›ems including the BIOS, MS-DOS ernel, internal stacks, routines, nd data structures.

'opics covered include:

- An Overview of MS-DOS
- A Fast File Search Utility
- PCnix: A UNIX-like Shell
- Adding Power to MS-DOS Programming
- Advanced MASM Techniques
- Undocumented MS-DOS Functions
- Terminate and Stay Resident Programming
- Data and File Security Techniques
- The Spy Utility: Investigating Windows
- MS-DOS Services for Device Drivers
- Sounder: A Musical Device Drive
- Programming the Enhanced Graphics Adapter
- Programming the Enhanced Graphics Adapter
- Enhanced Memory Specification (EMS)

400 Pages, 7½ x 9¾, Softbound
ISBN: 0-672-22594-8
No. 22594, $26.95

The Waite Group's Using PC-DOS™
The Waite Group

This is a complete introduction and reference for all users of PC-DOS, the dominant operating system of IBM® PC and PS/2 computers. The book combines a "quick primer" for beginning users with extensive tutorial chapters for intermediate-level users. A command reference section for advanced experts includes all commands and their options, with tricks for power users.

The book is compatible with PC DOS 2, 3, 4, and DOSSHELL and contains numerous hands-on examples for problem-solving, particularly in a business environment.

Topics covered include:

- Quick Primer
- DOSSHELL
- Files
- Managing Your Hard Disk
- All About Floppy Disks
- Creating Text Files
- Batch Files
- Advanced Use of The Command Line
- Customization and Installation
- International Language Support
- Command Reference Section

775 Pages, 7½ x 9¾, Softbound
ISBN: 0-672-22679-0
No. 22679, $26.95

The Waite Group's New C Primer Plus
Mitchell Waite and Stephen Prata

A thorough revision of one of our best-selling C titles, this user-friendly guide to C programming is an excellent tutorial for first-time students of C and a good reference for experienced C programmers. It is compatible with UNIX System V, Microsoft C, Quick C, and Turbo C.

The book moves through the fundamentals of the C language using practical, logical, interactive tutorials. It is based on the new ANSI C standard, and all programs include ANSI prototypes. Today's methods of structured code, step-wise refinement, and top-down design are emphasized.

Topics covered include:

- Getting Ready
- Introducing C
- Data and C
- Character Strings and Formatted Input/Output
- Operators, Expressions, and Statements
- C Control Statements: Looping, Branching, and Jumps
- Character Input/Output and Redirection
- Functions
- Arrays and Pointers
- Character Strings and String Functions
- File Input/Output
- Storage Classes and Program Development
- Structures and Other Data Forms
- Bit Fiddling
- The C Preprocessor and the C Library

638 Pages, 7 ¾ x 9 ¼, Softbound
ISBN: 0-672-22687-1, $26.95

The Waite Group's Microsoft® C Programming for the PC, Revised Edition
Robert Lafore

This entry-level programming book assumes no previous knowledge of C as it moves quickly through the fundamentals of the language using step-by-step, hands-on tutorials. The author shows exactly what to do and how to do it, from simple topics to advanced features, moving the reader in an orderly fashion. The new edition is based on the 5.1 compiler and includes a chapter on the newest graphics features, the newest updates to Codeview, ANSI C prototyping, VGA graphics, MCGA control, and details on the QuickC optimizing compiler have been added.

Topics covered include:

- Getting Started
- C Building Blocks
- Loops, Decisions, Functions
- Arrays, Strings, and Pointers
- Keyboard and Cursor
- Structures, Unions, and ROM BIOS
- Memory and the Monochrome Display
- Library Graphics
- Direct CGA, EGA, and VGA Color Graphics
- New Microsoft Graphics Functions
- Files
- Larger Programs and Advanced Variables

750 Pages, 7½ x 9¾, Softbound
ISBN: 0-672-22661-8
No. 22661, $24.95

Visit your local book retailer or call
800-257-5755

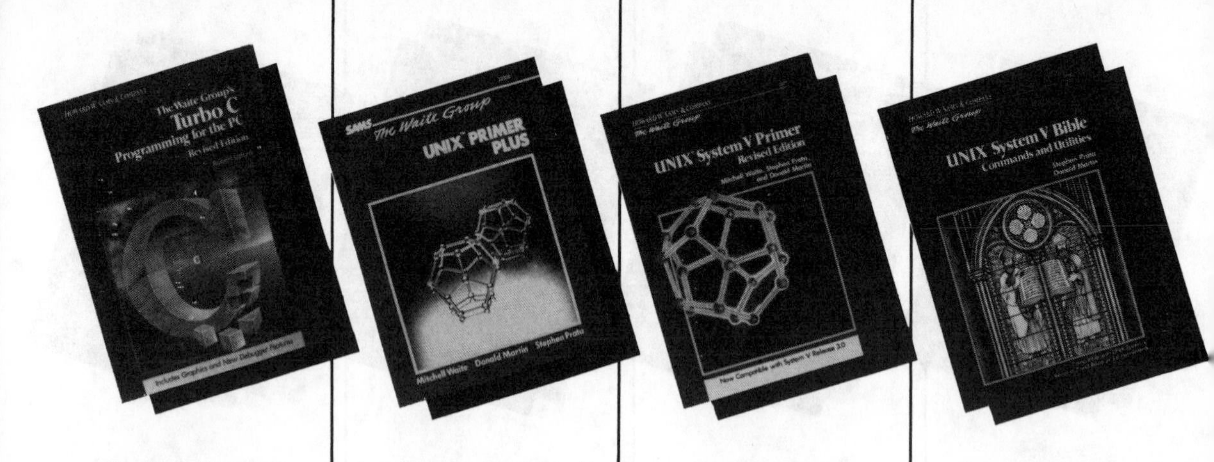

The Waite Group's Turbo C® Programming for the PC, Revised Edition

Robert Lafore

This entry-level book moves quickly through the fundamentals of the latest version of Turbo C, using step-by-step, hands-on tutorials to show readers how to write useful and marketable C programs.

Compatible with Turbo C 1.0 and 1.5, it contains new information on the Turbo C graphics library, the graphics model, and Debugging Tracer, as it highlights ANSI C features. The language concepts are presented in an orderly, graded fashion to allow readers to move smoothly from simple topics to the more advanced.

Topics covered include:

- Getting Started
- C Building Blocks
- Loops, Decisions, Functions
- Arrays and Strings, Pointers
- Keyboard and Cursor
- Structures, Unions, and ROM BIOS
- Memory and the Monochrome Display
- Direct CGA and EGA Color Graphics
- Files and Larger Programs
- Advanced Variables
- Appendices: Reference, Supplementary Programs, Hexadecimal Numbering, Bibliography, ASCII Chart, The Turbo C Debugger, Answers to Questions and Exercises

700 Pages, 7½ x 9¾, Softbound
ISBN: 0-672-22660-X
No. 22660, $22.95

UNIX® Primer Plus

Waite, Martin, and Prata, The Waite Group

Another excellent Waite book. For those who want to learn about the amazing UNIX operating system, this primer presents UNIX in a clear, simple, and easy-to-understand style. This classic is fully illustrated and includes two handy removable summary cards to keep near your computer for quick reference.

Topics covered include:

- An Introduction to UNIX
- Electronic Mail and On-Line Help
- Files and Directories
- Using The ed Line and Screen Editor
- Manipulating Files and Directories
- Using Programming Languages: Fortran, Pascal and C
- File Management Commands
- Adjusting Your Environment
- Special C-Shell Features
- Information Processing

416 pages, 7¼ x 9¼, Softbound
ISBN: 0-672-22028-8
No. 22028, $22.95

UNIX® System V Primer Revised Edition

Waite, Martin, and Prata, The Waite Group

This primer provides a comprehensive overview and introduction to the UNIX System V operating system for the beginning UNIX user. It gives the reader review questions and exercises at the terminal, for an applied, hands-on approach to learning not found in other books on the subject.

New material has been added to the second edition. It includes a new chapter on the extended electronic mail programs and new information detailing the use of the new shell layer manager for multiprocessing and the enhanced screen display page.

Topics covered include:

- Introduction to UNIX
- Getting Started
- Electronic Mail and On-Line Help
- Files and Directories
- Using Editors
- The *vi* Screen Editor
- Manipulating Files and Directories
- Using Programming Languages
- The UNIX Shell
- File Management Commands
- More Text Processing
- Information Processing
- Extended Electronic Mail Program

450 Pages, 7½ x 9¾, Softbound
ISBN: 0-672-22570-0
No. 22570, $22.95

UNIX® System V Bible

Prata and Martin, The Waite Group

You'll never have to open the UNIX manual again! This is a comprehensive reference to UNIX commands and utilities, focusing on the basic and advanced command groups found in standard UNIX System V manuals.

Commands are listed alphabetically and explained in down-to-earth language. Each entry states the purpose of a command, what it does, and how it is used. A graduated set of example programs goes far beyond the UNIX manuals, showing you each command in several different situations.

Features of this unique resource include:

- Detailed Table of Contents for Quick Reference
- Cross-Referencing of Commands and Features
- Friendly Format for Beginning and Advanced Users
- Coverage of All Major UNIX Features
- Guidance to UNIX Command Idiosyncracies

528 Pages, 7½ x 9¾, Softbound
ISBN: 0-672-22562-X
No. 22562, $24.95

Visit your local book retailer or call
800-257-5755

Understanding MS-DOS,
Second Edition

Waite Group Reader Feedback Card

Help Us Make A Better Book

To better serve our readers, we would like your opinion on the contents and quality of this book. Please fill out this card and return it to *The Waite Group*, 100 Shoreline Hwy., Suite A-285, Mill Valley, CA, 94941 (415) 331-0575.

Name ____________________

Company ____________________

Address ____________________

City ____________________

State ______ ZIP __________ Phone __________

1. How would you rate the content of this book?

- [ ] Excellent
- [ ] Very Good
- [ ] Good
- [ ] Fair
- [ ] Below Average
- [ ] Poor

2. What were the things you liked *most* about this book?

- [ ] Content
- [ ] Pace
- [ ] Writing Style
- [ ] Accuracy
- [ ] Compat. Boxes
- [ ] Listings
- [ ] Reference
- [ ] Format
- [ ] Examples
- [ ] Index
- [ ] Jump Table
- [ ] Cover
- [ ] Price
- [ ] Illustrations
- [ ] Construction

3. Please explain the one thing you liked *most* about this book. ____________________

4. What were the things you liked *least* about this book?

- [ ] Content
- [ ] Pace
- [ ] Writing Style
- [ ] Accuracy
- [ ] Compat. Boxes
- [ ] Listings
- [ ] Reference
- [ ] Format
- [ ] Examples
- [ ] Index
- [ ] Jump Table
- [ ] Cover
- [ ] Price
- [ ] Illustrations
- [ ] Construction

5. Please explain the one thing you liked *least* about this book. ____________________

6. How do you use this book? For work, recreation, look-up, self-training, classroom, etc?

____

7. Would you be interested in receiving a Pop-Up utility program containing the contents of this book? What would you pay for this?

____

8. Where did you purchase this particular book?

- [ ] Book Chain
- [ ] Small Book Store
- [ ] Computer Store
- [ ] Direct Mail
- [ ] Book Club
- [ ] School Book Store
- [ ] Other: ____________________

9. Can you name another similar book you like better than this one, or one that is as good, and tell us why?

____

10. How many Waite Group books do you own? ______

11. What are your favorite Waite Group books?

____

12. What topics or specific titles would you like to see The Waite Group develop?

____

13. What version of MASM are you using?

____

14. What other programming languages do you know?

____

15. Any other comments you have about this book or other Waite Group titles?

____

16. [ ] Check here to receive a free Waite Group catalog.

Fold Here

From:

Place Stamp Here

The Waite Group, Inc.
100 Shoreline Highway, Suite A–285
Mill Valley, CA 94941

Staple or tape here

27298